Effective Communication and Soft Skills

Strategies for Success

Consultant Editors
NITIN BHATNAGAR
MAMTA BHATNAGAR

The Pearson–ICFAI University Series is an outcome of a collaboration between Pearson Education India and ICFAI University Press.

Pearson

Editor–Acquisitions: Prasun Chatterjee
Associate Editor–Production: Amrita Naskar

ISBN 978-81-317-6034-5

First Impression

Published by Pearson India Education Services Pvt. Ltd, CIN: U72200TN2005PTC057128.

Head Office: 15th Floor, Tower-B, World Trade Tower, Plot No. 1, Block-C, Sector 16, Noida 201 301, Uttar Pradesh, India.

Registered Office: 7th Floor, SDB2, ODC 7, 8 & 9, Survey No.01 ELCOT IT/ ITES SEZ, Sholinganallur, Chennai – 600119, Tamil Nadu, India. Website: in.pearson.com,
Email: companysecretary.india@pearson.com

Compositor: Mukesh Technologies Pvt. Ltd
Digitally printed in India by Trinity Academy for Corporate Training Ltd, New Delhi in the year of 2022.

Effective Communication and Soft Skills

Contents

Introduction

The revolution in information technology and the rapid globalization have brought communication to the frontline of academia and industry. With the whole world becoming a global market and business getting varied and result-oriented, professionals, scientists, teachers, and students are facing newer challenges in communication every day. We have to communicate with the entire world—with the people of different nationalities, various backgrounds, and diverse experiences. The greatest need of the hour is to learn to work together as a team. To exist in this mode of working, organizations and institutions require a high level of proficiency in oral and written English, as well as skills in interpersonal communication. Moreover, we must have traits of leadership and take up challenges and responsibilities to renovate failure into success. In the phraseology of communication skill theory, these skills are called 'soft skills'. These are contrasted with 'hard skills' which are the technical competencies of an individual, that is, the skills gained through educational learning and hands-on training. Hard skills are quantitative, while soft skills are subjective in nature.

The present book has been designed comprehensively, keeping in mind the syllabi of P.G. programmes like Mass Communication, M.B.A., M.Ed., and all such courses that groom the learners for interpersonal communication, and have taken the responsibility to prepare them for the professional world. The book is an endeavour to study and understand the attributes of good communication vis-á-vis soft skills as well as hard skills; how to inculcate them and use them practically in contemporary life. One of the significant aims of the book is to strengthen 'teachers as effective communicators'. In addition, it will be valuable for all types of communicators, as well as researchers in similar areas since the chapters are also devoted to the theories of communication, its evolution, and models. The book, in fact, discusses all the four tenets of language learning, i.e., listening, speaking, reading, and writing. The chapter-wise briefs of the book are as follows:

Chapter 1: The first chapter is an attempt to draw guidelines in order to understand and acquire soft skills and hard skills, to learn the ways to have a proper co-ordination between these two significant skills, and to inculcate a feeling of self-confidence in order to become successful leaders, teachers, and communicators.

Chapter 2: The fundamental tenet behind all the types of skills is communication. This chapter deals with the issue of understanding communication. The discussion highlights the meaning and definitions of communication, along with the dimensions of intrapersonal, interpersonal, group, and mass communication. The chapter analyses various models of communication, its processes, barriers, theories, the basic forms of non-verbal and verbal communication, and the influencing factors. The chapter is also a useful critique on the importance of communication in an academic setting.

Chapter 3: After throwing light on the fundamentals of communication in chapter 2, chapter 3 acquaints you with the various channels of communication, providing an in-depth knowledge of the process, qualities, and the modes of communication. The channels of communication familiarize the reader with the psychological, social, and motivational aspects of communication, focusing on how communication works. The chapter further discusses the differences between verbal, non-verbal, and meta communication. This is followed by an evaluation of language and day-to-day communication, along with an explanation of persuasive communication. This section will equip the reader with an understanding to select the right channel of communication for a particular occasion.

Chapter 4: The in-depth study of communication remains incomplete without the study of the evaluation and theories of communication, which is the main focus of this chapter. This chapter provides a historical perspective of communication that deals with an interesting account of the evolution of communication, its roots, and growth to the modern era of technological advancement, including a brief note on the resulting social change. As a theoretical base is essential for understanding a concept, the chapter incorporates the major theories of communication. The aspects included in this chapter will enhance your knowledge on communication and at the same time will act as a useful material for research in the same field.

Chapter 5: In order to further understand the mechanism of communication, chapter 5 familiarizes you with different models that provide visual explanation of the communication process. With a purpose to avoid illusiveness generated through rigorous definitions, models of communication have been discussed to structure a clear grasp of the processes. Knowledge of the models will help you modify, change, and improve your own communication. Teachers will find them highly useful to advance their classroom interactions.

Chapter 6: This chapter deals with the psychology of communication. The personality of the speaker and the receiver plays an important role in the communication process. Differences in the traits of personalities affect communication in various interpersonal settings. The chapter examines these aspects, along with the role of the self in communication, interpersonal responses of the persons with low and high self-esteem, motivation, and communication apprehension. The acquaintance with communication psychology will assist you to reorient your own personality, understand the attitude of the listeners or the receivers, and will improve your whole communication process.

Chapter 7: This chapter will be highly beneficial to teachers as it highlights pedagogical communication and its components. It describes in detail some important aspects like the role of a teacher in a teaching and learning situation, conflicts that take place, and mutual feedback between the teacher and the taught. The chapter also deals with the issue of supportive pedagogical communication, wherein a teacher is considered as a facilitator and communication is just not a medium of sharing information, but becomes a supportive interaction between the pedagogue and the students.

Chapter 8: Communication is crucial to professional success of all kinds. Effective communication is a skill that can be developed by one and all. Chapter 8 takes into consideration the major barriers to effective communication such as criticizing, labelling, ordering, moralizing, etc., and the strategies to overcome them. In addition, this chapter gives some valuable tips to strengthen your non-verbal and oral communication skills. As good listening leads to good speaking, the chapter also deals with the dos and don'ts of an active listening.

Chapter 9: This chapter provides an in-depth account of the spoken element of communication skills in English. English is an unphonetic language as it does not maintain link between the written and the spoken form. Therefore, it is necessary for Indian students to make a systematic study of the English sound system. This part of the book covers the articulation skills by analyzing the individual sounds of English as represented by the International Phonetic Alphabet (IPA). It will help you to be familiar with the pronunciation of English sounds, stress and rhythm in connected speech, intonation and will provide you with the pronunciation improvement strategies. Professionals will find it helpful as it also deals with presentation and interviewing skills.

Chapter 10: Writing is a significant feature of communication. In chapter 10, the different aspects of writing as a means of communication have been dealt with in detail. The discussion elaborates upon the grammatical items of the English language, miscellaneous errors, and sentence clarity which will help you to write direct, correct, crisp, and unambiguous sentences. The vocabulary section will enable you to follow the right technique to enhance your word power. This unit will be especially rewarding for teachers as it incorporates items like structuring lesson plans, teacher's handbooks, annual reports, research papers, letter writing, etc.

Chapter 11 to 16: The various features of interpersonal communication discussed earlier, directly or indirectly, tend to add a lot of weight to the personality of a communicator. Keeping this fact in mind, the last six chapters have been designed to blossom from the earlier ones into units that deal with the aspect of personality development. These six chapters will be highly productive for all the readers as they effectively integrate the quintessential facets of interpersonal effectiveness, assertiveness, etiquettes, use of 'I' statements instead of 'you' or 'we' statements, self-esteem, conflict management, negotiation skills, leadership and team-building skills, and time management.

Another special feature of the book is the accompanying practice material with five sets of model question papers. Guidelines for answering the questions are also provided, along with solutions to some of the difficult problems.

Thus, it can be very well stated that this is not just a text book dealing with soft skills and hard skills, but is a complete manual for the development of a balanced personality, required for an all round success in the current scenario.

About the Editors

Nitin Bhatnagar is Professor of English, GLA University, Mathura. He has taught English language skills, professional communication and English literature at various levels for over two and a half decades now. His expertise lies in training learners for oral professional communication using Computer Aided Language Learning (CALL). He has also been guiding students for competitive examinations and preparing them for placements in companies. He has been associated with many reputed universities and institutes as a visiting faculty and has delivered expert lectures on various aspects of professional communication. He did his Ph.D. from Devi Ahilya University, Indore, and is currently supervising many scholars for their doctoral research. He has written many research papers, which have been published in various national and international journals.

Mamta Bhatnagar is Assistant Professor, E-Max Group of Institutions, Bhadauli, Ambala. She has several years' experience of teaching communication skills in English, English grammar, and professional interaction at various levels. She has also been engaged in imparting training in oral communication using computerized language labs. In addition to teaching, she has been actively involved in writing articles in magazines and newspapers as well as in editing magazines and newsletters for which she has received many awards. She has authored a book on communication skills and has written several papers in national and international journals.

1

Soft Skills: Growing Importance

After reading this chapter, you will be familiar with:

- Concept of soft and hard skills
- Categories of skills
- The importance of soft skills
- Process of skill acquisition
- Soft skills education and training

INTRODUCTION

It is not the strongest of the species that survive, nor the most intelligent, but the one most responsive to change.

—Charles Darwin

Darwin's words are still as relevant today as when they were first expressed during the early phase of the 19th century. Indeed, his words are more relevant now than ever before. The explosion of modern information technology poses a great challenge to the youth. As a result there is an increasingly emergent competitive global picture. In order to prosper and succeed in the era of technological advance, individuals, and organizations have *to be ready* to develop and adopt new skills and approaches. Otherwise, the chances of their survival may be at stake. Soft skills are the emotional sine qua non of psychological survival. Hence, they are the prerequisites to anyone who seeks a job. Soft skills also represent one of the fundamental attributes that the new knowledge-based economy seems to be demanding of the employers, employees, and organizations.

The educational scene in India is currently witnessing some upheavals. The challenges and demands that are placed on students are voluminous. They experience psychological ramifications due to the lack of skills. These skills are of two kinds namely, soft skills and hard skills. Although both the skills are deemed equally essential, soft skills should be the part and parcel of any course curriculum in view of its importance. Soft skills are essential not only for students, but also for teachers and other academic consultants.

Students seek employment at some point in life to advance into professional phase and to earn their bread and butter. It will not only be desirable but also essential for them to learn the aspects of soft skills. We know that teachers generally teach us how to solve a specific or complicated mathematical problem. They explain complex concepts in a manner that is easy to understand. However, it is witnessed that many teachers or academicians fail to teach us how to communicate, how to get along well in an interpersonal situation, how to make a career choice, and many such related problems. All these aspects fall under the domain of soft skills. On the other hand, some teachers are extremely good at teaching the prescribed material. They confine themselves only to teaching. However, they lack interpersonal skills like greeting students, communicating empathy, showing care and concern, helping students to grow, and to develop proactive and other related skills, counseling skills from a cluster of soft skills. It is imperative to examine what exactly soft skills are, how they differ from hard skills and why they are important to students. Primarily, however, let us look at the different aspects of hard skills.

HARD SKILLS

Hard skills are the technical competencies that an individual possesses. These are skills which are gained through educational learning and practical hands-on applications. Hard skills are quantitative in nature and can be measured. For example, Ravi, a 10th standard student can do any complicated mathematical problem within no time. Sita, a 10th standard student has a very good grasp over the concepts of science. Even she can solve complex problems very easily. Ravi's and Sita's skills in mathematics and science drive them to choose careers in engineering and medicine, respectively. Both their skills in engineering medicine can be termed as hard skills, which they have acquired through learning over a period of time. In other words, hard skills are essentially the technical abilities required to do a particular job or to perform a specialized task. A degree, diploma or certificate confirms that the relevant abilities necessary to perform a particular job have been sufficiently mastered. Hard skills are vital to get employed. However, hard skills alone might not be sufficient in order to survive successfully. Soft skills are important in addition to hard skills. While the term 'hard skills' or 'technical skills' is a relatively straightforward concept, soft skills are somewhat more difficult to pin down, referring as they do to a very diverse range of abilities. Let us examine these aspects of soft skills.

SOFT SKILLS

In contrast to hard skills, soft skills are generally interpersonal competencies and are more difficult to define due to their subjectivity, which consequently makes them difficult to measure. Typically, included in the ambit of the soft skills are the following:

- Listening skills
- Communication skills
- Team-building skills
- Leadership skills
- Problem-solving skills
- Time management skills
- Persuasion skills
- Negotiation skills
- Analytical thinking skills
- Conflict management skills
- Assertiveness skills
- Feedback skills
- Counselling skills
- Presentation skills
- Mentoring
- Flexibility
- Self-awareness

The above list of soft skills presents issues related to human capital. For example, Ravi, a B.Tech. graduate from Indian Institute of Technology, has problems in being assertive and is generally bullied by his friends. While Sita's professional skills are far more superior, she has difficulty in managing her time. Ravi's non-assertiveness and Sita's inefficient time management can both be regarded as a lack of soft skills being detrimental to their professional and personal success. Soft skills are as important and often even more important than technological skills for an individual to succeed. One can achieve synergy if one can combine both hard and soft skills.

CATEGORIES OF SKILLS

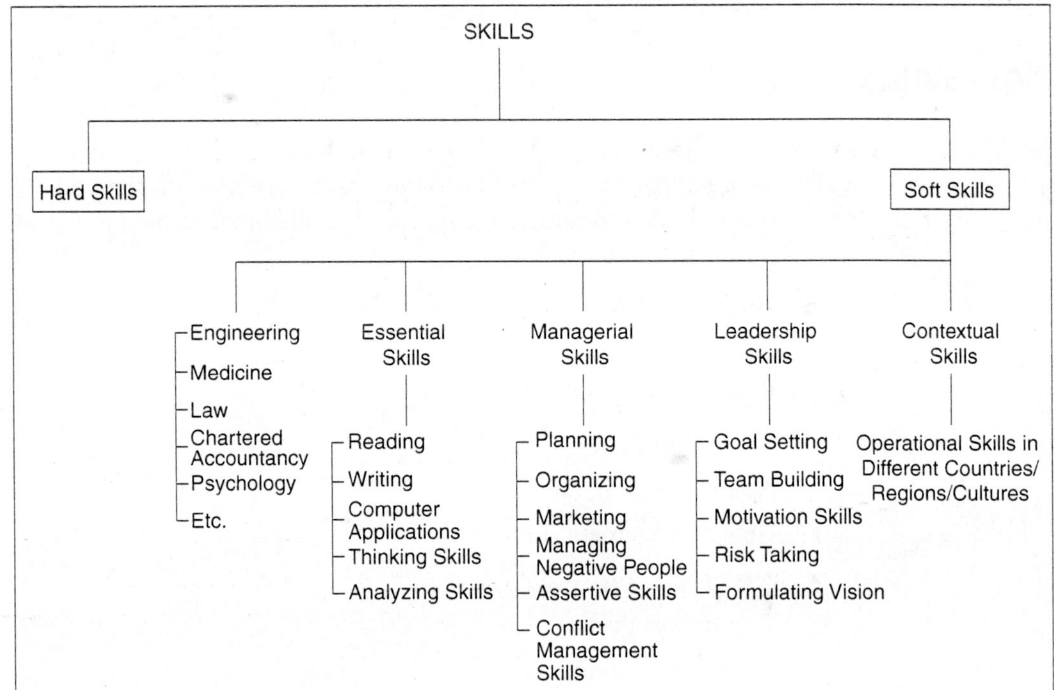

Figure 1.1
Skills and their types

The Expert Panel on Skills, in its report on 'Skills and Opportunities' in the *Knowledge Economy (March 2000)*, divided skills into five categories. They include the technical or hard skills referred above, and then four categories of 'soft skills'. According to the panel, soft skills encompass the following:

Essential Skills

Each and every student must possess the essential skills in order to strive and to survive in the competitive world. It is needless to mention that reading and writing are the most essential and fundamental soft skills through which all the students acquire competence. The onus lies on the teachers to help the students develop their potential for thinking, analyzing and developing problem-solving skills. Exercises, practice situations, and role-plays that address these essential soft skills in addition to regular curriculum will be instrumental in developing the personality of the students.

Management Skills

Managerial skills include the ability to manage people, capital, and budgets as well as the ability to undertake organizational activities such as planning, marketing, and evaluation. Managerial skills are essential for teachers and academic administrators. For an administrator or a school principal whose responsibility lies in managing the rest of the staff, the managerial skill is immensely important.

Leadership Skills

The ability to motivate and assist others to achieve their full potential, to take risks and to formulate a vision comes under the purview of leadership skills. These skills are essential for both teachers and students; teachers play a great role in helping students to acquire these skills.

Contextual Skills

The ability to operate successfully in different settings, such as different countries, different regions or a culturally diverse workplace is a contextual skill.

The authors of the above-mentioned report are careful to make the point that while technical skills are necessary by themselves, they are not sufficient for commercial success in the contemporary scenario.

THE IMPORTANCE OF SOFT SKILLS

In a survey of 400 employers concerning their perceptions of workplace, basic skills, and competencies required for current and potential employees, the employers explained that they wanted entry-level workers to possess employability skills rather than technology competencies. To them, the most important skills (rating over 92.6 per cent) were basic skills, thinking skills, personal quality skills, and interpersonal competencies; technology competencies and systems competencies rated the lowest at 54.5 per cent and 52.8 per cent respectively (Richens and McClain 2000). In another study, employers identified a lack of soft skills (e.g., general social skills that includes actions or behavioural patterns like callingto inform if one is going to be late or absent, staying on the job despite frustrations, etc.) as the primary barrier to employment (Owen et al. 2000).

In engineering, for example, communication skills are often considered more important than high-level mathematics, group work skills are more important than academic individuality, and a commitment to lifelong learning and continuing professional development more important than a theoretical contribution to research-focused projects and development.

Soft skills are very important to students for various reasons. Some of them are outlined below:

- To handle interpersonal relations,
- To choose career and make appropriate decisions,
- To communicate effectively.

An investment in student's soft skills ultimately affects the bottom line by building new knowledge in the student. Relationships play a vital role in human life. In today's fast-paced and continually changing technology, hard skills are continuously in need for being updated. A student who has interpersonal problem and another who has difficulty in making a choice about his career suffers from lack of soft skills. Hence, the need is for a continuous renewal of soft skills in terms of teaching and training the students. This will facilitate their potential towards being effective and successful.

According to Daniel Coleman, emotional intelligence, or EQ—referring to a combination of competencies that contribute to a person's ability to manage himself or herself and relate to other people—matters twice as much as IQ or technical skills in job success. Not only does it create happier and more successful employees, according to Coleman, it also helps create more successful companies. The results of one study on the opinion of the importance of soft skills indicated that the single most important soft skill for a candidate in a job interview to possess was interpersonal skills. This was followed by written or verbal communication skills and the ability to work under pressure. Technical skills and knowledge were found to be at the bottom of the list. It is interesting to note that another larger survey done in the US in 1998 indicates that more than two- thirds (68 per cent) interviewed, rated soft skills as very important compared to less than half (46 per cent) rating soft skills as very important in 1996. It is clear then that there are forces at play, which are changing the face of the working environment and leading to an increased emphasis on the deployment of soft skills at all levels of the management, irrespective of any organization.

THE LEARNERS AND THE LEARNING

The learners in the traditional educational setting predominantly constitute students preparing for a career. The learning system focuses on class-room based students and overarches the design and operation of the teaching. The courses are designed to provide a depth and breadth of knowledge, the relevance of which may not be fully understood by the students. The students are also aware that the possible application of any knowledge gained is at a distant horizon, leading to a perception of low relevance that results in low motivation. Their focus frequently shifts to the skills that are likely to yield higher grades and percentages as an immediate objective. Hence, skills related to 'examination techniques' acquire importance though there are not many situations in life that resemble the typically artificial nature of an academic assessment system. This kind of traditional learning system does not focus on the importance of soft skills. Hence, a major shift in the attitudes of the policy makers in necessary.

SOFT SKILLS—A PREREQUISITE FOR A TEACHER

The greatest potential for growth of an academic institute is its teaching community. To be an effective teacher, one should have both hard and soft skills. Possessing good soft skills will always strengthen teacher's confidence. Such teachers can prepare their students such that they learn to face the challenges of life better. Teaching is an emotional job, as it deals with teaching not only the academic material but also with the personal issues of the students. To inculcate soft skills in students, teachers themselves should be equipped with soft skills. One of the most vital soft skills required by a teacher is communication. To 'communicate' is to write, to persuade, to train, to present, to inspire, to inform, to entertain, and to teach. In addition to communication, soft skills such as mentoring and coaching are the essential pre-requisites of a teacher. A mentor is an experienced and trusted advisor. When asked who the most favourite teacher is, the image of that teacher who exhibits concern for students comes to mind than the teacher who is an expert in the subject. The reason is that s/he was not only an excellent teacher, but also made a lasting impression upon the students with his/her concerns, warmth, empathy, positive regard and communication. In times of crisis the teacher became a counselor. When a student is confronted with the dilemma to choose a career, the teacher helps him take a decision. There could be many teachers who have taught with great repute or explained difficult concepts with great ease. But, it is only that teacher who has exhibited a warm passion for students, who often comes to our mind, whenever we are a little nostalgic about school days. This is simply because of his or her excellent soft skills.

ROLE OF TEACHERS IN INCULCATING SOFT SKILLS IN STUDENTS

Teachers play a significant role in the transition phase of students' lives. This phase prepares the students for their adult life. It involves continuous teaching and supporting a student's growth and ability to handle the demands of this complex world. A key to the whole concept of transition is that while instruction is critical, it ultimately needs to be transferred into real-life settings in order to prepare the student for success beyond the classroom. To help achieve these outcomes, teachers work with students to set short-term goals, which are steps to prepare students for what they want to do after graduation. Teachers need to follow the student's school career to set goals and determine the activities, which will help students to achieve them. Transition actually commences in the school years of a student. Hence, many of the critical skills are taught while in school, including not only academic skills but also 'soft skills' such as social skills, teamwork, taking responsibility, following directions, attitude, and good attendance. Beginning at age 14, teachers should address transition planning, preparing the student for what or how he or she will be performing as an adult.

SKILL ACQUISITION

Soft skills come naturally to some people, or they can be learnt and consequently applied in practice. Let us examine the process of skill acquisition. Guthrie (1952) defined a skill as the ability to bring about some result with maximum certainty and minimum outlay of energy or of time and energy. Skill acquisition is an essential component of any learning system. The development of a skill, from playing basketball to resolving a conflict, will progress in levels of achievement. An individual will begin by struggling through attempts to perform the skill. In time, success and improved confidence will ensue. With enough practice, a person can become an expert in the performance of the desired skill. It has been described that this progression occurs through four steps (see Figure 1.2).

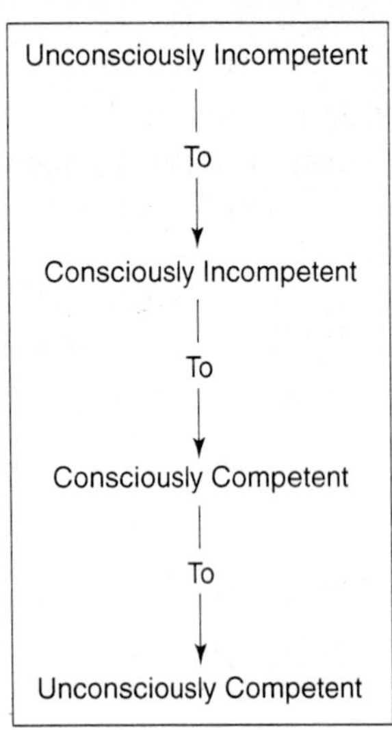

Figure 1.2
Four steps towards achievement of desired skill

Described further, a person can begin to learn a skill with no concept of it, and no ability to perform it. With some teaching and/or practice, the individual becomes aware of the skill and its goal, but still cannot perform the skill with any significant success. With vigorous teaching and practice, the skill is acquired and can be performed well, with higher levels of concentration. More practice positions the person to the highest level of function in which the skill can be performed with great success and without the need to concentrate intently. At this point, as one understands, the skill has become very repetitious. There are a great number of examples to illustrate this point. A child learning how to walk is an obvious case. At the earliest stages, the child will rise to its feet, will stagger and fall, and attempt again to rise and make a move. It does not know how to perform the skill and has no knowledge of how to improve. It is unconsciously incompetent. With more attempts, the child begins to realize the potential to walk or move, but is unable to perform the skill to any significant extent. With still more practice, the child can move about, but only with significant concentration. If it is distracted from its intent, it will quickly stagger and fall. In time, the skill becomes second nature and can be performed without conscious intent. The child has now become unconsciously competent. New skills are added in progression. The child will begin to run only to meet with a new series of challenges. Over the course of skill acquisition, the child will learn to run while catching and throwing, followed by more and more complex skills. At the highest level, very skilled athletes perform seemingly impossible tasks with relative ease. Just as the instance of learning to walk, further examples can be taken into consideration like training the thinking system to resolve conflict, to overcome non-assertiveness, to improve communication requires time, patience, and many repetitions. One school of thought vehemently argues that soft skills are innate and cannot be learned. The other school of thought holds the view that soft skills can be learned. Addressing the controversy whether soft skills are innate or not is a baffling issue and beyond the scope of this chapter. However, it is important to remember that acquiring soft skills needs tremendous effort on the part of the learner.

SOFT SKILLS EDUCATION AND TRAINING

Those who impart education and training should take action and expand programmes to include the training of soft skills. Another important consideration is that the training of hard skills is easier to define, and the returns of technical training are perhaps more immediately apparent—as a result it is much easier to ascertain whether someone has mastered a topic in Mathematics than ascertaining whether he has learnt appropriate listening skills. The training of soft skills is generally more nebulous and requires a considerable investment of time to acquire efficiency. The training begins with topics such as listening skills; assertiveness skills, conflict management skills, communication and other interpersonal skills should likewise be included in the course curriculum. Hence, teaching, training, evaluation, and a considerable follow up of soft skills have to be integrated in the learning system. This process helps the students to develop psychological well-being.

The case for improving soft skills is compelling, although it is worthwhile to remember that they are not a replacement for hard or technical skills. They are, in many instances, complementary, and serve to unlock the potential for highly effective performance in people qualified with the requisite hard skills. What is certain, though, is that soft skills will be taking on an increasingly important role in organizations across all sectors of the economy. It would seem that, given the nature of training required to develop effective soft skills, it may be necessary to start such training from the earliest years of schooling, and continue to expand them throughout all levels of education.

SUMMARY

- Due to the evolving nature of information technology, organizations and academic institutions have included soft skills as part of their curriculum.
- Hard skills are the technical competencies, which are gained through educational learning, and practical hands-on application.
- Soft skills are also interpersonal competencies and are as important as hard skills.
- According to the Expert Panel on Skills, four categories of 'soft skills' are essential skills, management skills, leadership skills, and contextual skills.
- Soft skills are very important for students in handling interpersonal relations, choosing a career and making appropriate decisions, and communicating effectively.
- Teachers play a significant role in inculcating soft skills such as communication skills, assertiveness skills, and conflict resolution skills.

REFERENCES

Drummond, I., I. Nixon and J. Witshire, 1998, 'Personal Transferable Skills in Higher Education: The Problems of Implementing Good Practice', *Quality Assurance in Education* 6(1):19–27.

Giddens, B. and C. Stasz, 1999, *Context Matters: Teaching and Learning Skills for Work*, Berkeley: National Center for Research in Vocational Education, University of California (ED 434 270).

Guile, D., 2002, 'Skill and work Experience in the European Knowledge Economy', *Journal of Education and Work* 15(3): 251–277.

Holmes, A. and S. Miller, 2000, 'A Case for Advanced Skills and Employability in Higher Education', *Journal of Vocational Education & Training: the Vocational Aspect of Education* 52(4): 653–664.

Hyslop-Margison, E. J., 2000, 'The Employability Skills Discourse: A Conceptual Analysis of the Career and Personal Planning Curriculum', *Journal of Educational Thought* 34(1): 59–72.

'Interview with Business and Industry What Do Employers Want?', *Techniques: Making Education and Career Connections* 72(5): 22–25.

Owen, G., E. Shelton, A. B. Stevens, J. Nelson-Christinedaughter, C. Roy, and J. Heineman, 2000, 'Whose Job Is it? Employers' Views on Welfare Reform', JCPR Working Paper 184, Chicago, IL: Joint Center for Poverty Research; St. Paul, MN: Wilder Research Center (ED 455 371).

Pucel, D. J., 1999, 'The Changing Roles of Vocational and Academic Education in Future High Schools', Paper presented at the Central Educational Science Research Institute, Beijing, China (ED 434 242).

Richens, G. P. and C. R. McClain, 2000, 'Workplace Basic Skills for the New Millennium', *Journal of Adult Education* 28(I): 29–34.

2

Understanding Communication

After reading this chapter, you will be familiar with:

- The meaning and definition of communication
- The dimensions and models of communication
- The basic forms and processes of communication
- Factors influencing communication
- Importance of communication in the academic setting

INTRODUCTION

Expression is the basic tenet of human communication. It is generally achieved either through signs or speech or by the method of writing. In order to express what we need, our signs, speech or writing should be meaningful. In other words, our communication should be effective; otherwise we fail to receive what we want. All means of communication should therefore be clear enough to stimulate action. Poor communication will only result in poor response.

Communication is employed extensively in the process of all types of interactions—social, educational, and official. According to Edgar Dale, 'Communication is a two-way sharing process, not a movement along a one-way track. To communicate is to make an idea common to two or more persons.' The analysis of the statement from the point of view of teaching will mean that (1) the communicator himself should be thoroughly acquainted with what he is going to teach, (2) the receivers—audience—should be equally interested in what is going to be taught to them, and (3) the process of stimulation should be heavily relied upon by the communicator.

WHAT IS COMMUNICATION?

To communicate with one another is a compulsive human need. Mutual understanding is the core of human relations. It cannot take place without communication. Man is not only a social animal but also a communicating being. He is empowered with the ability to express thoughts in words. Communication is the story of man and his efforts to express effectively. Without the aid of communication, civilization, and culture would not have progressed to this extent.

The word 'communication' is derived from the Latin word *communis*, which means 'common'. Precisely, it connotes a common ground of understanding. It is the transmission of and interaction between facts, ideas, opinions, feelings, or attitudes. Communication is an interdisciplinary concept and can be approached form various disciplines such as psychology, education, management, linguistics, and human resources, etc.

The process of communication involves sorting, selecting, and sending of symbols in such a way so as to help the listener perceive and formulate in his mind the meaning that exists in the mind of the communicator.

SOME DEFINITIONS OF COMMUNICATION

Communication is too broad a term to define. It is defined, understood, and used in different ways by people from different walks of life. Let us consider how researchers working on communication have formulated the various definitions of communication.

> The interchange of thought or information to bring about mutual understanding and confidence or good human relation.
>
> —The American Society of Training Directors

> Communication is an exchange of facts, ideas, opinions, or emotions by two or more persons. Communication is also defined as intercourse by words, letters, symbols, or messages and as a way that one organization member shares meaning and understanding with another.
>
> —Newman and Summer

> Communication is the sum of all the things one person does when he wants to create understanding in the mind of another. It involves a systematic and continuous process of telling, listening, and understanding.
>
> —Allen Louis A.

> Communication refers to a special kind of patterning: patterning which is expressed in symbolic form. For communication to take place between or

> among people, two requirements must be met: (1) a symbolic system must be shared by the people involved (we need to speak the same language or jargon or dialects) and (2) the associations between the symbols and their referents must be shared.
>
> —M.T. Myers and G.E. Myers

> The question to be asked of any administrative process is: How does it influence the decisions of the individuals without communication, the answer must always be: It does not influence them at all.
>
> —Simon

It can be seen that each of the definitions of communication seems to be self-sufficient. Though there is no consensus on a singular, categorical, and comprehensive definition of communication, it is evident that there is an overlap of constructs. Transmission and interchange of cognitions, emotions and feelings, and process of listening and understanding are the two integral and key components of the definition of communication.

DIMENSIONS OF COMMUNICATION

Communication has four broad dimensions namely intrapersonal, interpersonal, group, and mass communication. Each of these dimensions contributes to the process of developing good communication skills. The role of these dimensions in the educational setting cannot be underscored. Let us briefly examine these dimensions.

Intrapersonal Communication

It is very interesting to know what goes on in the minds of people as they think, feel, value, react, imagine, and so on. The statement 'we communicate to ourselves' may sound silly. However, it cannot be neglected as a fact. Language is nothing but sub-vocal speech. Communication is an ongoing and unending process, and it continuously takes place within us irrespective of whether we do or do not have an audience before us. This dimension is termed as 'intrapersonal' and has been the subject of psychological and cognitive studies, which attempt to learn how people respond to information and how they make decisions or store and retrieve data in their brains. It has also examined how bias, love, hatred, or even apathy can affect human interaction.

In developing a theory of meaning, Vernon Cronen and others write about what they call 'coordinated management of meaning', which necessarily starts inside people symbol-processing centres- interpersonally. 'The locus of meaning is intrapersonal, while the locus of action is interpersonal.' It is not possible to study one without the other.

How an academician forms perceptions about himself and the role of this self-perception in developing self-esteem is the domain of intrapersonal communication. How a communicator perceives himself/herself, how he estimates his self-worth, and the way he/she talks to herself/himself, positively or negatively is heavily reflected in interpersonal communication. In other words, it is a reflection of interpersonal communication. Do students like teachers who perceive themselves as inadequate persons or have low self-esteem? A teacher who is confident and has positive self-esteem may be liked by his students well. Similarly a student who is not confident may not be able to respond to the questions (of the teachers) without any anxiety. Students who are more confident would take the initiative of standing before a crowd or in an assembly and deliver a lecture. In these kinds of instances teachers are to identify those who have problems in intrapersonal communication and extend the desired help to the students so that they overcome them. Michenbaum, a cognitive-behavioural therapist, has done extensive work and named his method as 'Self-instructional training'. He holds the view that the way one instructs or talks to oneself can be modified. His research has proved that negative self-talk can be translated into positive self-talk. Intrapersonal communication is the first step towards interpersonal communication.

Interpersonal Communication

Interpersonal communication is a transaction between people and their environment, which includes other individuals such as friends, family, children, co-workers, and even strangers. Communication is now seen as a transaction in which both parties are active. The parties are not necessarily equally active—that is more likely in the case of interpersonal communication, less so in the case of mass media and their audiences—but the transaction is in some way functional to both parties. Information follows both ways to a greater and a lesser degree.

As mentioned earlier, interpersonal communication is a reflection of intrapersonal communication. The converse can also hold true. Sometimes problems in interpersonal communication result in problems related to intrapersonal communication. A teacher may approach the principal to seek approval for leave. The principal may refuse to sanction the leave. The teacher might then get involved in a verbal confrontation with the principal. The issue might remain unresolved as the teacher is expected to a class at that very moment. He, thus, starts perceiving himself as powerless, broods over the issue, and fails to attend to his students.

It is observed that most people who write about interpersonal communication appear to insist that the more communication one has, the better his/her relations will be. However, more may not always be better. It is also seen by researchers that how people see each other ('interpersonal perceptions') may have a significant effect on how those individuals interact.

What happens in interpersonal communication involves so much more than words that we must pay careful attention to people's habits of relating to each other if we are to be effective in either studying about or participating in these transactions.

Group Communication

Not all communication theorists agree on a definition of small group communication—how many people make up a group, what differences there are between dyads and other number of people in communication, etc. The field of group dynamics, however, represents a very interesting and special case of communication. It involves theories of leadership and management, small group discussion, and decision-making. A number of exercises and activities involving group dynamic, group discussion, leadership, and management principles are part and parcel of any academic setting. There is no way you can interact in your class without applying or taking into account the principles of group interaction. A teacher and an academic consultant play a vital role in enhancing group interaction and group communication.

Every teacher invariably handles a group of students. It is essential for him to understand group communication and group dynamics. Teachers need to pay careful attention to group communication which is a very sensitive issue. Therefore, any issues related to the group as a whole, such as strike or boycott, is to be handled sensitively. Similarly, when a group of teachers represents something to the principal, the issue has to be taken seriously and given due cognizance. Group communication in the academic setting cannot be ignored in view of its relevance and importance.

Mass Communication

One of the most popular areas of study in the recent times is that of the mass media—or 'Communication', as the term is used in sometimes—to indicate a broadened view of what was once termed simply as 'journalism'. At one time it was believed that audiences were a sort of homogenous group, which could be reached through a media source. This very simplified view of audiences was useful to some mass media practitioners but did not explain how complicated the process of communicating and the character of audiences are. While mass media study is beyond the scope of our chapter, there are many ties between interpersonal communication and mass communication. One-way transmission over mass media is no longer the only way to view information. As the significance of two-way (or interactive) communication grows, people studying and working in mass media will have to take into account many of the theories and principles of interpersonal communication; and merging of such fields of study is not too far away.

Each of the above detailed dimensions individually or collectively contributes to the academic field in terms of understanding and sharpening communication.

COMMUNICATION SEQUENCE

Communication sequences are punctuated while communication events are continuous transactions. There in no clear-cut beginning or end. As participants or observers of communication, we divide this continuous, circular process into causes and effects of stimuli and responses; that is, we segment this continuous stream of communication into a number of smaller pieces and label some of these causes or stimuli and other effects or responses.

Let us consider an example of a situation where the students are indifferent and the teacher does not prepare for the class. Figure (A) of 2.1 illustrates the sequence of events in which there is no absolute beginning and end. Each action (the student's indifference and the teacher's lack of preparation) stimulates the other; each serves as the stimulus for the other, but there is no initial stimulus. Each of the events may be regarded as stimuli and as responses, but there is no way to determine their specificities. Now, consider how the teacher might divide up this continuous transaction. Figure (B) illustrates the teacher's perception of this situation. From his/her point of view, the teacher sees the student's indifference as the stimulus for his/her own lack of preparation. This is seen as the response to the student's indifference. In figure (C) we see how the students might see this same sequence of events, beginning with the teacher's lack of preparation as the stimulus (or cause) and their own apathy as the response (or effect).

If communication is to be effective, if we are to understand what the other person means from his or her point of view, then we have to see the sequence of events as punctuated by the other person, that is, empathy. Further, we have to recognize that our punctuation is not a reflection of what exists in reality, but is a reflection of our own unique but fallible perception.

MODELS OF COMMUNICATION

Many influences and models have shaped the field of human communication. Communication not only is at the heart of humanity but is also the vehicle of our intentions towards each other. It is only through communication that we can realize our social potential. Without communication we would all be evolutionary misfits.

Before taking stock of the present understanding of the process of human communication, it will be useful to review briefly the major threads that run through the various approaches to the study of human communication.

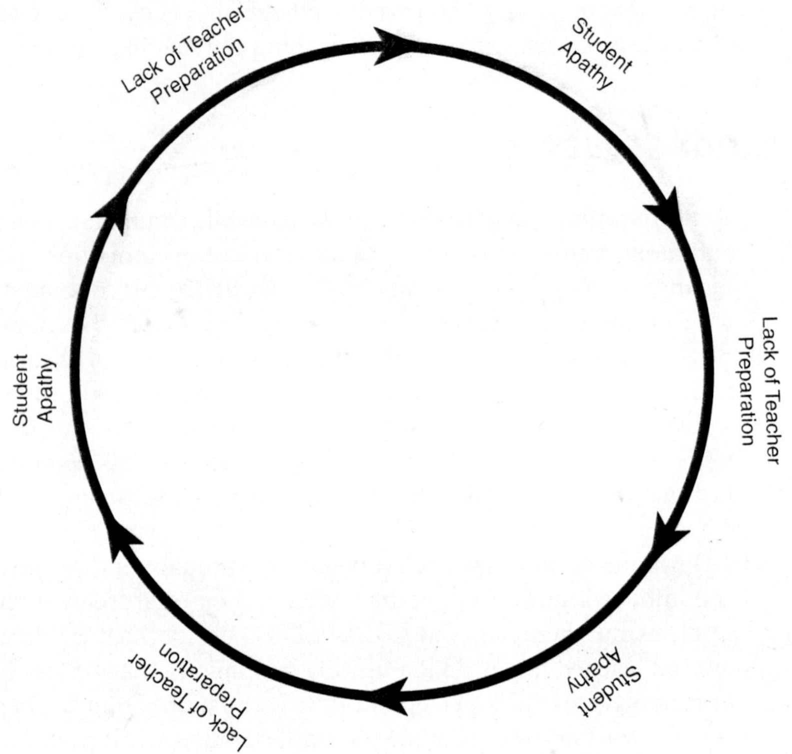

A. The Sequence of Events as it Exists in Reality

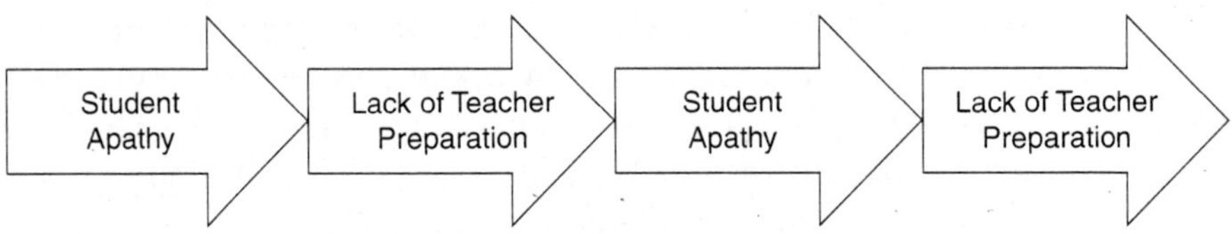

B. The Sequence of Events Punctuated by the Teacher

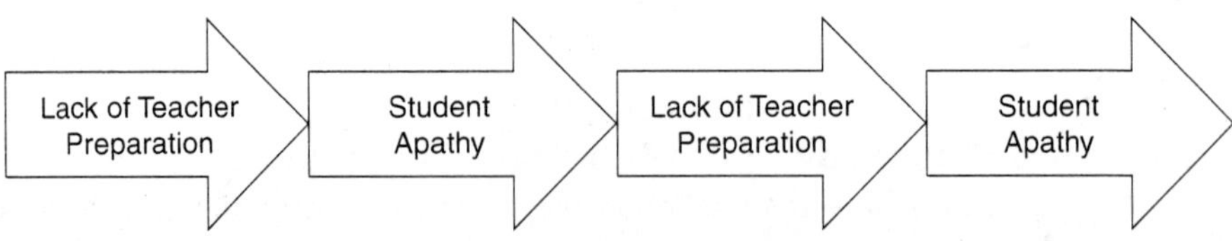

C. The Sequence of Events Punctuated by the Student

Figure 2.1
The sequence of events

The Action View: The Bull's-Eye Theory

The information theory perspective shares the view that communication consists of a one-way act like shooting an arrow into a target. You hit the bull's eye, you either get close or you miss. The whole activity of communication is centred on the one-way action of doing something to someone. How good you are depends mostly on how well you shoot the arrow, or how well you make your point. The emphasis is on the sender and his/her encoding skills. This means that how you construct a message, organize it, or deliver it, is just as crucial as sharpening your arrow, testing its feathers, flexing your bow, and shooting straight.

Another important aspect of this concept is that words actually have meanings. Therefore, if the sender knows the meaning of the words, the same meaning would be sent directly to the receivers—like a pipeline. In the simplistic view, misunderstandings would occur only if people did not know what words 'meant'. Further, if misunderstandings did occur, you would look to the way the speaker spoke/communicated to find the error. This view pays more attention to tools and skills than to the more potentially important aspects of communicating. It does not spend much time analyzing the reasons except that somewhere along the line you used the 'wrong' words, did not organize your message well enough, did not possess a good voice, did not possess enough credibility (as though credibility were a quality that a speaker could own); in essence you did not shoot straight at your target and therefore missed a little. This view is still quite widely believed, especially by those who sell their expertise to people on 'speaking success' which promises to make one an overnight success in the filed of communication if one follows a few simple rules of delivery.

The Interaction View: The Ping-Pong Theory

Another favourite way of looking at communication is to compare it with taking turns in a table tennis match: you say something, I answer; you say more, I reply; I serve, you respond. We take turns at being the sender and the receiver. This view accounts for more complexities of human communication than the bull's-eye theory. It does include the receiver by adding the concept of linear feedback, which permits the sender to exert more control over his or her communication. Yet, the communication process is still oversimplified by being treated as a process of linear cause and effect sequence. I speak, you answer.

The weakness in this view is that communication is not divided into ping and pong, stimulus and response, shot and return, action and reaction. Senders and receivers do not simply alternate in sending and receiving, and the simple linear model of cause and effect is inadequate to explain the complexities of communication. This is an ineffective model of communication from the academic point of view.

The Transaction View: The Spiral Theory

'Transactional communication' signifies that there is more than a simple interaction between senders and receivers. A transaction implies interdependency and mutual reciprocal causality among the parts of a system. Human communication, like any dynamic process, is best understood as a system where senders and receivers simultaneously change their roles. Communication is not the static picture like view of still photography. It resembles more of a continuous flow of motion pictures. Communication viewed as a process is characterized less by the actions of a sender and the subsequent reactions of a receiver than by the simultaneity of their reciprocal responses. Who starts the process is an irrelevant question, since processes have no specific beginning or end. Any communicative behaviour that we want to isolate for the purpose of analysis has a history and a future. They have lived in many places; they have said many things before, possibly to each other. In a transactional view of communication you are the cause and effect, stimulus and response, sender and receiver. Not only are you the product of your previous communicative behaviours; but also—equally importantly—what you see yourself to be is in a large measure affected by how you perceive others to behave towards you, that is, how you perceive others' communication. Your perception of other people's responses is itself the product of previous perceptions of previous responses, a lifetime of previous communication.

To view communication as a transaction does more justice to the complexities of the process than any other conceptualization we know.

THE PROCESS OF COMMUNICATION

It is abundantly clear that communication is the lifeblood of any institute, organization, or a social structure. It includes the structure through which messages pass and the way information is presented, as well as the actual content of the message themselves. Whether you are speaking or writing, listening or reading, communication is more than a single act. It's a dynamic, transactional (two-way) process that can be broken into six phases:

1. **The sender has an idea:** You conceive an idea and want to share it. A teacher has been given the task of explaining a concept. He first reads the concept and then understands it. This is the first phase of the process of communication.

2. **The sender transforms the idea into a message:** When you put your idea into a message that your receiver will understand, you are encoding, deciding on the message from word, facial expression, gesture length, organization, tone, and style, all of which depend on your idea, your audience, and your personal style or mood. Once the teacher understands the concepts, he translates it in his mind in the form of verbal structure or syntax. An active process of transforming the idea/concept into a message is the second phase of the process of communication.
3. **The sender transmits the message:** To physically transmit your message to your receiver, you select a communication channel (verbal or nonverbal, spoken or written) and medium (telephone, computer, letter, memo, report, face-to-face exchange, and so on). The channel and medium you choose depend on your message, the location of your audience, your need for speed, and the formality of the situation. Once the idea/concept is given a shape in the mind, the immediate task would be to transmit the message. To do so a communication channel is used, which involves both verbal and nonverbal communication. In the third phase of the process of communication, the teacher communicates the concept to his students.
4. **The receiver gets the message:** For communication to occur, your receiver must first get the message. If you send a letter, your receiver has to read it before he can understand it. If you are delivering a speech, your audience has to be able to listen to you, and pay attention. Once the teacher communicates the concept to his students, the students need to pay attention in order to 'listen' and process the communication.
5. **The receiver interprets the message:** Your receiver must cooperate by decoding your message, absorbing, and understanding it. The decoded message then has to be stored in the receiver's mind. If all goes well, the message is interpreted correctly; that is, the receiver assigns the same basic meaning to the words as you intended and responds in the desired way. Understanding of the concept follows by listening to it. Here the student makes an attempt to actively understand the concept. This understanding is nothing but interpretation according to communication researchers.
6. **The receiver reacts and sends feedback to the sender:** Feedback is your receiver's response, the final link in the communication chain. After receiving the message, your receiver responds in some way and signals that response to you. Feedback is the key element in the communication process because it enables you to evaluate the effectiveness of your message. If your audience does not understand what you

mean, you can tell by the response and refine your message. The student responds to and gives a feedback to the teacher either verbally or non-verbally. This is how the process of communication is completed.

Figure 2.2 illustrates how the process of communication is repeated until both parties have finished expressing themselves. The process is effective only when each step is successful. In other words, ideas cannot be communicated if any step in this process is skipped or is completed incorrectly.

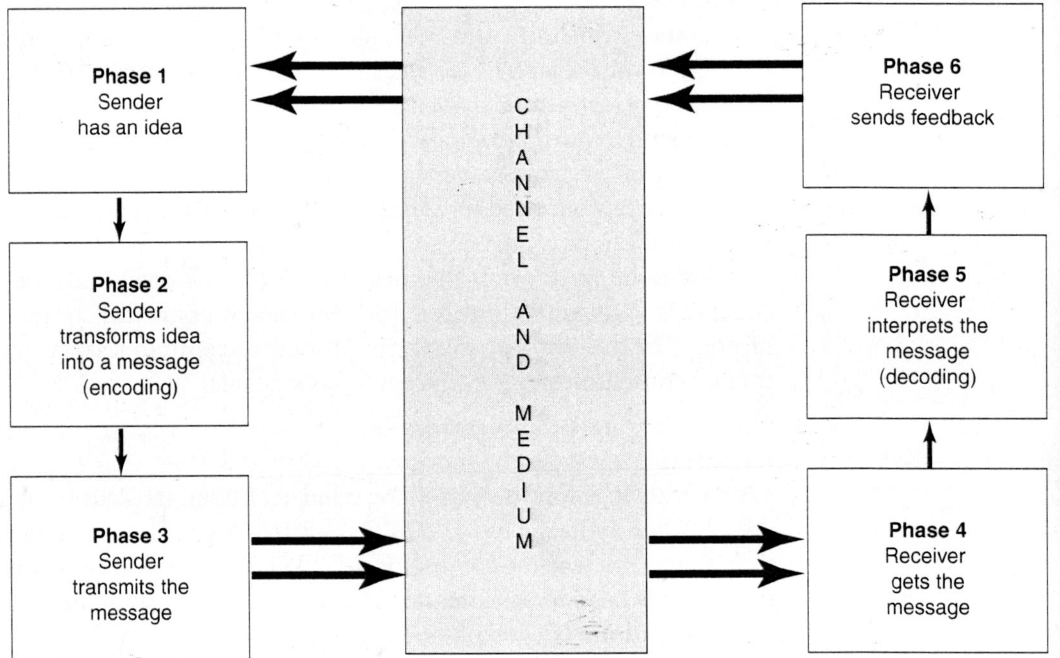

Figure 2.2
Repetition of the process of communication

Communication Barriers

Even if these six steps are successfully completed, other hurdles may prevent a speaker from communicating effectively. Communication is successful only when the receiver understands the message as intended by the sender/teacher. For example, noise is an interference in the communication process that distorts or obscures the sender's/teacher's meaning.

Communication Barriers Between People

When you send a message, you intend to communicate its meaning, but the message itself does not contain the meaning. The meaning exists in your mind and that of your receiver. To understand each other, you and your receiver must share similar meanings for words, gestures, tone of voice, and other symbols. Effective communicators do all they can to deal with barriers such as differences in perception and language, poor listening, emotional interference, cultural differences, and physical distractions. Let us look at each of these barriers in detail.

Differences in Perception and Language

The world around us constantly bombards us with sights, sounds, and other characteristic elements. Our minds organize this stream of sensations into a mental map that represents our perception of reality. Even when two people have experienced the same event, their mental images of that event will not be identical. Because your perceptions are unique, the ideas you want to express may differ from that of the other people. As a sender, you choose the details that seem important to you, a process known as selective perception. As a receiver, you try to fit new details into your existing pattern. If a detail doesn't quite fit, you are inclined to distort the information rather than rearrange the pattern.

Language is an arbitrary code that depends on shared definitions. However, there is a limit to how completely any two people can share the same meaning for a given word.

Poor Listening

Although most of us think we know how to listen, in actuality many of us are poor listeners. We all let our minds wander every now and then, as also we are especially likely to drift off when we are forced to listen to information that is difficult to understand or that has little direct bearing on our own lives. If we are tired or concerned about other matters, we are even more likely to lose interest.

Emotional Interference

It is difficult to shape a message when you are upset, hostile, or fearful. Your ideas and feelings often get in the way of being objective. Likewise, if the other person is emotional, he or she may ignore or distort your message. Although it is practically impossible to avoid all communication when emotions are involved, you should be alert about the greater potential for misunderstanding that accompanies emotional messages.

Cultural Differences

Communicating with someone from another country is probably the most extreme example of how different backgrounds and cultures may impede communication. In fact, it may be one of the hardest communication barriers to overcome-especially when your receiver's age, education, social status, economic position, religion, or life experience also differs substantially from yours. Figure 2.3 shows how shared experience contributes to shared meaning and understanding; the portion of each diagram where the circles overlap represents the level of understanding between the sender and the receiver.

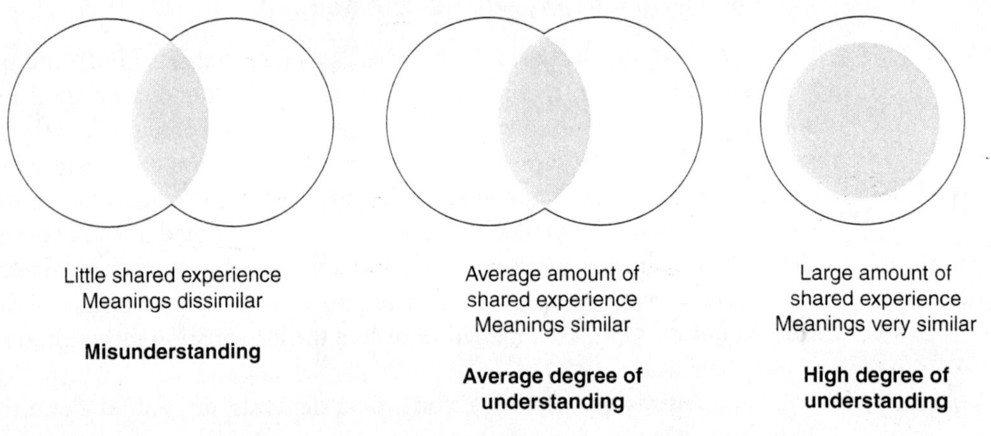

Figure 2.3
How shared experience affects understanding

Physical Distractions

Communication barriers are often physical: bad connection, poor acoustics, and illegible copy. Although noise of this sort seems trivial, it can block an effective message. Your receiver might be distracted by an uncomfortable chair, poor lighting, health problems, or some other irritating condition. These annoyances do not generally block communication, but they may reduce the receiver's concentration.

THE BASIC FORMS OF COMMUNICATION

Communication occurs in many forms. For example, Mr. Rao, the principal of a school can pick up the phone and have a conversation with Mrs. Radhika, who is a science teacher. He can choose, instead, to write her a memo. In turn, she can respond to his message in the form of her choice. He may decide to forward her message to other employees, and they may communicate it to all the other teachers and other outsiders. The process is fluid; the form in which a message is communicated changes constantly. Communication can be formal or informal, spoken or written, and internal or external.

Nonverbal Communication

Nonverbal communication is the most basic form of communication. All the cues, gestures, facial expressions, and attitudes towards time that enable people to communicate without words are different forms of communication. Anthropologists theorize that long before human beings used words to talk things over, they communicated with one another through their bodily gestures. They gritted their teeth to show anger; they smiled and touched one other to indicate affection. Although we have come a long way since those primitive times, we still use nonverbal cues to express superiority, dependence, dislike, respect, love, and other such feelings.

Most people deceive each other quite easily with their words, but since actions speak louder than words, their body language gives away their real intentions. Words are relatively easy to control; body language, facial expressions, and vocal characteristics are not. By paying attention to these nonverbal cues, you can detect deception or affirm a speaker's honesty.

Nonverbal communication differs from verbal communication in fundamental ways. For instance, it is less structured, and hence is more difficult to study. You cannot pick up a book on nonverbal language and master the vocabulary of gestures, expressions, and inflexions that are common in our culture. Even experts do not really know how people learn nonverbal behaviour. No one teaches a baby to cry or smile, yet these forms of self-expression are almost universal.

Nonverbal communication also differs from verbal communication in terms of intent and spontaneity. You generally plan your words. When you say, 'Please get back to me once you finalize you annual report,' you have a conscious purpose; you think about the message, if only for a moment. However, when you communicate nonverbally, you sometimes do so unconsciously. You don't mean to raise an eyebrow or to blush. Those actions come naturally. Without your consent, your emotions are written all over your face. Good communicators generally recognize the value of nonverbal communication and use it to enhance the communication process.

One of the famous communication researchers, Virginia Johnson, holds the view that nonverbal communication is so reliable, that people generally have more faith in nonverbal cues than they do in verbal messages. It can also be argued that nonverbal communication is not reliable. One may put forth a view that somebody may fake crying. However, it is very possible to differentiate a person who cries with agony and who fakes crying. You explain a complex concept to your students. In response to your question- whether they have understood or not- some may respond verbally in terms of 'yes' or 'no' and some may respond nonverbally by nodding their head. Do you straightaway take them for granted that they have understood the concept? Or, can you make out fake nonverbal response? In the same way it is equally possible to differentiate a vague smile and warm smile. Sometimes nonverbal communication alone may occur without verbal communication. Hence, one has to be very careful in interpreting nonverbal cues as the meaning of nonverbal communication lies with the observer, who both reads specific signals and interprets them in the context of a particular situation and a particular culture. Chances are, if you can read other people's nonverbal messages correctly, you can interpret their underlying attitudes and intentions and respond appropriately.

Nonverbal communication is important for another reason. When you have a conscious purpose, you can often achieve it more economically with a gesture than you can with words. A wave of the hand, a pat on the back all are streamlined expressions of thought.

Characteristics of Nonverbal Communication

Communication researchers have identified some characteristics of nonverbal communication. These may be found in all forms of nonverbal communication and should provide a kind of framework through which the specifics of nonverbal communication may be viewed. Nonverbal messages are characterized by being: (i) communicative, (ii) contextual, (iii) believable.
Let us examine each of these characteristics briefly.

Communicative

Nonverbal behaviour in an interactive situation always communicates. This observation is true of all forms of communication, but it seems particularly true of nonverbal communication. Regardless of what one does or does not do, regardless of whether it is intentional or unintentional, one's nonverbal behaviour communicates something to someone.

Sitting silently in a corner and reading a book communicates to the other people in the room just as much as verbalization. Staring out of the window during the class communicates something to the teacher just as much as saying, 'I am bored'. The important difference between the nonverbal communication and the verbal statements here should be noticed. The student looking out of the window, when confronted by the teacher's question- 'why are you bored?', can always claim to be just momentarily distracted by something outside. Saying 'I am bored' however prevents the student from backing off and giving a more socially acceptable meaning to the statement. The nonverbal communication, however, is also more convenient from the point of view of the teacher. The teacher, if confronted with the student's statement- 'I am bored' must act on that in some way. Some of the possibilities include saying, 'see me after the class', 'I am as bored as you are', 'who cares', 'why are you bored', and so on and so forth. All of them, however, are confrontations of a kind. The teacher is in a sense forced to do something even though he or she might prefer to ignore it.

Even the less obvious and less easily observed behaviours communicate. The smaller movements of the eyes, hands, facial muscles, and so on also communicate just as much as do the gross movements of gesturing, sitting in a corner, or staring out of a window. These small movements are extremely important in interpersonal relationships. All nonverbal behaviour, however small or transitory, is significant as each has a meaning, and each communicates.

Contextual

Like verbal communication, nonverbal communication exists in a context, and that context helps to determine the meanings of any nonverbal behaviour. The same nonverbal behaviour may have a totally different meaning when it occurs in another context. A boy's wink of an eye to a beautiful girl in the school bus means completely different from a student's wink of an eye to another friend of the same gender; it signifies a put-on or a lie. Similarly, the meaning of a given bit of nonverbal behaviour will differ depending on the verbal behaviour it accompanies. When separated from the context, it is impossible to tell what any given bit of nonverbal behaviour may mean. Sometimes, even if we know the context in detail, we still might not be able to decipher the meaning of the nonverbal behaviour.

Believable

Why we are quick to believe nonverbal behaviours when they contradict the verbal behaviour seems to be an unanswered question till date. Consider, for example, a conversation between a teacher and a student. The student is attempting to get a good grade for the course and is in the process of telling the teacher how much hard work was put into the classes and how much enjoyment was derived from them. Throughout the discussion, however, the student betrays his or her real intentions with various small muscle movements, inconsistent smiles, a lack of direct eye contact, and so on. Somehow, the teacher goes away with the feeling, based on the nonverbal behaviour that the student really did not put in a good deal of work. For the most part, research has shown that when the verbal and nonverbal messages differ, we believe the nonverbal.

Types of Nonverbal Communication

The types of nonverbal communication can be grouped into the following general categories:

Facial Expressions and Eye Behaviour

Your face is the primary site for expressing your emotions; it reveals both the type and the intensity of your feelings. Your eyes are especially effective in indicating attention and interest, influencing others, regulating interaction, and establishing dominance. In fact, eye contact is so important that even when your words send a positive message, averting your gaze can lead your audience to perceive a negative one. Although the eyes and the face are usually reliable sources of meaning, people sometimes manipulate their expressions to simulate an emotion they do not feel or to mask their true feelings. Maintaining eye contact is not important in some cultures. In fact, it can be considered impolite.

Gestures and Postures

By moving your body, you can express both specific and general messages, some voluntary and some involuntary. Many gestures—a wave of the hand, for example—have a specific and intentional meaning, such as 'hello' or 'good-bye'. Other types of body movements are unintentional and express a more general message. Slouching, leaning forward, fidgeting, and walking briskly are all unconscious signals that reveal whether you feel confident or nervous, friendly or hostile, assertive or passive, powerful or powerless.

Vocal Characteristics

Like body language, your voice carries both intentional and unintentional messages. On a conscious level, we can use our voices to create various impressions. Consider the sentence 'What have you been up to?'. If you repeat that question four or five times, changing your tone of voice and stressing upon various words, you can convey quite different messages. However, your vocal characteristics also reveal many things that you are unaware of. The tone and volume of your voice, your accent and the pace of your speaking, and all the little *um*'s and *ah*'s that creep into your speech say a lot about who you are, your relationship with the audience, and the emotions underlying your words.

Personal Appearance

Your appearance helps establishing your social identity. People respond to others on the basis of their physical appearance. Because you see yourself as others see you, these expectations are often a self-fulfilling prophecy. When people think you are capable and attractive, you feel good about yourself, and such a feeling affects your behaviour, which in turn affects other people's perceptions of you. Although an individual's body type and facial features impose limitations, most people are able to control their attractiveness to some degree. Grooming, clothing, accessories, 'style'—all modify a person's appearance. If your goal is to make a good impression, adopt the style of the people you want to impress.

Use of Time and Space

Time and space can be used to assert authority. Some people demonstrate their importance by making other people wait; others show respect by being on time. People can also assert their status by occupying the best space. Apart from serving as a symbol of status, space can determine how comfortable people feel talking with each other. When others stand too close or too far away, you are likely to feel ill at ease.

Verbal Communication

Although you can express many things nonverbally, there are limits to what you can communicate without the help of language. If you want to discuss past events, ideas, or abstractions, you need symbols that stand for your thoughts. Verbal communication consists of words arranged in meaningful patterns. To create a thought with these words, you arrange them according to the rules of grammar, putting the various parts of speech in the proper sequence. Once the syntax is formed in the mind of a person who communicates, he then transmits the message in spoken or written form, anticipating that someone will hear or read what you have to say. Therefore, language is the main aspect of verbal communication. To begin with let us examine language as a symbol system.

Language as a Symbol System

Language may be thought of as the code, the system of symbols, utilized in the construction of verbal messages. Language may be defined as a specialized, productive system capable of displacement and composed of rapidly fading, arbitrary, culturally transmitted symbols. The six characteristics of verbal communication are (i) specialization and productivity (ii) displacement (iii) rapid fading (iv) arbitrariness (v) cultural transmission.

- *Specialization and productivity:* Language is a specialized communication system and it produces creative responses and learned utterances. Introduction of new words is another dimension of productivity.
- *Displacement:* Human language can be used to talk about things that are remote in both time and space; one can talk about the past and the future as easily as the present. It has the ability to displace concepts and sometimes statements uttered in one place today may have effects elsewhere tomorrow. Displacement, together with productivity, also makes possible the ability to lie.
- *Rapid fading:* Speech sounds fade rapidly; they are short-lived. They must be received immediately after they are emitted or else

they will not be received at all. Speech signals are probably the least permanent of all communicative media.

- *Arbitrariness:* Language signals are arbitrary; they do not possess any of the physical properties or characteristics of the things for which they stand. Names are largely arbitrary: there is no real relationship between the name and the individual. And yet, names are not totally arbitrary; many names indicate the ethnic group to which an individual belongs and usually indicate sex.
- *Cultural transmission:* The form of any particular human language is culturally or traditionally transmitted. One of the consequences of cultural transmission is that any human language can be learned by any normal human being. All human languages are learnable.

Language as Meaning System

If it were not for the desire of one person to communicate a meaning to another person, language would probably not exist. Of all the functions of language, the communication of one person's meaning to another is surely the most significant. Consequently, meaning must be placed at the centre of any attempt to explain language. Although a variety of types of meanings may be identified, two general types essential to identify in communication: denotation and connotation. The denotation of a word is its objective definition. The connotation of a word is its subjective or emotional meaning. In order to explain these two types of meanings, let us take an example of the word *fail.* To an examiner this word might simply mean or denote that the student did not get 50 or more than 50. It is an objective description of a particular event. On the other hand, to the person who failed in the examination, the word means much more than getting 50 or more than 50. He or she recalls his or her preparation, stress involved in understanding the concepts, losing time, pain involved in preparing again for the exam, his or her classmates being promoted to another class, he or she remaining in the same class, and so on. To him or her it is a highly emotional word, or a highly subjective word. These emotional or subjective or personal reactions are the word's connotative meaning. Denotative meanings are relatively unchanging and static. Although definitions of all words change through time, denotative meanings generally change very slowly. But the connotative meaning changes rapidly from person to person.

Speaking and Writing

Educationists have witnessed that people tend to prefer oral communication channels to written ones. In general, talking to somebody is quicker and more convenient than writing a memo or a letter. Furthermore, when you are speaking or listening, you can pick up added meanings from nonverbal cues and benefit from immediate feedback. Even though oral communication is the preferred medium, there are times when written communication is more appropriate and effective—when the information you are conveying is very complex, when a permanent record is needed for future reference, when the audience is large and geographically dispersed, and when immediate interaction with the audience is either unimportant or undesirable. The most common types of written communication are letters, memos, reports, and proposals.

Over the past few decades, technological advances have led to the development of electronic communication. Teleconferencing, e-mail, and computer networks have revolutionized both oral and written communication and have become vital elements in achieving organizational goals. However, it is worth noting that, each form of communication also has its limitations. Protocols must be followed, and individuals must learn when it is appropriate to use each form.

Listening and Reading

Listening and reading are as important as speaking and writing. People spend more time receiving information than transmitting it. Most of us are not very good listeners. Immediately after hearing a ten-minute speech, we typically remember only half of what was said. A few days later, we have forgotten three-quarters of the message. Even worse, we often miss the subtle, underlying meaning entirely. To some extent, our listening problems stem from our education, or lack of it. We spend years learning to express our ideas, but few of us ever think of giving importance to the concept of listening. Nevertheless, developing better listening abilities is crucial for anyone in general. Reading again, is a skill in itself. One is required to read and comprehend quite a number of times during one's student or professional life. Reading with improper articulation and understanding may lead to erroneous interpretations, which, in turn, may result in further complications.

FACTORS INFLUENCING COMMUNICATION

A common experience between two or more people is essential for an effective communication. Several factors, which influence the process of communication, are outlined below and these are to be viewed carefully in view of intrinsic contradictions:

1. **Age factor (we are young or old):** A teacher's method of teaching a 4th standard student is entirely different to that of a 10th standard student. Like the age of the student, the age of teacher also matters

in communication. It is generally perceived that the experienced are more effective teachers than the inexperienced. However, this may not be true always.

2. **Sex factor (we are men or women):** Male teachers are perceived as stricter than female counterparts. Women teachers are generally perceived as effective as language teachers, while men as effective as Mathematics or science teachers. Girl students are perceived as more obedient than boys. Hence the sex factor plays a significant role in communication. However, these perceptions may no be generalized.
3. **Mental factor (we are bright, slow or average):** Teachers come across a group of students wherein some are bright and some are slow or average. Teachers generally focus much on the bright in view of the fact that they are rewarding to work with. Some teachers equally work with both the groups and strike a balance and are loved by both the groups. All teachers should strive to strike the balance with regard to the interest of students.

This is not the complete list of factors, which influence communication. There are several others but the above list includes only the major factors. The background of the student influences his receptivity to varied communications. The teacher has, therefore, to keep his mind open and go about in his work keeping in view the factors, which influence the process of communication (Prakash 1975)

COMMUNICATION IN ACADEMIC SETTING

After having discussed communication, its meaning, definition, scope, dimensions, forms, process, factors, and various other aspects, we now come to the most important factor which helps in the process of teaching. A teacher who is to teach has to be a good communicator. A teacher has, besides having complete knowledge about his subject, the following qualities:

1. He possesses is a good and pleasing personality.
2. His voice is clear and intelligible.
3. He makes is adequate preparations to present his subject.
4. He makes is a lively presentation that will instill and sustain the interest of the students.

It is beyond doubt that a teacher should be a good teacher. He should be well informed, well aware of his subject, having good personality, and should be interested in the profession. The statement that 'anyone who knows his subjects can teach it' can be misleading. So is the belief that the method is more important than the subjects matter.

Desirable features to develop good communication:

- Good physical health and personality.
- Above average intelligence.
- Creativity, imagination, and resourcefulness.
- Good grooming, poise, refinement in voice, and action.
- Courtesy, kindness, sympathy, and tact.
- Patience.
- Sincerity and honesty.
- Firmness.
- Promptness, efficiency, and ability to organize.
- Positive and encouraging attitude.
- Democratic leadership.
- Professional status.

Undesirable features to develop good communication:

- Superiority complex, arrogance.
- Inferiority complex, insecure, defensive.
- Imperfect voice- shrill or harsh.
- Ill-mannered.
- Insincere, dishonest.
- Unfriendly, unsocial.
- Disrespectful of the opinions of others.
- Lacking imagination.

Some other indications of a poor teacher are:

- Plays with chalk or some other object while teaching.
- Leans on the furniture, moves back and forth.
- Misinformation.
- Using very few teaching aids.
- Sticking to only one method of imparting instruction.
- Does not answer questions.

- Does not evaluate his work or that of his students.
- Humiliates students.
- Looses temper frequently.

In order to be an effective teacher and academician, it is important that one should have good communication skills. The practical aspects of communication as to how to develop and sharpen communication skills will be detailed elsewhere.

SUMMARY

- Good communication skills shape the impressions you make on your students. They enable you to perceive and respond to your students' needs and to influence your students to think in a particular way. Successful communicators will often turn out to be effective teachers.
- Communication connotes a meaning of common ground for understanding. It is a process of exchange of facts, ideas, and opinions. Transmission and interchange of cognitions, emotions, and feelings and the process of listening and understanding are the two integral and key components of the definition of communication.
- The scope and subject matter of communication is very broad. It has applications in virtually all the fields. It is an interdisciplinary subject involving both one-way and two-way processes. It uses a set of symbols. Both written and oral or verbal media are used to transmit messages.
- The four dimensions of communication namely interpersonal, interpersonal, group, and mass communication contribute to the process of developing good communication skills. These dimensions contribute individually or collectively to the academic field in terms of understanding communication and sharpening it.
- Significant models such as the Bull's-eye theory, the Ping-Pong Theory, and the Spiral Theory have shaped the field of human communication. Each of these theories represents action view, interaction view, and transaction view.
- Communication is a six-phase process: the sender has an idea, transforms the idea into a message, and transmits the message; the receiver gets the message, interprets the message, and reacts to the message by sending feedback.

- Communication occurs in many forms such as verbal, nonverbal, spoken, and written. The important types of nonverbal communication include facial expressions and eye behaviour, gestures and postures, vocal characteristics, personal appearance, and use of time and space. Verbal communication include speaking, writing, listening, and reading.
- Dealing with communication barriers such as differences in perception and language, poor listening, emotional interference, cultural differences, and physical distractions is an important task for all people in academic sphere.
- Several factors, which influence the process of communication, are age, sex, economic state, location, mental state, education and organization, vocation, social, and racial factor. The background of the student influences his receptivity to varied communications. In order to be an effective teacher and academician, it is important that one should have good communication skills.

REFERENCES

Bovee, Courtland L. and John V. Thill, 2000, *Business Communication Today*, New Jersey: Prentice-Hall.

Leathers, Dale G., 1986, *Successful Nonverbal Communication: Principles and Applications*, New York: Macmillan.

Prakash, Daman, 1975, A *handbook of Communication and the Cooperative Teacher*, New Delhi: International Cooperative Alliance.

Joseph, Derito A., 1978, *Communicology: An introduction to the Study of Communication*, New York: Harper & Row.

______________, 1985, *Human Communication: The Basic Course*, New York: Harper Row.

Myers, Gail E. and Michele T. Myers, 1985, *The Dynamics of Human Communication: A Laboratory Approach*, USA: McGraw-Hill.

3

Channels of Communication

After reading this chapter, you will be familiar with:

- Various channels of communication
- The importance of and reliance on communication
- Various processes of communication
- Differences between verbal, nonverbal, and meta-communication
- Your own communication style

CHANNELS OF COMMUNICATION

Source conveys messages through the channel to the receiver. Channels are vehicles that carry messages from one point to the other. Communication that the channels convey is either interpersonal within a group or mass media. In an interpersonal and group communication an individual becomes the channel. Newspapers, magazines, films, radio, television, and such other things which address a wide range of audience are mass media channels.

Depending upon the development of technology, communication process can be divided into different periods. Before the invention of electricity communication was based on primitive methods. With the invention of electricity, methods of communication attained incredible speed. In the electronic communication, messages began to be carried out or transferred with the speed of light. It is hard to imagine if further advances in communication technology are possible at all.

Here are the details of communication in different periods. Communication is also studied from the stand point of the smallest unit i.e., one to one communication, as well as from the stand point of mass media.

Channel Attributes

Depending on the effectiveness and efficiency as well as the nature of the communication, channels are also divided. These are:

- The speed with which they transmit signals.
- The ability to separate their own signals from those of other channels.
- The accuracy with which meanings are conveyed.
- The effectiveness with which channels communicate emotional information.
- The effectiveness with which channels communicate factual information.

The different major interpersonal channels are: (i) facial, (ii) gestural, (iii) postural, (iv) proxemic, (v) artifactual, (vi) vocalic.

Nonverbal Communication

Nonverbal communication has three categories: sign language, action language, and object language.

Sign language is a kind of nonverbal communication in which gestures are used in place of words or numbers. These may vary from the hitchhiker's thumb to systematic gesture languages such as the language of the deaf and dumb. We can also assimilate symbolic information by touch as in the method devised by Louis Braille, which is a form of tactile communication. Action language embraces all movements that can be used as signals. Examples of action language are to be found in the creative arts, pantomime, and ballet, and, also for instance in Japanese *No* plays and formalized church liturgy.

Signs and Words

Primitive forms of communication have been used by human beings since time immemorial. Even after the development of different technologies some societies still use the primitive forms of communication after refining them. To be able to externalize their feelings and needs, individuals first used their bodies to communicate. 'Body language' and other nonverbal languages (e.g., facial expressions, gestures, mime, dance, images, music, songs, drawings, paintings, sculpture, sport, etc.) while being used for millennia in traditional societies for a variety of purposes have not lost any of their validity and importance today despite their obvious limitations.

If we attribute significance to the symbol which we come across, we would understand how it carries a social meaning. Because people are different and unique in their own ways, the meaning they attribute to the symbol also varies. A particular symbol, word, or object has no inherent meaning and symbols do not mean the same way to everyone. Meanings reside in people and not in words. People develop meanings in accordance with their individual personality, learning, experience, and perception. This notion is crucial to an understanding of how communication works.

Object Language

If words fail in communication nonverbal languages become important. Photographs, paintings, material samples, or three dimensional models are indispensable, for instance, to an appreciation of the distinctions between temple architectures of different periods of the Indian history. Object language, because of its time-enduring qualities, plays an enormous role in archaeology, anthropology, and history. Tools and weapons were known as early as the Stone Age, and the fact that material articles almost always carry either implicit or explicit instructions with them makes it possible to reconstruct events of prehistoric times, even though we lack knowledge of the verbal language of a particular period.

Object language comprises the international and non-intentional displays of tangible things; for instance, art objects, the arrangement of flowers, architectural structures, and finally the human body and what clothes it. The choice of code will depend on the nature of communication. The use of object language may be preferred because of its direct and immediate nature; for example, the presentation of flowers, or a person tying a knot on the handkerchief to remind himself of something. The arrangement of the physical environment also conveys information. The furniture may be so arranged in a library so as to say to the reader 'make yourself at home' or 'come in if you must, but keep quiet'. Three dimensional models are useful in the appreciation of architectural structures. Object language, because of its enduring qualities, plays an important part in the transmission of documents of our cultural heritage and deforms the subject matter of the branches of knowledge such as archeology. Until the discovery of the first written document, the only clues we had to the remote past were those that survived in the form of objects (artifacts) and buildings.

Action Language

Action language is transitory, and the most universal king of language. Among animals auditory and visual perception of movements tend to set in motion other actions on the part of the perceiving animal. These actions may in turn influence the animal which initiated the first signal. This is true of human behaviour as well; for example, the deaf depend upon this phenomenon in the interpretation of lip-reading. Action language is the principal way in which emotions are expressed; for example, a person slamming his fist upon the table, friends hugging each other when meeting after a long time, a person avoiding eye contact while lying, etc. Closely related to action language are sign language and gestures. Every social group has developed definite systems of communication in which particular words, signs, and gestures have been assigned communicative significance so that it cuts across verbal language barriers.

A verbal language can be divided into vocal and non-vocal. A vocal sound need not always be symbolic; for example, a scream may be vocal and nonverbal at the reflex discharge level. At the same time a scream when interpreted by a passerby may be of a different meaning than that of the screamer. Thus, the passerby's meaning being the result of his past experience—actual or vicarious—is interpreted by him in terms of this world of experience. Frank Dance suggests that the situation and communicators determine what is and what is not nonverbal. Mark Knapp defines the field of nonverbal based on the premise that, if words are not spoken or written, they become nonverbal in nature. Nonverbal communication would then include such factors as tone of voice, and nuances surrounding words. Nonverbal communicators can either reinforce of refute the verbal messages. A good communicator will seek to reinforce the verbal message with the nonverbal message.

Paralanguage, dress, physiological, behavioural characteristics, and spatial and timing qualities are important components of nonverbal communication. The primary function of the voice is to carry words while a secondary function is to carry additional information about the words. This is accomplished through each individual's distinct, unique vocal apparatus and his manner of using it. One's speech is determined by the rate, intensity, and pitch, while linguistic variables contribute to meaning. Rate of speech is sometimes faster or slower depending upon a mental state of anxiety or a state of relaxation.

Silence is a form of nonverbal communication in addition to verbal punctuations such as 'Ah…', 'Ugh', 'You know', 'Well…', etc. Among the nonverbal aspects of communication it is important to include these features of speech that are concerned with HOW something is said rather that with WHAT is said. It includes a rise and fall in the pitch, stress, and loudness of speech as well as the tempo of speech and the unsure utterances that interrupt it. The same verbal content can be expressed in a variety of ways, and each time a different message is received, it is even possible to contradict the verbal content para-linguistically and to say 'no' in such a way that one obviously means 'yes'. These nonverbal aspects of speech are often referred to as a paralanguage.

An individual's appearance also contributes to nonverbal communication. Attire influences the way you feel about yourself, the way others feel about you and the way you communicate. Apparel that reflects the personality and attitude of an individual are termed as artifacts.

- **Emblem:** An emblem is an insignia. It is a symbol or feature of dress worn to suggest who or what the person wearing the dress is and how he desires to be identified by: a tattoo, an earring, etc.
- **Posture:** One's emotions or general state of being is revealed in the posture. Standing, sitting or walking—or putting into action such inherent

or learned/acquired qualities—can reveal one's emotions or general state of being; for example, arms tightly folded across the chest, hands in pocket, leaning against the wall, leaning forward, and so on. During a conversation, individuals interact by a turn or tilt of head and shoulders at various angles, adopt a variety of positions for their arms and legs, and generally hold themselves at different levels of tension and relaxation. These aspects of posture explain one's social relationships.

- **Gesture:** Sometimes people talk with hand gestures and facial expressions. Gestures are used to regulate or control. Not all gestures have the function of emphasizing upon what is being said. There are the two types of movements, namely, motor-primacy movements and speech-primacy movements. The speech primacy movements are subservient to speech; the motor-primacy movements replace speech to some extent. Gestures may accompany a spoken language, merely punctuating and emphasizing it, or they may take over some of the content of the message that remains partly unarticulated in verbal form. Both types of gestures are related to the intent to communicate (Kurt Danziger 1976).

The emotional and attitudinal state of the communicator is related to the non verbal form of communication. An arm around the shoulder shows friendliness, whereas legs folded one over the other while sitting may indicate a state of stress. People do not keep still when they interact. They use their hands, in gestures, shuffle their feet, nod their heads, and assume different facial expressions continuously. Certain movements seem to play a role in the setting up and maintenance of basic relationship between the interacting individuals; for example, nodding of heads, pleasantness of facial expression, and frequency of hand and arm gestures indicate affiliation or solidarity. Some people utilize such movements in addition to verbal and paralinguistic techniques (Mehrabian 1971).

- **Physiological qualities:** These are involuntary features as they are beyond one's control, like, the nervous twitch of the eye.
- **Behaviour qualities:** The extremely active communicator has an energy level which keeps audience overwhelmed. For the moderate communicator the energy level is seemingly natural and unforced. The extremely passive communicator is characterized by such a low level energy that one might be tempted to label his or her as apathetic.
- **Spatial qualities:** Communication behaviour is influenced by the space around us and between us. One can create a space for oneself in various ways: by decorating one's room, arranging books etc. Secessionist groups have resorted to the nonverbal communication of graffiti to territorialize a section of the city. This would be a spatial

quality in communication. In the home environment also there could be territorialization like grandfather's chair, father's study room, mother's prayer room, etc.

The Characteristics of Nonverbal Communication

According to DeVito (1978), all nonverbal behaviour in an interactive situation is communication. It is inevitably bound to the context, highly believable and occurs in 'packaged' forms. Nonverbal communication is frequently meta-communicative; for example, a person staring vacantly out of the window during a class gives the impression of boredom or pre-occupation. Participants are quick to believe nonverbal behaviours even when these behaviours contradict the verbal behaviour; for example, an unenergetic handshake while proclaiming happiness in the results of a discussion, avoidance of eye contact when lying.

Packaged Nature of Nonverbal Communication

Nonverbal behaviours whether of the hands, the eyes or the muscle tone of the entire body, are normally accompanied by other nonverbal behaviours that reinforce and support each other. Nonverbal communication can occur in packaged forms. We do not express fear in our eyes, for example, when the rest of the body is as relaxed as if sleeping. We do not express anger through our posture while our face smiles. Rather the entire body expresses the emotion in consensus. In fact, it is difficult to express an intense emotion with only one part of the body. It is even more difficult to express widely different or contradictory emotions with different parts of the body.

Meta-communication

According to the anthropologist Gregory Bateson, every communication simultaneously conveys two messages- the basic message and the meta-message. Meta-message is encoded and superimposed upon the basic, which indicates how one wants the other person to receive/interpret the basic message. The prefix 'meta' is a Greek word and means 'higher'. For example, a playing dog often tends to show its enthusiasm and affection by chewing or working its teeth on the object it is playing with. We understand from the basic message that the dog is biting. The meta-message is conveyed when we see that the grip of the dog's teeth is gentle, not aggressive and that the dog is wagging its tail or performing some other such gesture simultaneously. According to John Gumperz, each successful message carries with it a second meta-message which tells the listener how to interpret the basic message. A basic message by itself cannot be interpreted without the help of the meta-message. Meta-communication can be quite simply termed as 'communication about communication' (Rom Scollon and Suzanne Wong Scollon 1995).

THE FUNCTIONAL IMPORTANCE OF NONVERBAL COMMUNICATION

Nonverbal communication is important for a variety of reasons:

- Nonverbal or verbal factors are the major determinants of meaning in the interpersonal context.
- Feelings and emotions are more accurately exchanged by nonverbal rather than verbal means.
- The nonverbal aspect of communication conveys meanings and intentions that are relatively free of deception, distortion, and confusion.
- Nonverbal cues serve meta-communicative functions that are indispensable in attaining high quality communication.
- Nonverbal cues represent a much more efficient means of communication than verbal cues.
- Nonverbal cues represent the most suitable vehicles for suggestion. We can communicate our true feelings and emotions by nonverbal means accurately and frequently. Messages conveyed non-verbally are often involuntary, or the result of reflex action.

There are several types of nonverbal communication. The most important among these are kinesics—the movement of our bodies, like, smiling; proxemics or the use of space; and our use of time (Ron Scollon and Suzanne Wong Scollon 1995).

Kinesics

Smiling and laughter are universal actions but the meanings attached to them are different depending on the context. When two persons meet in Europe, the first thing they might do is to shake hands as a matter of social courtesy. For the same reasons, two people meeting in Asia would perhaps hug each other or just bow their heads. If the meanings attached to these nonverbal signs are not understood, the very same actions can lead to misinterpretation and the whole process of communication would collapse. Kinesics can be divided into three major areas—**prekinesics, microkinesics,** and **social kinesics.** Prekinesics is concerned with the physiological aspects of bodily movements. Microkinesics is concerned with bodily emotions that communicate different meanings, while social kinesics is concerned with the role and meaning of different bodily movements (DeVito 1978).

Paul Ekman and Wallace V. Friesen classified the body movements into five types. This was done on the basis of the origins, functions, and coding of the behaviour. They are **emblems, illustrators, affect displays, regulators,** and **adaptors.** Emblems translate words or phrases. Illustrators are nonverbal behaviours that accompany the verbal messages. Affect displays are the movements of the facial area that convey emotional meaning e.g., anger, happiness, surprise, etc. Regulators are nonverbal behaviour that regulate, monitor, maintain, or control the process of speaking by another individual; for example, we nod our heads, purse our lips, adjust our eye focus, etc. Adaptors are nonverbal behaviours that resorted to in private or in public—but without being seen; for example, when you are alone, you may sit with your legs flung over the arm of the chair or you might talk loudly, something that you may not do in public.

Proxemics—The Use of Space

When individuals interact with one another they maintain some distance that is termed as proxemics. The usual nose to nose distance in ordinary conversation is four to five feet and variations of even a few inches may create feelings of discomfort. The narrowing of this distance by one individual may be interpreted as a higher degree of intimacy, which may no be to the liking or comfort of the other person. In different parts of the world individuals of differing cultures have their own sense of a comfortable distance between them and the person they are talking to. The orientation of two people in a discotheque will be different from that between a professor and a student in a classroom, even though unknown to the two in the discotheque; one may well be a professor and the other a student (Berg and Boguslaw 1985). It has been observed that this distance is the maximum in North America and the distance is the closest in the far Eastern regions with Mediterranean countries falling somewhere in between. Effective communication takes place if one knows and respects these differences in nonverbal signs in intercultural communication.

Use of Time

Different cultures have different attitudes towards time management and work. This has always been the basis of argument, when people of differing cultures meet at a common forum. The speed with which different cultures achieve their goals reflects their agreement with Utopian time or the Golden Age concept of time to a considerable extent. In the advanced countries of the West, the trend is towards modernization and progressive thoughts. Most westerners seem to be time-conscious while people from the East, traditionally have been observed to take a more relaxed view of time.

SPEECH

Speech is an important part of communication. It serves a number of different functions. There are four basic functions of human speech—to teach, to please, to move, and to defend oneself. The functions of speech are based on the five essential elements in communication—source, channel, code, receiver, and referent. Each of these components has a specific category of speech associated with it.

Types of Speech and Their Functions

Emotive speech serves a psychological function and is readily used to express the feelings, attitudes, or emotions of the speaker:

- Phatic speech, which creates social relationships.
- Cognitive speech, which makes reference to the real world and is frequently referred to as referential, denotative, or informative.
- Rhetorical speech, which is also referred to as directive or connotative.
- Meta-lingual speech, which is used to talk not about the objects and events in the real world but about speech itself.
- Poetic speech, which serves to structure the message to which it had its primary orientation (DeVito 1978).

ORAL COMMUNICATION

It is the most common form of verbal communication. Speech is more natural than writing and is the source of all languages. Oral communication has distinct advantages over written communication. It is direct and personal; it has a wide variety of styles ranging from highly formal to completely informal. The grammar of spoken language is more flexible than the grammar of written language; it is not permanent (unless tape recorded); it tells the receiver more about the sender (through accent, dialect) and so on.

Facial Communication

The face indicates quite a number of things. It functions primarily as an affect display system. No other communication system serves this function as effectively or efficiently. The person, who is being communicated to, can identify consistently and accurately the emotions of the communicator through his facial expression. These facial expressions are usually a reliable source of meaning provided the person communicated to can interpret or understand:

- what the communicator's facial expression could mean,
- how such meanings are apt to relate to the actual intentions and feelings of the communicator, and

- how he or she can develop his capacity to encode and decode meanings via facial expression.

Ten classes of meanings can be communicated by facial expressions: happiness, surprise, fear, anger, sadness, disgust contempt, interest, bewilderment, and determination. These facial expressions accurately reflect an individual's internal state. The face is often called 'the index of the mind'. To quote—'the human face has evolved as the most potent transmitter of information that we know and the transmitter we most readily learn to tune in to'. The face, furthermore, gives a high level of feedback that may be isomorphic to the transmissions one is making; for example, blushing, smiling, holding a stern/stiff upper lip. When we blush, the message is conveyed to others and through a multitude of ways we receive that same message and feel humbled, foolish, and confused. However, the expressions on the face can be effectively controlled to mask one's true emotions, if and when a person wants to.

Gestural Communication

Gestures have been an integral part of communication, since time immemorial, especially when one needed to address large gatherings of people. It was however, more suitable for communication among smaller groups because of the close physical proximity of the group members. Gestures represent a form of nonverbal communication. Even today, a communicator's gestures are reliable indicators of the intensity of his or her feelings. Gestures serve two functions:

1. They are reliable cues to a communicator's behavioural predispositions, whether cooperative, defensive, or hostile.
2. They function to regulate interactions among group members by communicating the member's attitudes and feelings.

Gestures comprise the form of communication, to which all physical movements or postures to which meaning is ascribed. These forms of expression range from an involuntary reaction reflecting one's personal attitude, to the conscious use of an elaborate code of signals, as in the occupational codes of railway men, supervisors, structural workers and scouts, or the deaf-mute sign language. Symbolic gestures may have the same, varied, or exactly opposite meaning in different cultures. Gestures are related to the group opinion process in many ways. Within group situations like crowds, mobs, audiences, and other face-to-face groups, the membership is affected not only by the gestures of leaders, but by the gestures, physical postures, and facial expressions of their fellows. Such gestures may be profoundly indicative of their attitude.

Postural Communication

Posture functions to define the nature of relationships that may endure for a considerable period of time. Posture often functions symbolically to communicate what one sees as the type of relationship with other persons that is expected or even demanded because of one's position.

The sociologists introduced several constructs to identify nonverbal communication. They first distinguished emblems, which are gestures that replace words and are encoded arbitrarily and with intent (for example, the hand signals of a football coach or a cricket umpire). Next they identified different types of gestures that are used in conjunction with speech:

(a) batons—movements that accent a particular word or phrase;

(b) ideographs—movements that trace the flow of an idea;

(c) deistic gesture—movements that point to available referents;

(d) spatial gestures—movements that portray relationships in space; and

(e) kinetographs—movements that depict a bodily action.

Nonverbal Communication and Intent

Verbal messages can be controlled better than our nonverbal messages. The greater the awareness of one's messages, the greater is the likelihood of precise communication. Nonverbal communication is not always unintentional. Many communicators are able to skillfully reinforce or even combine their verbal messages with their nonverbal messages, combinations of the verbal and the nonverbal may be employed not only to enlighten but also to obscure the issues involved, especially in politics, business, and advertising. Indeed, in every walk of life, words may be used to conceal forthcoming actions; and contradictory expressions are constantly used to create confusions in communication. The principles on which verbal language are based are very different from those of the nonverbal. Words enable us to express abstractions. A single word can denote a single idea or event, but to be more specific, one has to use a string of words. Nonverbal language is analogic and continuous, but not as versatile as verbal language.

VERBAL COMMUNICATION

Language is called the 'vehicle of expression'. There are three known forms of language—the sign (pictorial) language, vocal (spoken) language, and the symbolic (written) language.

Language can be defined as a system of orderly vocal sounds and combinations of sounds manipulated by one individual (the sender) to form a message which will facilitate the creation of a meaning in the mind of another individual (the receiver). Language is essentially a system of interrelated parts working together as a whole. Communication is most effective when all the parts of the system are working together smoothly. Orderly vocal sounds help the receiver to recognize and identify the sounds or the combination of sounds. As we learn to talk, we learn not only to produce sounds that will be recognized, but also to combine units of sounds into more complex structures, for example, expressions such as 'Want water' becomes 'May I have a glass of water?'. What makes human language unique is that humans are able to manipulate language in a manner that satisfies their needs. Individuals, thus, make functional use of language. We vocalize some sounds to another person to achieve some results. The intent of the communicator is not just to vocalize, but also to create a message with those sound combinations, so as to receive particular response from the receiver. The message so formulated is focused on the receiver. If the receiver understands the message, then, the first step has been taken in the creation of a communication cycle between sender and receiver. Recognizing the signs transmitted by the sender, the receiver can assign a meaning to those words. A meaning is assigned when the receiver interprets the message sent. The language system is functioning properly when the meaning received is vquite similar to that intended.

Language has sound and form and is made up of parts that work together. These parts may not mean anything individually. Language has context, and is influenced by the social context in which it operates. The signal that has one effect in a particular context may have an entirely different effect in another context. Words have numerous meanings. The meaning is determined by the context in which the word is used. Language has symbols. When we voice sound in a particular way, we are creating stimuli. As we learn to use language we learn that these stimuli stand for certain objects or referents. Thus, we know that the utterance of the word 'table' stands for a piece of furniture. Language has utility. It is functional and is used for specific purposes. Language has capacity because it is used as a tool. It has the ability to adapt to changing social conditions.

LANGUAGE AS A MEANS OF COMMUNICATION

There are a number of languages that are used in verbal communication. There are approximately 3,500 languages identified worldwide as of now. However, while speech is common to all societies, writing is not. The number of written languages is much lower, with one estimate indicating not more than 500 in all. It is estimated that there are at least 16 languages spoken by more than 50 million people. These include Chinese, English, Russian, Spanish, Hindi, Portuguese, Bengali, German, Japanese, Arabic, Urdu, French, Malay, Italian, Telugu, and Tamil. About 1,250 languages are spoken on the African continent alone. Some of these such as Swahili, Wolof, and Hausa cover large areas and even nations. In Europe, there are 28 official languages. The people of South Asia use 23 principal languages. Most countries have a large number of internal languages, In the US, the number of such languages are 89. India recognizes 15 for official and educational use alone, with a total number of languages and dialects exceeding 1,650. In Ghana, the total number of languages is 56 and Mexican Indians have more than 200. This multiplicity of languages, each the incarnation of long traditions, is an expression of the world's cultural richness and diversity. Language problems inevitably occur, but the development of a truly national communication system covering the entire population cannot be achieved unless more languages are used for information and cultural activities, and the ideology that any language policy should be an intrinsic part of communication policies is recognized.

Language is necessarily ambiguous. It means that in order to communicate, we must always arrive at immediate conclusions about what other people mean. Meaning is the process of assigning a particular significance to a particular stimulus. The individual receiving the stimulus assigns meaning or significance on the basis of his ability to understand and experience. Language works in a comparable way. When someone says something, we must be able to recognize what he or she means. We draw inferences based on two main sources—the language they have used, and our knowledge about the world. Such knowledge includes expectations about what people would normally say in such circumstances. Understanding both the meaning of the sentence as well as the speaker's added meaning requires two kinds of knowledge. Sentence meaning depends on knowledge of grammar, speaker's meaning depends on knowledge of context. Often, some of the components of communication are manifested in a very explicit from, while other components remain tacit, that is unexplained; for example, the structure of a business organization is always presented in an organization chart. This is an explicit manifestation. At the same time the unofficial power structure or authority structure by which decisions are directly taken is normally not explicitly given—it remains tacit (Ron Scollon and Suzanne Wong Scollon 1955).

The study of the relationship between language and meaning is called semantics. Since the assignment of meaning is a psychological process or mental activity, semantics is the study of the relationship between language and thought as well.

Action Language

Action language is transitory. But at the same time it represents a universal kind of language. When people wish to convey the exact nature of a situation to others, such as, ideas involved in the performance of music, in the servicing of machinery, in teaching flying, painting, photography, or dance, this can often be done more efficiently in a nonverbal way. It is also the way in which emotions are expressed, like the slamming of a fist on the table during the course of a deadlocked argument, or showing joy when one watches one's favourite team winning match.

Pictorial Language

Gesture and speech were man's first means of communication. The pictograph was probably the first stage in codifying his ideas. In the early beginnings of man's social history, there were pictorial symbols denoting a real object, person, or institution and these formed the primitive system of writing used by the Egyptians, Sumerians, and the Babylonians. Still these symbols did not satisfactorily express ideas, actions, or emotions. The 'ideograph' was developed, denoting a combination of actions and ideas, like, a drawing of the sun and the moon to denote time or light. Among the more recent uses of pictorial language are the diagrams of the botanist, or the use of Venn Diagrams in mathematics.

LANGUAGE AND EVERYDAY COMMUNICATION

Linguistic Functions

Depending upon the linguist's importance distinctions are made between 'linguistic' and 'non-linguistic' is made. Linguistics refers to the degree to which signals are integrated into the verbal content of an utterance. Since it uses words, the verbal language is the clearest example of a linguistic signal. An overall classification of all the different types of verbal and nonverbal signals is possible only on a scale of linguistic-ness. Figure 3.1 exhibits the completed scale of linguistic-ness).

Linguistics does not prescribe rules of correct usage. In any given situation, the setting and the circumstances must dictate the appropriate usage. It is impossible to generalize what is linguistically right or wrong. One can only be concerned with appropriateness. Communication failure could be a result of language failure. If you cannot understand someone's language, communication cannot take place easily. If we cannot speak each other's language we have a language failure. Sometimes we speak the same language and fail to communicate because of the way we use the language.

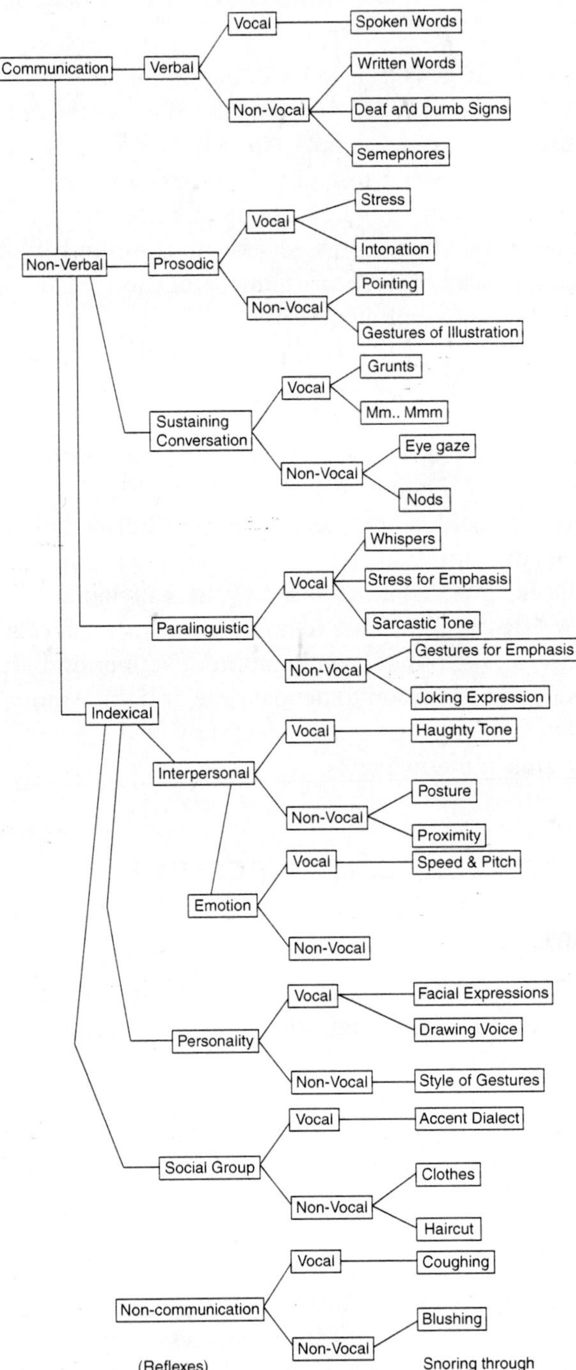

Figure 3.1
Completed scale of linguistic-ness

When language becomes a barrier to the creation of meaning rather than a tool for its facilitation, it is again a language failure. Language is a system of symbols. Its success depends upon the skills of the communicator in using those symbols. Languages are situation-specific, but, at the same time, person-specific as well. In any communication situation, the communicators (senders and receivers) are more or less skilled in the use of language. The objective of all communication must continue to be understanding, and language can be considered effective only to the extent to which it facilitates understanding. Language is designed to help a communicator, create meaning in the mind of the receiver. This creation of meaning can also be called understanding. If the communicator has created the desired and appropriate meaning in the receiver's mind, one can then say that understanding has been achieved and proper use of language has contributed to the effectiveness of communication.

WRITING AND PRINTING

Man extends himself through media. Writing made it possible for man to transmit his message to his people without direct contact. It also allowed man to record his history, works of art, and knowledge for the present and future generations. The Chinese gave the world paper to replace expensive Egyptian parchment. In 1450 John Gutenberg, by printing his book, enabled man to communicate with more people than ever before in the history of communications.

Speech is transitory. Writing gives permanence to communication, preserves the record, and makes it accessible. Without writing there can be little organization and permanence of knowledge. Pictorial and phonetic writing ensured that complete records of incidents, of history, of folklore, wisdom and sayings, of legal forms, thought, and opinions could be preserved.

VISUAL AND AUDIO-VISUAL MEDIA

Through the visual media, man can share with others any language or image form he wishes by reproducing it via a printed and/or photographic process. The visual media has made it possible for people all over the globe to receive new and valuable information through books, magazines, newspapers, photographs, and other visual material. With the advent of the Internet, visual medial facilities like e-mail and chatting has been made available.

Any meaningful sound can be converted into electrical or light waves and transmitted instantly in the audio communication media. Man can now talk to his neighbor on a telephone, send voicemail via the Internet, listen to the news on the radio, play his favourite music on a cassette/CD player, record on tapes or discs, and speak to his fellowmen as they walk on the moon.

Man in the audiovisual communication world becomes seen and heard at the same time. TV has brought a new world of entertainment, information, and influence into the living rooms of millions of people. In the classroom, motion pictures have brought the world close at hand. Telephones now combine audio with a visual aid allowing the receiver to hear and see the sender. New heights of success have been reached with such inventions, contributing towards faster, easier, more efficient, and far-reaching communication.

EXTENSION OF VISUAL EXPRESSION

Visual communication is a form of expression which in this century has been dramatically vitalized by the invention of moving images carried by cinema or television screen. Despite the instant appeal of such images, the older static picture has lost none of its importance, as the frequent and widespread use of wall sheets, posters, hoardings, illustrations, and comic strips and 'picture novels' testify. The poster, either handwritten or printed, often illustrated, is a traditional example of a simple means of communication between the producer of goods or ideas and potential consumer. It fulfils multiple functions. Advertising, informing, exhorting, persuading posters have also been a favoured communication medium at particular moments in history, such as World War II, the anti-nuclear armaments movement, the collapse of the Berlin Wall, the October Revolution in USSR, the students' movements in 1960s and during various periodic changes in China.

Photography

Photography is the art of the process of producing images on a sensitized surface by the action of light or other radiant energy. The picture is a visual message that was encoded by the photographer. The message is transmuted when someone looks at the photograph. It is one of the several means of communicating ideas. The first photograph was taken 150 years ago. Photography has grown to become one of the most common types of medium for communicating. It is used by the media producer to attract the attention of the receiver, to inform, influence, and support the written message.

Cartoon

The cartoon is simply a pictorial crystallization of a current thought. It was the English periodical *Punch* which first labelled some of its illustrative drawing as 'cartoon' in the early 1840s, and the term has been used since that time to designate any drawing that illustrated a social issue. The cartoonist may effectively use humor. In crisis situations a humorous cartoon may be especially effective in influencing opinions. Laughter provides a welcome release from tensions. Over the years the cartoons have variously touched subjects like strikes, international situations, public issues, interactions of husband and wife, parents and children, leisure time situations, and work situations.

Caricature and the Cartoon—The Difference

The caricature is an instrument of satirical and sometimes spiteful personal attack. It has been a weapon of venomous attack, used as an instrument for the manufacture of public opinion, while the cartoon has come to be regarded as a humorous and sarcastic comment on the topic uppermost in the nation's mind. The caricature is a subtle exposing of the individual's physical peculiarities or idiosyncrasies, whereas the 'cartoon, in the modern sense is—with or without humor—a forceful presentation by means of exaggeration of a topic political or moral issue' (W. Murrell 1933).

The Comics

During the latter half of the 19th century, various series of humorous drawings began to appear in the back pages of American magazines. But it was well towards the close of the century before the now popular comic strip was presented in the newspapers around February 1896 that the readers of the *New York Sunday World* were presented with funny drawings in colour, the first comic strip by 'Outcault'. Comics are a number or series of pictures which present an episode in the life of the characters, and thus tell a story. There are usually some additional verbal captions, explanations or dialogues, encapsulated in what are known as 'speech balloons'. The most celebrated are syndicated in thousands of newspapers or published as comic books reaching worldwide audience of millions. Others may be disseminated to smaller audiences, but nevertheless more often attain high quality, aesthetic value and socio-political influences.

The theme of the early scripts was mainly the playing of practical jokes of a crude slapstick variety. These picture comics were indigenous to America, bearing little resemblance to anything in the European, or the Oriental tradition. According to A1 Capp, the legendary American folklore comic strip artist 'the true function of the cartoonist is to hold up to his fellowmen a mirror of their own foolishness, and join them in the laughter'. Since the comic strip has come to be devoted to purveying pictured stories, often not humorous, the range of stereotypes acquired from them has widened. Children's idea of life in the jungle, life on Mars, life in the 25th century, life as a gangster or a detective and so on must have been influenced by these pictures. In addition to entertainment, the comics have been somewhat involved in matters of economic, political, and general social significance. During World War II, comic strips and books were used to sell abound, keep citizens alert for sabotage, promote salvage drives, solicit blood donors, for recruiting, and numerous other campaigns.

Charts, Graphs and Statistics

The way of showing the relationship of quantities to one another is to present them in charts and graphs. These are intended to make intelligible at a glance certain relationships that otherwise would have to be described at great length. Straight-line graphs, cumulative charts, bar charts, maps, circle charts, various designs of comparable size, and the like, are presented to newspaper and magazine readers with increasing frequency. Promoters in various fields use graphs to present information. Advertisers, government bureaus, and special-interest groups use charts, graphs to the audience to explicate the concepts. If the data are accurate the unbiased theses may be extremely useful tools for transmitting ideas.

MASS COMMUNICATION

Among the four major forms of communication, mass communication is at the extreme end, beginning with dyadic, interpersonal, and the small group communications. Since public speaking can be broadcast over the radio, the mass media level of communication can greatly expand the potential audience of any given speaker. A larger part of mass communication can be carried through print and electronic signals. While we know and can control the audience in the other three levels of communication, it is not so in the case of the mass media. A single electronic signal is beamed out from the control tower of a TV station, and there is very little control over who is going to receive it. Further, while only a finite number of people become the receivers at a public communication level, the number of potential receivers in the mass media is enormous—in some situations the number can turn into millions.

The Nature and Influence of Mass Communication

The different media have variously been charged with responsibility for:

1. lowering the public's cultural tastes;
2. increasing rates of delinquency;
3. contributing to general moral deterioration;

4. lulling the masses into political superficiality; and
5. suppressing creativity.

This is a very alarming list, and if the apparently innocent device in our living rooms is actually guilty of such vicious influences, they should, of course, be viewed carefully. On the other hand, advocates of opposite points of view tell us that our newspapers, radios, and television sets are not insidious devices. In fact, they are our faithful servants or even saviours in that they are:

1. exposing sin and corruption;
2. acting as guardians of precious free speech;
3. bringing at least some culture to millions;
4. providing harmless daily entertainment for the tried asses of the labour free;
5. informing us of the world's events; and
6. making more beautiful our standard of living by their unrelenting insistence towards the purchase and consumption products to stimulate our economic institution.

If such claims are true, to reject such benefactors or even to suggest that their content is uninspiring would appear to be premature.

The Functions of Mass Communication

The proof of usefulness of any idea, object, or process is its ability to satisfy a need, partially or completely. Mass communications have the capacity to perform many functions either individually or in conjunction. The immense popularity of the medium testifies to the degree in which it performs these functions. Its pervasive influence is a measure of the satisfaction derived by its audience. Some of the most important functions are discussed in the following pages.

Entertainment

The mass media entertain in order to secure the attention of group of people so that they may in turn sell their attention to advertisers. This seems to be the major reason why mass communication exists. They exist so that they may sell viewers to advertisers. In Western societies, if the media did not entertain they would no longer have viewers and would quickly be out of business. In countries like India, where the State supports the media to a certain extent, the existence may not entirely be based on the advertisement lobby. By entertainment is meant the diffusion of cultural and artistic products through signs, symbols, sounds, and images, of drama, dance, art, literature, music, comedy, sports, games, etc. for personal and collective recreation and enjoyment.

Reinforcement

Another aspect of this function is that we actively search for the reinforcement that the media provide. Thus, individuals who continue to smoke, although they may have wavering doubts that they should quit, may well seek out cigarette advertisements in the newspapers and magazines. These advertisements will reinforce their behaviour is just fine; as cigarettes are enjoyed by their role model, they are low in tar and notice and in the process they feel that they are getting all the pleasure they seek.

PERSUASIVE COMMUNICATION

Communication–Persuasion Matrix

The prime components involved in the process of persuasive communication have been identified as source, message, channel, receiver, and destination (independent variables) and presentation, attention, comprehension, yielding, retention, and overt behaviour (dependent variables).

A convenient framework for understanding the entire process in the form of a matrix greatly facilitates the study as set out in Table 3.1.

Table 3.1 Communication–Persuasion Matrix

Dependent variables	Independent Variables				
	Source	Message	Channel	Receiver	Destination
Presentation					
Attention					
Comprehension					
Yielding					
Retention					
Overt behaviour					

Source: Handbook of Communication, W. J. McGuire, 1973.

When, for theoretical or practical reasons, we want to estimate the persuasive efficacy of a campaign or hypothesize the relation to persuasion impact of some communication variable, then we can analyse the communication aspects of the situation into the various volume headings and estimate row. Such a column-by-row analysis makes the question more manageable and also calls our attention to aspects that we might otherwise overlook.

One pervasive complexity revealed by this matrix is that a communication factor that is conducive to persuasion via one of the behavioural steps (for example comprehension) tends to be detrimental to it via another step (such as yielding).

We have such a situation in the case of 'fear appeals' where pointing out more vividly the dangers of non-compliance might increase 'yielding' but decrease 'comprehension' and 'retention' of the relevant message content. It also occurs with certain personality characteristics like self esteem, which are conducive to attitude change through increased 'attention' and 'comprehension' but are detrimental via increased 'yielding'.

Again one can with some analytic skill compare the level at which the maximum impact occurs in one situation with that in other situation. For e.g., if we learn empirically in a particular public health campaign the level of fear arousal that is optimal for getting to public to take adequate health measures in a given situation, we can then with some interpretative skill state in other analyses the situation taking into account how much of the variance in attitude change impact will derive from each of the six mediating steps in the matrix.

Education/Persuasion

The purpose of education has always been that of providing useful information and adding to the storehouse o knowledge. Transmission of knowledge so as to foster intellectual development, the formation of character, and the acquisition of skills and capacities at all stages in life are the basic exemptions out of the process of education. But education and persuasion have always had something in common. Both employ communication from one source to change the views of the target receiver, except that education aims at changing the beliefs, while persuasion and propaganda aim at changing the feeling and dispositions to a purpose, i.e., action to go for the product or service being offered. Changes or conversions seldom occur with extremists but they do occur with those in the middle of the road. Political preference, religious attitudes, social commitments and the like however, are not as easily changed as a decision to switch from one brand of toothbrush to another. All these have to be kept in mind while analyzing educational or persuasive communication using the matrix form.

Socialization

The media provide the viewers with the values that form their opinions. They do this in stories, in discussions, in articles, in comics, in advertisements and commercials, in all of these situations we are taught how to dress for different occasions, the proper way to eat, what a proper meal should consist of, how to hold a discussion, how to respond to people of different national and racial groups, how to behave in strange places, and so on.

As with all human attributes there are individual differences, but most of us to a greater or lesser degree show a desire to be with others just for the sake of it. We particularly value and seek out contact with those of similar attitudes and experience, where interaction offers rich communication potential. The experience of separateness arouses anxiety. Separate means being cut off, without any capacity to use the human powers of interpersonal communication. The importance of social communication is perhaps reflected by the observation that deafness is often found to be greater burden to bear than blindness. Loss of sight, our dominant sense, may make performing everyday tasks immeasurably more difficult, but deafness cuts off our primary mode of contact with others. Thus, socialization and communication are intertwined.

SUMMARY

In this chapter, we have been acquainted with the various channels—both verbal and nonverbal communication. This gives us an in-depth knowledge of the processes of communication, qualities of communication and the differences between different modes of communication. The channels of communication familiarize a teacher with the psychological, social, and motivational aspects of communication, which is very important for the teacher to know, understand an d practice communication effectively, the objective here is to familiarize the teacher as to how communication works, and that, to be an effective communicator, one has to be familiar with the different form, aspects, processes and channels of communication. A teacher also needs to understand, decipher, and respond to students' communication pattern, interest, motivation, etc. The knowledge of the channels of communication will equip the teacher to handle interpersonal and didactic communication effectively.

4

Evolution and Theories of Communication

After reading this chapter, you will be familiar with:

- Historical perspective of communication
- How communication evolved from a very simple process to the most complicated process in the present time
- Theoretical underpinnings to understand communication
- Trends in communication study
- Communication theories that help development of concepts

THE EVOLUTION OF COMMUNICATION

We start our journey towards the understanding of communication by examining it as it has been perceived over the years. When we make an attempt to study a subject, it is essential to know the historical evolution of the subject in order to understand its present status and future trends. This chapter follows this methodology in dealing with communication per se.

Systems

A system is any entity or a whole that is composed of interdependent parts. Systems have characteristics and capabilities, which are distinct from those of the separate parts. It evolves from the combination of the parts.

The Evolution of Communication Study

The history of communication is as long as the history of human civilization. It has a rich and long history, which can be traced back to the Babylonian and Egyptian writings prior to the 5th century BC. The initial contributions to communication study came from scholars who were trained in the discipline of rhetoric. They viewed communication as the practical art of persuasion.

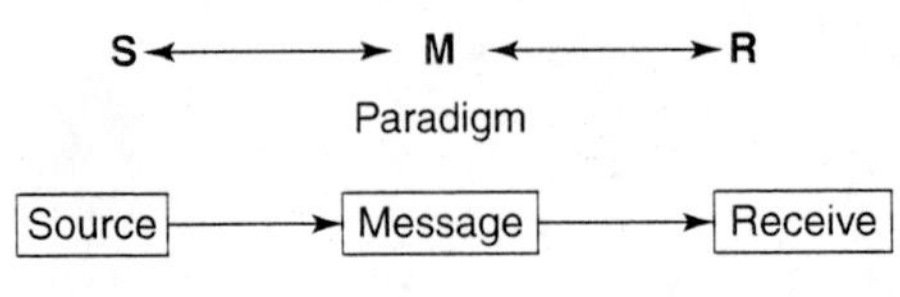

Figure 4.1
The classical S > M > R perspective (paradigm)

Aristotle and Plato, who were particularly significant to early communication study, saw rhetoric and public speaking not only as an art but also as a legitimate area of study. From its early beginnings, communication was seen as a process in which a speaker constructed messages to be transmitted to a receiver to bring about desired responses in his or her receiver—as set out in Figure 4.1.

This perspective also has been termed as a paradigm by many scholars of sociology like Thomas Kuhn because this broad framework guided the thinking of researchers in their studies.

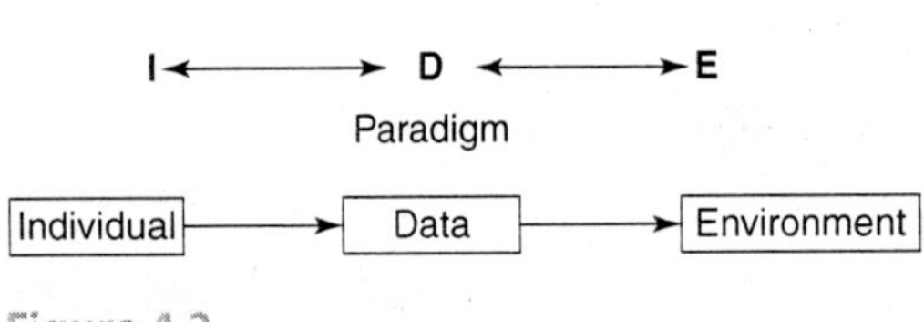

Figure 4.2
IDE paradigm

Soon the SMR paradigm gave way to a revision in thinking and the IDE paradigm took its place. This was a view of communication as the process through which individuals {I}—all animals and human systems—create and use data {D} to establish the communis-commonness-with the environment and its inhabitants {E}—what could be termed an I-D-E paradigm as shown in Figure 4.2.

Along with rhetoric and speech, journalism also contributed to the heritage of communication study. As with rhetoric, initially journalism was considered to be an area that primarily dealt with practical rather than theoretical matters. By the beginning of the 20th century rhetoric and speech were clearly established as disciplines in their own right and journalism began to take shape as a field as well.

During the early 20th century, interest in communication continued in rhetoric and speech, and the advent of the radio and later TV led to the wider application of journalistic concepts and the development of more theories of the overall process. The late 1940s and 1950s were years of interdisciplinary growth. Scholars from various disciplines advanced theories of communication that extended beyond the boundaries of their own fields. Among those to provide such descriptions of communication were Lasswell, Shannon and Weaver, Schramm, Katz and Lazarfeld, and Westley and MacLean.

The 1960s was a period of integration. A good deal was done to synthesize the writings of rhetoric and speech, journalism, and mass media as well as other disciplines. The decade of the 1970s was a time of unprecedented growth within the field. It was also a period in which much specialization took place giving rise to research and writing in interpersonal group, organizational, political, international, and inter-cultural communication. During this most recent period of history, a number of additional models of the communication process were advanced, extending the work of the earlier scholars. Among these were the writings of Berlo, Newcomb, Dance, Watzlawick, Beavin and Jackson, and Rogers and Kincaid.

History of communication reveals a number of changes during the nearly 2,500 year heritage of the field—changes both in the theory of the communication process and the discipline in which it is studied. The earliest perspectives in communication were concerned with public speaking with persuasion as the goal. With increasing evidence that the messages sent and that received seldom equaled one another, that is MS ≠ MR, or to put it in another way, D ≠ I, that is, data sent are not equal to the information received, a movement away from the S>M>R paradigm has taken place, providing impetus for a broadened view during the 1970s and 1980s, with the models of Newcomb, Dance, Rogers and Kincaid as presented in Chapter 5.

Communication is ancient and newly emergent, interdisciplinary in heritage, the home of scholars and professionals, a science and an art, belonging to the humanities, and is also concerned with technology (Harper 1979).

Body positioning and gestures in particular cultures form a part of the research in anthropology. These studies laid the down the groundwork for more general studies of non-verbal communication. In psychology, interest focused on persuasion, social influence, and specifically, attitudes—how they form, how they change, their impact on behaviour, and the role of communication in these dynamics.

Sociologists and political scientists studied the nature of mass media in various political and social activities, voting behaviour, and other facets of life. In Zoology, communication among animals began to receive considerable attention among researchers. During the same years, scholars in linguistics, general semantics, and semiotics—fields that focused on the nature of language and its role in human activity—also contributed to the advancement of communication study. Studies in rhetoric and speech in the late 1940s and 1950s broadened to include oral interpretation, voice, and diction, debate, and thereafter, physiology of speech, and speech pathology. In journalism and mass media studies, growth and development were even more dramatic and spurred on in no small way by the popularity of television and efforts to understand its impact. In a number of classic works in the 1950s the focus on specific media—newspapers, magazines, radio, and television—began to the replaced by a more general concern with the nature and effects of mass media and mass communication.

By the end of the 1950s a number of writings had appeared that paved the way for the development of more integrated views of communication. It was during these years that the National Society for the Study of Communication (now the International Communication Association) was established with the stated goal of bringing greater unity to the study of communication by exploring the relationships among speech, language, and media. These developments set the stage for the rapid growth of communication as an independent discipline (Ruben 1984).

Symbols as Concepts

All animals, including man, live in a world made up of signs and stimuli from the physical and non-physical objects in the world. There are two types of signs, which are defined by the ways in which animals respond to them—signals and symbols. With the exception of man, all animals are restricted to the use of signals. Signals are stimuli which have come to be associated with various physical objects. Pavlov's dog salivating at the sound of a bell is a good example of an animal responding to a signal. A bell immediately precedes a notion of food to the dog. The dog is hungry and salivates when he sees and smells food. After a while he associates the bell as a signal that is associated with the notion of food. Hence, he salivates when he hears the bell.

Man has the capacity to use signs as symbols. He can conceptualize a plate of food. Symbols are signs, which lead to the conceptualization of their referents (Hawes 1975).

From Smoke Signals to Printing

Early humans (around 2000 BC) first carved symbols on the walls of caves and used drums and smoke to signal one another. With these very primitive common devices, the foundations of our modern information processing technologies were put firmly in place. While smoke signals and cave drawings served their purposes well, the development of the first systems of writing dramatically increased the possibilities of making coded data more permanent and portable. By about 1000 BC early pictographic writing had given way to systems of writing that made use of an alphabet. Paper was invented by about 100 AD and the oldest known printed piece was a *Sutra* printed in Korea in 750 AD.

HISTORICAL DIMENSION

The human voice reached only those within its range and the written message travelled no faster than a runner, a horse, a bird, or a sailing ship. The Hindu temples in the countries of Southeast Asia are striking evidences of this mobility of ideas and flow of information. The teachings of Buddha, Christ, and Mohammed were effectively carried to remote places at a time when travel was slow, arduous and dangerous.

The Roots of the Present

Invention of printing started the modern age in the field of communication. The technique of multiple reproductions, by the printing of images and writings initially engraved on stone or wood, first appeared 2,500 years ago. The impact of this invention was more spectacular initially in promoting the spread and proliferation of knowledge and ideas than in developing mass information as this came to be understood later. The important advance in book production came with the invention of paper. The next invention was of printing and when the age of printing and diffusion of books arrived, the way was open for the transformations, which led to the Renaissance and the Reformation.

STAGES IN THE DEVELOPMENT OF HUMAN COMMUNICATION

A Theory of Transitions

It is the mastery of the communication system used for information storage, exchange, and dissemination that represents the critical points of change in human history and even prehistory. It was the increasing ability to communicate fully and accurately that led to the escalating development of complex technology, and to myths, legends, explanations, logic, and the complex rules for behaviour that make civilization possible.

The age of signs and signals started very early in the progression of pre-hominid and early pre-human life, long before our primitive ancestors walked upright. Inherited or instinctual responses played a significant role in such communication, and learned communication behaviour was at a basic minimum. As brain capacity slowly increased, the processes and their importance were reversed. Literally, millions and millions of years passed before it became possible to adopt at least some standardized—learned and shared—gestures, sounds, and other kinds of signals that could be used by succeeding generations to engage in the basic exchanges needed for a social life. This could be achieved through the category of speech. Many animals use cries, shrieks, and bodily postures to signal danger, the presence of food, availability for mating, and conditional hunting.

A radical change occurred rather quickly (in terms of the sweep of time we are considering) when humans moved into the age of speech and language. Compelling evidence now exists that this age began rather recently with the sudden appearance of the Cro Magnon, a new form of Homo sapiens. Although this conclusion is not universally shared, it appears that these—our most immediate ancestors—began to talk somewhere between 90,000 and 40,000 years ago. About 35,000 years ago language was in use.

It was only about 5,000 years ago that human beings made the transition into the age of writing. 'The skill was invented independently in several places in the world at various times. This important ability to communicate using written symbols spread slowly over the centuries as alphabets became increasingly standardized and as lighter and more portable surfaces became available. The printing press and the process of manufacturing paper were important technological advances that eventually led to the use of print as a mass medium.' (Lewis and De Fleur 1983)

The Print Media

We entered the Age of Print approximately in 1455, in the city of Mainz, when a press with moveable type was set up. Books, of course, were the oldest print medium, but by their very nature of dependency on literacy, they remained a medium for the elite for centuries. They had to wait till the nineteenth century to become and remain the most respected mass medium till today, when they are read as textbooks, as contributions of the literature of the times, and as scientific reference works.

Again it was not until 1834 that the first daily newspaper was brought out in New York. Soon when the experiment was successful, other imitators followed suit and, in a few years along with industrialization there was a daily newspaper in every major city in the western world and the Age of Mass Communication was ushered in. And they held their sway over the mass society till the birth of the movies and the growth of broadcasting. Unlike books, magazines had a greater readership, but were latecomers into the field of mass communication. They catered to specialized tastes, and their profitability and continuance therefore, became unpredictable.

THE MODERN AGE

The Era of Technological Inventions

Telegraphy and Telephony

The first telegraphic message was transmitted in 1844 between Washington D.C. and Baltimore, Maryland. Samuel Morse sent this message through a copper wire. Sir Charles Wheatstone and Samuel Morse discovered telegraph in 1840 which opened a new era in communications. Alexander Graham Bell sent the first telephone message by wire. Again in 1895, when the waves could be successfully converted into coded signals, Marconi and Popoff succeeded independent of each other in transmitting and receiving wireless messages across vast distances.

Next to the postal system the telephone remained the largest organized interpersonal communication network for more than two centuries. In a way it can be called an extension of the oral communication system. Now with the Internet, virtually linking all nations, the telephone has become the largest single integrated communication system ever devised so far. The e-mail, the voice mails are only off-shoots of the telephone system.

The Films

The film industry has its beginnings in and around 1839 when the lens, on which both photography and projection techniques are based was first invented and when Daguerre devised a practical method for photography. From the crude 'nickelodeons', of around 1910 in the cities of USA, the industry has graduated with the star systems, the formula themes, the horror stories, the science fiction with stereophonic sounds to an endless variations of the basic idea of entertainment. From the silent movies, the industry has taken the route of the talkies, from the 'black and white' to the 'technicolor' picture, and from the millions of big theatres outdoors to the millions of 'small screen' television sets inside the living rooms. As an audio-visual mass medium the television has the biggest reach ever, with the cable TV, the pay TV, and satellite broadcasting adding to its technological capabilities.

Radio

Fessender transmitted the human voice by radio in 1906. The age of broadcasting was made possible with the invention of the vacuum tube. Since then, radio—the audio medium, which, unlike the print medium, did not depend on the requirement of literacy, has grown into the single largest mass communication system with the widest coverage on this entire planet. Again, unlike the press, it could manage to transmit messages across great distances without having to depend on conventional forms of transport over land, sea, or by air. Broadcasting has changed the way of lives for most of us on this earth than any other invention of the 20th century.

Television

The chief attraction of television lies in its properties for revealing a panorama beyond our immediate horizon, for reflecting a world of possibilities that would otherwise be denied to the people.

As a medium, television is basically an extension of the sense of touch, which involves maximum interplay of all the senses. The influence of television is all pervasive and subtle. The advertisements persuade to constantly hanker after things that we really do not need in the first place. Television coaxes us to change, to be modern, to cast away the old, and to go in for the new. Skornia points out how TV is a very keen political weapon in elections as a propaganda tool to sway the viewer's minds. Wars can be started by TV, and like the Vietnam War, TV can end a prolonged and obstinate battle by influencing the viewers in their own living rooms (Andal 1987).

We have recently lurched quite unprepared into the Age of Computers.

This theory of transition is one of accumulation rather than an account of serially arranged but distinct periods, that is, our primitive ancestors learned to use signs and symbols very early, and we still use them rather widely. Speech and language were added; writing was followed by printing and mass communication. The use of computers is now fast spreading. Thus, the history of human communication has been one of corresponding communication systems rather than simply a passing from one to another, as each of the major media of communication emerged in our society.

The New Technology

New technology signifies the converging technologies of microelectronics computing and communications. And a consequence of this would be a mass production of science fictional characters—complex, sinister, and out of our control. On the other hand social and economic progress also entirely depends upon this new technology—computer controlled aircraft, computer aided design, tele-medicine, etc. In a way this is the second industrial revolution. While the first one affected limited areas of the West, the current revolution promises to touch the personal lives of almost everyone around the globe because of the vast transfer of technologies that are taking place between distant nations. The effects will be profound and no less disturbing to many of those involved, as were the effects of the first revolution. In our society technological change is justifiably equated with progress and so it would be pointless to question if it is desirable. Information Super-highways have revolutionized the style of work, leisure and life of the people though the years. The chart below shows how the introduction of new technologies has over the years reduced the time taken to send a hundred words message from Edinburgh to London.

1760 —— stage coach on rough tracked roads —— 10 days
1830 —— stage coach on modern road —— 3 days
1850 —— telegraph —— 4 minutes
1950 —— telex —— 1 minute
1980 —— modern data transmission —— 0.1 second

Oral Communication

It is a known fact that folklore and legendary grandmother's tales form part of a chain that extends backward for many centuries, and without doubt will extend forward into the distant future as long as humans, who talk, laugh, and cry are people of this planet. The childhood games that we played have been passed on to us down the generations, and will live on without the aid of literacy and reading. The artist Bruegel has preserved a vignette of the childhood games for posterity through his well-known painting. From the earliest times most communications have been by word of mouth, including the Indian scriptures. If this chain of communication is broken, the passage of time will dilute traditions and cultures, and unless these are retrieved through artifacts and excavations and symbolic structures, they will be lost.

On the other hand, the reach of oral communication in space is limited by distance reached by human voice. In ancient Persia important news was transmitted at the rate of fifty miles a day. As late as the beginning of the nineteenth century diplomatic bags from London to Washington took 60 days. The invention of telegraphy changed all this drastically. The technology of information transmission was advanced through the transistor and the computer by leaps and bounds. Man today has overcome the natural messages for later retrieval. Man has at once removed the dilution of the messages by the mere passage of time. By speeding up the transmission of messages man has effectively reduced the time gap between the actual happenings and the news transmission. In live transmission the raw event is witnessed through its images the same instant. By bridging any spatial gap man has effectively crunched the distances between the event and the spectator, the communicator and his audience, the creative artist and his patrons, the scholars and their material to be examined, the physician and his patent, and the tutor and the taught.

Written Communication

Indians knew the art of writing as early as 2500 BC. Their earliest decipherable records do not go beyond the 3rd century BC. Ashoka's edicts were scattered all over the country except the down south—and were scattered even in Afghanistan. The *Vedic* literature is considered to be the oldest in India—1500 BC, but the earliest manuscripts were not older than the 10th century AD. The Vedas were something that has been heard. In the written forms of communication the earliest period witnessed the prevalence of the *Vedic* style (*shlokas*) in law books, epics and *Puranas*. The two epics, Ramayana and Mahabharata were similar in this aspect.

Inscriptions

A record carved in stone and set in a public place had the advantage over the spoken word. The spoken word is a means of communication only to those present at a given occasion. The tree inscription declared its message to any one who might pass by that spot. Plainly to carve letters in stone is an expensive and laborious business. It was mainly used by those who wished their message to be conveyed to the future generations. Two examples of major inscriptions used for propaganda are the inscriptions in Ankara in Turkey and that of the epicurean philosophy of Diogenes at the town centre of Oenoanda in Asia Minor. The Ashoka pillar in Old Fort, Delhi, in the 3rd century BC is yet another example.

The Written Word

Written word had certain advantage as a means of communication. Even though one has to take into account the advantages of printing, the advantage of the written word still remains. The most obvious advantage was that it was a means of communicating from a distance. Secondly, it made anonymous writers publish their works. Everyone can see a person delivering a speech. However, one can tell who has composed a piece of writing. This is important for the purposes of propaganda. Words, whose genuine source might obviously be tainted, could circulate freely. The written word made possible the consultation of the work as a permanent record. The historical writings are, thus, a kind of reference for the statesmen. The written word made the development of prose style easier.

We have started from non-verbal communication and ended with the written word. There was a Greek myth about Cadmus of Thebes. One of his achievements was to introduce the alphabet. His other achievement was to sow the dragon's teeth and reap a harvest of armed soldiers. McLuhan wrote, 'Like any other myth this one encapsulates a prolonged process into a flashing insight. The alphabets mean power and authority and control of military structures at a distance.'

THEORIES OF COMMUNICATION

The history of theories of communication is a record of the tensions between material and in material networks, biological and social paradigms, nature and culture, technical device and speech, economics and culture, micro and macro perspectives, village and globe, actor and septum, free will and social determinisms.

The notion of communication theory poses just as many problems as that of communication itself and that, too, has given rise to contradictory debate. First, as often happens in the human and social science, there is a strong opposition between one school or epistemology and another concerning the status and definition of the theory. It is left to the discerning reader to judge whether it is the clearer formulae of one theorist or the weighty philosophical constructions of another, and which of the two has more radically influenced him or her.

The world of communication is divided into two kinds. One faction concerns itself with communication about the environment, while the other with communication among the humans. The former is impersonal in its pure form, but human communication is always enmeshed in a personal matrix. Just as signs represent the referent in terms of a shared code, when a communicator chooses a certain form of address, the tone of voice or position vis-à-vis his audience, he does not represent their mutual relationship. On the other hand, he presents it. Communication scholars and sociologists have developed a few major theories concerning them.

Primarily communication is based on signs, symbols and shared meanings, whether verbal or non-verbal, vocal or non-vocal. But there are also some scholars who view communication as a function of behaviour and research on all these aspects as a part of communication research is an ongoing process. In the following pages are discussed the major communication theories which have further led to a conceptualization to be represented in the form of communication models.

The entire subject of communication can be studied through two schools of thought, the Semiotics School and the Process School.

THE SEMIOTICS SCHOOL

Charles Morris laid down the foundations for the study of semiotics fifty years ago. Morris divided semiotics into three areas of general study: syntactic, semantics, and pragmatics. By syntactic he meant the area in which to include a study of how symbols relate to each other—a sort of symbol-to-symbol relationship. In semantics Morris discussed a study of how symbols relate to their referents, that is the things that symbols represent—a symbol-to-referent relationship. Pragmatics refer to the study of how symbols relate to people, i.e., the symbol users—users that is a sort of symbol-to-user relationship. These three divisions of semiotics remain as a reasonable and popular analysis of language and communication study to this day. The semiotics school approaches communication as the generation of meaning, a mixture of signs, symbols and messages, which the sender wants to convey and expects a specific reaction from the receiver of the messages—the sign itself.

Signs are of different varieties. There are differences in the ways they carry meanings, and the ways they relate to the people who use them. Signs are human constructs and can only be understood in terms of the uses people put them to. The codes are systems in which the signs are organized.

The Process School

This school looks at communication as a process, a simple transmission of messages or meanings, which the sender wants to convey irrespective of the reaction of the receiver or his interactions. On one extreme end of the scale, the works of art, sculpture, music painting, etc. fall in the process category, because the messages are created not with any motive, but as an expression of the sender's feelings or emotions. Besides, each receiver may interpret the message in his own individual way. On the other extreme, in the second category of semiotics, belong the messages of commands, instructions, warnings, and propaganda. Here the sender expects the receiver to interpret the messages in an accepted conventional way and react accordingly. All the other forms, news, documentaries, films, dramas, entertainment, etc. fall in between these two extreme ends of the scale. In the study of communication by semiotics, the focus of common concern is the sign. The study of signs and the way they work is called semiotics or semiology.

Equally important is the status of the receiver or reader who in semiotics is seen as playing a more active role than in most of the process schools (George Gerbner's model of communication is an exception).

Semiotics prefers the term 'reader' (even of a photograph of a painting) to 'receiver' because it implies a greater degree of activity and also that 'reading' is something that we learn to do. It is, thus, determined by the cultural experience of the reader. The reader helps to create the meaning of the text by bringing to it his own experience, attitudes, and emotions. Assimilation of meanings and understanding messages is a continuous process of human activity.

The human brain is in perpetual interaction with the environment from which the learner receives stimulation, which activates the sensory apparatus that n turn is transformed into neural information. Initially the information enters a structure called selective perception. This activity depends on the learner's ability to attend to certain features of the sensory register. Transformed and identified information then enters the short-term memory where it persists for a limited period—say 20 seconds. The given evidence explains the three forms of short-term memory storage.

The first form is acoustic information—information internally heard by the learner. The second is the articulated form, in which the learner finds himself re-iterating the information, for example, in retrieving a telephone number for the first time. The third is visual—remembering—pictures of scenes witnessed.

A critical transformation of the information now occurs when it leaves the short-term memory and enters the long-term memory. Perceptual information is converted into concepts (like darkness, light, colours, etc.). Such storage in memory can also be in a coded form or in a semantic organization or in hierarchical structures of meaning. Retrieval is resorted to in decision-making and problem-solving situations. For this, certain cues must be provided. This process of recalling sometimes requires a reconstruction of events remembered so that the retrieval helps to complete the communication process.

Whether through the process or semiotics school the subject of communication can be studied through

(a) the models of communication and the basic theories evolved by sociologists—the issues that communication throws,
(b) the process or flows involved in communication,
(c) the different styles and forms of communication,
(d) the development of communication as a science,
(e) the codes, ground rules, and factors that govern communication,
(f) the findings on the intentions, impact, and effects of different communications.

Of all the above, the study of communication through models is the most satisfactory since the theories are generally evolved around the models.

The Two-step Flow of Information

A hypothesis that aroused considerable interest was that the influences stemming from the mass media first reach opinion leaders, who, in turn pass on what they hear and read to their acquaintances over which they have some influence.

This hypothesis was proposed by Paul Lazarfeld, Elihu Katz, Bernad Berelson, and Hazeldaudet and is known as the 'two step flow of information'. These theorists themselves were intrigued by the implications of such a hypothesis for a demographic society. It meant that the influence of mass media per se was less automatic and less potent as was generally believed. Also that opinions and decision-making was more by interaction among the people themselves. It also meant that the earlier assumption of audience as a mass of disconnected individuals, who were attuned to the media had to be modified in view of the two-step flow theory of mass communication, which implied a society of individuals in perpetual contact with each other through which mass communication is channeled. Several studies have been undertaken in the West, which could evaluate the extent to which it has found confirmation for this theory and the ways in which it has been extended, contracted, and reformulated. It was revealed by these studies that opinion leaders were generally interested more in the events affecting the lives of the people like elections, government regulations, etc. There was an even distribution of opinion leaders throughout every class and occupation and they were much like the people whom they influence, be they friends, coworkers, or relatives. The study also threw up the fact that opinion leaders were more exposed to the radio, to the newspaper and to magazines than the people over whom they had influence. Therefore ideas often flow from radio and print to opinion leaders, and from these to the less active sections of the population.

The findings of modern day studies in the light of the original statement of the two-step-flowhypothesis, suggests the following picture. Opinion leaders and the people they influence are very much alike and typically belong to the same primary group of family, friends, and co-workers. Most spheres of influence focus the group's attention on some related part of the world outside the group and it is the opinion leader's function to bring the group into touch with this relevant part of the environment through whatever media are appropriate. Even though opinion leaders appear to be more in contact with the outside world through the mass media, it is also true that they are also primarily affected not by the communication media but by still other people. The main emphasis of this two-step-flow theory appears to be only on one aspect of interpersonal relations, that is. interpersonal relations as channels of communication. But studies have revealed that such interpersonal relations influence the making of decisions at least in two additional ways.

In addition to serving as a network of communication, interpersonal relations are also sources of pressures to conform to the groups' ways of thinking and acting. Examples of the working of such group pressures are evident during the election time in the homogeneity of opinion and action observed among voters. A similar situation is found among doctors. The social support that comes from being a part of the respected medical community gives the doctors the confidence needed to adopt a new drug. Similar examples abound in our every day experience, repeatedly verifying the working of the two-step-flow of communication, the role of opinion leaders, and the potency inherent in interpersonal relations.

The two-step-flow theory of communication and influence offered new perspectives on the mass communication process. Family members, friends, and others brought ideas from the media to the attention of common public who were not exposed to it directly. Thus, to re-iterate, there was an indirect but important flow of ideas and influences from the media to those who were directly exposed, and from them to additional people who had not read or heard the original messages.

In his study on this matter, Katz and Lazarfeld found that 'position in the life cycle' was a critical variable determining who would influence whom and in what area. For example, young working-women in close contact through media sources with the world of fashions, hairstyles and cosmetics sought

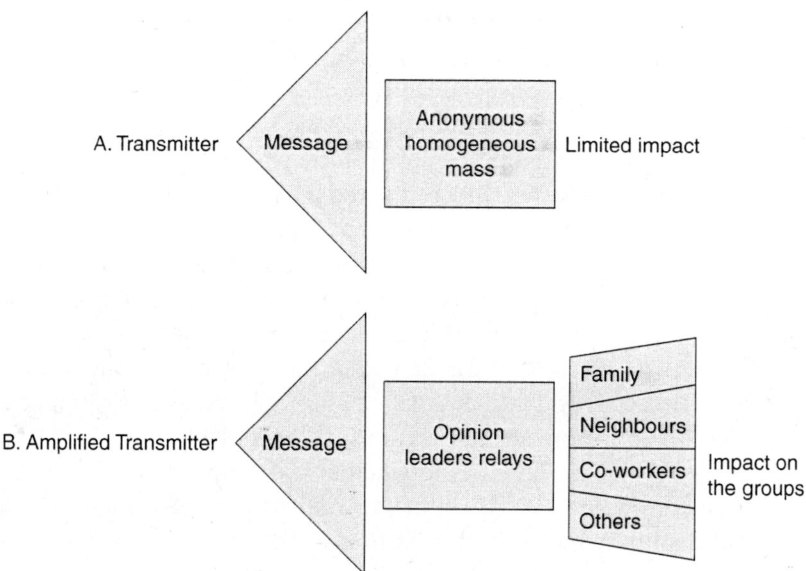

Figure 4.3
Situation A: Classic diagram of mass diffusion

as leaders by full time housewives who were less aware of these nuances. Married women with large families on the other hand were sought for advice about household products, marketing bargains at the supermarket, and so on. Thus, such considerations of the social category like age, marital status, family size, and employment predisposed some to monitor the mass media selectively so as to be knowledgeable about specific topics and, as a result, they appeared as good sources for advice on those issues to those who lacked such media exposure.

Theories of Selective Influence

This term was applied by later day scholars to a body of explanations of the mass communication process by earlier researchers. They mailnly consist of three distinct but related formulations. These emerged from the social scientists' increasing recognition of patterning in the behaviour of individuals and groups. These were called the individual differences theory, the social differentiation theory, and the social relationship theory.

As the limitations of the existing theories came to be better understood it was obvious that new theories of mass communication were needed to guide research in a more realistic manner. Like the earlier theories, the new approaches would be derived from the basic paradigm that was being developed in both psychology and sociology. Those two fields actively sought to understand human nature from a personal perspective on one hand and from a collective or interactive point of view on the other.

Numerous concepts, hypothesis and generalization about process and effects of communication were yielded by an increasing number of studies. At the same time the structure of the emerging theoretical development in the early years was uncoordinated and even chaotic. It did not follow the neat and orderly model of an unfolding science where latter day investigators systematically tested the idea, pioneers of those who went before. In spite of this unorganized nature of mass communication research in the early years, there gradually accrued a body of knowledge about the media and their effects as well as an increasing consensus about how they should be studied. Out of that accumulated body of knowledge a discipline called mass communication eventually emerged decades later.

Yet the argument as to whether the study of mass communication can be considered as a discipline, or only as a loosely organized field of interdisciplinary interests, still continues. Therefore a body of explanation of the mass communication process was developed that can collectively be called selective influence theories (De Fleur 1975).

Two events occurred early in the twentieth century that would eventually make it necessary to abandon the idea that exposure to mass communications had immediate, uniform, and direct effects on the audiences. First, large-scale empirical research on the process and effects of mass communication was begun. The findings from such research slowly revealed a picture inconsistent with the magic bullet theory.

The second event was significant as new conclusions were developed by psychologists and sociologists concerning the personal and social attributes of human beings. These conclusions resulted from a radical revision of the basic theory concerning both the sources and the characteristics of human nature. The new paradigms had clear implications for understanding the influences of mass communication and they were completely inconsistent with the basic theories from which the magic bullet theory had been drawn.

The Uses and Gratification Perspective

During the 1940s the realization of the consequences of individual differences and the social differentiation of behaviour related to mass communication led to a new perspective in the relationship between audiences and the media. It was a shift from the view of audience as passive to the realization that its members are active in their selection of the preferred content and messages from the media. Earlier theories (e.g., the magic bullet formulation) considered the audience as relatively inert, passively waiting for the media to transmit the information, which was then perceived, remembered, and (presumably) acted upon more or less uniformly.

Once the powerful role of cognitive variables and subcultures became clear, it was no longer possible to conceptualize audience in this manner. Some, critics feel that the uses and gratification approach is less than an independent theory in its own right; rather, it is a limited restatement of certain aspects of selective theories. They point to the fact that its main proposition is that the needs and rewards, which the individuals obtain from the mass media and influence people's patterns of attention to media content, and the uses to which they put the information obtained there from. This is essentially a simple version of the individual differences theory based on considerations of cognitive structure.

Another limitation is that using the uses and gratification perspective for research has generated little more than lists of 'reasons' (various kinds of self identified 'needs') for which people claim that they select and attend to different categories of media content (e.g., self identified 'gratification'). The perspective does not provide much in the way of systematic explanation beyond that.

Selective Perception

The difference between selective perception and selective exposure is that in the latter one chooses what to see, while in selective exposure one chooses how to interpret what one sees. Selective perception is the tendency for an individual to interpret what he sees, reads, or hears in a way which supports his own viewpoint.

Retrieval, Retention and Recall

These refer to a tendency to recall things on a selective basis. It would mean that elements, which fit in with one's own point of view, are remembered. All of the above ideas on selectivity refer to trends in the processing of information received via mass communication. In effect they are very similar despite their obvious differences. They all imply that the response to mass media is an active and manipulative process. But it is likely that activity is far from being a complete explanation of the failures of the mass media to affect the audience. The failure to absorb a great deal of information from the mass media is more likely to be because the news is of very minimal interest or because there is simply too much information to cope with. Although there is good evidence of certain amount of selectivity, care is needed to avoid the glib assumption that it applies to every case where a viewer or reader fails to be affected by mass communication.

The Principle of Selective Perception

A second underlying principle operates in much the same manner. Because of differences in such cognitive factors as interests, beliefs, prior knowledge, attitudes, needs, and values, different individuals will perceive—that is, attribute meaning to—virtually any complex stimulus differently based on the different cognitive structures. For example, a given newspaper article, movie, radio programme, or TV presentation can be viewed by a number of individuals, and each one will come away with a somewhat different interpretation of what he or she has been exposed to. Perception refers to be a psychological activity by which individuals organize meaningful interpretations of sensory stimuli they receive from their environment. Variations in cognitive structure cause individuals to put together different patterns of meaning and interpretation for any given pattern of stimuli such as media presentation.

Similarly, members of specific social categories who support subcultures will attribute distinctive patterns of meaning to particular media content. For example, in US, often news stories about capital punishment, racial discrimination, school dropouts, and other social issues have an impact on black people in ways that are not the same as the interpretations of whites. Veterans of World War II read different meanings into media messages about Germans and the Japanese than do young people who did not participate in that conflict.

Selective perception and attribution of meaning are also influenced by social relationships. Parents with young children may interpret a particularly violent or sexually explicit TV programme with a different set of sensitivities than do childless people. Lovers may read deep shared meanings into songs or movie scenes that might leave others yawning.

Thus, the principles of selective perception are that the people of distinct psychological characteristics, sub-cultural orientations, and social network membership will interpret the same media content in very different ways. Selective perception has been linked to sets of variables in literally thousands of studies conducted by social scientists, and it is one of the most significant of all the factors for understanding the selective influence theories.

Selective Attention

People screen out media content in which they have little or no interest and attend to what they like, for example, those motivated to keep up with current events pay more attention to the news than do those with little interest and understanding. Similarly, those with deep concerns about their health pay closer attention to content dealing with medical issues than do those who are more reluctant.

Members of different social categories select the programmes depending on their social strata. For example, religious broadcasts hold little interest for secular audiences but are enthusiastically received by the devout. Those with limited education and income may avidly follow wrestling on

TV, while those with more schooling and money might often avoid such programmes. Similarly the rural, the urban, males and females and those of the other social categories with distinctive subcultures show clearly defined differences in attention to different forms of media content.

Thirdly, people who have deeply established social ties are more likely to attend to issues and topics that they know are of interest to their friends and families than to unrelated themes. Furthermore, patterns of friendship can be powerful influences on people in directing or even redirecting their reading, viewing, and listening habits. Social relationships can even lead to attention to media content that the individual does not like. Many a wife has endured live cricket telecasts to suit a husband's taste and many a male has viewed episodes of Indian family drama soap operas just to keep peace in the family. Thus, the principle of selective attention is that cognitive structure, category membership, and meaningful social linkages result in paying of attention to media content that are linked to those factors.

Selective Recall

In the same way people act in their own way as a result of being exposed to a given media message. Action is the final link in the chain before it takes place, a member of an audience has to attend to the media presentation, perceive the meaning, and remember its content.

The selective influence theories can be summed up as following: one is in terms with the nature of the intervening conditions that they pose between media content and the responses people make. Secondly, in terms of the four principles of selectivity lead individuals to attend to, interpret, recall, and act upon media messages in distinctive ways.

The Individual Differences Theory

As psychologists undertook studies in human learning and motivation, it increasingly became clearer that people are all different in their psychological makeup. Like fingerprints, the personality of every human being was found to be unlike that of any other, while they all shared the behavioural patterns of their cultures. Each individual had a different cognitive structure of needs, habits, perceptions, beliefs, values, attitudes, skills and so on.

Therefore the study of individual differences and their distributions in their populations eventually became an important focus of psychological research. To summararize, therefore, the progress of research on the process and effects of mass communication had the beginnings in the simplistic beliefs of the magic bullet theory, and proceeded through the more complex selective influence theories to culminate in the theories of long range and indirect influences.

Mass Society and the Magic Bullet Theory

According to the magic bullet theory, media messages were perceived as magic bullets. In the aftermath of war, there emerged a general belief in the great power of mass communication. The media was thought to be able to shape public opinion and to sway the masses towards almost any point of view desired by the communicator. To name the tool—'the new hammer and anvil of social solidarity' is propaganda. The basic theory of mass communication that is implied by such conclusions is not quite as simple as it would appear. Of course it is based on relatively straightforward stimulus-response theory. But there are also certain underlying presumptions of the social organization of the society and the psychological structure of the human beings who are being stimulated and who are responding to the mass communication message.

The first set of beliefs about the nature and power of mass communication was never actually formulated at the time into any systematic statement by any communication scholar, but in retrospect it has come to be called as 'the magic bullet theory'. It has also been called by other names such as the 'hypodermic needle theory', and the 'transmission belt theory. The basic idea is that the media messages are received in a uniform way by every member of the audience and that immediate and direct responses are triggered by such stimuli.

The tremendous impact of wartime propaganda was a solid and valid proof that the media were powerful in precisely the manner so dramatically described by Lasswell when he concluded that they were the new 'hammer and anvil of social solidarity'. There were also the seemingly indisputable facts from the mass advertising of the time that the media were capable of persuading people to buy goods in degrees and variety hitherto unheard of. This belief added to the conviction of great power and it reinforced the seeming validity of the magic bullet theory. It has also been termed as 'effects model' or the 'hypodermic' approach of the 'stimulus-response' approach. The idea that the mass media inject into the audience a dose of persuasive communication, which has a fairly uniform effect on the audience, was easy enough to understand. The hypodermic model draws attention to the analogy on which it is based; the assumption explains that there is nothing intervening between the media and audience, and the effects are direct. It is, thus, like a syringe entering the flesh directly.

Some people considered media as powerful one, due to its impact through the advertisement. In this regard several assumptions have been made which appear to be unwarranted. The first is that advertising cannot persuade us to do that we do not want to. Most advertising campaigns are failures and the history of advertising is littered with products, which could not be sold. Certainly there are some products which were first brought to the attention of the consumer through advertising but this is a different matter and there is no evidence at all that anything can be sold by proper advertising. The second assumption is that a product's success can be attributed to advertising. Advertising is merely one of the many marketing tools, which include special sales promotions, in-store display, competitions, discounts, and other strategies. Any or all of these could be contributing to the success of the product. The third assumption is that advertising increases the sales of the particular product rather than strengthening a particular manufacturer's version of the product. Most advertising is directed towards enhancing the sales of one particular brand rather than selling more of a particular type of consumer goods.

The role of advertising is seldom a very powerful one. It is not a matter of persuading or manipulating the ignorant consumers, since consumers of heavily advertised products are most highly experienced. They have already bought the product often and have used a wide range of different brands. The magic bullet theory simply did not work for advertising the way it was expected to. Subsequently, however, sociologists attempted to modify this theory because they felt that the target was not always a passive one. Most often they found that the audience resisted any response when hit by the bullet and refused to play dead. The change was not apparent and it was as if nothing had happened at all.

The explanation for this apparent failure of the magic bullet theory was furnished by scholars in the form of the 'category theory' of communication. Especially for the advertisers and heads of media it was necessary to find a simple way of classifying audiences so that their responses to a given communication or a type of communication can be predicted more or less correctly. Sustained research threw up some interesting findings. People who held certain clusters of attitudes and beliefs would react differently from others—like college educated people, the teens, the elderly, the men and the women, people from the southern parts of the country, and the northerners, the rich, the poor, the middle class and the elite, and so on. It could be easily seen that these different kinds fall under distinct categories. The category theory held that educational television would appeal much more to the educated class than the other categories just like the soap operas telecast during the day appeal to the women and the music channel to the teenagers.

Media System Dependency Theory

It is not at all clear as to which of the competing theories best explains the relationship between the mass media and the people who make up the societies in which they disseminate messages. No single explanation predicts that relationship fully. Furthermore, some of the theories openly contradict each other. One says that there will be immediate, universal, direct, and powerful influences on audience members from exposure to mass communication. Another elucidates that such influences will be long-term, indirect, selective, and limited. The dissimilarity among contemporary theories of mass communication exists because each focuses on different configurations of independent and dependent variables and therefore each use different assumptions in uniqueness to make predictions about influences on people and society. For example, one focuses on beliefs, attitudes, and behaviour at an individual level while another attempts to explain shared conventions of meaning and their influences on social organization, society, and culture. Few scholars today would maintain that the 'magic bullet' theory provides adequate explanations on how the media influences people. The accumulated research evidence has failed to support its claims. Other earlier formulations have similarly started to come into question. Yet, most of the theories still remain as sources of important research hypotheses and until totally convincing data have been gathered it is not time yet to dismiss them completely. Some of these theories of communication are:

- Congruence theory
- Conspiracy theory
- Dependency theory
- Play theory
- Reflective-projective theory
- Uses and gratification theory
- Hypodermic syringe theory
- Effects theory

Sleeper Effects of Communication

It is described to be the unconscious effect upon subjects that do not become apparent until unspecified subsequent occasions are spontaneously aroused.

Cognitive Dissonance

The basic need of man is information and a structure by which to interpret it. Man is an inquirer regulating his life and behaviour by forming hypotheses about his environment and the events within it, and by noting the criteria that will assist him the most. Individuals, more over, may differ in this respect. When information that an individual receives is already familiar to him, a range of inner motivational and cognitive factors affect his reactions to it. On the other hand, when it is not as Festinger (1954) indicates that the individual is forced to use more tenuous external criteria for evaluating the world around him, and a range of quite superficial cues can determine judgments not only of the personal interest value of the incoming information but also of its credibility (i.e., cognitive dissonance).

The Social Environment of Communication

One early and important concept with which to analyse if the mass media is a part of a social system is that opinion leadership. As might be expected, opinion leaders are influential within relatively restricted spheres. There are opinion leaders for domestic appliances but nothing else apart from that. In some aspects opinion leaders differ from followers, but how they differ depends on the sort of innovation in question, (Katz 1961, Katz and Lazarfeld 1964). The development of the idea of opinion leaders leads directly to the concept of a two-step-flow of communication. A one-step-flow of communication exists when the influence of the mass media is direct on the individual. This in fact is the classic assumption of mass communication 'affects' research.

The two-step-flow of communication inserts the opinion leader as part of intermediary step or link between the mass media and the person influenced. So the process is one in which the mass media influences the opinion leader, who then influences a second party. Of course, there is absolutely no reason why there should not be a three, four or five step flow of communication or more. Likewise we may have just a single step. Research suggests that direct influences by the media opinion leaders can serve merely to inform others about an innovation. Being informed about new developments however, does not necessarily lead to their adoption. This conceptualization has bred a whole specialization in social sciences—the diffusion of innovation, which studies the way in which important innovations contraception, agricultural methods, etc.) lead to adoption in society. It tends to concern itself more with the problems of modernization in Third World countries but obviously is by no means limited to this.

Selective Exposure and Congruence Dissonance

The reader, viewer, or listener may not watch, read, or hear even one item of the vast output of mass media—he may not even pay attention to that which he is nominally viewing or read everything chosen by his newspaper. The point is simple—people select which of the devices of mass media to use. This would be fairly banal, but for certain findings. People tend to expose themselves to mass media, which reflect points of view, which are mostly like their own. The theoretical basis of this is a little clouded. One suggestion would be, of course, a psychological abhorrence of ideas, which conflict with one's own. Contradictory ideas are avoided because they are psychologically uncomfortable. This idea is strengthened by the congruence dissonance theory (Festinger 1957), which suggests that individuals should keep the psychological world balanced; ideas that do not fit in with one's belief system cause a psychologically unbalanced state, which motivate an individual to correct the imbalance by whatever means he can. For example,, most people do not read 'x' ideas not because they do not read any books at all. It is rather because 'x' ideas would necessarily cause their discomfort.

Perception

Perception is the process by which we become aware of objects and events in the external world through our various senses—sight, smell, taste, touch, and hearing. Perception is an active rather than a passive process. Out perceptions is only in part functions of the outside world in large measure. They are a function of our own past experiences, desires, our needs and wants, our causes of love and hate. Therefore, each perception is the beneficiary of all previous perceptions, and in turn, each new perception leaves its mark on the common pool. A percept is, thus, a link between the past which gives it its meaning and the future which it helps to interpret. In communication we are particularly concerned with that area of perception and the judgments we make about them.

To understand Perception there are three principles or rules that perceptual process follows. They are: subjectivity, stability and, meaningfulness. Perception is active and perceived as some structured whole. Stability or invariance focuses on an object. The meaningfulness lies in viewing a film of a dream scene, that is, at the time of viewing without any meaning.

- **Perceptual processes:** Interpersonal perception is an extremely complex affair. Perhaps the best way to explain some of these complexities is to examine at least some of the psychological processes involved in people's perceptions.
- **Psychological processes:** Primary recency, self-fulfilling prophecy, perceptual accentuation, implicit personality theory, consistency, and stereotyping.
- **Primacy recency:** In a class half the students are dull and other half are extremely exciting. At the end of the semester if the results are evaluated it would be found that what portions were taught earlier had been remembered best by some students while others had remembered what had been taught the last. In the former case it is called the primacy effect and when what had come later had the most influence it was called the recency effect. The principle here is that we utilize early information to provide us with a general idea as to what the subject is like and we utilize the later information to make this general idea or impression more specific.

- **Perceptual accentuation:** Perceptual accentuation is similar to the fact that bitter gourd may taste horrible but when you are starving, it can taste like any sweet dish and so it goes down easily. There is a rather strong tendency to maintain balance or consistency among our perception.

SELF-FULFILLING PROPHECY

Psychologists argue that we live by scripts which are given to us by our parents and that essentially we act in the way in which we are told to act. All of us, according to transactional psychology, live by the scripts given to us as children. For example, people who enter a group dispute are convinced that the other members will dislike them. What they may be doing is acting in such a way as to encourage people to respond negatively. When we enter a classroom and expect that it will be a dull class, it turns out, more often than not to be a dull class. Now it might be that it was in fact a dull class. But it might also be that we defined it as dull, and hence made it dull. We made a prophecy and then fulfilled it (Devito 1978).

So far we have been discussing the evolution of communication theories over the years as developed by successive sociologists and psychologists. As a sequel to the development of theories there has always been a conceptualization of these theories in the form of models. In the next chapter, an attempt has been made to review the different models developed by the scholars in communication studies in different contexts.

SUMMARY

A theoretical base to any knowledge is essential in understanding any concept. In this chapter, we tried to familiarize you with the evolution of the theories of communication to give you a historical perspective of communication. This knowledge will not only help you to understand in depth the communication process—a mind blowing growth and movement—but also take you into an interesting and intriguing voyage into one of the most important aspects of our civilization—communication. This information and scholarly knowledge is very important for any learning institute and especially for a teacher who cannot function with superficial knowledge. An in-depth knowledge of this part is essential for future growth and effectiveness.

5

Models of Communication

After reading this chapter, you will be familiar with:

- Different models that provide visual explanation of the communication process
- Models that are best-suited to classroom teaching
- Techniques that improve your own communication
- Programmes that help develop effective communication

MODELS OF COMMUNICATION

There is a paradox about the term 'communication'. It is obvious and obscure at the same time. Its meaning seems to be obvious in contemporary usage but very illusive when we try to capture its essence in a rigorous definition. In order to understand the communication process we must use various devices to structure our thinking. These devices are called communication models.

According to Devito (1978), communication models serve to organize the various elements and processes of the communication act. No model can organize all the data pertaining to communication but we can expect reasonably good models to organize at least some of the data in a meaningful and interesting way. These models aid in the discovery of new facts about communication. Thus, they serve a heuristic function. These models help to generate questions concerning communication that can be researched further and hopefully studied and understood. These models enable us to make predictions concerning communication, for example, to theorize what will happen under certain conditions. Such knowledge can help fine-tune the understanding and grasp of technical literature and matters involving ideas and concepts. The models to a great extent can provide a means of measuring the elements and processes involved in communication. Feedback is one such element of considerable value to the communicator to enable him to enhance the quality of his message.

Communication models allow the researcher to account for different variables in different communication situations. Models only represent systems or processes. Since they are not real, they are just symbolic ways of looking at systems to help us to think about them more lucidly. Again since models do not show every part of a system, they are usually incomplete in that sense. Even those that are shown are represented only in enough detail to help us look at the processes or features in which we are interested. Models give us an idea of complicated objects or events in a general way. They enable us to see how a particular communication event fits into the general pattern. They provide a classification for an orderly nature of events and suggest new ways of looking at old problems and familiar events. They help us by providing a structure of reference for purposes of study. Theories are not models and the most fundamental difference between a theory and a model is that, the former is an explanation whereas the latter is a representation.

DEFINITIONS OF MODEL

In social science research, a model is a tentative description of social process. In the similar way, communication model is also the description of communication process or a system. It is a tool of explanation and analyses, very often in a diagrammatic form. It shows how various elements of a situation being studied relate to each other. Models are not statements of reality. Only after much further research and testing would the model be considered viable. It could then be developed into a theory.

Additionally, the model can be a person whose behaviour others wish to emulate or who they wish to model themselves after.

The simplest definition of a model is that it is an analogue. A model is a relatively well-developed analogy. Given two objects or processes, which are dissimilar in many respects, one is an analogue of the other to the extent that the physical or logical structure of one represents the physical or logical structure of the other.

INTRODUCTION TO MODELS OF COMMUNICATION

In the following pages, twenty-two models of communication will be discussed briefly. They cover a period of about 2,300 years, commencing with the Greek philosopher and orator Aristotle and concluding with present day communicologists. The aim of the exercise is to examine how different sociolgists down the years have approached the theory and process of communication. A summation of all of their approaches will perhaps give us the most accurate concept of this process called communication.

Simple Models of Communication

The model shows a sender S and a receiver R with a message passing from S to R shown by the direction of the arrow.

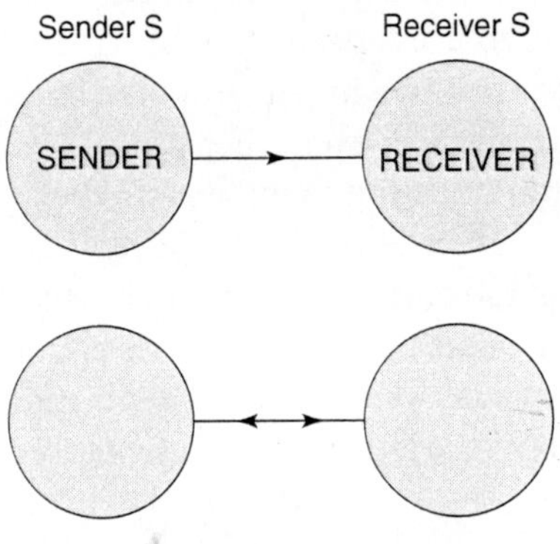

Figure 5.1
Model A: One way and two way communication

The model shows the process in the situation above working in both directions. Because each sender is also a receiver, S and R have been left out of the models. The arrows still show the direction of the communication.

As in situation B, the arrows show the direction of communication and S and R have been left out. Models [A] and [B] help us to see the differences between one way and two way communication. For instance [A] is clearly a good way of showing what happens in a radio or TV broadcast or a newspaper where a receiver cannot directly respond to the sender. The model helps us to see the difference between radio, TV or newspaper, and a lecture or a briefing session, because in these the receiver becomes the sender by (for instance) asking questions, coughing, growing restless, pulling a face, 'heckling', etc. Body language (gestures, how you sit or stand and so on) is communication too. So is silence.

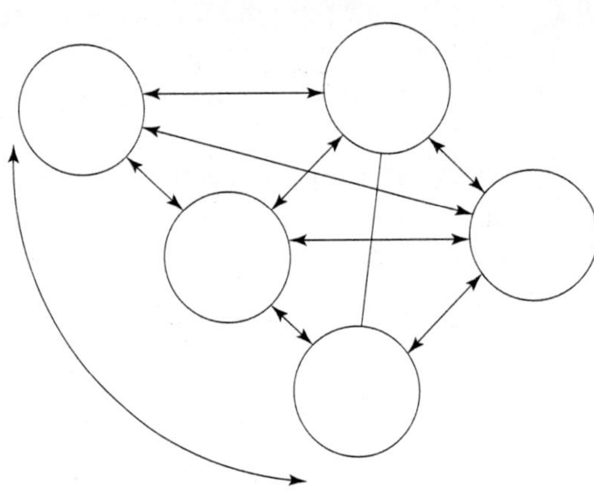

Figure 5.2
Model B Multiple way communication

The whole series of models A, B and C is useful for showing us how dramatically the act of communication increases in complexity as soon as more than two people are involved. This increased complexity can be shown by two things—the larger number of lines pointing away from or towards each sender/receiver and the complicated crisscrossing of the lines in the model. Models then can be used in explaining why committees, parliament and other formal groups have rules to decide who speaks when and to whom. The model may also prove useful to chairmen of meetings or groups because it assumes that every sender/receiver in the group is communicating with every other member. A chairman who is thinking about this model will be able to identify members who are flocking the discussion and those who are sending their messages in the form of silence, restlessness, etc. instead of words. The fact that a member of a group says nothing can be just as important as what those who do speak have to say.

The Cultural Ratification Model

This approach is based on the central assumption that the mass media are 'allied to the power structure of the society; that it is inevitable that they serve to support and maintain the power structures, and dominant ideologies. The mass media in particular present a world view to members of the society, which regenerates continually, and pervasively the ideological structure that are required for the maintenance of the existing power structure' (De Fleur 1989).

Thus, the media is seen in this approach as agencies in aiding the political control of the society. The contribution of the mass media is also seen as having the effect of preventing radical changes in attitudes, values, beliefs, perceptions, etc. of the members of the society.

The drawback of this approach is again lack of empirical evidence. For at last this reason the model is not especially popular with psychologists interested in mass communication research. It is included in this text for the purposes of record.

Communication Models

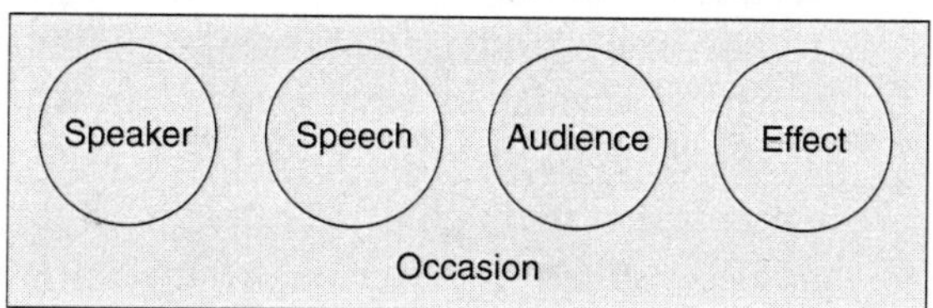

Figure 5.3

Aristotle's Model of Communication

Devito (1978) discusses Aristotle's Model of Communication. The earliest model of communication was the symmetrical and simple model developed by the great Greek philosopher Aristotle some 2,000 years before. Aristotle in his model includes the five essential elements of communication, i.e., the speaker, the speech or message, the audience, the occasion, and the effect. In his rhetoric, Aristotle advises the speaker on constructing a speech for different audiences on different occasions for different effects. This model is most applicable to public speaking.

Lasswell's Model (1948)

Lasswell has given us another simple model. His model belongs specifically to the area of mass communication. He has argued that to understand the process of mass communication one needs to study each of the stages in his mode: 'Who says what, in which channel, to whom, and, with what effect'.

Figure 5.4

This is the verbal version of Shannon and Weaver's original model. It is still linear. It sees communication as the transmission of messages. It raises the issue of the effect rather than meaning. Effect implies an observable and measurable change in the receiver that is caused by identifiable elements in the process. A change in one of these elements will change the effect. We can change the encoder as well as the message. We can change the channel and each one of these changes would produce the appropriate change in the effect. Most mass communication research has implicitly followed this model.

The work of institutions and their process on the producers of communication on the audience and how it is affected clearly derives from a process based linear model.

Lasswell's Model—Comments: Until the 1960s Lasswell's four questions (of who says what, by what channel, to whom and with what effect) dominated studies of the mass media in France. Not only his exemplary expression defines the different research areas for communication investigations, but also seemed to prescribe the appropriate concepts and methodological orientation to be followed. Thus, Lasswell's paradigm served the entire scientific community of communication scholars.

Lasswell's model was represented by Michael Buhler.

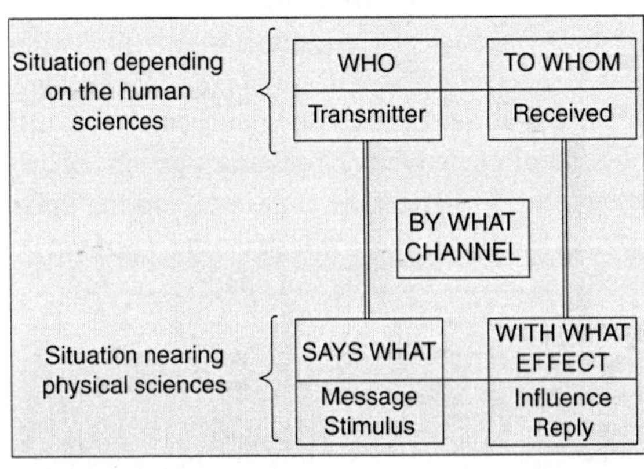

Figure 5.5
Lasswell's Model (1948)

It was Harold Lasswell who first precisely delineated the various elements with which constitute a 'communication fact'. According to him, one cannot suitable describe a 'communication action' without answering the following questions—who said what, by what channel, to whom and with what effect. Identification of transmitters, analysis of message content, study of transmission channels, audience identification and evaluation of effects; these are the five parameters of communication studies. Michel Buhler represents the Lasswell's model with the above diagram.

Lasswell's view of communication, as had Aristotle's some two thousand years earlier, focused primarily on verbal messages. It also emphasized the elements of speaker, messages, and audience, but used different terms. Both men viewed communication as a one-way process in which one individual influenced others through messages. Lasswell offered a broadened definition of channel to include mass-media along with verbal speech as a part of the communication process. His approach also provided a more generalized view of the goal or effect of communication than did the Aristotelian perspective.

Shannon and Weaver (1949)

The pre-conception of communication was heavily influenced by the engineering model of Shannon and Weaver (1949). Communication was conceived as a linear act of transmission of a message from a source to a receiver via a signal producing transmitter. A component called 'noise' acknowledged the presence of context in the electrical engineering model.

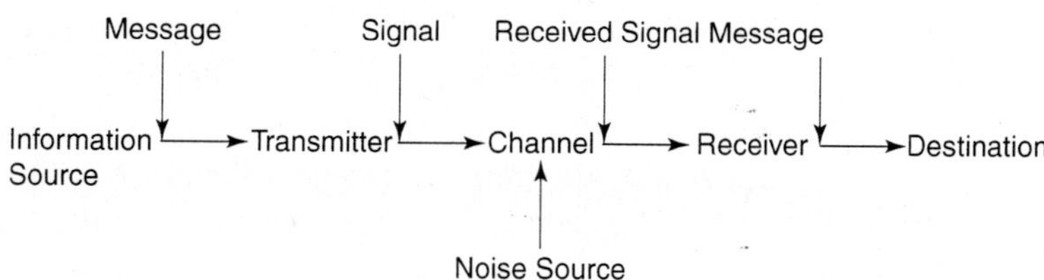

Figure 5.6

Shannon and Weaver's mathematical theory of communication (1949) is widely accepted as one of the main seeds out of which communication studies, has grown. It is a clear example of the process school, seeing communication as the transmissions of messages. The work developed during the Second World War in the Bell telephone laboratories in the US and their main concern was to work out ways in which channels of communication could be used most efficiently. For them the main channels were the telephone, cable and the radio wave. They produced a theory that enabled them to approach the problem of how to send a maximum amount of information along a given channel to carry information. This concentration on the channel and its capacity is appropriate pertaining to their engineering and mathematical background, but they claim that their theory is widely applicable over the whole question of human communication.

Shannon and Weaver's model (1949) presents communication as a linear process. Its simplicity has attracted many derivatives, and its linear process centred nature has attracted many critics. Its obvious characteristics of simplicity and linearity standout clearly. Shannon and Weaver identify three levels of problem in the study of communication. These are:

- Level A—Technical problems: How accurately can the symbols of communication be transmitted?
- Level B—Semantic problems: How precisely do the transmitted symbols convey the desired meaning?
- Level C—Effectiveness problems: How effectively does the received meaning affect conduct in the desired way?

Level A problems are the simplest to understand and these are the ones that the model was originally developed to explain. Level B problems are easy to identify but hard to solve. Level C problems may at first sight seem to imply that Shannon and Weaver see communication as manipulation or propaganda. The sender X communicated effectively with receiver Y when Y responds in the way X desires him to. They claim that three levels are not water-tight, but are interrelated and interdependent and that their models, despite its origin in level A, work equally well on all three levels. The source is seen as the decision-maker and decides which messages to send or rather selects one out of set of possible messages. This selected message is then changed by the transmitter into a signal which is sent through the channel to the receiver. For a telephone the channel is the wire, the signal, the electrical

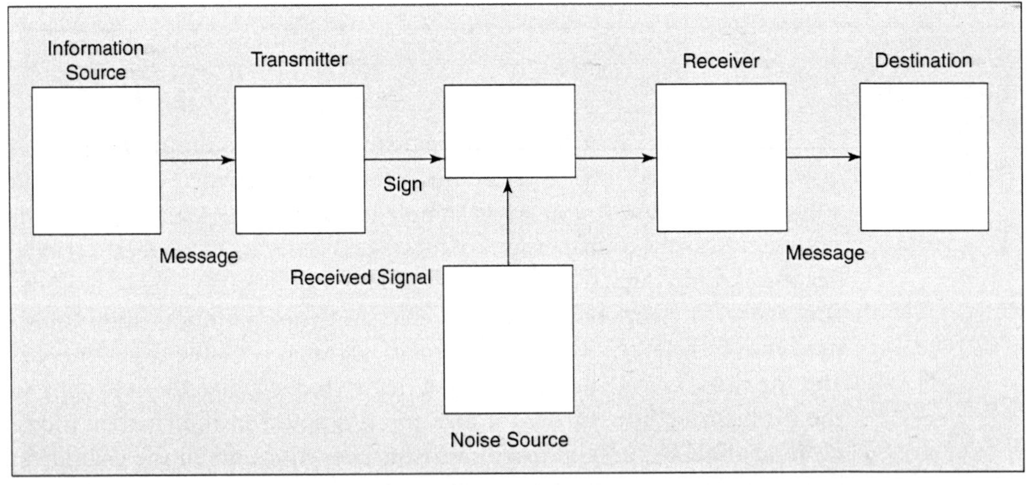

Figure 5.7
Shannon and Weaver's Model (1949)
Source: The Mathematical Theory of Communication, Claude E. Shannon and Warren Weaver, 1949.

current it carries and the transmitter and the receiver are the telephone handsets. In conversation the mouth is the transmitter, the signal is the sound wave, and which pass through the channel of the air, and ear is the receiver (John Fiske 1982).

This model was given its definitive formulation in 1949 by Claude Shannon and Warren Weaver. As the diagram above indicates, this communication model comprises four elements. A source of information with a greater or lesser number of messages to communicate; a transmitter or sender with the capacity to transform a message into a signal; a receiver which decodes the signal in order to retrieve the initial message, and finally, the destination, a person or thing for whom the message in intended. Communication, according to this model, follows a simple left to right process. The information source (say speaker), selects a desired message from all the possible messages. The message is sent through a transmitter (microphone) and is changed into signals. The signals are received by a receiver (say earphone), changed back into a message and given to the destination or a listener. In the process of transmission certain distortions are added to the signal which is not part of the message and these will be called noise.

The basis of all contemporary Western theories of communication—Shannon-Weaver model stresses the idea of inside and outside and assumes that communication is a lineal matching rather than making. The source of information changes the message into the signal which is actually sent over the communication channel from the transmitter to the receiver. In the case of telephony the channel is a wire, the signal a varying electrical current on this wire, the transmitter in the set of devices (telephone transmitter, etc.), which change the sound pressure of the voice into the varying electric current. In oral speech, the information source is brain; the transmitter is the voice mechanism producing the varying sound pressure (the signal) which is transmitted through the air (the channel). In radio the channel is simply space, and the signal is the electromagnetic wave, which is transmitted. The receiver is a sort of inverse transmitter, changing the transmitted signal back into a message and handing this message on to the destination.

During the process of transmission certain things are added to the signal, which were not intended by the sender. These additions are distortion of sounds as in telephone, or static in radios, or errors in transmission in telegraphy or facsimile etc. Such changes in transmission signals are called noise.

Comments on Shannon and Weaver's Model by Brent

Bell Telephone Laboratories conducted the research to study the engineering problems of signal transmission. In their book *Mathematical Theory of Communication* Shannon and Weaver described the nature of communication process—'communication will be used here in a very broad sense to include all the procedures by which one mind may affect another. This of course involves not only written and oral speech, but also music, the pictorial arts, the theater, the ballet, and in fact all human behaviour'.

The view of the authors in this model represented an important expansion of the idea of communication that includes such activities as music, art, ballet and the theater—in fact all human behaviour—although far reaching implications were not to be elaborated upon for some time. The Shannon and Weaver perspective, like that of Lasswell included not only verbal and mediated channels, but also gestures, body position, and other forms of nonverbal behaviour.

Shannon and Weaver also advanced the new notion of a correction channel, which they regarded as a means of overcoming problems created by noise. An observer operates the correction channel. He compares the initial signal that was sent with what was received: when the two didn't match, additional signals would be sent to correct the error.

Since the Second World War attention to communication problems per se—as an explicitly practical matter—has been paid by engineering and social scientists. The concept of electrical engineering in particular, originally applied to human communication by Shannon and Weaver (1949) have played a formative role in the development of socio-psychological approaches to the subject, and continue in currency within media research even today.

Comments on Shannon and Weaver's Model (1949)

Both European and American scholars recognize that Shannon and Weaver's model provided the basic paradigm for effects—oriented communication research by setting forth the main elements (source, channel, messages, and receiver) of a simple linear model of communication. This model became tremendously popular with communication researchers enabling the field of communication study to take off about 30 years ago. It formed the main paradigm for many researchers around the world. Less well known is the contribution by Shannon and Weaver in defining the concept of information as a central notion for the field of Communication. Shannon and Weaver's model was used in the field of electronics for many purposes from the design of telephone networks to matrices of computer memories.

An important distinction has been identified by an eminent Finnish scholar between the two central concepts—(a) communication and (b) information. These two concepts trace from Aristotle to the Shannon and Weaver mathematical theory of a single transmission and to other models of information and communication. Although Shannon and Weaver's concept of the probabilistic model of communication has been fruitful in leading to further research, it was never intended to describe linguistic information and human communication.

Bolton and Cleaver Model (1949)

Many communication models assume that provided the message can be made clear and strong, good communication will result because there are no significant differences between senders and receivers. However, the Bolton-Cleaver model assumes that every sender and receiver is different and that every act of communication has to make allowances for these differences. The differences are those that exist in every human being who communicates like background, social standing, attitudes to other people/communicators, experiences in communication, etc. To put it simply, these personality differences can make messages mean exactly different to its receiver from what the sender intended. A good example of this problem at its most acute is the difficulty of describing emotions (love, joy, hatred, frustration etc.). Emotions are intensely personal and are inescapably linked to a person's background and upbringing. This makes it very difficult to communicate them accurately and we usually manage to get across only a part of the idea.

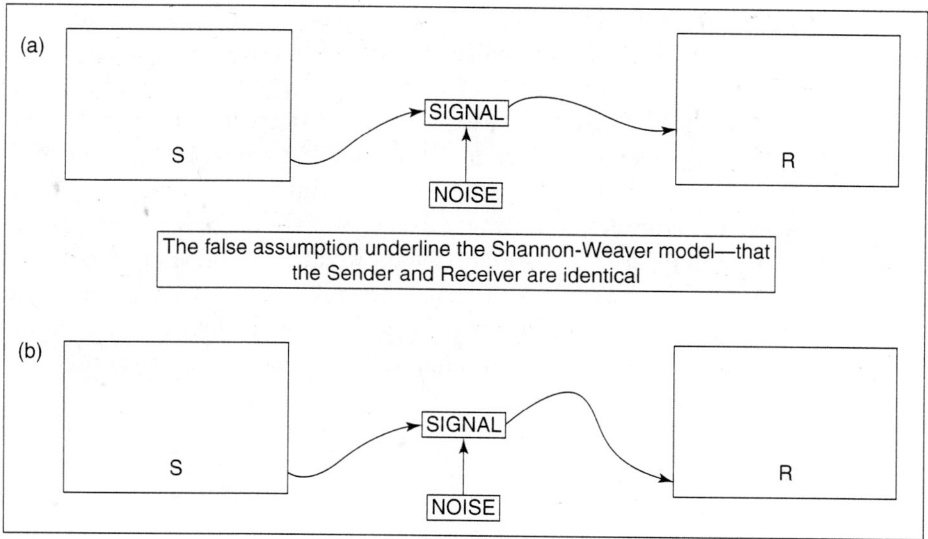

Figure 5.8
Bolton and Cleaver Model (1949)
Source: Everett Rogers and Francis Balle, 1985.

Wendell Johnson Model (1951)

One of the most insightful models and most clear is a model of interpersonal communication which was proposed by Wendell Johnson.

The model indicates that communication takes place in a context which is external to both speaker and listener and to the communication process as well. Figure 5.9 with curved loop indicates that the various stages

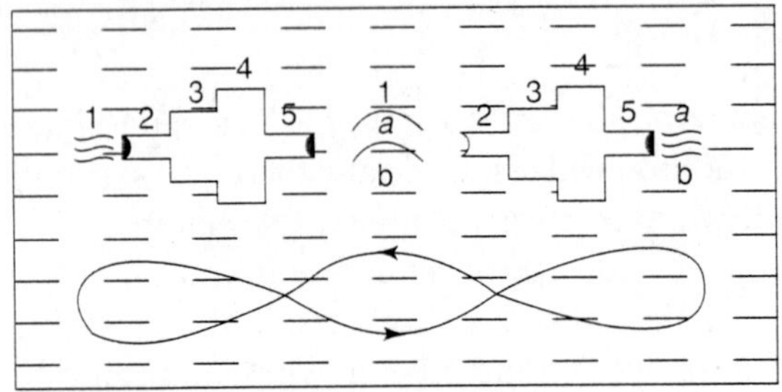

Figure 5.9
Wendell Johnson Model (1951)
Source: Communicology, Devito, 1978.

of communication are actually interrelated and interdependent. The actual communication process begins at stage 1 which represents the occurrence of an event, anything that can be perceived. This event is the stimulus. Although not all communication occurs with reference to such external stimuli, communication makes sense. Johnson argues that only when it does in some way relate to the external world. At stage 2 the observer is stimulated through one or more sensory channels. The opening at stage 2 is purposely illustrated as relatively small to emphasize the out of all the possible stimuli in the world, only a small part of these actually stimulate the observer. At stage 3, organismic evaluations occur.

Audibility never impulses travel from the sense organs to the brain which effect certain bodily changes in, e.g., muscular tension. At stage 4 the feelings aroused at stage 3 are beginning to be translated into words, a process that takes place in accordance with the individual's unique language habits. At stage 5, from all the possible linguistic symbols certain ones are selected and arranged into some pattern. At stage 1 the words that the speaker utters, by means of sound waves, or the words that are written, by means of light waves, serve as stimulation for the hearer, much as the outside event at stage 1 served as stimulation for the speaker. At stage 2, the hearer is stimulated; at stage 3 there are organismic evaluations; at stage 4 feelings are beginning to be translated into words; at stage 5 certain of these symbols are selected and arranged; and at 1 these symbols, in the form of sound and/or light waves, are emitted and serve as stimulation for another hearer. The process is a continuous one (Devito 1978).

Newcomb's Model (1953)

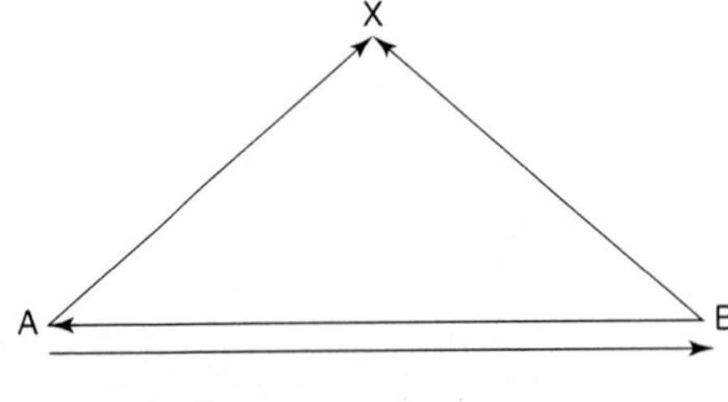

Figure 5.10
Newcomb's Model (1953)
Source: Introduction to Communication Studies, John Fiske, 1982.

As we have seen Lasswell's model was linear like the earlier model of Shannon and Weaver or G. Gerbner. But Newcomb's model introduced to us a fundamentally new and different shape. Its main significance however lies in the fact that it is the first of the models to introduce the role of communication in a society or a social relationship. The role according to Theodore Newcomb is to maintain equilibrium with the social system. The model works as follows:

A and B are a communicator and a receiver, respectively. They may be in individuals or management or government and people. X is part of their social environment. ABX is the system which means that its internal relations are interdependent. If A changes the X then B will change as well, or if A changes his relationship to X, then B will have to change either his relationship to X. Again if A and B are friends, and if X is something or someone known to both of them it will be important that A and B have similar attitudes to X. If they do, the system will be in equilibrium.

On the other hand, if A likes X and does not like B, then A and B will be under pressure in communicating effectively until they reach a broad agreement on their attitude to X. Again X may not be a thing or a person. It may be a part of the environment. For example, A may be a union of bank employees, B the government, and X a change in government policy, like bank privatization. If A and B like each other they will hold frequent talks to agree on X. If A and B are not in the same camp then there will be less pressure to agree on X. The system is till in equilibrium.

Newcomb's proposition was based on consistency or balance theory. His approach described the communication process in terms of interpretive processes that occur within individuals rather than on the transmission of information between them. His contribution is way from transmission-oriented theories. He is concerned with explaining the relationships between two or more individuals and an object. He stipulates that the people involved in the communicative act must be in one another's presence and the object must be familiar to both of them.

Schramm's Model (1954)

Wilbur Schramm's model presents a complete treatment of the fundamentals of communication. His model offers a classic general explanation of the nature of communication. He presents a schematic diagram of human communication as elucidated below:

When the encoder is the microphone and decoder the earphone—Figure 5.11 represents electronic communication. If you consider that the source and encoder is one person, decoder and destination are another and

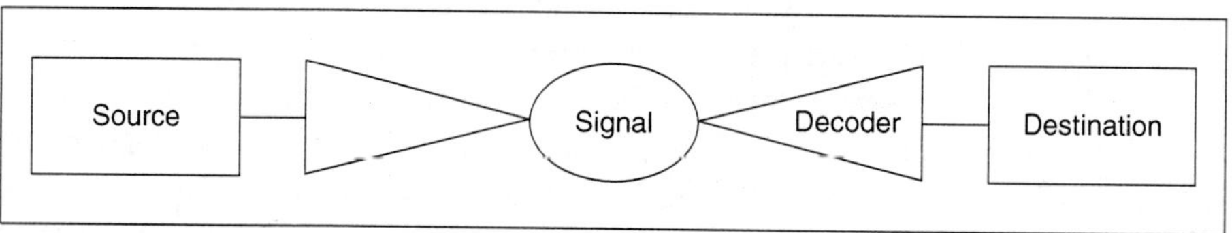

Figure 5.11
Schramm's Model (1954) (a)

the signal is language the same diagram represents human communication. Schramm felt that such a system is also only as strong as the weakest link.

For example, there may occur a situation in which the source does not have adequate or clear information or the message is not encoded fully, accurately and effectively in transmittable signs. Those messages are not transmitted fast and accurately enough despite interference and competition to the desired receiver. Those are not in a pattern that corresponds to the encoding and finally, if the destination is unable to handle the decoded message so as to produce the desired response, then obviously the system is working at less than top efficiency. When we realize that all these steps must be accomplished with relatively high efficiency, if any communication is to be successful, the everyday act of explaining something to strangers or writing a letter seems a minor miracle.

Schramm also felt that the most important thing about such a system is one we have been talking about all too glibly—the fact that receiver and sender must be in tune. This is clear enough in the case of a radio transmitter and receiver but somewhat more complicated when it means that a human receiver must be able to understand a human sender.

His modified the diagram therefore and it looked as in Figure 5.12.

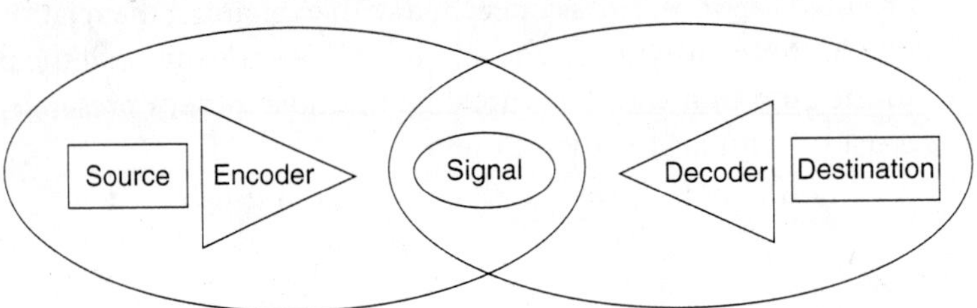

Figure 5.12
Schramm's Model (1954) (b)
Source: The Process and Effects of Mass Communication, Wilbur Schramm (Ed.), 1965.

According to Schramm the circles are to be perceived as the 'accumulated experience of the two individuals trying to communicate'. The source can encode and the destination can decode only in terms of the experience each has had. If the circles are huge and are in common then communication is easy. If the circles do not meet—if there has been no common experience—then communication is impossible. If these circles have only a small area in common i.e., if the experience of the source and destination have been strikingly unlike—then it is going to be very difficult to get an intended meaning across from one to the other. This is the difficulty we face when we try to communicate to one with a culture much different from our own (Schramm 1954).

There were several additional models by Schramm dealing with the dynamics of the communication process.

It was in the model that Schramm introduced the concept of field of experience which he thought to be essential to determining whether or not a message would be received at the destination in the manner intended by the source.

Schramm's view of communication was more elaborate than many others developed during this period and added new elements in describing the process in addition to re-emphasizing the elements of sources, message, and destination. It suggested the importance of encoding and decoding processes and the role of field of experience. Further, whereas other models had acknowledged that the receiver might either be a single person or a large audience, this model suggested that a source could also be one individual or many, and in actual operation, the source and the receiver were often indistinguishable.

Schramm went on to modify his models further to enable us to understand the process of communication completely. According to Schramm each person in the communication process can be called as both an encoder and decoder because he learns to transmit and receive the message in the form acceptable to both on the basis of individual's accumulated experience. He portrayed the sender or receiver, thus, in Figure 5.13.

Schramm felt each individual to be 'switchboard centres, handling and re-routing the great endless current of communication'. He said, 'we can accurately think of communication as passing through us—changed to be sure by our interpretations, by our habits, our abilities and our capabilities, but the input still being reflected in the output'. According to Schramm there is now need 'to add another element of our description of the communication process', that is, the role of the interpreter.

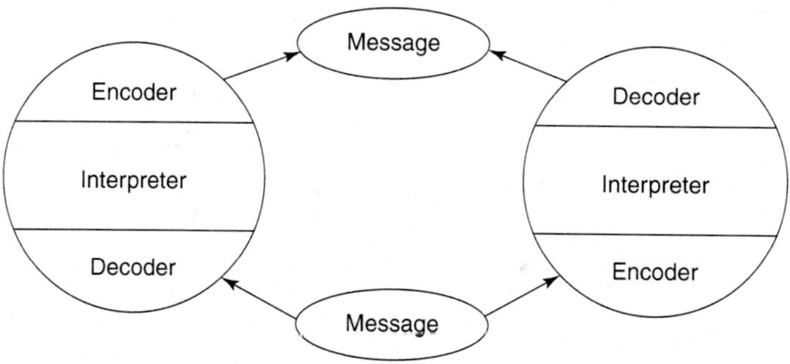

Figure 5.13
Schramm's Model (1954) (c)
Source: The Process and Effects of Mass Communication, Wilbur Schramm (Ed.), 1965.

In Figure 5.13, the model is basically the one proposed by Wilbur Schramm, based on work by C.E. Osgood. It presents communication as a circular process and identifies three elements in the behaviour of a sender/receiver: encoding (putting the message/feedback into the mode or channel of communication), decoding (getting it out again) and interpreting (the mental process of forming message or responding to it).

C.E. Osgood–Schramm Model

To the circular model, we have added boxes and arrows showing the influence of noise and personality, is helix, used as a model by Frank E.X. Dance. He felt that circular models were better than straight-line ones like Shannon-Weaver, but that they had a built-in-error since they showed communication ending up where it started off. In fact as an act of communication goes on, the noise gets lessened (because the communicators gets more used to handling the channel/mode) and personality becomes more helpful (because, as communicators get to know each other and the subject, they adjust to each other and fill gaps in their knowledge). Ideally figure 5.14 (Osgood–Schramm) and figure 5.15 (Katz and Lazarfeld's Model) should be a single, three dimensional model. As the helix widens and ascends, the personality box would get bigger and noise box would get smaller. The two models should always be used together.

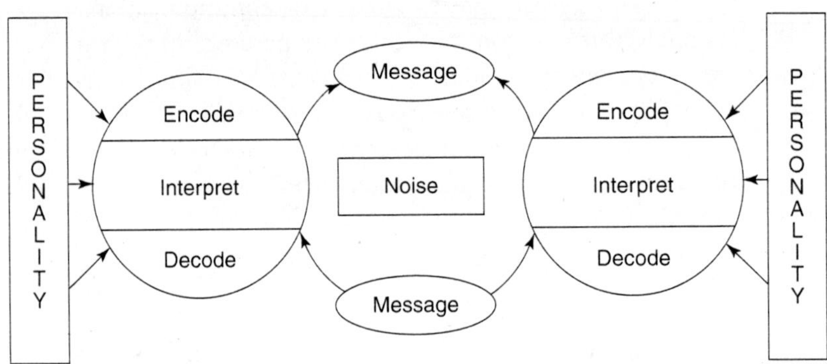

Figure 5.14
C.E. Osgood–Schramm Model

Katz and Lazarfeld's Model (1955)

The model of 1955 was based on earlier research in which they found that information presented on the mass media did not have the reach and impact upon the receivers as previous views of communication seemed to suggest it would. Specifically their research indicated that political radio and print messages seemed to have a negligible effect on the individual's voting

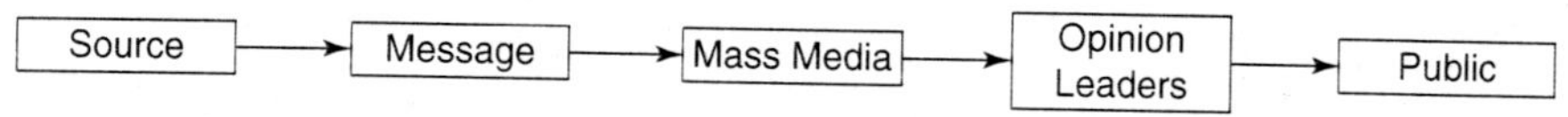

Figure 5.15
Katz and Lazarfeld's Model (1955)
Source: Personal Influence, Eilhu Katz and Puai Lazarfeld, 1955.

decisions. Their research also indicated the some people were consistently more influential than others, leading them to conclude that ideas often seemed to flow from radio to print to opinion leaders and from them to the less active sections of the population in a two-step flow.

Gerbner's Model (1956)

Communication processes can be seen as consisting of two alternating dimensions—the perceptual or receptive, and the communicating or means and control dimensions. The main elements of Gerbner's model are shown in Figure 5.16.

The process begins with an event E, something in external reality, which is perceived by M (where M can be a human or a machine such as a camera or a microphone) M's perception of E is a percept E_1. This is the perceptual dimension at the start of the process. The relationship between E and E_1 involves selection, in which M cannot possibly perceive the whole complexity of E. If M is a machine the selection is determined by its engineering and its physical capacities. If M is a human, however, the selection is more complex.

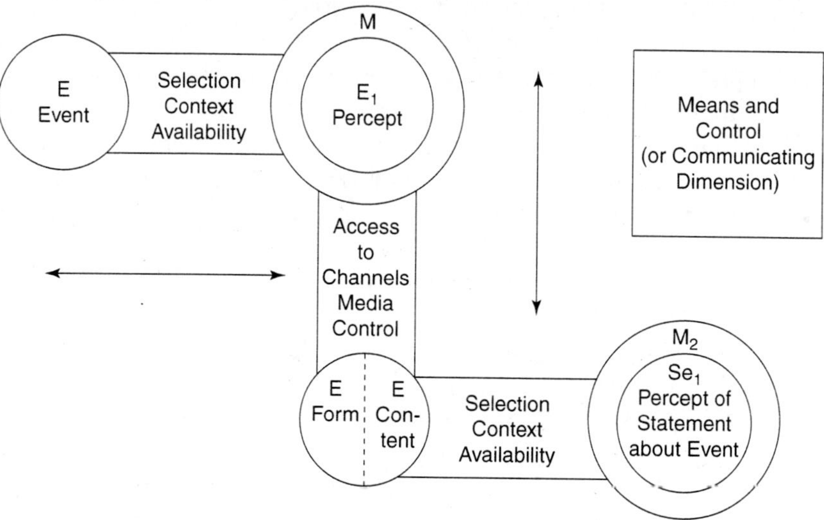

Figure 5.16
Gerbner's Model (1956)
Source: Introduction to Communication Studies, John Fiske, 1982.

Human perception is not a simple reception of stimuli but is a process of interaction or negotiation. What happens is that we try to match the external stimuli with internal patterns of thoughts or concepts when this match has been made, we have perceived something, and we have given it meaning. So meaning in this sense derives from matching the external stimuli with internal concepts. Consider what happens when we fail to hear a word clearly, cannot decipher someone's handwriting, or try out puzzles of photographs of familiar objects taken from unfamiliar angles in unfamiliar close ups. Once the matching or recognition has occurred, the photograph is easily perceived for what it is. Until this moment we are in a stage of frustration, for although we can see the tones and shapes of the photograph we cannot say we perceive it yet for perception always involves the drive to understand and organize. Failing to see meaning in what we perceive puts us into a state of disorientation. This matching is controlled by our culture, internal concepts, or patterns of thought.

We now move into the second stage of vertical dimension. This is when the percept E_1 is converted into signals about E or to use Gerbner's code SE. This is what we generally call a message or a signal or statement about the event. The circle representing the message in divided into two: S refers to it as a signal, the form that it takes and E refers to its content. It is clear that a given content or E can be communicated in a number of different ways—there are a number of potential Ss to choose from. Finding the best S for a given E is one of the crucial concerns of the communicators. It is important to remember that SE is a unified concept, not two separate areas brought together in that a chosen S will obviously affect the representation of E.

The relationship between form and content is dynamic and interactive. In this vertical dimension selection is as important as in the horizontal. First there is the selection of means the medium and channel of communication. Then there is the selection from within the percept E_1. Just as E_1 cannot be a complete and comprehensive response to E so too a signal about E_1 can never in its turn attain completeness and comprehensiveness. Selection and distortion must occur.

Westley and MacLean's Model (1957)

Bruce Westley and Malcolm S. MacLean (Jr) (1957) make two distinctions between face-to-face communication and mass communication. Face-to-face communication involves more sense modalities than mass communication. Visual cues, paralinguistic cues, olfactory cues, and kinesic cues are available to the participants in face-to-face communication but not available in mass communication. In face-to-face communication participants have access to immediate feedback from the receiver whereas in mass communication the feedback is delayed. The rationale Westley and MacLean provide for constructing this model of mass communication is to highlight these differences between the two modes of communication. Newcomb's (1953) theory of communicative acts is used as the analogue for the model.

Social need for information underlines Westley and MacLean's (1957) extension of Newcomb's model. They adopt it specifically for the mass media. They introduced a new element, C, which is the editorial-communicating function. It is the process of deciding what and how to communicate.

Westley and Maclean argue that in mass communication, situations the people involved are not in one another's presence and the object may not be familiar to them. When person B cannot receive the information about other persons and objects he needs to re-orient himself to his environment. For this he must rely on a gatekeeper (C) to select relevant information from the environment and pass it on to him. The gatekeeper in this model is the mass media and it functions to select and transmit information otherwise unavailable to B. The mass media, insofar as it functions as a gatekeeper, survives only if it satisfies B's needs for information to orient himself to his surroundings. In a sense, the function of the mass media is to extend selectively people's information environments.

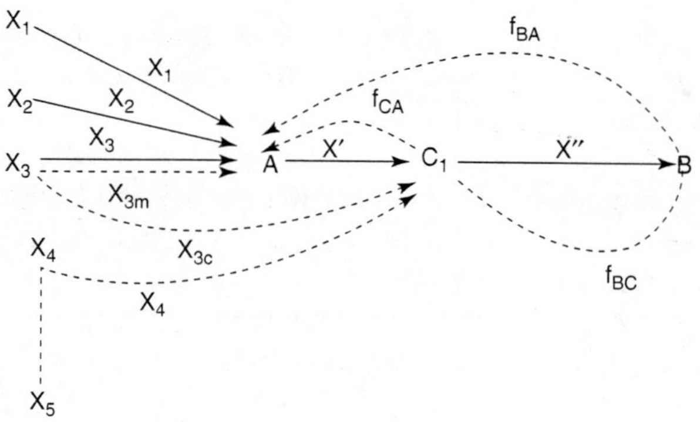

Figure 5.17

Westley and MacLean's Model (1957)

Source: A Conceptual Model for Communication Research, Bruce Westley and Malcolm S. MacLean Jr 1957.

The messages C transmits to B(X") represent his selections from both messages to him from As (X') and Cs selections and abstractions from Xs in his own sensory field (X_{3c} X_4) which may or may not be Xs in A's field. Feedback not only moves from B and A (f_{BA}) and from B to C (f_{ac}) but also from C and A (f_{CA}). Clearly, in the mass communication situation, a large number of Cs receive from a very large number of As and transmit to vastly large number of Bs, who simultaneously receive from other Cs.

The authors argue that one of the advantages of this model is its generality. The gate keeping function, C, may be any form of mass media. They also contend that unintentional acts are objects Xs, whereas intentional acts are As, or specific senders. The model represents communication occurring without the presence of a sender transmitting intentional messages to specific receivers. The gatekeeper transmits X to Bs in the absence of As. The gatekeeper is a conduit for messages rather than the source of messages per se.

At the same time—their model departed from previous popular approaches by suggesting, 'that communication did not begin with a source but rather with a series of signals or potential messages'. The Westley and MacLean model was considerably more complicated than previous models and the additional components, lines, arrows, etc. led to a view of communication that was expanded in several significant ways. The model accounted for both mass-communication and interpersonal communication as well as the relationship between the two. Additionally it broadened and elaborated the feedback concept. Under the Westley and MacLean model not all messages were intentionally sent or necessarily the result of human activity. Finally the model suggested that messages are transformed as they are transmitted from individual to individual.

Hypo Model (1958)

As in the case of the early days of other fields the infant communication field in search of academic legitimacy and distinct identity gave precedence to affirmative studies of the process of communication as an independent variable leading to behaviour change. Thus, in the optimistic 1960s promises made on behalf of communication technology were to be qualified by considerations of their interactions with different international, national, and sub-national contexts. The popular retrospective myth called the magic bullet theory or hypodermic needle model was presented as if media messages were all powerful. Thus, the specific time and country context of the source of this model (the US as a site for early mass communication research in the 1940s) was not expected to make a difference in spite of Lazarfeld and Merton's warning that the social effects of the media would vary with the nature of media ownership and control system prevailing in each society.

Jakobson's Model (1958)

Jakobson's model has similarities with both the linear and the triangular models. But he is a linguist, and as such is interested in matters like meaning and the internal structure of the message. He, thus, bridges the gap between the 'process' and 'semiotic' schools. His model is a double one. He starts by modeling the constitutive factors in an act of communication. These are the six factors that make any communication possible. He then models the functions that this act of communication performs for each factor. He starts on a familiar linear base where an addresser sends a message to an addressee. He recognizes that this message refers to something other than itself which he terms as the context. This gives the third point of the triangle whose other two points are the addresser and the addressee. He further adds two other factors: one is contact, by which he means the physical channel and psychological connections between the addresser and the addressee. The final factor is the code, a shared meaning system by which the message is structured. He visualizes his model as in Figure 5.18.

	Context message	
Addresser	———————	Addressee
	Contact code	

Figure 5.18
Jakobson's Model (1958)

The Constitutive Factors of Communication

Each of these factors determines a different function of language and in each act of communication we can find a hierarchy of functions. Jakobson produces an identically structured model to explain the six functions (each function occupies the same place in the model as the factor to which it refers.) This is shown in the Figure 5.18 below:

	Referential	
Emotive	Poetic	Conative
	Phatic	
	Metalingual	

Figure 5.19
Source: Communicology DeVito 1978.

The Functions of Communication

The emotive function: The emotive function describes the relationship of the message to the addresser. In some messages such as love and poetry this emotive function is paramount. In others such as news reporting, this is repressed.
The connative function: At the other end of the process is the connative function. This refers to the effect of the message on the addressee. In commands or propaganda this function assumes paramount importance.
The referential function: The referential function or the 'reality orientation' of the message is clearly of prime priority in objective, factual communication. This is communication that is concerned to be true or factually accurate.

These three are obvious common sense functions performed in varying degrees by all acts of communication and they correspond fairly closely to the A, B, and X of Newcomb's model. The next three functions may appear less familiar.

The phatic function: The phatic function is meant to keep the channels of communication open. It generally maintains the line of communication and confirms that a communication is really taking place.

The meta-lingual function: The meta-lingual function is that of identifying the code that is being used. All messages have to have an explicit or implicit meta-lingual function.

The final function: The final function is the poetic. This is the relationship of the code to itself. In aesthetic communication this is really central.

Examples are to be found in the symbols that the political parties adopt at the time of elections. The symbol and the logo tells us about the man who stands, with the logo pinned on his chest, his personal standing in the society (emotive function), the values and the political programme of the party supporting him (connative function), refer to the existing man and the programme (referential function), and finally the phatic function helps to bring the man and the party closer to his audience, maintain and strengthen the fellow feeling that exists among the members of that community of voters.

Riley and Riley Model (1959)

The model illustrates the constant two-way communication between the primary groups in the social systems comprising the mass society.

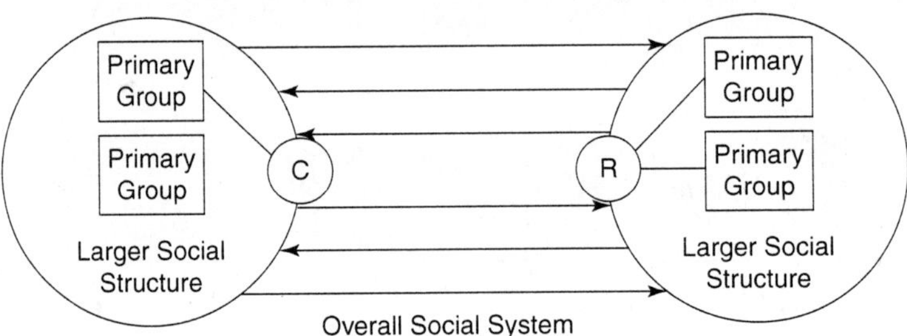

Figure 5.20
Riley and Riley Model (1959)
Source: Mass Communication, Riley and Riley, 1959.

David Berlo's Model (1960)

In the last 25 years a number of models of communication have been developed by communicologists, each one expanding the earlier presentation, David Berlo's model is one among them, which has been profusely quoted and frequently mentioned in discussions. In his book, *The Process of Communication* written in 1960, he presented his model, which had a close similarity to the earlier Aristotelian model, including the traditional elements of source, message, channel, and receiver. Berlo's model attempts to explain the various components in the communication process. For each of these, basic components controlling factors were listed.

For each of these four components there are five elements that need to be considered. The source and receiver are treated in essentially the same way. To study either we need to consider their communication skills (speaking and writing for the source and listening and reading for the receiver); their attitudes, their knowledge, the social system of which they are a part and the culture in which they operate. The message consists of both elements and structure, each of which may be broken down into content, treatment, and code. For the channel Berlo lists the five senses emphasizing that the messages may be sent and received by any and all of the senses.

Berlo, more than the others, emphasized the idea that communication was a process, and the idea that 'meanings are in people, not words....' His model reinforced a shift away from views of communication that emphasized the transmission of information to perspective that focused on the interpretation of information. Berlo writes, 'People can have similar meanings only to the

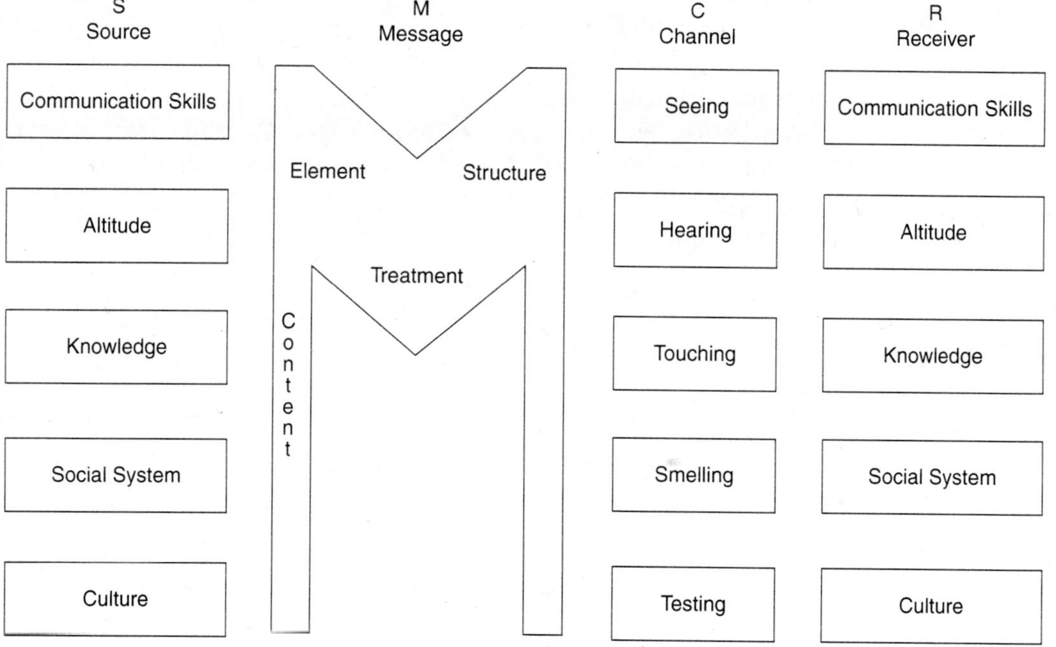

Figure 5.21
David Berlo's Model (1960)
Source: The Process of Communication—An Introduction to Theory and Practice, David Berlo, 1960.

extent that they have had similar experiences'. Berlo also felt that human communication always had a purpose 'our basic purpose in communication is to become an affecting agent, to affect others, our physical environment, and ourselves... we communicate to influence—to affect with intent'.

Watzlawick, Beavin, and Jackson's Model (1967)

In the year 1967 Paul Watzlawick, Janet Beavin, and Don Jackson wrote *Pragmatics of Human communication,* which provided a general view of communication on the basis of psychiatric study and therapy. Their approach and many of the concepts and propositions they provided have been influential in communication thinking since that time. The Watzlawick-Beavin-Jackson's view of communication presented in a general form in Figure 5.22 portrayed it as a process involving a give and take of messages between individuals. The perspective stressed the view that communication is not something that occurs only when a source chooses intentionally to send messages. Rather, they asserted, in the tradition of Shannon and Weaver, that because we are always behaving, 'one cannot but communicate'.

Communication was seen as an ongoing, cumulative activity between individuals who function alternatively as source and receiver. As with other works of this period their writings suggested that in order to understand how communication worked, one needed to look beyond the messages and channels to the meanings the individuals involved attach to the words and actions they created.

Watzlawick, Beavin, and Jackson proceed from the tenets of the information theory in order to explain behavioural choices in an evolutionary form of explanation. They feel that humans choose a behavioural alternative in terms of a 'limitations' principle of communication that in a communicational

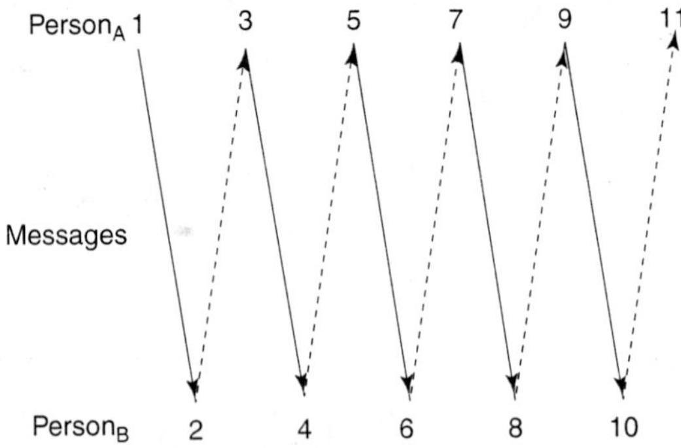

Figure 5.22
Watzlawick, Beavin, and Jackson's Model (1967)
Source: Adapted from *Pragmatics of Human Communication,* Paul Watzlawick, Janet H. Beavin and Don D. Jackson, 1967.

sequence every exchange of messages narrows down the number of possible next moves. In fact, the pragmatic perspective is by far the newest of the four perspectives of the aspects of human communication and has assumed great force in the discipline of communication study and its development steers from the basic studies of Watzlawick, Beavin and Jackson.

Frank Dance Model (1967)

A model that appears relatively simple and says a great deal that is not obvious about the process of communication is the helical spiral proposed by Dance.

The model presented below emphasizes that communication has no clear observable beginning and no clear observable end. The spiral continues indefinitely. No communication transaction can be said to have fixed boundaries. Each transaction is in part a function of previous communication and each transaction in turn influences future communication. The message becomes less serious and personality helps more as the helix ascends and widens. 'At any and all times it gives geometric testimony.' It combines the desirable features of the straight line and of the circle whole avoiding the weakness of either. The choice of the form was intended to reflect a sense of communication as a complex and evolutionary process—'If communication is viewed as a process, we are forced to adapt our examination and our examining instruments to the challenge of something in motion while we are in the very act of examining it.'

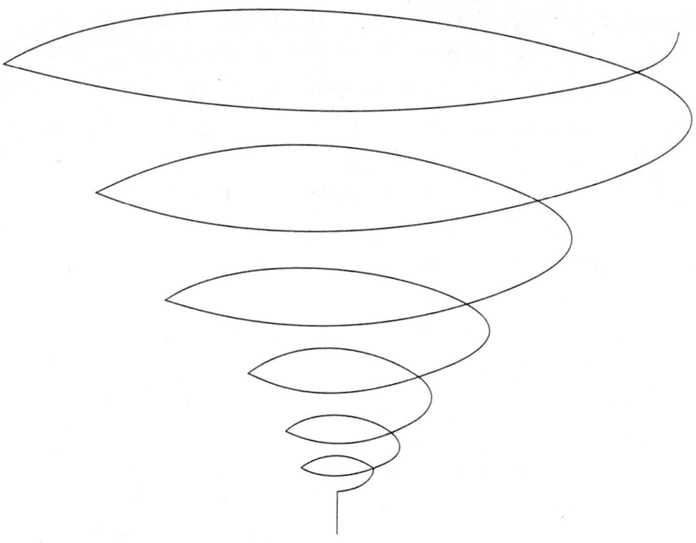

Figure 5.23
Frank Dance Model (1967)
Source: Toward A Theory of Human Communication, Frank E.X. Dance, 1967.

As shown in the Figure 5.23 the helix was seen as a way of combining the desirable features of the straight-line models with those of the circle, while avoiding the weaknesses of each. The Dance perspective added a concern with the dimension of time to the circular feedback models, suggesting that each communicative act builds upon the previous communication experience of all the parties involved.

Becker's Mosaic Model of Message Environments (1968)

Samuel L. Becker (1968) has portrayed the modified nature of information as a time-space mosaic symbolizing a conglomeration of numerous 'bits' of messages available. The individual moves almost randomly through the mosaic and is bombarded with these mini messages. Becker views the concept of messages in the sense of a unified whole as an archaic concept in the present times. Rather the contemporary communicator is exposed to multiple pieces of messages from multiple sources.

Message 'Bits'

It is a common human experience that whenever there is an assassination of a powerful public figure, the news about the event reaches us in small bits and pieces; from the hotel waiter, from the car driver, the local bar, the colleagues at the office, the eveningers, the TV, and so on. We form the complete picture within ourselves based upon these pieces, from a multitude of differing sources. A few hours later, there come other pictures- the filmed footage of the memorial service, the funeral, the events of last day of the victim, etc. Every time we hear about the event we relive our experience.

Becker felt that enough studies had been done on the effects of single messages on well defined audiences. His model focuses on the effects of multiple and diffused messages presented repeatedly over time to a large and constantly changing audience.

Becker's argument is that we are exposed repeatedly to sets of message in our everyday lives, yet very few studies have been conducted to assess the effects of such messages on both attitudes and overt behaviours. To represent more adequately the message environment in which we constantly find ourselves. Becker constructs a model using McLuhan's metaphor of the television as 'a mosaic mesh of light and dark spots'. An illustration of Becker's mosaic is presented in Figure 5.24.

The mosaic consists of infinite message bits on any given topic. These bits are scattered over time, space, and modes of communication. Each cell of the mosaic has the potential of containing a message pertaining to any given topic. The blanked cells represent and absence of a message.

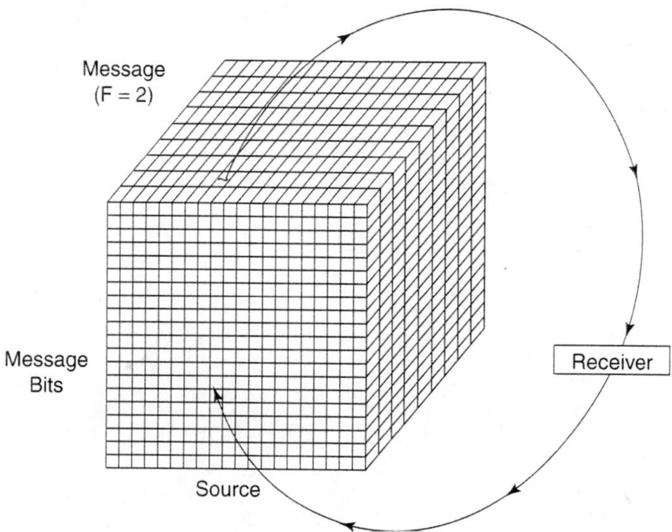

Figure 5.24
Becker's Mosaic Model of Message Environments (1968)
Source: Pragmatics of Analoguing—Theory and Model Construction in Communication, L.C. Hawles, 1975.

The model represents two processes—first, the ever increasing number and variety of messages and their sources, and second the repetitiveness of going through the same or similar transactions again and again. The mosaic should be thought of as a changing cube through which the receiver is constantly moving. Some of the cells are empty because at any point in time some messages are not available from some source. Each vertical slice or layer of the mosaic represents a particular message set. The cells represent the messages. The receiver goes through cells of the mosaic in continuous loops. The frequency of the loops varies; some people expose themselves to the messages more frequently that others; some expose themselves to a wider variety of messages than others. Becker's model is conceptual land function of the model is descriptive rather than explicative or simulative. (L.C. Hawles 1975).

Andersch, Staats and Bostrom (Models of Communication) (1969)

Environmental or contextual factors are at the centre of the communication models devised by Elizabeth G. Andersch, Lorin C. Staats and Robert N. Bostrom. Like Branlund's transactional model this one stresses the transactional nature of the communication process, in which messages and their meanings are structured and evaluated by the sender and subjected to reconstructing and

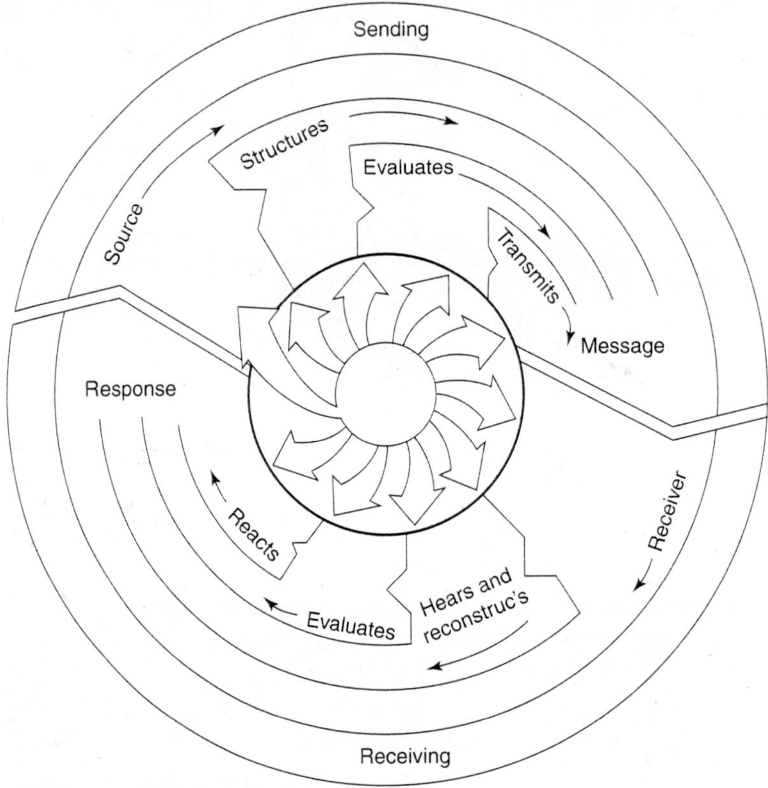

Figure 5.25
Andersch, Staats, and Bostrom (Models of Communication) (1969)
Source: Model devised by Elizabeth G., Andersch, Lorin C. Staats and Robert N. Bostrom and presented in *Communication in Everyday Use*, 1969.

re-evaluation on the part of the receiver, all the while interacting with the factors (or the stimuli) in the environment.

Branlund emphasizes the transferability of cues. Public cues can be transformed into private ones. Private cues may be converted into public ones, while environmental and behavioural cues may merge. In short the whole process is one of transaction and few models have explored so impressively the inner dynamics of this process as Branlund's. Branlund illustrates a form of one-way communication as a situation in which receivers are 'expected to listen and not talk back'. Such situations probably result from an overly autocratic parent or teacher of boss.

This is not necessarily a one-way communication situation but reflects the limited capability of decoding messages by the sender. The autocratic boss in the factory probably also receives feedback responses if he were to decode the efficiency reports, production quality reports, absenteeism, labour turnover, employee morale reports, and so on as feedback responses. If the autocrat in a bureaucratic organization receives feedback responses at all, the situation is probably attributable to an overtly restrictive gatekeeper mediating the response to the autocrat from the worker. Probably some such situation developed in the last phases of the World War II just before the fall of Berlin. The generals who were close to Hitler in the chancellery kept the grim reports from the battlefronts and the imminent collapse of the German Army away from the dictator till the last, and patiently listened to his hysterical tirades of the German superiority and so on.

Branlund traces a major change in the field of communication when theorists began viewing communication as a process. Branlund considers process to emphasize the actual operations involved in communicating. Process, thus, stresses the significance of the communicative functions—that is what goes on during communication—rather than simply visualizing the structural components of the phenomenon of human communication in relative isolation. Thus, process inherently refers to events or occurrences—actions and behaviours fundamental to the process of human communication.

Rogers and Kincaid Model (1981)

One of the more recent models of the communication process is provided by Everett Rogers and D. Lawrence Kincaid in *Communication Networks: Toward a New Paradigm for Research*, published in 1981 (Figure 5.26). The authors described what they termed a convergence model of communication that stressed the importance of information and the manner in which information link individuals together in social networks. They described communication as a process in which individuals create and share information with one another in order to reach mutual understanding.

This cyclical process involves giving meaning to information that was exchanged between two or more individuals as they move towards one another, and to unite in a common interest or focus. In explaining the matter in which the convergence process was thought to operate, they indicated that communication always begins with 'and then'- to remind us that something has occurred before we begin to observe the process. Participant A may or may not consider the past before he shares information (I_1) with participant B. This individual must perceive and then interpret the information which A creates to express his/her thoughts, and then B may respond by creating information (I_2) to share with A individual. A interprets this new information and then may express himself again with more information (I_3) about the same topic. Individual B interprets this information, and they continue the process (I_4........I_n) until one or both become satisfied that they have reached a sufficient mutual understanding or one another about the topic for the purpose at hand. As in a number of early views, the convergence

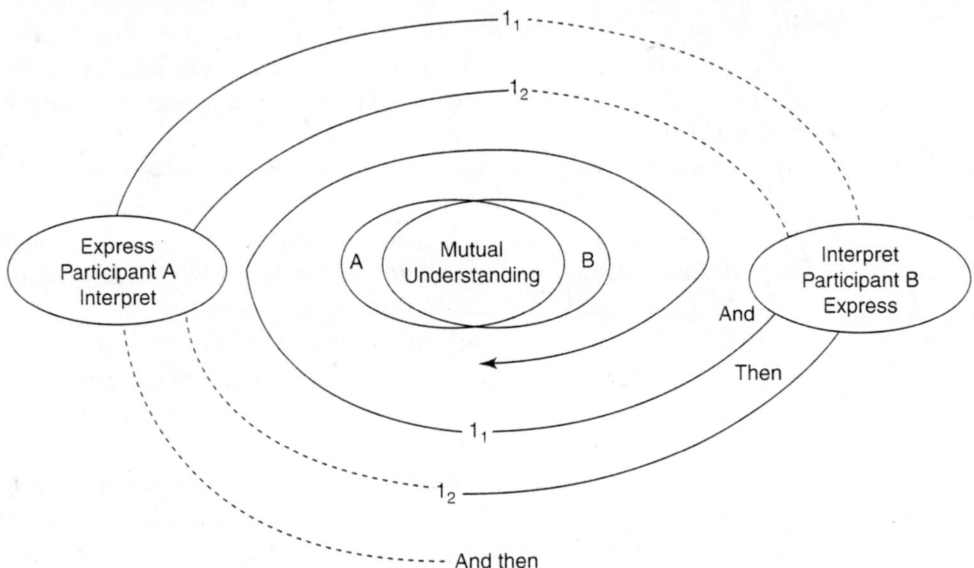

Figure 5.26
Rogers and Kincaid Model (1981)

model explained communication in terms of a progressive sending and receiving messages between two individuals in which the goal and predicted outcome are mutual understanding of a topic. Although acknowledging the role of interpretive process, that occurs within individuals, the Rogers and Kincaid view emphasized the information exchanges and networks them. Their perspective also carried forth the view of communication as a process rather than a single event, a point of view emphasized in nearly all models in recent years.

Toulmin Model

Stephen Toulmin has made an important contribution to understanding of argumentation. His model can be used to evaluate the strength of an argument before it is actually presented to audience, or locate the weakness of the arguments. According to Toulmin all arguments share three basic elements- data, acclaim, and a warrant. On the basis of data the speaker makes a claim, but there has to be a reason or warrant, for the listeners to accept the claim. For example, the fact that a company is a monopoly (just offering data) by itself does not justify government action. We must also know something about how monopolies operate. This is something that is supplied by the warrant. When the data and the warrant are taken together the full implications of the claim become apparent.

GENERAL COMMENTS ON ALL MODELS

As all of the models point out communication consists of several different elements in constant interaction with one another. The elements most frequently mentioned are source, receiver encoder, decoder, feedback, message, noise, context, effect, and channel. Each element, as both Lasswell and Gerbner note, may be associated with a specific area of research. Each element in communication may be further broken down into more specific elements or components as Berlo's in his SMCR model. Communication has no clear observable beginning or end. Communication transactions do have fixed boundaries. This is illustrated most clearly in the models of Dance and Branlund.

Each communication act influences future transactions and is influenced by past transactions- an assumption that is visualized most clearly in Dance's helical spiral. Noise in inevitable in any communication transactions—a point made most vividly by Shannon and Weaver. As both Branlund and Johnson note, communication is dynamic. Communication is not a static event but rather one constant process. Communication is transactional, each element influencing every other element, something that is most adequately recognized by Dance and Branlund. Communication is complex. This is also a point made by Branlund. Encoders and decoders are interchangeable. This characteristic exists in any conception of communication, but is made most forcefully by Branlund. Feedback messages come from the sources as well as from the receiver and provide the source with information as to the relative effectiveness of various messages.

Westley and Maclean made the role of feedback an essential part of their model. Communication as Johnson notes makes sense only to the extent that the message relates to the external world. Communication messages may be verbal as well as nonverbal. Communication can take place when we squint as well as when we speak. Berlo, Branlund, and Johnson make this explicit. Communication takes place in a context—a point that has been made clear in the models of Aristotle and Johnson. Communication is inevitable and all behaviours communicate, as all the models propose. Each communication event is unique. No two communication acts are ever identical or repetitive. Communication takes place through the continual encoding and decoding of signals which is most clearly visualized in Shannon and Weaver's models. All models are abstractions and are incomplete representations of the actual communication act.

No model is flawless, nor is there much hope for a complete isomorphic geometric model of something as complex as human communication. However, although not perfect, models succeed in helping us visualize the reality of human communication.

SUMMARY

Models are experiential guide to understanding any process. The scholarly display of models in this chapter will help you to understand how communication works. It will also help you modify, change, and improve your own communication style. Teaching–learning process is exclusively interactive, and communication is the main vehicle; the knowledge of the models will help the teachers understand the communication patterns intent in the classroom. The knowledge of models will help the teachers in developing effective patterns of communication in the student.

6

Psychology and Communication

After reading this chapter, you will be familiar with:

- Models of impression formation
- Personality and communication
- Motivation and communication
- Values, beliefs, and attitudes
- Emotion and communication

COMMUNICATION: A CHAIN OF REACTIONS

Communication is the basis of all interactions. The body is an important tool of communication. The psychology of communication includes different stages of interaction in an individual such as:

(i) **Absorption of external information:** Absorption occurs through sense organs when we simply absorb the sounds and colours, the spoken elements, and all facts provided to us. Absorption is an objective process.

(ii) **Interpretation of the stimuli received:** Interpretation involves analyzing external stimuli as well as details such as expressions and fine verbal and non verbal messages. Interpretation is a subjective process.

(iii) **Reaction to the information:** Reaction uses physical communication such as speech, language, or expressions through facial and bodily movements. Reactions are the result of a subjective and an objective process which takes place because when presented with certain stimuli we all have a set of expected responses which are objective but depend on how we interpret the situation subjectively. Reactions can be imitative or it can be just the opposite as when someone tries to look at you and you try to look away.

This reaction or response evoked in an individual can become a stimulus for another chain of responses. Psychologists have suggested that communication is directly related to how we instinctively perceive the external information based on our own experiences. So interpretation of stimuli is an important feature of communication according to psychoanalysis. Thus according to behavioural psychology, we identify an object and react to it via communication. It sounds strange that the importance of mind and consciousness in communication has only been recently acknowledged in psychology as a sign.

Communication is almost motivated or intentional as we obviously anticipate a response from people we communicate with. In fact all communication is based on expectation of response from others. Thus communication has a direction or purpose. However the communication gap can generate problems in the process and the purpose of communication may remain unfulfilled when communicated ideas are indistinct or indirect. The ambiguity increases when channels of communication between two or more individuals are remote rather than proximal.

As a physiological process, a person's perception follows some basic principles—we shall now see what these principles are:

Principle 1: Your reactions to others are determined by your perception of them, and not by who or what they really are. For example, you may be reluctant to choose a fellow student to work with you in the project, who has got an unfriendly expression. Based on this fact, you feel that he may not be a co-operative worker. Your behaviour towards him is based on your perception and not on facts. It is based on your subjective perception of him.

Principle 2: Your goal in a particular situation determines the amount and kind of information you collect about others. Your goal in this situation is clear—you need to select some student who will work with you in the project. Hence, you focus your attention on the characteristics of fellow students that seem to be relevant to your goal, thus, ignoring other details.

Principle 3: In every situation, you evaluate people partly in terms of how they are expected to act in that situation. Whether you are in a restaurant, public gathering, or classroom, your behaviour is governed by social norms—the 'rules' or expectations for appropriate behaviour in that social situation. Your objective here is to choose ten co-workers who will assist you in your project. The rules and regulations of this 'working together' are not written down anywhere. So, you decide your own norms in that particular situation to meet your objectives. You will evaluate your co-workers in terms of how efficiently and co-operatively they can work with you in the project.

Principle 4: Your self-perception also influences how you perceive others and how you act on your own perceptions. Your decision about whom to choose to work with you in the project is also influenced by how you perceive yourself. If you think you are a slightly difficult person to work with, you may look for people who are more adjustable and obedient, rather then people who are assertive and non-compromising.

In combination, these four basic principles underscore that person-perception is not a one-way process in which we objectively survey other people and then logically evaluate their characteristics. Instead, our self-perception, or the perception we have of others interact collectively and influence our understanding of the other person. Each component plays a role in the judgments we form of others.

Consider the following events:

- You receive a lower grade in a term paper than you expected.
- You leave several messages for a friend on her answering machine, but she never returns your calls.
- You have applied for a job and feel that you are highly qualified for it, but you do not get it.

What questions would arise in your mind in each of these situations? Certainly, you would want to know why? This is the acid test we face in most situations. We want to know why other people have acted the way they do, or why events have turned out in the way they do. Such knowledge is crucial for us to understand the causes behind others' action or behind events that occur; only then can we hope to make sense of the social world and perhaps do better socially in the future.

Attribution

The knowledge of others, current moods, or feelings can be useful in social perception in many ways but in actuality, this is only the first step. In our quest to know the 'other' we also want to know the causes behind their behaviour. We do not simply want to know how others have acted; we would also want to know why they have done so. The process through which we seek such information is known as attribution. Thus, we can say that, attribution refers to our efforts to understand the cause behind others' behaviour as well as the cause behind our own behaviour.

Attribution Error

We tend to get the idea that attribution is a highly rational process in which individuals seeking to identify the causes of others' behaviour follow orderly cognitive steps. To a large extent, this is so, but we should not overlook the fact that, attribution is subject to several forms of error-tendencies that can lead us into serious errors concerning the cause of others' behaviour.

Suppose you are sitting in your college library when you notice two men trying to lift and move a large cupboard. They lift and tip the cupboard; as they do this, four drawers come flying out and one hits one of the men on his head. You think to yourself, 'Obviously they are a pair of dim-witted men'. Why did you arrive at this conclusion? Perhaps both the men were not dim-witted. May be the lock of the drawers broke. Or may be there is some other reason for the mishap.

We tend to spontaneously attribute the behaviour of others to internal and personal characteristics, while downplaying or under-estimating the effects of external situational factors. This bias is called **attribution error**. Even though it is entirely possible that situational forces act behind another person's behaviour, we tend to automatically assume that the cause is an internal and personal one.

Let us look at another aspect of attribution, which is an interesting exception to the fundamental attribution error. When it comes to explaining our own behaviour, we tend to be biased in the opposite direction; we are more likely to use an external-situational attribution than internal and personal attribution. This common attributional bias is called the **actor–observer discrepancy** because there is a discrepancy between the attribution you make when you act in a given situation and those you make when you are the observer of other people's behaviour.

Impression Formation and Impression Management

What exactly are first impressions? How are they formed? What steps can we take to make sure that we make a good first impression on others? And finally how accurate are first impressions and social perceptions in reality?

Some aspects of social perception, such as attribution, require a lot of hard mental work; it is not always easy to draw inferences about others' behaviour or traits by looking at them. In contrast, forming first impressions seems to be relatively effortless. We look at a person and immediately a certain impression of his character forms itself in us. A glance or a few spoken words are sufficient to tell us a story about a highly complex personality.

1. Have you ever wondered how we manage this feaure? How do we form unified impressions of others in the quick and seemingly effortless way that we often do? First impressions, it is believed, are very

important. Most of us assume that the initial impression we make on others will shape the course of our future relation with them in crucial way. We also believe, that such impression may be quite resistant to change over time and situation.

2. Whether the information is positive or negative in nature—we tend to weigh negative information about others more heavily than positive information.
3. The extent to which the information describes behaviour or traits that is unusual or extreme. The more unusual and extreme, the greater is the weight placed on information and finally.
4. The sequence of input—information received first- is weighted more heavily than information received later.

MODELS OF IMPRESSION FORMATION

According to the Cognitive model, impression of others' involves two major components: concrete examples of behaviours that are consistent with a given trait; and mental summaries that are abstracted from repeated observations of others' behaviour. They are usually termed as abstractions. Some models of information formation stress the role of behaviour exemplars. These models suggest that, when we make judgments about others, we recall examples of their behaviour and base our judgments and our impressions based on them. For example, you meet a person for the first time and he or she smiles warmly at you and comes running to your help when you drop your books—all these actions are examples of the trait of kindness, and hence we include this trait of kindness in our first impression of this individual.

In contrast, other models stress the role of abstractions. Such views suggest that, when we make judgments about others, we simply bring our previously formed abstractions to mind and use these as the basis for our impression and our decisions. A growing body of evidences suggests that, both exemplar and mental abstraction play a role in impression formation. In fact, it appears that the nature of impressions may shift as we gain increasing experience with others. At first, our impression of someone we have just met consists of largely of exemplars (concrete examples of behaviour they have performed). Later, as our experience with this person increases our impression comes to consist mainly of mental abstractions derived from the many observations of the person's behaviour.

The modern view of impression formation emphasizes the cognitive basis of our mental pictures of other persons. While we seem to form impressions of others in a rapid and seemingly effortless manner, recent research suggests that in fact, these impressions emerge out of the operation of many cognitive processes relating to the storage, recall and integration of social information. In short, there appears to be a lot more going on beneath the surface than we might first suspect.

Impression Management

Impression management is the art of looking good. Most of us do our best to look good to others when we meet them for the first time. The desire to make a favourable impression on others is a strong one. Social psychologists use the term, impression management or appropriate self-presentation to describe this. Research efforts have shown that those who perform impression management successfully do gain important advantage often in many situations.

Techniques of Impression Management

Individuals use many conscious and unconscious techniques to boost their image. These are divided into two major categories—self-enhancement, or efforts to increase ones' appeal to others and other-enhancement, or efforts to make the target persons feel good in various ways.

The techniques for self-enhancement include our effort to boost our physical appearances through style, personal grooming, and the uses of various props.

Describing oneself in positive term is another technique which is used by many an individuals. Many people use this technique to increase their adversely affecting reactions to the persons who use them. Coming to other-enhancement, we may use many different tactics to induce positive moods and reactions in others. The most commonly used tactics of other-enhancement is flattering statements that praise the other person, his or her trait or accomplishments, or the organizations with which the person is associated with expressing agreement, doing small favours for them. You may probably recall many instances when you were the target of such strategies. But do these tactics succeed in generating positive feelings and reactions on the part of the person towards whom they are directed? The answer is yes, provided, they are used with skill and care. But if overused or used ineffectively, it can backfire and produce negative rather than positive reactions from others. The moral is, while tactics of impression management often succeed, this is not always the case as sometimes they may turn around as boomerangs.

Impression Management and Communication

The function of identification and identity management is grounded in an encoder perspective, examining how communication manifests 'who they are' through nonverbal signals. Impression formation is grounded in a decoder perspective, examining how receivers use the same signals to form judgments of communicators. Impression management returns to an encoder perspective, examining the ways in which communicators strategically craft their nonverbal performances to create desired images projecting 'who they want to be'.

The flip side of impression formation is impression management. How can communicators use nonverbal cues to foster desired impressions? Impression management is often, but not always, strategic—strategies which a communicator can use to project desired images along dimensions of believability, expertise, attraction, status, etc. Impression management is strategic self-presentation which centres on those features of behaviour affected by power augmentation motives designed to elicit or shape others' attributions of the actor's dispositions. Simply put, it is also described as communicative behaviours that people use to regulate their social identity.

An individual's attempt at impression management may not always be successful. According to violations theory of Burgoons (1993), the impression can be negative if the individual violates expectations. Central to the theory are two premises: (a) nonverbal behaviours engender strong expectations that govern interaction patterns and outcomes, and (b) nonverbal behaviours have message value. When meanings are unequivocal and/or congruent, a social meaning model prevails such that interpretations and evaluations associated with the behaviours are predicted to influence outcomes directly.

When meanings are ambiguous or conflicting, communicator reward valence is posited to moderate the cognitive-affective assessment process. Communicator reward valence is a summary term for all the combined communicator characteristics that, on balance, cause the communicator to be regarded positively; characteristics that, on balance, cause the communicator to be regarded positively or negatively. The interpretation and evaluation process results in a net valence for the nonverbal act. Positively valenced act produces positive outcomes, and negatively valenced act results in negative outcomes. Violations of expectations are hypothesized to intensify this process by causing an intentional shift to the source of the violations and the behaviours themselves, thus, making communicator characteristics more salient.

In conclusion, we can summarize the 'expectancy violation theory' in terms of impression management strategy in the following ways:

1. Proximics violations and non-intimate touch promote favourable impressions of positively valanced communicators but undermine impressions of negatively valenced communicators.
2. Increases beyond normative levels in conversational involvement and immediacy behaviours such as gaze are positive violations that

improve impressions, regardless of communicator valence, whereas reduced involvement and gaze aversion and negative violations.

3. Hypo- and hyper-relaxation are negative violations that produce largely unfavourable social judgments, although hyper-relaxation may create an impression of power and dominance.

Other relevant appropriateness or acceptability include:

(a) physical attractiveness (apparel, grooming, etc.);

(b) warmth and pleasantness (expressive behaviours such as smiling, nodding of the head, raising of the eyebrows, pleasantness of the voice);

(c) immediacy (eye contact or gaze, touch, closeness/proximity, open body positions, direct body orientation, leaning forward); and

(d) dominance (e.g., relaxed, asymmetrical posture with slight backward leaning and frequent gesturing but infrequent nodding; louder, faster, more fluent voice, with shorter response latencies, and longer turn lengths).

Many of these cues are employed to manage impressions of credibility and power in a like manner. Credibility is a multidimensional construct that includes judgments of competence, character, sociability, dynamism, and composure.

Many of the kinesic and proxemic cues that convey dominance are very important communication tactics. Taken together, these cues help speakers to manage others' impressions of their poise, competence, trustworthiness, credibility, and power. The number of relevant cues points to the powerful and dramatic effects of nonverbal signals in fostering desired impression.

Relational Communication

Relational communication, impression management, and identity have close resemblances with regard to specific nonverbal cues used to signal evaluations and self-images. However, relational communication is distinct in at least four aspects.

1. Relational communication follows a participant as opposed to an observer's perspective.
2. A relational message is directed towards a specific target as opposed to a generalized audience.
3. Relational communication typically focuses on dyadic interaction between the sender and the receiver and may use the dyad as the

unit of analysis, whereas impression management focuses on the individual sender.

4. Relational communication focuses on meaning attached to non verbal-behaviour, as opposed to common cause-effect approach to identify an impression management.

The traditional approach to relational communication has identified only two or three dimensions (e.g., dominance, affection, inclusion, or involvement) along which messages may be exchanged. Such perspectives can underestimate the variety and richness of message themes that are present in interpersonal task versus social orientation.

SELECTIVE PERCEPTION AND ATTENTION IN COMMUNICATION

People selectively expose themselves to information with which they basically agree. The term 'selective attention' refers to the fact that people see what they want to see and expect to see. In the same way, people interpret information on the basis of part experiences. Selective perception is governed by family background, physical and personality characteristics, cultural differences, organizational affiliation and position, professional experience, and other such factors.

The term selective perception and retention refers to the phenomenon whereby people forget much of what they perceive. A large amount of the information that is perceived by an average person is dumped into the subconscious. People maintain their equilibrium by filtering out dissonant or uncomfortable information. Factors that have been found to mediate people's responses to dissonant information are the extent to which people are well informed on the issues to the extent to which they have affiliation to the strength of their convictions, and their educational level.

PERSONALITY AND COMMUNICATION

Since the emergence of Psychology as a science, the concept of personality was contained in and intrinsic to it. However, this concept has been interpreted in different ways by different psychologists, yet most of them are unanimous in affirming that personality is something integral; it is not simply a cluster of mental or physical qualities, propertics, or tokens, but rather the unique and unrepeatable combination of characteristics of each individual. Psychologists also agree that, in that last analysis it is precisely personality, which determines the concrete behaviour of a given person, his or her discrete thoughts and deeds.

The famous nineteenth century psychologist, William James, described personality as the 'master' of mental functions. But what lies at the basis of this integrality? What makes it the 'master' of man's mental life? How is it related to the way we communicate, receive message, perceive others motivation, attitude and beliefs? In order to answer these questions, we need to know a little more about personality.

We can simply explain personality as the product of the 'equally influential' effects of innate hereditary psychological characteristics, and, environment and culture. Of course personality takes shape as the result of absorbed socio-historical experience, and on the basis of innate preconditions; but one does not end up with personality just by adding the two together; just as one does not end up with the steel by simply mixing iron ore with carbon.

The Self in Communication

The self is the most important agent in the study of interpersonal communication. Who we are, how we see ourselves, how others see us, what roles we play for the various audience, what we need and value—all of these are fundamental questions because what we think we are determines so much of what we do and which role we choose to play. Again, who we think we are, is to a large degree, determined by responses we get from others to our behaviours. These responses shape in many ways the way we see ourselves, and so we are in an ongoing, spiraling, transactional process called 'communication'.

A fundamental assumption shared by sociologists such as George Herbert Mead and Charles Hertonlodey, and by psychiatrists and psychologists such as Harry Stack Sulivan, Haren Horney, R. D. Laing, Carl Rogers, and Abraham Maslow, is that the concept of self is learned through interpersonal communication. What they mean is that, we come to see ourselves as the product of who we see and how others se us. Cooley, for example, developed the concept of the 'looking-glass self' as the process of imaging how the self appears to be for another person. The concept of self is but a reflection from the mind of others. Through the process of socialization we learn what is good and how we should behave. This process of personification occurs also in our perception of us. All these develop because of our interaction with people and on their interpretation of our behaviours. Thus, we can say that, the transactional nature of self-identity is like a merry-go-round, that is, how we view ourselves is largely determined by our perception of how others see us; it is also largely a function of our self-conceptual action as a filter which shapes our perceptions of other people's reactions to us. This entire cycle frequently turns into a self-fulfilling prophesy[1].

What is the Role of Communication in 'Self-concept'?

The view we hold of ourselves is by no means a static state. Our self-concept develops through interpersonal communication; it is also maintained and changed through communication.

Each person and each new experience that we encounter to some extent confirms, but may also change, how we view the world, other people, and ourselves. The impact of all these may be tremendous and obvious at times, but more often it may be subtle and go unnoticed. We can understand this better through the confirmation and disconfirmation process

Confirmation and Disconfirmation

Our image needs verification and support from others, and much of what we communicate will, in indirect ways, contain subtle demands to have our image confirmed. Every message we send includes the request: 'validate me'. We seek confirmation not only of the way we view ourselves, but also of the way we view others, and the way we experience the world. The process of confirmation and disconfirmation has been described by Sieburg as:

Communication with others is a basic human need for it is through communication that relationships are formed, maintained, and expressed. It was theorized that in attempting to establishing messages with the expectation is met—if response is direct, open, clear, congruous and relevant to the prior communication attempt. The persons involved are likely to experience the benefit of genuine dialogue as well as the advantages of 'therapeutic interpersonal communication'. If response is absent, tangible, unclear, ambiguous, or otherwise inadequate, the participants are likely to feel confused, dissatisfied, misunderstood, and alienated.

Confirming Responses

Confirming responses include:

1. **Direct acknowledgement:** when we respond directly to another person's message and, thus, indicate that we heard what was said and that the person is included in our perceptual world;
2. **Agreement about content:** when we reinforce our support to the opinions and ideas expressed by another person;
3. **Supportive response:** when we give assurances, express understanding, or somehow attempt to make the other person feel better or encouraged;

4. **Clarifying responses:** when we try to get the other person to express more, to describe their feelings or information, to seek repetition or make part remarks clearer;
5. **Expression of positive feelings:** when we share positive feeling about what the other person has done or said.

Disconfirming Responses

Disconfirming responses include the following:

1. **Impervious response:** when we do not acknowledge or ignore what was said, when we give no indication that something has been said.
2. **Interrupting response:** when we interrupt or cut off something that is being said, or begin a new thought while the first person is still speaking.
3. **Irrelevant response:** when we introduce a new train of thought or a new topic, or in some way indicate that what the first person said is so inconsequential that it is not worth commenting upon.
4. **Tangential response:** when we make a slight attempt to relate a new thought to what was said previously, but when in fact we take the discussion in a new direction.
5. **Impersonal response:** when we use generalizations, clichés, pronouncements, and intellectualizations abundantly.
6. **Incoherent response:** when we ramble, when we use words in special idiosyncratic ways that are unclear to our listeners, when we leave sentences incomplete, or reword and rephrase so much that our main ideas get lost.
7. **Incongruous response:** when our nonverbal communication is completely at odds with our verbal statements.

Why is Self-concept So Important in Communication?

Self perception is a major filter mechanism, and it plays a significant part in how we generally perceive the world and hence how we behave. Hence, the formation of self-concept and the ways it is maintained and changed through interpersonal communication needs to be discussed in detail. Who we think we are is confirmed or denied by the responses others make to our communication with them. Unless we get clear and supportive message, we are not likely not to have effective communication experiences.

Very early in our lives, we learn how to give each other many different kinds of responses, and we should recognize that. What we do to each other has an effect on our feeling of worth, or our self-esteem, and also how we can get the job done, because without some internal support for our activities, the outside work we do will remain undone. Much of the development and maintenance of our self-concept is intimately related to our work, and the roles we learn in the formal organizations we participate in. Much of our sense of inner worth comes from performing the roles that the society provides, and we always try to measure up to it. Inability to do so leads to the loss of our self-esteem. Let us now look at how we build a sense of self-esteem.

In the process of developing a self-image, we develop feelings about who we think we are and also tend to look at other people for confirmation of those feelings. And when we get that confirmation, we feel that we are entitled to have that particular image of ourselves.

Self-esteem is the feeling we get when what we do matches our self-image and when that particular image approximates an idealized version of what we wish we were like. in the process, if we are confirmed by others, it validates our feeling of our self-worth and self-esteem.

Self-concept and Patterns of Communication

A study of the verbal patterns of persons with low self-concept and high self-concept shows some tendencies, which can be identified. Self-concept may vary with situations of topics, and the relations of the others with whom a person is communicating. The way people see themselves in relation to others has a great effect on the changing patterns of communication.

The following are some verbal patterns, which may characterize low self-concept:

- Frequent use of clichéd phrases or a few words which are used not so much to help identify something in common with others as because the person with low self-concept does not trust his or her ability to be original.
- A need to talk about self in terms of criticism, weaknesses, and difficult experiences, which help explain why he or she is not in a better state of mind.
  - An inability to accept a praise gracefully, often expressed by a superficially-worded disclaimer, which invites additional proof.
  - Defensiveness about being blame to the degree that the person may be more anxious about who gets credit or blamed in a project than about actually getting the project accomplished.
  - A cynical attitude towards accomplishment or possession of others.

- A persistently whining or sneering tone of voice or posture as assumed in relation to one's own or other's successes, as if to dismiss any accomplishments by anyone as luck or special privilege.
- An unsporting attitude expressed about competition.

High Self-concept

On the other hand, here are some verbal patterns which may characterize a high self-concept:

- Use of original expressions; a rich vocabulary used in appropriate settings; an ability to 'find the right word' or to use the balanced correct forms of address with others (for example, Mr, Miss, first names, or nick-names).
- A tendency to talk about the self less frequently and to talk about others easily in terms of their accomplishments is an apparent ability to get along without constant reassurance of personal worth.
- The ability to accept, praise or blame gracefully; in working on projects, taking risks and verbalizing positions other than the 'correct' ones; not spending much time figuring out the 'safe' way of approaching problems in order to avoid blame.
- A willingness to look at accomplishments with the balance of credit and with the ability and the circumstances, and give credit to others for their part in what is done.
- A confident tone of voice; avoidance of a condescending tone or attitude; ability to say 'I don't know' or 'I was wrong'.
- Admission of wide range of feelings and of empathy for others without considering these are not popular.
- An optimistic attitude about competition; willingness to try new games, to enter into discussions about new topics with questions (to risk displaying ignorance in an effort to learn more).

We want to emphasize that this list is partial and that it does not necessarily describe a person. It describes some verbal patterns which may, in some circumstances or if found persistently, indicate low or high self-esteem for that particular relationship.

Individual Differences in Communication

Each individual is unique. And the idea that people differ from one another in systematic ways is as old as man himself. Scholars today, in various academic disciplines, continue this tradition. In the field of communication researches too, personality dispositions have a long and distinguished history. Indeed, some of the empirical studies of communication revolved around individual differences in peoples' proclivities to be comfortable in speaking in front of others. And if one were to tabulate the phases of academic work in the field of interpersonal communication over the past fifty years, one would discover, unsurprisingly, that the greatest proportions of articles in journals have explored topics directly related to personality.

Given the enormous number of studies on topics related to individual differences in communication, we shall touch upon the major dispositional differences associated with communication, most importantly, interpersonal communication. First we shall try to understand what individual difference is, and secondly see the catalogue of various individual differences that affect communication and social interaction.

Are Individual Differences Important in Communications?

For many years, there have been debates about the validity of personality constructs. Are there really individual differences? Moreover, if there are, how important are they in the explanation and production of communicative behaviour? Let us find out about some of the researches relevant to the various communication-related predispositions that is, the nature of personality difference as they relate to communicative behaviour.

Oslon, Vernon, Haris, and Jang (2001) found that a number of communication-related behaviours (e.g. enjoying big parties, enjoying public speaking, being assertive) have significant heritability. Beatly, McCrosky, and Hiesel (1990) found genetic predispositions and communication, such as communication apprehension. Krants Price (1976), gives the explanation of personality variables such as reinforcement, social norms, and modeling. Each of these alternative explanations is, to some degree, relevant to the development of various communication related predispositions.

The motion behind these alternative approaches is that, genetics may predispose a person to certain traits, but environment factors exacerbate or ameliorate the development of these traits. For instance, in the case of social-communicative anxiety, evidence exist that the anxiety of the people may be shaped by the sort of reinforcements they received for communicating as children, the level of social skills they were taught, and the adequacy of the models of communication to which they were exposed. What we are trying to see here is that, both hereditary and environmental factors are responsible for individual differences in communication.

Besides, the heredity and environmental factors and differences in culture are also responsible for individual differences in communication. The cultural construal decides how skilled individuals are when they are working, living or communicating in culture other than their own, a concept that has been labelled as intercultural communication competence. People with higher levels of intercultural communication competence interact more effectively with people from different cultures.

Cognitive Disposition

Cognitive complexity: In the past twenty years probably no cognitive disposition has received more attention from scholars in communication than cognitive complexity. Cognitive complexity may be defined as the number of different constructs an individual has to describe others (differentiation), the degree to which those constructs cohere (integration), and the level of abstraction of the constructs (abstractness). The bulk of research has demonstrated positive consequences for complexity. Individuals, who are cognitively more complex, offer more people-centred responses (Applegate 1980, Burleson 1998), whether in terms of comforting, persuading, or using of regulative message. The reason for this appears to be that, cognitively complex individuals are better able to perform a variety of tasks related to communication, such as recognizing affect (Burleson 1994), decoding nonverbal behaviours (Woods 1996), and integrating information (O' Keefe).

Cognitive disposition and cognitive complexity locus of control: Locus of control means an individual's beliefs about his or her control over the environment (Rotter 1966). There are two types of individuals with two types of locus of control - the internal and the external. At one end of the continuum are individuals with internal locus of control; these 'internals' believe that they have mastery over what happens to them. They believe that they themselves are the 'origins' of their actions. If they want something to happen, they can make it so.

At the other end of the continuum are those with external locus of control; 'externals' believe that they are 'pawns' and their lives are shaped by chance, luck, and other powerful variables over which they have no control; that they have little control over their fates. Communicatively, internals are more attuned to information that have bearingss on their lives and are less likely than externals who, experience negative stressors (Thoits 1995). Internals are more attentive listeners, more socially skilled in conversations, more sensitive to social cues (Lefcourt, Martin and Fick 1985), and less likely to withdraw in conflict situations (Canary, Cunningham and Cody 1988).

Authoritarianism and Dogmatism

In the early years of the empirical study of communication, authoritarianism and dogmatism were of special importance to researchers. In many ways the constructs give the same broad idea as tolerance of ambiguity. Some people are more rigid than others, and this rigidity affects both on how they communicate and how they respond to communication. For instance, authoritarians choose not to accept information that may change their attitudes, (Dillehay 1978), and dogmatic individuals are more responsive to source cues when it comes to persuasion (DeBono and Klein 1993).

Emotional Intelligence

Though the concept of emotional intelligence was proposed long back, it received the attention of the researchers in recent years. Thorndike presaged the concept early in the 20th century when he discussed social intelligence as one of the three sorts of intelligence. In popular literature, Daniel Goleman (1995) has suggested that the construct has five components: self-awareness, managing emotions, motivating oneself, empathy and handling relationships. Salovey and Mayer (1990) have defined emotional intelligence as the ability of people 'to monitor their own others' emotions, discriminate among them, use the information to guide their thinking and actions'.

Individuals with high emotional intelligence are higher in empathy, social assertiveness, more socially perceptive, are more social, and socially skilled, has better relational quality and the ability to manage one's mood, as well as emotionally stable, optimism, stress tolerance, and self-regard. Individuals with emotional intelligence are found to have more effective communication and interpersonal relationships.

Self-esteem

Cooley's looking-glass self theory is the most important model for understanding the self in communication. His premise is that, how we see ourselves is determined by how we believe our 'significant others' see us. We construct our self-images from how we internalize what we believe others think of us. Consequently, the stability of self-esteem is affected by the interactions people have with others, such as family members. There are multiple sorts of self-esteem: (a) global versus specific esteem; (b) trait versus state esteem; and (c) personal versus social esteem. Self-esteem has clear relationships with a variety of communication-related outcomes. People lower in self-esteem are less likely to take decisions, less likely to ask questions in the classrooms, more lonely and depressed, more verbally aggressive, and poor in interpersonal communication and relationships.

Extreme self-esteem might reach the point of narcissism, that is, denying negative feedback, engaging in greater self-enhancement and always looking forward to being the centre of attention in any social interaction.

In communication, such individuals mostly indulge in monologue; they are inner-directed and not outer-directed. Their preoccupied conversation is termed as 'conversational narcissism'.

Communicative Disposition

Individuals have certain dispositions in communication. We shall discuss two of them—argumentativeness and verbal aggressiveness. Argumentativeness is considered to be constructive as it involves an individuals' willingness to attack another's arguments while defending his or her own position. Compared to people lower in the skill of argumentativeness, highly argumentative individuals are perceived as better decision makers as well as more interesting, dynamic, competent, and credible. They are more resistant to persuasive attempt; consequently, they are less likely to withdraw from conflicting situations.

There is a difference between aggressiveness and argumentativeness. Verbally aggressive people have lower communication and interpersonal skills as well as low level of argumentative skills. They attack the self-concept of others by threats with a motive to cause psychological pain.

Communication Apprehension

The most studied individual difference in the field of interpersonal communication has been communication apprehension. Communication apprehension is more interpersonally oriented.

Behaviourally, people with high levels of communication apprehension are less likely to talk in social settings, and when they do participate, they engage in mostly acknowledgements and confirmation. They also engage in less eye contact and are more self-protective and disclose less. Perceptually, they are seen less positively by others in a variety of settings, such as interviews and social interactions.

Apprehensive people are less assertive or argumentative, less conversationally sensitive, and less independent. They have lower self-esteem, are more insecure, not willing to take risk, and suffer from inferiority complex. Not surprisingly, shy individuals suffer more from social isolation and more emotional and psychosomatic health problems.

Developmentally, communication apprehension affects identity formation and it is inversely related to academic achievement and cognitive performance. Occupationally, this disposition affects career development and career choices, and apprehensive individuals are less likely to be successful in positions that require communication like teaching.

MOTIVATION AND COMMUNICATION

The most important element in defining personality and to best understand its influence on communication, are the social relationships a person enters into and in which he or she is both the subject and the object. A person enters into these social relationships through his or her activity.

When we speak of activity we do not intend it as a synonym of behaviour as the behaviourist understands it. For the behaviourists, man is, in effect, an automaton albeit a very complex one. Like an automaton, he 'switches on' when external forces somehow exert and influence him, by pressing a button, inserting a coin—as soon as such influence is exerted, man starts to 'behave', to act in some way, and to react. This influence need not always be direct and immediate. The influencing factor or 'stimulus' itself need not necessarily have physical reality; it might be nonverbal, that is, it might take the form of a sign.

A person's activity is relational and significant, he or she does not simply 'behave', nor does he or she perform abstract deeds. Each of his actions is an interaction with objects outside himself, and it can influence and alter them. There is no abstract subject of activity in the act of communication; there is always an object as well as a subject that is another person and the content in communicative activity. The nature and effectiveness of communication in any interaction depends upon the object, the contents, and more importantly the subject. The qualitative characteristics of this activity depend upon the cognitive, affective, native, as well as social characteristics of a person, and embody his or her social relationships. Since it is a social phenomenon, the person shows the socially elaborated prerequisites necessary for the act of communication.

The task of education is to determine the structure of a learner's personality with significance to society because personality is the fundamental propulsive force for the person's activity in the society. The students must be taught to evaluate their own behaviour and that of others' objectively in any act of communication or interaction. The teacher's, personality, too, plays an important role in fulfilling the task.

As far as psychology is concerned, communication is identical to any other activity. It has definite aims and is impelled by a motive or more often by a system of motives. These motives may be internal; for instance they may grow out of some needs. Internal motives may be of a social nature. For example, the teacher, who asks his pupil a question on the lesson, is at the same time shaping a motive or a series of motives for the pupils' subsequent utterance. But the pupil may at the same time be guided by self-assertive motives and by the desire to gain or maintain prestige in the eyes of the teacher or in the class.

The psychological aspects of motives in the act of communication can be summed up under two headings. This is something which the teacher has to take into account while teaching. On the one hand, the pupil should learn how to convert the motives into effective communicative act, how to apply to nonverbal tasks and make it a part of his nonverbal activities; the pupil must learn to think about what to say and how to say, as well as learn to establish a communicative activity, that is to say, an activity, the aim of which is not only the immediate satisfaction of concrete practical objectives, but the setting up of constant and mutual understanding, the establishing of interaction with the members of his or her social group. These are all forms of communicative activity.

In such communicative activity, the student is not speaking for the sake of speaking; he or she speaks for a different purpose. Their motives take them beyond the limits of mere communicating. They say not only what they have to say, but also as it needs to be said in order to influence or to promote interaction. In the psychological sense, the teacher helps the student to insert into the communicative activity a different motivation and direct it to a different aim—to use language for nonverbal purpose as well as to include in it a structure of nonverbal activity.

At the psychological level, the mastery of effective communication entails the constitution of individual operation (arising initially as independent acts); this is followed by their combination into an integral communicative act; and finally refining the communicative act according to the situation and the purpose of the communication. Thus, we see that motivation plays a very important role for the students' 'will' to communicate effectively; It plays a significant as well for the teachers to communicate effectively to accomplish the didactic task, build effective interpersonal relationships, and develop the desire to communicate effectively in the students'.

Motivation refers to the forces acting on or within an organism to initiate and direct behaviour. There are three characteristics associated with motivation. They are- activation, persistence, and intensity. Activation is demonstrated by the initiation or production of behaviour such as the motivated student who initiates going to the library to finish a term paper. Persistence is demonstrated by continued efforts or the determination to achieve a particular goal, often in the face of obstacles. Finally, intensity is seen in the greater vigor of responding that usually accompanies motivated behaviour such as the highly motivated student who studies harder to qualify for a scholarship.

Maslow's Hierarchy of Needs

Maslow's theory is based on two fundamental assumptions:

1. People have basic needs, which are arranged according to a hierarchy of importance. Only when the first basic level of needs is satisfied

can people devote energy in seeking satisfaction of the needs on the next level.

2. Only unsatisfied needs can motivate behaviour. Once a need is satisfied, it no longer acts as a motivator.

Maslow identified five basic need levels. They are as follows:

- **Physiological needs:** Physiological needs include the most basic necessities which sustain life - the needs of air, water, food, sleep, excretion, and sex. They are the most basic of all needs and, if frustrated, take precedence over other needs. If you have not eaten for several days you will be solely motivated by your desire to get food. It is difficult to lift the spirit of a person with an empty stomach. If you have not slept for a long time the need for sleep will take precedence over any other need.
- **Safety needs:** The second level of needs in Maslow's hierarchy is the need for safety or the desire for protection from danger, threat, and deprivation. People look to their home as a generally 'safe' place to be. From an organizational standpoint, safety needs are manifested in a desire for job security and steady or increasing monetary income.
- **Social needs:** It is only when physiological and safety needs are relatively well satisfied that social needs - those on Maslow's third level of hierarchy - motivate people's behaviour. Social needs are related to people's desire for companionship, belonging, acceptance, friendship, and love. Some people will go to great lengths to belong to particular groups they value. Family reunions, searching for 'roots', and keeping in touch with relatives are all related to the social needs of a family unit. The need to belong, formally as well as informally, to a variety of human groups is indeed a powerful motivator for those who derive their sense of identity from their membership in social or professional groups.
- **Esteem needs:** Esteem needs on the fourth level do not act as motivators until the previous levels of needs have been reasonably well satisfied. Esteem needs consist of (1) the need for *self-esteem,* which is characterized by a desire for self-confidence, self-respect, and feelings of competence, achievement, and independence; and (2) the need for esteem from others, which includes a desire for recognition, status, appreciation, and prestige. You look to your friends and family members to help you fulfil this need at a very personal level. In most large organizations there are relatively few opportunities through formal channels for the satisfaction of the esteem needs at the lower levels of the organization. However, one of the functions of the informal system which exists in all organizations is to provide a means for

the satisfaction of the esteem needs at all levels of the organizational structure. Respect from coworkers often means more to a person than recognition from the boss.

- **Self-actualization needs:** Self-actualization needs on the fifth level include the need for self-fulfilment, creative expression, and the realization of one's potential. It is not unusual to meet people who are highly respected in a field, whose lower needs are satisfied in large measure, yet, who feel restless and experience discontent. The highly successful executive who suddenly turns an artist or the eminent scholar who starts a business venture are not uncommon examples of people motivated by the need for self-actualization who shift gears in mid-career.

Schutz and the Theory of Interpersonal Needs

William Schutz has identified three basic interpersonal needs, which underline most of your behaviour around other people. These needs can be best represented as dimensions or continuums along which most people fall. Schutz terms these interpersonal needs the 'need for inclusion', the 'need for control', and the 'need for affection'.

- **Inclusion:** According to Schutz, the need for inclusion is the need to be recognized as an individual distinctively from others. A person with a very high need for inclusion needs recognition and attention from others. Such a person likes to be in the spotlight, to be signed out, and to be noticed. At one of the extremes of the continuum, we find the prima donna, or the obnoxious little kid who does anything simply to attract some attention, even if it results in punishment. For him/her to be punished is better than to be ignored. On the other hand, a person with a low need for inclusion prefers not to stand out, would rather not receive too much attention, and does not like to be prominent in the public eye.

  Schutz holds that people at both extremes are motivated essentially by the same fear of not being recognized as individuals. The people high on the inclusion need will combat the fear by forcing others to pay attention to them Those low on the inclusion need have convinced themselves that they will not get any attention, but that it is just the way they want it. Most people are probably somewhere in the middle of that continuum. Your needs for inclusion may change as the people you associate with differ, and as the situations you find yourself in change. We may want very little recognition from a professor when we have not done an assignment and do not wish to be called upon. At the same time we may have a strong need for attention from the person sitting next to us, whom we are interested in getting to know better.

- **Control:** The need for control involves a striving for power, for being in charge, for running things, and for influencing one's environment. The need for control is not necessarily related to the need for inclusion. Some people enjoy being in charge of things even if no one is aware that they are running the show. These people are high on control while low on inclusion-power, behind-the-throne types. On the other hand, some people may seek leadership or prestige positions not for the power they bring but for the attention they produce. This is why it is not always easy to determine whether a person's behaviour is influenced by one need or the other.

  Naturally, some people are quite low on the need for control and are not interested at all in taking initiative, in assuming responsibilities, in making decisions, or in leading a group. As is true for the inclusion need, a mixed group composed of highs and lows on the control dimension has a better chance of getting things done.

  Too many 'leaders' and not enough 'followers' may result in a constant struggle for leadership and the ensuing climate of competition may not be conductive to accomplishing much. On the other hand, too many 'followers' and no 'leader' may result in apathy as not much may get done.

- **Affection:** The need for affection has to do with how close people want to be to one another. Some people like to be very intimate and enjoy warm relationships even with relatively casual acquaintances. They enjoy talking about themselves on a personal level and expect similar behaviour on the part of others. They want and need to be liked. Sometimes, people high on the need for affection are perceived by as too friendly or coming on too strong. Affection is closely related to disclosing a kind of behaviour which can have a great effect on our interpersonal relations.

  On the other hand, some people prefer to keep others at a distance. They do not like to become too friendly too quickly. They do not wish to be too personal with others or to share too much of themselves with people they do not know well. They may have a strong distaste for closeness and intimacy except with carefully selected people. These people are usually perceived as aloof, cold, or 'superior'.

  In the case of affection a mixed group is not the best combination for productive interpersonal relationships. Cold people and warm people do not mix well. Each type makes the other uncomfortable and they find it hard to figure out each other. Neither is able to satisfy the other's needs.

Interpersonal communication is satisfying to you when you manage to satisfy your needs. In the case of interpersonal needs you depend solely on others for their satisfaction. If others give you the recognition you seek, or give you a chance to exert influence when you wish to, or provide you with the close intimate atmosphere you like, you feel satisfied and seek these people again in other interpersonal situations. You tend to avoid, when you can, the type of interpersonal communication situation where your needs are generally thwarted.

An understanding of interpersonal needs is essential not only in facilitating your insights into group processes but also in helping you predict the situations that will be more or less satisfying and productive for you.

VALUES, BELIEFS AND ATTITUDES

You may often feel that your personal world is unique, peculiar to you, and unshared by anyone else. You have great difficulties explaining a feeling or an experience to someone else. Even when you manage to describe the feeling or the experience with words you doubt that others know it as you do.

However, people are peculiar. At the same time that you intuitively believe in your uniqueness, you also assume that you live in the same world as others do. You assume that what you see is what others see. Despite your feelings of uniqueness your daily life is usually spent in a world you assume is shared as much as unique.

This may be the vital function of communication. Were it not for human communication or human contact you would live alone exclusively in your world of uniqueness without getting confirmation of your experiences.

Confirmation of your experiences (or disclosing) not only involves the physical world—checking your perceptions with others to test their reliability. It also involves the social world—comparing your ideas about religion, politics, morals, etc. with others to test their validity.

Because human beings are symbol-using creatures, they can create for themselves rules of conduct which go beyond the mere needs for survival of the species. When a animal raises her young, she does so because she is programmed to do so in order for the young to survive and for the species to continue to exist. When human parents raise their children, they are considerably more involved with regard to feelings, societal expectations, laws, duty, etc. Human beings create value systems from beliefs about the nature of their world and as a result, learn to respond to their environment in some ways more than in others.

In the remainder of this chapter we will examine how values, beliefs, and attitudes—the ingredients of a person's assumptive system—are formed, held, and changed through interpersonal communication.

Values

Values are fairly enduring conceptions of the nature of good and bad, of the relative worth you attribute to the things, people, and events of your lives. Values are usually embodied in complex moral or religious systems that are found in all cultures and societies, from the most 'primitive' to the most complex and industrialized. Values define for people the parameters of their actions. They indicate to those who share them what is desirable, to that degree it is desirable, and therefore what one should strive for. They also provide people with a guidance system which is supposed to enable them to choose the 'right' alternative when several courses of action are possible.

Words you use in making your value judgments, such as 'bad', 'good', 'moral', 'immoral', do not stand for any quality of the object or people you apply them to. Value judgments, those are in turn applied by human beings to the objects. They are not 'in' the objects. Something is good to a particular individual or group only because it is defined as good.

Values grow out of a complex interaction between basic needs and the specificity of a given environment. For example, all humans need to eat in order to survive, but they do not all value the same foods. In America beef is commonly eaten, while in India the sacred cow must not be touched. What is valued in a particular area, a region, or country is partly determined by the availability of certain foods. Values thus differ from place to place because of the variety of ways specific needs can be fulfilled.

What people value at a given time is based on the needs they try to fulfill at that particular time. The indictment of 'materialism' directed as the generation who lived through the great depression in the United States, by a generation who lived mostly in post World War II affluence, may reflect a change of need levels. Once people know a certain level of material affluence which satisfies physiological and safety needs, they can reject what they no longer need, since it fails to fulfill the next need level, which has become more prominent.

Beliefs

Beliefs represent the way people view their environment. Beliefs are characterized by a true-false continuum and probability scale. The existence of ghosts, for example, may be closer to the 'false' end of the continuum for some people than for others. That humans evolved from apes is still debated by many who place Darwin's theory of evolution closer to the 'false' end of the continuum and place the story of Genesis closer to the 'true' end of continuum. Beliefs represent what you agree with and what you usually think is true. There are certain things that you believe to be absolutely true, some you believe to be probably true, some you are not sure about, and some you think are false, probably or absolutely. According to the social psychologist Milton Rokeach, a belief system 'may be defined as having represented within it, in some organized psychological but not necessarily logical form, each and every one of a person's countless beliefs about physical and social reality'.

You cannot observe a belief. You can only observe a persons behaviour and assume that it came about because of a particular belief. Beliefs are not necessarily logical. They are largely determined by what you want to believe, by what you are able to believe, by what you have been conditioned to believe, and by basic needs which may influence you to have a certain belief in order to satisfy those needs.

Some belies are more central than others. The more central a belief is, the more likely it is that it will resist change. If it does change, however, the repercussions on the whole belief system will be widespread.

It is not always easy to determine which of the beliefs a person holds are central and which ones are less important. According to Rokeach, the importance of a belief depends on how it is connected to other beliefs and what consequences it has on those other beliefs. Central beliefs are connected to other beliefs and have deeper consequences on this large number of beliefs than less central beliefs do. Connectedness and consequences are more likely to be strong in the case of beliefs about your own existence and who you are. Relatedness to your existence is also evident in your attachment to your own name; you want it pronounced and spelled correctly; in some cases you can hear your own name spoken when nothing else in the conversation can be accurately discriminated. Beliefs learned from direct experience and shared by others are much connected to you and hence very central. By examining some of your beliefs in relation to their centrality for you, it is possible for you to distinguish among the following five types of beliefs which Rokeach identifies.

Primitive Beliefs: 100 Per Cent Consensus

Primitive beliefs are the most central beliefs of all. You learn them from direct experience. They are supported and reinforced by unanimous consensus among the people with whom you associate. They are fundamental, seldom questioned, taken-for-granted axioms, which rarely come up for controversy. It is as though you were saying, 'I believe this and I also believe that everyone else believes it too'. Beliefs in the existence and constancy of things are primitive beliefs. Even though you see a rectangular table from many angles, you continue to believe that it remains a table and that its shape does not change.

Your belief that things remain the same in the physical world and in your social world is extremely important in the development of a sense of self-constancy. If such beliefs are disrupted, you begin to question the validity of your own senses, your competence to deal with reality, and sometimes your sanity. Because so much would be called into question, disruption of primitive beliefs is extremely upsetting and seldom occurs. Primitive beliefs are the most central, important, and clung-to beliefs of all. They are very resistant to change. They include things that your parents taught you and that have been reinforced by teachers, the media, peers, and your own experiences. For instance, day of the week and time of day are verifiable beliefs on which you base much of your day-to-day personal activity

Primitive Beliefs: Zero Consensus

Some primitive beliefs are not shared by others, and do not depend on social consensus, but arise from deep personal experiences. Because those need not be shared by others, in order to be maintained, they are usually quiet resistant to change. Many of these unshakable beliefs are about yourself. Some are positive (what you are capable of) while some are negative (what you fear). These beliefs are held on pure faith. For example, you may have always thought that you were totally inept in mathematics, no matter what other people have told you about your mathematical ability. You kept your belief in spite of other evidence. Perhaps you feel you live in a very hostile world; no matter what others tell you, your belief stays unshaken. As a matter of fact, even when you want to change these beliefs about yourself because you are intellectually convinced that they are unfounded, they are still extremely resistant to change. It often takes the help of a therapist, a counselor, or some other professional to really modify these deep-seated beliefs.

Authority Beliefs

When you were a child all your beliefs were of a primitive nature. At the time you assumed that they were shared by the rest of the world. A 3-year-old may not only believe in Santa Claus, but also believe that everyone else holds the same belief. At some point, however, the realization comes that not all beliefs are shared. At that time, the child usually turns to authorities to figure out the issue. As you mature, you wrestle with the question of which authorities to trust and which ones not to trust, which reference group to identify with. You generally worry over the question of how to evaluate information about your world. Naturally, in the beginning, your family serves as reference group, but later you diversify your experience and expand the number of groups with which you identify.

These non-primitive beliefs do not have the same taken-for-granted character that primitive beliefs have.

Derived Beliefs

Once you put stock in an authority for a particular belief, you tend to buy other beliefs from that authority, even in unrelated areas. The derived beliefs may not be based on any direct experience, but they may be held simply on the strength of the trust put in the authoritative source. This is the principle behind endorsement practices in advertising. If your favourite actor shaves with a particular brand of shaving cream, you may believe his testimonial and buy the product out of faith.

Inconsequential Beliefs

Matters of taste are usually considered inconsequential because they seldom have connections with other beliefs. If and when they change, there are usually few consequences on other beliefs that you hold. To say that these are inconsequential beliefs does not mean that they may not be held strongly. Nor does it mean that you don't think of them as important. They are occasionally important. You may be absolutely convinced that vacations in the mountains are better than vacations at the shore. This belief is inconsequential, however, because if you change your mind, it will not necessitate a massive reorganization of your belief system

Attitudes

Attitudes are relatively lasting organizations of beliefs which make you tend to respond to things in particular ways. Actually, attitudes are never seen directly. You infer their existence from what people do. If people seem to act consistently in a similar fashion in a particular set of circumstances, you infer the existence of an attitude which predisposes them to act that way. Attitudes include positive or negative evaluations, emotional feelings, and certain positive or negative tendencies in relation to objects, people, and events.

Attitudes are human responses and they can be examined along three dimensions: their direction, their intensity, and their salience.

Direction

'Direction' of an attitude refers simply to how favourable, unfavourable, or neutral one tends to be in relation to an object, person, or situation. It refers to whether one is attracted to, repulsed by or simply indifferent to a particular course of action; it also refers to whether one evaluates a thing positively or negatively. You may or may not like someone, or on the other hand, might not care at all. You may or may not approve of birth control, or you are ambivalent about it, oscillating between one direction and the other. You have attitudes on just about everything you know about. You will judge what people communicate to you in relation to the background of your existing attitudes about that 'message'. When you do not know much about something, and, thus, have no particular attitude about it, what people communicate to you will usually help you form one.

Intensity

'Intensity' of an attitude refers to how strong it is - to how much you like or dislike someone or something. You may not like science courses. Attitude has been defined as predisposition to respond, either positively or negatively to an object situation. Classical consistency theories seek to explain how people respond to information that does not fit with existing perceptions and attitudes. Many different terms have been used to explain this: balance and imbalance, congruity and incongruity, consonance and dissonance, in which people tend to avoid or alternatively rationalize their psychologically uncomfortable situations. All these situations involve internal conflict, in which the person confronts inconsistencies in what he or she knows and believes.

Newcomb (1953) discussed a situation in which cognitive imbalance results when two people who like and respect each other—a teacher and the pupil—disagree on an issue, in such circumstances, the desire to maintain the relationship can stimulate attitudinal shift on the part of both. The final position will be somewhere in-between the two original positions. The teacher and the taught can experience change of attitude towards the object of discussion as well as the person, with the greatest attitude change occurring towards the least valued. Second, the person can distort the position of the other person in his or her own mind. Finally, the person can disassociate his or her thoughts, even his or her physical self from the uncomfortable situation. It is obvious, that the last two situations are not required in any interpersonal context and certainly not in a teaching and learning situation. Hence the knowledge of attitude on the part of the teacher is essential for effective communication, or it would lead to imbalance, incongruity, dissonance, and conflict.

The aim of the teacher through communication would be to try toward co-orientation rather than direct attitudinal change. Co-orientation refers to the extent to which parties are willing to change to accommodate the positions of persons or groups with opposing points of view, that is, achieve a perceived consensus towards attaining symmetry. Here, neither the teacher nor the learner is trying to change each others' attitude for effective communication. In any institute of learning, the aim of the communication process is not to direct the learners attitude toward dominant coalition (teachers') perspective but rather moving toward each other for mutual understanding and increasing communication.

The psychological knowledge of values by the teacher is essential for effective communication and this knowledge which is available through psychographics, is constructing a psychological profile of the learner. Among the learning community there will be sub-group of value-grouping ranging from poor struggling survivors to highly motivated, integrated, sustainers, belonging individuals, emulators and achievers with their distinct value patterns. For example, the belonging individuals, emulators and achievers share in common the fact that they are outer-directed. To specify, they respond to how others in society expect them to behave. Belonging individuals always aspire to be a part of the mainstream because they believe in a puritanical code of behaviour. Emulations are competitive and upwardly mobile. Sustainers are always angry with the system and distrust the system. On the other hand, the achievers value hard work and success. There are also groups that belong to the inner-directed. Whereas, outer-directed group tries to meet the expectations of others, the inner-directed people are more individualistic in their responses, they are inventive, impulsive, and liberal in orientation; they take up leadership roles and social reforms. The integrated are more matured people, self-assured, self-experienced and actualized individuals according to Maslow's developmental model. In every full-fledged classroom, every one of these will appear, as will the values making the task of teaching a challenge.

Now let us take this psychograph and put it in a classroom. What would be the role of the teacher? What kind of communication would be most effective to cater to the needs of all the different groups? We shall try to see the role of values in communication.

It is said that classroom communication creates 'gigantic magnetic fields' of common and conflicting items of knowledge, beliefs, and values. A teacher by his or her imaginative and effective and empathetic mode of communication shall be able to bridge these cultural and individual differences in values spanning across a message, effectively. At the same time the teacher must make access to the value system in a relatively ambiguous manner. Ambiguity allows the students to identify with the values rather than explicit appeal to bring attention to that which divides the students.

But how do the teachers plan their communication to get access to their universally held values? For this the teacher has to understand the process of communication and the methods. A teacher needs to link the peripheral beliefs to more centrally held beliefs about the nature of reality. These peripheral beliefs become the gateways or entry points into the central value system. Next is the use of the trigger stimuli to carry the preferred messages. These triggers activate needs and interests and open the door to the central value system of the students. Triggers stimulate our signal behaviour.

Signal behaviour means responding without thought - a witty remark by the teacher, an impressive audio-visual aid, and an interesting anecdote can act as stimulus in classroom interaction. Semantics define signal behaviour as immediate, automatic, and uncritical responses, which are followed by symbolic behaviour, which is a more critical response and marked by more self-awareness. The learner, therefore, internalizes the messages and interprets it. Once the pathway has been established and learned, the later occurs easily.

The next stage leads to metaphors. Metaphor puts beliefs, attitudes, values, people, activities, scene, etc. side by side with the communicated content, and converts this contiguity into meaningful relationship. For example, a teacher may start an unfamiliar lesson with a familiar experience. In tying the unfamiliar to the familiar, metaphor exploits similarity and differences simultaneously, that leads to relationship. Here the teacher makes imaginative transportation from the plane of feeling to the plane of comprehension. He or she, thus, stresses the similarity between the planes and minimizes the differences.

Another important aspect of psychology of communication *is* its relation to needs and personality of the learner. Maslow's (1954) hierarchy of needs indicates that all people have motives and drives that influence their susceptibility to learning from messages. This staircase of needs includes physiological, safety, love, esteem, and self-actualization factors. At the bottom of the staircase are the needs that are physiological and related to safety and love. The individual must find a way to satisfy these needs before the higher-level needs assume any real importance. A starving man will think only about food, a homeless man of shelter, giving little though to matters of esteem or self-actualization. In institutes of learning, the appeal must be made to the self-actualizing needs of the learners. They offer the challenge to the learners to 'become all that you are capable of being'. Successful communication in classroom interaction implies that the teachers know the learners' position on the staircase of need.

We have examined here the influence of beliefs, attitudes, and values on students. We have also discussed the impact of needs and personality on how people receive messages. The communicator who wants to impart knowledge or information, change or reinforce attitude or more people to action must consider these variables. Each individual does not hear the same messages. Nor does everyone have the same motivation or incentive to act on the messages. A keen understanding of students' psychology lies at the heart of effective communication.

Formation of Values, Beliefs, and Attitudes

The point we wish to emphasize strongly here is that values, beliefs, and attitudes are learned. People are not born prejudiced, conservatives, atheists, or football fans. They are not born fearing God and valuing freedom and human dignity; nor are they born convinced that a steady use of mouthwash will make them social successes. All values, beliefs, and attitudes are learned from the people with whom you live and associate. Because they are learned, they can be unlearned, that is, changed, although change may often be resisted.

It is essentially through interpersonal communication that people develop prejudices, assumptions, and outlooks on what life is like or ought to be like. Your values, beliefs, and attitudes were formed through the various human groups you were and are exposed to, which 'indoctrinated' or 'socialized' you—and still do—in those values, beliefs, and attitudes they hold dear.

To communicate with others is to influence them and to be influenced by them, because any time that you have human contact with others, their behaviour and what they tell you affect you. Any time you learn something new, you change and become a little more like those who taught you. This is what makes society possible. Interpersonal communication, thus, fosters the minimum uniformity necessary for people to live and work together. Sometimes the indoctrination is successful. Sometimes it has a reverse effect; the child of an ultraconservative parent becomes a radical. This common phenomenon may be explained in terms of what social psychologists call 'reference group theory'.

EMOTION AND COMMUNICATION

No feature of communication has more meaning and significance than the one identified by the word emotion or affect—love, hatred, anger, sadness, courage, anxiety, and frustration are emotional states or feelings. Positive or negative emotion constitutes a very general predisposition. Individuals with positive affect are marked more by enthusiasm, favourable expectations, and general optimism, than individuals with negative affect. The communication-related outcomes of emotion are that people with positive emotions are better communicators because positive emotions are highly correlated with concept of self, sensitivity, empathy, and interpersonal skills. The impact of negative emotion in communication can lead to communication apprehension, miscommunication, aggression, etc. The impact of negative emotion in teaching is far more critical for it involves a teacher's overall attitudes about students and teaching. Emotion is the source for the words and expressions we use, and since we know the relation of emotion with communication, negative emotions also disrupt relationships between the teachers and the students indeed, the emotional tie or relationship between the teacher and the taught serves as the channel for all the messages that each arouses in the other.

Teachers are human and can experience a range of emotions but the question is, should a teacher let his or her emotions reflect in her communication with the students? The answer is 'yes'. In case of positive emotion (as we shall see in the next chapter on pedagogy and communication) the show of love, kindness, empathy, concern are all very important for effective communication in teaching and learning. Teachers who have made a difference in our lives were for us real people. Those who were not flesh and blood did not help us internalize whatever they taught. A teacher without clearly expressed emotions is more like a teaching machine than a teacher.

IMPLICATIONS

The question upper most in one's mind at this point is: just because we find that certain sorts of people behave differently than others in interpersonal setting and in communication, why is that important? To the degree that traits are basic to a person, and to the degree that they are very difficult to change, what is the value of studying them? One answer is that, given enough knowledge, we can aid people varying in dispositions to be more successful. In educational settings, personality differences are often chosen as a way of segmenting student population. Alternative kind of instructional methods are used. There are successful therapies for social anxieties such as communication apprehension. Communication competence can be improved with training.

Finally, individual differences deepen our understanding of the phenomenon of interpersonal communication. Science is about making distinctions in that matter. Clearly, the study of personality has long played an important role in scholarship in interpersonal communication. It has survived so long because it offers an intellectually and practically viable ground for understanding and developing effective communication.

SUMMARY

- The role that personality plays in communication is clear: individual difference affect how people communicate in various interpersonal settings. Over and above, contexts and the psychological dimensions to communication add to our understanding of the intent, motive, context and the process of communication. Teachers who deal with 'people' and whose job needs communication cannot but know and understand the interplay of personality and individual differences in communication.

- It is very important for teachers to understand and be cautious when examining the traits. People are composed of a multitude of traits and these traits certainly interact. For example, people low in communication apprehension may behave very differently from one another, depending on the degree of conscientiousness. On the other hand, an argumentative person with high self-esteem may act very differently in arguments than an equally argumentative person with low self-esteem. Looking at how different traits combine to create a behavioural predisposition is important in understanding both personality and communication, which requires scholarship, motivation, and sensitivity on the part of the teacher.
- We have seen that psychology plays in communication in a very subtle but very powerful way because the act of communication involves the whole person—his or her personality, beliefs, motives, emotions, attitudes, and so on. Hence it is essential for the teacher to have a comprehensive knowledge of psychology not only at a theoretical level but his or her day-to-day dealings with the students. The knowledge of psychology of communication will also help the teacher, reorient his or her own personality, question his or her own values attitudes, improve her motivation and most importantly improve the communication process, with the ultimate objective to carry on the pedagogic task effective and to have effective interpersonal relationship with the students

7

Pedagogy and Communication

After reading this chapter, you will be familiar with:

- The components of pedagogical communication
- The processes of supportive communication
- The importance of pedagogical and supportive communication
- The essential skills required to be a better communicator and teacher

INTRODUCTION

In any progressive institute of learning, educational communication (i.e., communication and relationships between teachers and class and between teacher and pupil) is an exceptionally important socio-psychological requirement. Much has been written—and rightly so—about the socio-psychological demands made on the personality and activity of the teacher. Yet, the way these demands are formulated and put into effect in relation to the teacher needs a much in-depth study. To put it mildly the grasp of most teachers over socio-psychological notions or over those of general psychology leaves something to be desired. There is nothing surprising in this; in pedagogical institutes and institutes for further training of teachers, the latter simply receive no information about social psychology and those of its problems which are relevant to education.

Everything here depends on the personal pedagogical experience and the general level of culture of the teacher. For this reason, the acquisition of pertinent socio-psychological knowledge, skills, and habits of pedagogical communication represents an extremely important task, and it requires special research and active attention from those who are responsible for the training, professional activity, and further qualification of teacher.

Obviously, it is not accidental that the problems of pedagogical communication are examined at great length especially in America and former

West Germany, focusing on those aspects of psychology, which can help us uncover the mental processes of perception and communication, as well as skills and habits. Pedagogical communication is based on the methodological principles of a new form of communicative teaching, following the techniques of 'Suggestopaedie', an emotionally significant and intensive method based on the principles of psychotherapy. It is a system of procedure for the creation of a positive emotional and psychological climate in teaching and communication.

PEDAGOGICAL COMMUNICATION

Communication can be defined as a complex process of establishing and developing contacts between people, which is rooted in the need for joint activities. On the technical side, pedagogical communication comes out as a system of method intended to provide interaction between the pedagogue and the pupil. It is the exchange of information and maintenance of mutual understanding, and proper relationship between the pedagogue and the pupil with the help of appropriate communicative means.

Definition

Pedagogical communication is understood to be the system of interaction between the pedagogue and the students. It is based on appropriate methods and habits and consists of exchange of information, exercising of appropriate influence on the pupils for didactic and educational purposes, and the promotion of their mutual understanding. The pedagogue must initiate and control this process.

Pedagogical communication comes out, on the one hand, as the emotional background of the process of training and education and, on the other, as its immediate content. Pedagogical communication is a joint activity, and as such, the pedagogue must unite with the students and communicate with them, that is, establish contacts, strive for mutual understanding, receive necessary information, and transmit information in response. Communication appears here as an important informative aspect of activity. Interestingly, activity is an important aspect of pedagogic communication. Communication and activity constitute an inseparable entity.

Pedagogical communication assumes the form of interpersonal interaction, that is, the sum total of ties and mutual influences arising in the process of individuals' joint activities. Interpersonal interaction is a sequence of individual's reactions to one another's actions: an action of individual A, changing the behaviour of individual B evolves the latter's reactions which, in turn, influence the behaviour of individual A.

Pedagogical communication is based on social norms and social control. This is because joint educational activities and communication proceed under the conditions of social norms. The pedagogue should also have the knowledge of the laws of communication and of the sociability and communicativeness, which is particularly important for his or her professional task. For, a teacher will be effective only, when he or she succeeds in drawing the pupils in joint activity and in establishing interaction and mutual understanding.

Didactic and educational tasks confronting the teacher in his or her activity cannot be effectively executed without productive communication between the body constituting the teacher and the pupil. First, communication for the pedagogue primarily refers to the effective execution of the didactic task. Secondly, it means a system of socio-psychological support of the process of education, and a method of promoting a definite system of relations between the teacher and the pupils conducive to the success of education and training. Thirdly, it is a process of moulding the students' personalities. To sum it up, we may say that, pedagogical communication means teaching the content effectively as well as providing an emotional support to the process of education and training.

The Role of the Teacher in the Communication Process

In pedagogical communication, social control in processes of interaction is exercised in accordance with the roles performed by participants in communication. By role, psychologists mean the normatively approved model of behaviour expected of every individual of a given social status, like post, age, group, position and so on; and every role must meet definite requirements and justify different expectations of the surrounding people. A person also plays different roles in different communicative situations. Playing multiple roles leads to conflict with each other; this is termed as role conflict.

A teacher, as an individual, cannot afford to have role conflicts because the post of a teacher is regulated by role expectations, and is subject to social control and assessment. Any substantial deviation from the standard is condemned. Teaching behaviour is very important in the process of education and communication, and a teacher can only be successful if the behaviour of communicating to individuals meets their mutual expectations. Teaching behaviour requires tact in communication, that is, we are capable of accurately predicting the expected behaviour, violation of the rules of 'tactful' behaviour leads to serious consequences in pedagogic communication.

Psychological Contact in Pedagogic Communication

A teacher must be keenly aware of the fact that, the body of pupils consists of living human beings and that due regards should be given to every individual though the group may be treated as a single whole. Even a temporary loss of psychological contact with pupils may have consequences, which are difficult to foresee. Regular impairments of mutual understanding between the teacher and the pupils which become a rule rather than an exception are bound to create a gulf between them. Thus, pedagogic tact helps the teacher to establish necessary contacts with his pupils, and gives him broad possibilities for moulding and developing the pupil's personality.

Contact between persons presupposes reciprocity in the process of communication between them. Communication can only be maintained, and effectively developed, if parties mutually respect and trust one another. For establishing contact with the pupils for teaching and other educational purposes, the pedagogue requires due respect, but the reciprocal character of contact in communication calls for respect and trust for the pupils as well from the teacher.

The relation between the pedagogue and the pupil depends to a greater or a lesser degree on the general climate in the school and on the psychological culture in general. A teacher, who can mix discipline with empathy, can create a favourable psychological atmosphere. Empathizing pedagogues know how important it is to rely on a pupil's self-respect for establishing and maintaining close psychological contact with them. By contrast, the loss of psychological contact is likely to result in an interpersonal crisis.

How Conflicts Take Place in Teaching and Learning Situations

The process of communication does not always proceed smoothly and should not be conceived as something devoid of inner contradictions. At times, the communicating individuals enter into an interpersonal conflict.

Interpersonal Conflict

Interpersonal conflicts may arise due to possible antagonistic stands. The social and educational significance of such conflicts may be different, and depend on the values providing the base for interpersonal relations. Between the pupil and the pedagogue, it leads to tension, emotional distancing, communication gap, and blocks the way to the common goal.

Semantic barriers in communication create conflicts preventing the establishment of interaction between the pupil and the pedagogue. A semantic barrier in communication consists of a different interpretation by the partners regarding a demand, request, or order leading to a lack of mutual understanding and, thus, hampering their interaction. For instance, a semantic barrier in the relation between a pupil and the pedagogue may arise due to the fact that, the child cannot comprehend the teacher's demand as they run counter to his experience, views, and attitudes. Semantic barriers arise because of age differences, life experiences, interest, and 'adult errors' and its removal is very important in pedagogic communication.

Semantic barrier can only be overcome if the pedagogue knows and takes into account the pupils' age and past experiences and understands their psychology as well as their personal limitations. To reduce semantic barriers, children should be taught to use adult language and adults should be taught to understand children's language. Communication between two people may have contrary meanings and intentions. For a teacher, a fight between two boys in school is a breach of discipline, whereas, for the student it may be yet another attempt to prevent the bully from teasing him.

A pedagogue has every reason to expect the child to master a language not only in its proper context, but also from a personal sense, which would provide a common platform for mutual understanding and respect. But a teacher while expecting a student to learn an adult language with its system of personal senses should also try to understand the personal sense of the child. The objectives of teaching and learning will be facilitated if teachers can identify themselves with the child. Interpersonal conflicts in pedagogic communication arise mostly due to pedagogue's lack of ability or his/her lack of desire to understand and acknowledge the student's system of interpersonal senses.

Influence of Interpersonal Relations

Communication is not just based upon words, intonations, and pronunciations. It is also the transmission of one's personality, feeling, and intents. In pedagogic communication, the 'transmission' of one's personality into the communication process, is essential for the purpose of social influence, and acquires particular importance when we consider the psychological aspects of teaching.

Teaching is primarily an informative process. The teacher imparts knowledge to the pupil and gets feedback from the students in the form of answers and test results, which gives the teacher information about the pupil's assimilation of the received information. Here, interaction takes place at the level of meanings. But the pedagogue's role in communication does not stop at meaning, forming notions and other such criteria. The pedagogue plays a crucial role in transmitting the sense of these notions as he or she sees it to the pupils.

For example, when a teacher is teaching a poem, or issues related to history or social studies, the teacher is not only teaching the content but also much more- he is passing on the values. He/she is providing meanings, appreciation, as well as his personal attitudes to the topics he/she is discussing. This part of communication is crucial in education, which is inseparable from teaching just as sense is inseparable from meaning. Behind the influence exerted by the pedagogue on his or her pupil, he or she should also have the capability to impart his or her personal senses to them; this influence shows the impact of the teacher's character on the process of education and the efficacy of his or her pedagogic communication.

Friendly Communication

Friendship is a specific form of interpersonal communication. It is characterized by every individual's selective interpersonal relationships and interaction, mutual attachment of its members and a high degree of satisfaction with the communication process and by mutual expectation of reciprocal feelings and preferences. The development of friendship presupposes adherence to its unwritten 'code', which affirms the need for mutual understanding, frankness, and openness in respect of each other, as well as active mutual assistance and mutual interest in the affairs of one another with sincerity and selflessness. Breaches of this friendship 'code' result either in a cessation of the relationship, or in the transformation of friendship into superficial comity or into its opposite-enmity.

The problem of friendship and friendly communication is particularly important with teenagers. Friendly relations enable the teenager to participate in a process of communication where, he or she may extend his or her self to many of the peers with the help of traits and abilities that are meaningful to him or her.

Communication as Mutual Understanding

Besides the interactive and communicative aspects, communication also has a perceptive aspect, which surfaces in the process of mutual perception of the participants in communication. In pedagogic communication, communication is possible if and when the pupil and the pedagogue are in a position to assess the level of mutual understanding and seek to reproduce in their consciousness each others' inner world, and understand each other's feelings, motives of behaviour, and attitude. It is not very easy to enter into this 'inner world' because we often try to judge and understand others by their appearances, behaviour, and actions used as communicative means. Yet, a pedagogue has to make a deliberate attempt to understand on the basis of the information he or she has, the pupil he or she deals with , and draw conclusions regarding their abilities, thoughts, and intentions. Here interpersonal perception in communication acts as the key to the solution of psychological problems in communication and interpersonal relationships.

The perceptive aspect of communication lies in the perception, understanding, and assessment of one individual by another. In getting to know the other person, the pedagogue needs to accurately assess the prospect of the joint activity, and the success of the joint activity will depend upon the joint effort of accuracy of his insight into the pupil's inner world.

Mechanism of Mutual Perception

Let us try to understand the mechanism of mutual perception. How can a pedagogue and the student 'construct' an image of the other, or each other's inner world, from their external characteristics of behaviour? We shall answer this question with the help of three mechanisms of interpersonal perception. They are identification, reflection, and stereotyping.

Identification is a method of understanding another individual by consciously or unconsciously identifying oneself with the other. During the process of communication, we tend to make queries about the other person's inner state, intentions, thoughts, motives, and feelings by putting ourselves in the other person's position. But the subject of communication needs to understand the other not only in an abstract manner, but to know how we ourselves will be perceived and understood by the other person. The awareness of the subject of an individual's own image formed in the 'other person's' mind is called reflection.

To sum up, reflection may be understood as to how in order to understand the other person, we must be aware of our own attitudes, as well as that of the person perceived. It is like a double mirror image; we see ourselves being reflected in others' perception. In the process of communication, identification, and reflection comes out as a single whole as both of them are very important in pedagogic communication in order to avoid casual attribution or casual interpretation. An erroneous casual interpretation of a pupil's behaviour by the pedagogue will hamper the process of communication.

Stereotypes

Stereotyping is the classification of the forms of behaviour and their casual interpretation, at times without any valid reason, by rating them with already known or seemingly known phenomena matched with social stereotypes. Stereotype in this sense is a fixed image of an individual used as a cliché. It may be the result of generalization by the subject of interpersonal perception of his personal experiences, and the knowledge based on such experience may not only be doubtful, but also absolute nonsense. Unfortunately, our stereotypes often form the standard for understanding other persons.

Prejudice and Subjectivity

In pedagogic communication, stereotypes on the part of the teacher would lead to subjectivity. Unfortunately they are formed in the mind of the teacher by the initial information he or she gets about a particular pupil, and this biased attitude of the pedagogue may eventually lead to poor performance, lack of self-concept, and inferiority complex on part of the students, who are being biased against. Unfavourable impression always results in negative assessment, and favourable impression may lead to favouritism. Pedagogic principles do not allow a pedagogue to be biased or show favouritism, because these have adverse effects on the performance, psyche, and the communication process of the pupil.

Feedback in Communication

By now we know, communication is much more than the exchange of words and ideas; and to be effective, pedagogic communication must include along with all other things a system of feedback, that is, the 'other' person should receive the information about the result of interaction with another. Students constantly receive information from the teacher; such communication necessarily requires reflection because it forms the basis of this information on which the student modifies his or her behaviour, restructures the system, and the process of communication in order to attend the end objectives. A student, consciously always relies upon the feedback from the teacher. Similarly, the teacher too needs feedback from the student as to how he or she is understood, accepted and perceived by the student. Effective communication and interaction will become impossible, and the pedagogic contact will snap without any feedback in the process of communication. The more there is reciprocation of feedback, the more dialogic communication will take place, or the communication process will be mostly a monologue. An experienced and empathetic pedagogue can understand the expression, hopes, grief, and intonations of his or her students' inner world, and accordingly modifies his or her behaviour to choose the most suitable methods of interaction with the students. Thus, feedback in pedagogic communication becomes informative and a self-regulatory function.

Communication Training

The skills of communication may develop spontaneously or can be developed by training. Training aimed at developing communication represents an important task for a pedagogue. To train students in the process of effective communication, the teacher, need to train him or her in effective communication.

Socio-psychological Training

Socio-psychological training has two kinds of objectives. First, knowing the laws of communication in general, and second, knowing the special laws of pedagogic communication, which means learning the habits and skills of professional pedagogic communication. Hence, psychologists distinguish between the theoretical and practical aspects of the problem of socio-psychological training. The practical aspects include exercises aimed at helping teachers in developing habits and skills of communication with pupils, to act consistently, the ability to achieve muscular relaxation during lessons, the ability to distribute voluntary attention, and the ability of observation—special attention is to be given to elocution exercises for improving oral speech standards based on the use of feedback, audio and videotape recording, mimicry, and pantomime.

Psychological—pedagogical training may be conducted in the form of professional games, which stimulate the object—oriented social context of the future specialists for professional activity, thereby providing more realistic modeling than in traditional training setups. Communication training as a method of psychological influence enhances the individual's ability for communication and teaching activity, thereby improving is personal characteristics.

SUPPORTIVE COMMUNICATION

If we define a teacher as a facilitator, then communication is not only a medium of sharing information or passing knowledge, supportive communication and interaction are ubiquitous in any institution of learning. Teachers also provider support to the students which has a positive effect on supportive interaction, social relationship, and emotional anchoring. Effective support fosters psychological adjustment and perception of self-efficacy, improves coping with upsetting events, and enhances task performance under stressful conditions.

Moreover, supportive interactions are a primary means though which the social and emotional connections are created and sustained and, it leads to the development of personal relationships. Supporting communication has a therapeutic value and develops moral character because it displays the highest expression of the human spirit.

The recent focus on supportive communication owes much to the tradition of interdisciplinary scholarly inquiry centred on the concept of social support. At the same time the sociological and psychological perspective on social support were being articulated and refined, roughly between 1975 and 1990. Scholars in several different academic disciplines were developing research programmes examining what eventually would be called supportive communication.

Especially the work of Albrecht and her colleagues within the academic discipline of communication provided much of the initial impetus for an articulation of a communication perspective on social support. This emerging perspective was also informed by a variety of other empirical traditions and these diverse literatures remained largely segregated through the early 1990s. Since that time, however, growing number of scholars have appreciated the common focus in the varied research traditions on communicative efforts directed at helping others in need. As a result, a distinctive communication or interactional perspective on social support has emerged over the past 10 years.

Nature of Supportive Communication

Let us now see the underlying mechanisms through which supportive messages have their effects. Any explanatory model for supportive messages must account for relationships among three elements: message feature, theoretical mechanisms, and outcomes. Message behaviour is verbal and nonverbal represent components of a helper's behaviour, directed at assisting a target; there are isolated units of behaviour that have characteristics structure. Theoretical mechanism discusses the actions performed by message features; such a mechanism identifies what the enacted or presence of message components does. Finally, outcomes are the events or states that follow (more or less reliably) from the action of some mechanism; when messages are successful, outcomes reflect the goals, which helpers seek to achieve.

At least four features influence the effectiveness of supportive messages: (a) the presence of a discernible supportive intention, (b) the use of politeness or face work, (c) the informative or prepositional content of the message, and (d) the person centred quality of the message. Here, we discuss each feature in conjunction with the particular outcomes.

Supportive Interaction

Supportive interaction can be understood as multi-turn conversational sequences or episodes focused on support seeking, provision, receipt, processing, and response. Two sets of issues pertaining to supportive interaction should be borne in mind by the pedagogue: (a) the structure of supportive interactions, especially the nature and sequence of the events composing these interactions; and (b) the factor that influence the behaviour of both pedagogue and the pupil during the course of supportive interactions.

Supportive Intention

Supportive intentions are the pedagogue's underlying desires to provide aid or assistance to students. Here, the most important aspect is the intention of the pedagogue to be supportive. It is this intention that makes the message supportive. The supportive intention of the pedagogue has to be clear as the variation in the quality of the pedagogues' intentions that affect the pupil. Most of the time, the intentions are 'read off' or inferred from the behaviour of the pedagogue. However, pedagogues need to make their supportive intentions explicit through overt statements of availability, for example, when the pedagogue says, 'I am here for you', or 'I really want to help however I can', or 'Don't worry I am with you', and so on; these overt statements enhance the pupil's perceptions of the clarity, intensity, purity, and sincerity of the pedagogue's intention, and is, thus, comforted, and opens up for further communication. It creates affiliation because of the pedagogue's empathy, as well as develops the motivation, interest, and involvement in solving the problem. The pupil may also feel that the pedagogue likes him or her and, thus, value the relationship.

In supportive communication, the pedagogue has to be careful that the supportive intention does not make the pupil feel that he or she cannot manage the problem on his or her own. This implication can negatively affect the target's self-esteem and sense of self-efficacy. Once the pedagogue keeps this in mind, supportive communication is very effective in building interpersonal relationship and a sense of belonging among the pupils.

Face Work or Politeness Strategies

As mentioned, a pedagogue has to be careful in showing his or her supportive intention. Supportive intentions may imply that the pupil needs help, and is unable or is incompetent to solve his or her problem, or acted unwisely in creating (or failing to avoid) a problematic situation. At times, supportive communication can be threatening. Asking questions can challenge privacy, offering advice may undermine autonomy, and making suggestions can imply criticism.

To offset this possibility, the pedagogue has to use certain devices. Face work or politeness strategies are communicative devices for redressing the face threats inherent in supportive messages. Positive face work aims to protect the pupil's desire to be evaluated positively. It includes verbal devices that express positive regard for the pupil, admiration for the courage or effort shown by the pupil, respect for the pupil's own understanding of difficulty and confidence in the pupil's capacities and qualities to overcome problems.

Positive face work when used by the pedagogue, results in the following favourable outcomes: (a) increase in the pupil's willingness to consider the substance of the helpers message (b) interest in interacting with the helper, revealing potentially sensitive thoughts and feelings; and (c) liking for the pedagogue. Face work achieves these and regard outcomes through the mechanism of conveying the pedagogues positive regard and respect for the pupil. Supportive intentions, along with sensitive face work helps to cultivate 'Supportive conversational environment'.

The third important feature of support message for the pedagogues is its effectiveness in passing informative context. Supportive message can be declaratives like factual statements, observations and opinions, intended to enhance the pupil's awareness or understanding of classroom interactions; or they may be directives like suggestions, proposals, advice, etc.—all intended to enhance the pupil's appreciation or motivation to improve or solve the problem.

Declaratives present information in an adequate and appropriate manner and quantity, expressed in an empathetic manner. Helpful directives present sound proposals and solve the problem effectively and efficiently. Sometimes, there is cognitive or emotional deficit in the learner. In this situation, the pedagogue has to provide 'instrumental support' that would facilitate learning and task accomplishment. At times, the pedagogue may find the pupils lacking information about themselves, lacking confidence, doubting their competence and self-efficacy or their likeability and social acceptance. Under these conditions, the pedagogue needs to provide appraisal support to the pupil to make them able and competent, and emotional support to make them feel accepted and loved as also to manage their grievances.

However, one key point that a pedagogue needs to remember is that, supportive communication is not a commodity or a resource that can be delivered. Rather it arises through the interactions occurring in the relationships. Besides, the pedagogue may face problems in conceptualizing supportive communication that would serve the purpose.

Supportive Communication is Pupil Centred

An important and interesting feature of supportive message is that, it is pupil-centred as it acknowledges the pupil's emotional and cognitive state and the affection reactions, expression of compassion, and understanding. Person centred supportive communication avoids evaluating pupils or asking them to act or behave in a particular way, because such acts undermine the reflective processes that supportive communication seek to achieve.

Person centred supportive communication assists the pupil in developing greater comprehension skills for a problematic situation and improved perspective on it. These messages may also help the student to modify personal goals and feelings as a result of increased appreciation for the character of the situation and possibilities inherent within it. In the long run, supportive communication leads to enhanced understanding, acceptance, and adjustment between the pedagogue and the pupil.

Supportive Interactions

Supportive communication requires supportive interactions. Supportive interactions can be understood as multi-turn conversational sequences or episodes focused on support seeking, provision, receipt, processing, and response.

Supportive interactions between the pedagogue and the pupils have a typical structure composed of four phases or events that are sequenced in a characteristic order. These events, in the order in which they typically occur are: (a) support activation by the pupil, (b) support provision by the pedagogue, (c) support receipt and accompanying reactions by the pupil and (d) responses to the pupil's reactions by the pedagogue.

Support activation may be intentional (that is, the pupil may seek support) or unintentional (that is, the pedagogue may notice that the pupil is not doing well or is looking upset and indicates the need for concern). The term support seeking is described as support activation when it appears that the pupil is intentionally acting to elicit support from the pedagogue. Support provision involves the pedagogues producing messages directed towards assisting the pupil. A pupil's reactions encompass immediate behavioural replies, both verbal and non verbal, to the pedagogue's supportive message. Finally, the pedagogue responds to the reactions of the pupil.

Process of Supportive Interaction

First, supportive interaction is a logical structure, a schema or a script or Memory Organization Packet (MOP) that channels expectations, interpretations, and actions in support episodes.

Second, supportive communication is naturalistic, requires interaction analysis, experimental and message perception.

Third, each of the four support events has a variable internal structure and may consist of anything from a brief bit of behaviour to long complex behavioural sequence: for example, a pupil's distracted look in a class to a series of dysfunctional behaviour. Support activation may consist of a single simple sigh or a very long multiple narrative like, 'I am not being able to cope up with all these. I am a failure. I am useless. I don't think I can do all these.' Let us see how support activation extends over multiple turns by this following example:

Pupil: (Sighing dejectedly)
Pedagogue: 'Is everything alright?'
Pupil: 'Not exactly.'
Pedagogue: 'Would you like to share it with me?'
Pupil: 'Well.' (Pause)
Pedagogue: 'Come on let's sit together and see what we can do. Let us discuss and work it out.'
Pupil: 'Well I have a problem. I cannot express myself clearly. I feel shy to communicate and as a result my classmates ignore me.'

What is important to be noticed here is that the pupil and the pedagogue collaboratively construct the support activation event; in this case, the actions of both the parties are required to complete support activation and set the stage for support provision.

Fourth, the events identified in this analyses are open structures, or slots that can be filled appropriately by a variety of content. That is, pedagogues may pursue each of these broad events by performing several possible actions. For example, a pupil may seek help by direct verbal acts (asking) indirect verbal acts (hinting or complaining), direct nonverbal acts (crying or sulking). Pedagogues can provide support by engaging in problem-focused approach acts, which suggest solution to problems (solve); emotion-focused approach acts, which strive to elicit positive emotions (solace); problem-focused avoidance acts, which minimizes the significance of the problem (dismiss); or emotion-focused avoidance acts, which distract the pupil or discourage the expression of negative emotion (escape).

Fifth, the actions that take place in one event influence the interpretations, experience, and actions occurring in subsequent events. Finally, every phase of supportive interactions is filled with perils, pitfalls, paradoxes, and predicaments for both the pedagogue and the pupil. These problems of supportive interactions stem from a variety of sources, including threats, inherent in seeking and providing support.

It is clear, that every phase of supportive communication and interactions—seeking, providing, reacting, and responding—represents a challenging task for the pedagogue and many lack the skills which are necessary to meet the challenges successfully. Additionally, many features of support situations increase the difficulty of seeking and providing support even for pedagogues who are skilled communicators. We now consider some of the individual and contextual factors that influence communicative activities in support situations, particularly, the efforts that lead to the effectiveness in providing support.

Research studies by Barbee and Cunningham (1995); Barbee; Rowatt and Cunningham (1998); Dunkel—Schetter et al., (1992); Stroebe and Stroebe (1998); Vause (1988); found that behaviour by both the pedagogue and the pupil is influenced by numerous variables, including demographic factors (e.g., sex, age, social class, etc.); personality traits (e.g., attachment styles, trait empathy, pro social values, gender orientations); cognitive variables (e.g., cognitive complexity, social perspective taking, attribution processes); affective states (e.g., helper mood, pupil mood, specific emotional states of pedagogue and pupil), relationship factors (e.g., type of relationship between the pedagogue and the pupil, quality of the relationship, length of the relationship), international contingencies (e.g., type of support, activation behaviour, success of support effect), and situational variables (e.g., problem severity, responsibility for the problem, interaction setting, etc.).

Factors Influencing Effective Communication in Supportive Interactions

As we have seen, providing emotional support through effective communication is a challenging task because effective behavioural strategie, pursue multiple goals and service multiple rhetorical demands, e.g., signalling, intent, attending to face concerns, incorporating appropriate information, exhibiting person centredness). Thus, highly effective communication for providing support requires complex and sophisticated behavioural structures as well as considerable skills including the ability to retrieve relevant knowledge from memory (of persons, situations, and message options). They acquire new information with existing knowledge and integrate new information with existing knowledge so as to generate optimal and appropriate messages. Supportive communication, thus, requires behavioural skills.

In addition to having sophisticated behavioural skills, a considerable amount of effort too is required. Hence, the pedagogue must possess the motivation to initiate and pursue what may prove to be a challenging task.

Further, the motivation to provide support can be affected by a host of situational factors such a competence, skills, and motivation factors. The competence, skill, and motivation involved in an effective supportive communication can be summarized step-wise as follows:

1. **Interpretation:** Defining the situation; making attributions about the causes of others' actions; inferring others' internal states; and determining relevant situational roles and rules.
2. **Goal generation:** Forming intentions pertaining to primary and secondary instrumental objectives; and forming intentions pertaining to relational and identity objectives.
3. **Planning or action assembly:** Building 'behavioural programmes' or cognitive representations of action lines.
4. **Enactment:** Executing behavioural plans or output representations.
5. **Monitoring:** Observing and evaluating the outcome of one's behaviour—a directed form of interpretation, the result of which may lead to
6. **Reincoding:** Recycling processes 2 through 5 in light of the monitored outcome.

This analysis of message production processes needs to be supplemented by a parallel analysis specifying the cognitive and affective structures that are generated by one set of processes and subsequently execute another set of processes. Specifically, interpretation proceeds through the application of cognitive schemata or constructs the activation and operation which are influenced by features of the current situation as well as enduring interpretive abilities, that is, social information processing abilities, and motivational orientations and personality dispositions. The output of the interpretive process is a situational representation or definition of the situation. This gives rise to emotional states aroused both directly and through the mediation to interaction goals. Goals activate elements of procedural memory that contain action-outcome specifications. These elements are selectively synthesized through an 'action assembly' or planning process into specific behavioural plans, that is, representation of action lines. Subsequently, the enactment process produces the behavioural structure called the act or message.

The Communicative Perspective

The communicative perspective on social support is distinct from the sociological and psychological perspectives in several respects. First and foremost among these perspectives is the central role allotted to communication. The social and psychological perspectives assume that communication contributes to the origins or effects of social support. In contrast, the communication perspective conceptualizes social support as assistance that people seek to convey to those they perceive as in need of some form of help. In this perspective, social support is not a by–product or perceptual outcome of social interactions; rather, it is fundamentally communicative in character. Thus, from a communication perspective, the study of 'social support' is the study of supportive communication including both verbal and nonverbal behaviour which is intended to provide or seek help.

A second (and most important for teachers) distinguishing feature of the communication perspective is the assumption of a relatively direct connection between communication and well-being. The communication perspective takes as its primary focus those communicative acts specifically intended to improve the well-being of another person who is currently experiencing a problematic or emotionally distressing situation. Thus, the communication perspective examines the behaviour enacted in pursuit of such an objective as reducing emotional upset and promoting the resolution of problems.

This perspective is very important for the teachers in dealing with the behaviour problems in the classroom, as well as emotionally disturbed children and for counseling and guidance. A teacher needs supportive communication for all these.

The third perspective emphasizes the study of intentional responses to currently required needs. Such needs may stem from a variety of acute stressful experiences. The teacher's role here is understanding, intentional helping in response to the perception of such events in the students' life, and providing support to influence cognition, emotion, behaviour, and physiological processes in ways that facilitate mental health through communication.

The fourth distinctive characteristic of the communication perspective is that it does not assume that well-being and other outcome will be improved simply by more supportive communication. Rather, the communication perspective believes that not everything individuals say and do when seeking or providing support is equally effective. This is very important for the teachers because the teacher needs to be aware of this fact that, some forms of supportive communication are better than others, at least in some situation with respect to certain goals, and as evaluated by certain criteria. The fact that there are functional differences in form of supportive communication motivates the teacher's efforts to determine the form of support that is more effective than others.

The fifth characteristic of the communication perspective is its emphasis on interaction and relationship outcomes, that is, whether communication behaviours achieve 'primary goals'. For example, does a particular communication behaviour actually reduce emotional distress or improve problem solving ability? Attention has also been given to the effect of supportive communication on the quality of relationships between the helper and the persons being helped. These effects are of special interest in teaching because emotional support is viewed as a key provision of close relationship between the pedagogue and the pupil and it places high value on the supportive communication skills of the teachers where quality emotional support is associated with relationship satisfaction and commitment.

The most important aspect of pedagogical communication is improving the general well-being of the students, their heightened motivation, improved interpersonal skills and effective learning by the pedagogical mastery of the pedagogue and on his or her techniques of communication with his or her pupils.

Pedagogical communication does not only teach the teacher how to communicate with the pupils but also develop a positive attitude towards them. His or her position is that of a concerned, loving, knowledgeable, and empathetic person who organizes and guides the pupil's collective effort, interest, aspirations, and striving so that each individual manifests whatever is best possible for him or her. With his or her skills the pedagogue with effective communication, creates an atmosphere of acceptance, ease, directness, and absence of any feeling of pressure or fear. Stimulation and the development of personality are its main focus as well as the development of the personality of the teachers to be able to keep up with their pedagogical convictions.

Pedagogical communication is a creative communication directed towards a complex development of its intellectual, emotional, and motivational aspects.

HOW DOES PEDAGOGICAL COMMUNICATION HELP A TEACHER IN CLASSROOM INTERACTION?

To begin a controllable relationship, not only within the group, but also in the teacher—learner system, the authority of the teacher lies herein on the basis of his affiliations as a facilitator and for his outstanding personality and informal quality of the relationship and not by his status or power.

Secondly, it is not only the control of the class but also the control of one's impact on others through effective and empathetic communication. For this, the pedagogue requires orientation in pedagogic communication.

Thirdly, pedagogic communication is not just words, instructions, directions, or content—here the pedagogue projects his or her personal characteristics into the communication process. Besides, pedagogical communication requires professional qualification or else it degenerates into self-parade. It is believed, most of the psychological problems in the classroom is directly reducible to some extent by the personality of the teacher and by his or her activity of communication within the framework of the learning process, as well as to the communicative contracts between the pupils and the teacher.

CONCLUSION

We have reviewed the scholarly literature on supportive communication which is a part and parcel of pedagogic communication. We now have an improved understanding of the features contributing to effective supportive communication, characteristics of message influence, evaluation of effectiveness and sensitivity to emotional, cognitive, behavioural, and social outcomes, giving special attention to the message reception process through which message characteristics have their effects.

The social context in which supportive communication and interaction takes place needs social integration in the institutes of learning. Social integration may have important effect on patterns of support seeking and provision, both within and across relationships. Similarly, perceived support availability may influence ways in which support is sought and received, as well as effect how pupils interpret, experience, and respond to specific supportive message.

Application of what we know about supportive communication interaction not only offer the hope of improving the pupil's performance, behaviour, and interpersonal relationship but also improve the quality of their lives. Supportive communication when incorporated in educational and training programmes can facilitate the didactic task as well as build the relationship of mutual trust, respect, and support on part of both the pedagogue and the pupils. Tangible support can also help pupils solve their problems and cope with stress. The pedagogue can do much for the pupil whether in response to crises or everyday upsets. Support becomes tangible when conveyed through supportive messages and interactions that add warmth, love, and meaning to life.

Pedagogical communication is a system to uncover the maximum unused reserves in the personality of the pupil and the pedagogue—physiological, social and psychological. Each of these are of equal significance—the behaviour of the teacher, the atmosphere he or she creates in the classes, the contents, the message, and his or her approach to the students.

SUMMARY

- Pedagogic communication consists of three aspects—communicative, interactive, and perceptive. These three aspects of communication are a means of carrying our joint activity between the pedagogue and the pupil. The knowledge of the laws of communication and the development of sociability and communicativeness are particularly important for the pedagogue because he or she can succeed only if he or she can carry on a joint activity and establish interaction and mutual understanding in compliance with the objectives and goals of education; that is, if he or she manages to establish viable pedagogical communication.
- Pedagogic communication is a system of methods intended to provide interaction between the pedagogue and the pupil. It essentially means an exchange of information and maintenance of mutual understanding and proper relations between the pedagogue and the pupil with the help of appropriate communicative means. For a pedagogue communication basically means a process of carrying on the didactic task, providing a socio-psychological support of the process of education as well as facilitating interpersonal relations between the pedagogue and the pupil for effective development of personality.
- Pedagogic communication is understood to be the system of interaction between the pedagogue and the pupil based on appropriate methods and habits consisting of exchange of information, exercise of appropriate influence on the pupil for didactic and educational purposes, and the promotion of their mutual understanding. The pedagogue, thus, needs to know and understand how to initiate, organize, and control the process.
- A classroom is not only a place for learning; it is also a place where students learn social interaction and build social relationships and

emotional affiliation. The need and importance of affiliation between the pedagogue and the taught and the increasing importance of effective communication on part of the pedagogue made us more mindful of this essential form of human communication the way in which it is conducted through varied messages, within ordinary and in response to myriad of professional demand. Thus, supportive communication becomes the part and parcel of pedagogic communication.

- Supportive communication has several clear objectives. On the most general level, messages exhibiting an emotion focus are viewed as broadly helpful, especially when they reflect a descriptive (rather than evaluative) orientation to teaching, learning, and interactive situations.
- More concretely, supportive communication are most useful when: (a) exhibit a clear supportive intent, (b) use politeness strategies, (c) contain adequate information and sound proposals, and (d) take a person-centred approach in providing support, especially with respect to the pupils' understanding, learning process as well as developing a sense of well being.

8

Communication Skills

After reading this chapter, you will be familiar with:

- Barriers to effective communication
- Skills for overcoming the barriers to communication
- Effective verbal and nonverbal communication skills
- Dos and don'ts of good listening and active listening

INTRODUCTION

If I had eight hours to chop down a tree, I'd spend six sharpening my axe.

—Abraham Lincoln.

In communication, sharpening your axe is learning about and developing yourself. This shines through in all your communication.

Communication is a central part of our lives. Verbal or written, symbolic, nonverbal, intentional or unintentional, active or passive, communication is essential to almost everything we do. Communication is critical to our success. We can accomplish many of our aims and ambitions through communication. Effective communication is a skill that can be developed by one and all. Conscientious practice and the application of straightforward and simple techniques will enhance our skills.

BARRIERS TO EFFECTIVE COMMUNICATION

The inability to communicate effectively can create conflict and also impede its effective management. Our ability to communicate often degenerates because of barriers. Let us examine what are these barriers to effective communication and why they lead to ineffective communication.

Table 8.1 The Barriers and Why They Lead to Ineffective Communication

Barrier	Why it leads to ineffective communication
Criticizing:	Criticism is often inappropriate and excessive, leading to defensive and/or aggressive responses. It is often justified as a way of getting another to improve or perform better. There are often better alternatives.
Name calling and labelling:	Labels tend to put barriers between us and others, creating a 'box' into which we place others. The result is often to distance others from us.
Diagnosing:	A more sophisticated form of labelling practised often by professionals of various kinds. It can damage communication for the same reasons as labelling.
Praising evaluatively:	Unrestrained praise is often insincere. It can also be manipulative if the person has an ulterior motive. The result is often resentment.
Ordering:	If ordering is used with coercion, it will create resistance and anger. Response can range from sabotage to submission.
Threatening:	Threatening has the same effects as ordering, but often more pronounced
Moralizing:	Bolton describes this behaviour as people putting '.... a halo around their solutions for others'. (1987). Moralizing creates many problems including resentment and increased anxiety.
Excessive or inappropriate questioning:	Questions are unavoidable and valuable tools of communication but when used excessively, can create boredom and unnecessary distance between the people. There are often better, more direct, ways of communicating.
Advising:	Advice is sometimes valuable but when used inappropriately (which is often) it may damage the other's confidence or fails to enhance his or her own problem-solving abilities. It often prevents a full exploration of the issues.
Diverting:	Diverting is used often to avoid the unpleasant, or the uncomfortable. It creates tension.
Logical argument:	Logic is necessary but using a logical argument when the emotions are running high may be inappropriate because it creates a distance.
Reassuring:	Sometimes reassurance is a way of avoiding the issues whilst having the appearance of providing comfort. It can, in some cases, be very frustrating for the person.

HOW TO OVERCOME BARRIERS AND IMPROVE COMMUNICATION

Successful communicators share the following traits:

1. **Perception:** They are able to predict how you will receive their message. They anticipate your reaction and shape the message accordingly. They read your response correctly and constantly adjust to correct any misunderstanding.
2. **Precision:** They create a 'meeting of the minds'. When they finish expressing themselves, you share the same mental picture.
3. **Credibility:** They are believable. You have faith in the substance of their message. You trust their information.
4. **Control:** They shape your response. Depending on their purpose, they can make you laugh or cry, calm down, change your mind, or take action.
5. **Congeniality:** They maintain friendly, pleasant relations with you. Regardless of whether you agree with them or not, good communicators command your respect and goodwill. You are willing to work with them again, despite your differences.

Effective communicators work hard at perfecting the messages they deliver. When they make mistakes, they learn from them. If a poorly written memo does not get the response they hoped for, they change their approach. If a meeting they are running gets out of control or becomes unproductive, they do things differently in the next one. If they find themselves having to explain themselves over and over again, they reevaluate their choice of communication medium or rework their message.

It is essential to understand what it means to communicate effectively. Four themes emerge as effective guideline for overcoming barriers and improving your communication skills:

1. Fostering an open communication climate.
2. Committing to ethical communication.
3. Adopting an audience-centred approach to communication.
4. Creating and processing your messages effectively and efficiently. Let us examine each of these themes in detail.

Fostering an Open Communication Climate

An organization's or educational institute's communication climate is a reflection of its culture: the mixture of values, traditions, and habits that give a place to its personality. Some academic institutions tend to block-off the upward flow of communication, believing that debate is time-consuming and unproductive. Some other institutions work to maintain an open communication climate. They encourage openness and honesty and their employees feel free to confess their mistakes, to disagree with the superiors and to express their opinions.

Facilitate Feedback

Giving your audience a chance to provide a feedback is crucial in maintaining an open communication climate. Psychologists opine that the thing employees wanted the most from their employers was personal feedback (money was rated second). But eager to avoid conflict or to be cast in the role of critical boss, many managers avoid giving a frank feedback to under performing employees until it is too late.

If you encourage people to be open and to tell you what they really think and feel, then you have to listen to their comments objectively. You can't say, 'Please tell me what you think' and then get mad at the first critical comment. Your goal is to find out whether the people in your audience have understood and accepted your message. If you find that they haven't, don't lose your temper, and try not to react defensively. After all, the fault is at least partially yours. Instead of saying the same thing again, try to find the source of the misunderstanding. Then revise your message. Sooner or later, you will succeed. You may not win the audience to your point of view, but at least you will make your meaning clear, and you will part with a feeling of mutual respect.

Let us take an example. Radha is a content writer in a software company. She was asked to develop content for three modules. Sastry, who is the project leader, gave clear instructions as to the content to be developed by Radha. Sastry helps Radha, by giving the accepted structure followed by the company and suggests her to strictly adhere to the pattern. After a fortnight, Radha submits the work. Sastry is annoyed at her work. She did not follow the pattern and she has written two modules afresh in addition to the modules assigned to her. The two modules have already been written and finalized by another content developer. Sastry was wondering whether to really give a feedback on her performance in terms of time and efforts she has put in. In this kind of circumstances, it is essential to offer a feedback as Radha's work is detrimental to the productivity, and team-work. Time, effort, and manpower of the company is also at stake, if a constructive feedback is not given to Radha.

Committing to Ethical Communication

The second guideline for effective communication is a commitment to ethics, the principles of conduct that govern a person or a group. Unethical people are selfish and unscrupulous, saying or doing whatever it takes to achieve an end. Ethical people are generally trustworthy, fair, and impartial, respecting the rights of others and concerned about the impact of their actions on society. Former Supreme Court Justice Venkata Chalamaiah defined ethics as 'knowing the difference between what you have a right to do and what is the right thing to do'.

Ethics plays a crucial role in communication. Language is made up of words that carry values. So merely by saying things a certain way, you influence how others perceive your message, and you shape expectations and behaviour. Ethical communication includes all relevant information, and is not deceptive in any way.

When sending an ethical message you are accurate and sincere. You avoid language that manipulates, discriminates, or exaggerates. You do not hide negative information behind an optimistic attitude, you don't state opinions as facts, and you portray graphic data fairly. An ethical message makes you honest and selfless, keeping the well-being of the organization in mind.

Recognize Ethical Choices

Every academic institution has responsibilities towards various groups: students, parents, teachers, non-teaching staff, like a company has towards its customers, employees, shareholders, suppliers, neighbors, the community, and the nation. Unfortunately, what is right for one group may be wrong for another? Moreover, as you attempt to satisfy the needs of one group, you may be presented with an option that seems right on the surface but somehow is wrong. When people must choose between conflicting loyalties and weigh difficult trade-offs, they are in a dilemma.

An ethical dilemma involves choosing among alternatives that aren't clear-cut (perhaps two conflicting alternatives are both ethical and valid, or perhaps the alternatives lie somewhere in the gray area between right and wrong). Suppose you are a principal of a school that's losing money. You have a duty to your employers to try to cut your losses and to your employees to be fair and honest. After looking at various options, you conclude that you will have to fire 10 people immediately. You suspect you may have to fire another 10 people later on, but right now you need those 10 employers to run the school. What do you tell them? If you confess that their jobs are at stake, many of them quit just when you need them the most. However, if you tell them that the future is rosy, you will be stretching the truth. Unlike a dilemma, an ethical lapse lies in making a clearly unethical or illegal choice. How do you decide between what's ethical and what is not? A thorough examination of the situation, articulating, or airing out your views, doing adequate brainstorming on the related topic, taking a group consensus is one way of resolving this kind of dilemma.

Make Ethical Choices

One place to look for guidance is the law. If saying or writing something is clearly illegal, you have no dilemma—You obey the law. However, even though legal considerations will resolve some ethical questions, you will often have to rely on your own judgment and principles. If your intent is honest, the statement is ethical, even though it may be factually incorrect; if your intent is to mislead or manipulate the audience, the message is unethical, regardless of whether it is true. You might look at the consequences of your decision and opt for the solution that provides the greatest good to the greatest number of people, and one that you can live with.

Adopting an Audience-centred Approach to Communication

The third guideline contributing to effective communication is adopting an audience-centred approach, or keeping your audience in mind at all times during the process of communication. You care about your audience, and you take every step possible to get your message across in a way that is meaningful to your audience. In fact, empathizing with and being sensitive to your audience's feelings is the best way to overcome such communication barriers as differences in perception and emotional interference.

In reality, the audience-centred approach is more than an approach to business communication; it is actually the modern approach to business in general. By focusing your attention on your audience, you accomplish the other factors that contribute to effective communication. You want to know what your audience's needs are and what they think of your message. You sincerely wish to satisfy the needs of your audience, you approach communication situation with good intentions and high ethical standards. Finally, because you value your audience's time and make a practice of anticipating your audience's expectations, you create and process your oral and written messages effectively and efficiently and use technology wisely and responsibly to obtain and share information.

Creating and Processing Your Messages Effectively and Efficiently

In Chapter 2, we discussed the six-phase process of communication. The six steps we presented involve transforming your idea into a message and transmitting it. Let us understand how to plan messages, generate ideas, organize your thoughts, and turn your words into effective messages.

Learn About Your Audience

Creating an effective message is difficult if you are unfamiliar with your audience or if you do not know how your message will be used. For example, if you are writing a report and you do not know the purpose of the report, it is hard to know what to say. What is the content, what aspects are to be covered, what are the issues to be viewed with caution, how long should the report be, should it provide conclusions and recommendations or simply facts and figures, are the dimensions to be taken care of. Unless you know why the report is needed, you can not really answer those questions intelligently. You are, thus, forced to create a very general document, one that covers a little bit of everything.

Likewise, you need to know something about the biases, education, age, status, and style of your receiver in order to create an effective message. If you are addressing strangers, try to find out more about them; if that is impossible, try to project yourself into their position by using your common sense and imagination. Whatever the tactic, the point is to write and speak from your audience's point of view.

Adapt Your Message to Your Audience

The best way to create messages carefully is to adapt your message to your audience so that you can help them understand and accept it. If you are writing for a specialist in your field, for example, you can use technical terms that might be unfamiliar to a lay person. On the other hand, if you are communicating to someone who might not share your understanding of a topic or someone who might not have your wealth of experience, you can minimize language barriers by using specific and accurate words, especially the ones that your audience will understand. Decisions about the content, organization, style, and tone of your message all depend, at least to some extent, on the relationship between you and your audience. If you don't know your audience, you will be forced to make these decisions in the dark, and at least part of your message may miss the mark.

Develop and Connect Your Ideas

Deciding what to say is the first hurdle in the process of communication. Many people make the mistake of trying to convey everything that they know about a subject. Unfortunately, when a message contains too much of information, it becomes difficult to absorb. As you decide what to include and what to leave out, keep in mind that if you try to explain something without first giving the receiver adequate background, you will create confusion. Likewise, if you recommend actions without first explaining why they are justified, your message may provoke an emotional response that inhibits understanding.

It is also important to make written messages visually appealing and easy to understand by balancing general concepts with specific illustrations. Use specific details such as numbers, tables, and figures, and using memorable words such as colours, objects, scents, sounds, and tastes to create a picture in your audience's mind. You can also call attention to an idea visually by using headlines, bold type, and indented lists and by using charts, graphs maps, diagrams, and illustrations. Furthermore, be sure to show how new ideas are related to concepts that already exist in the minds of your audience. Such connections help make the new concepts acceptable.

Finally, keep your messages as brief and as clean as possible. With few exceptions, one page is easier to absorb than two. However, because it is important to develop each main idea adequately, it is better for you to cover three points thoroughly rather than skimming through eight points superficially. Remember, by highlighting and summarizing your key points, you help your audience understand and remember the message.

Reduce the Number of Messages

Limiting the number of messages you send, is another way of being effective. One useful way to reduce the number of messages is to think twice before sending one. It takes time and resources to produce letters and memos, and hence organizations have to be concerned with how many messages they create. If a written message merely adds to the information overload, it is probably better left unsent or handled some other way, like a quick telephone call or a face-to-face chat. By holding down the number of messages, organizations will maximize the benefits of their communication activities.

Choose the Correct Channel and Medium

Even the most carefully constructed message will fail to produce results if it does not reach your audience. Try, as far as possible, to eliminate potential sources of interference. Begin by eliminating the number of channels a message must pass through, before it reaches its intended target. Follow this by making sure of the fact that your choice of communication channel and medium does not interfere with your message.

When you plan a message, think about the amount of feedback you want to encourage, and choose a form of communication that suits your needs. Some channels and media are more compatible with feedback than others. Media richness is the value of a medium in a given communication situation. Richness is determined by a medium's ability to (1) convey a message by means of more than one informational cue (visual, verbal, and vocal), (2) facilitate feedback, and (3) establish personal focus. Face-to-face communication is the richest medium because it is personal, it provides both immediate verbal and nonverbal feedback, and conveys the emotion behind the message. However, it is also one of the most restrictive modes of communication because the person and his audience must be in the same place, at the same time. To ensure effective communication, use richer media for messages that are complex, ambiguous, and non-routine. Use rich media to extend and humanize your presence throughout the organization, to communicate consideration for employees, and to gain employee commitment to organizational goals.

HOW YOU SAY IT IS WHAT COUNTS

Our words are only a fraction of the message that we send. In fact, how we say those words often matters more than the words themselves. It is required for each one of us to have an assessment of how we sound like. The following questions proposed by Kris Cole, may help you to understand what you sound like:

- Is your voice tone harsh, soft, sharp or neutral?
- Is your pitch high or low?
- Is your volume loud, quiet or in between?
- Is your inflexion rising, falling or sing-song?
- Is your voice speed fast or slow?
- What emphasis do you place on words?
- Do you articulate clearly or do you mumble?
- How much energy do you speak with?
- What rhythm do you speak with?

IMPROVE YOUR NONVERBAL COMMUNICATION SKILLS

To improve your nonverbal communication skills, pay more attention to the kinds of signals. It is particularly important to avoid giving conflicting signals to others. For instance, if you tell an employee that you are free to talk to about her raise but your nonverbal signals suggest that this is not the best time to discuss the subject, she will be confused. So try to be as honest as possible in communicating your emotions. The following are some strategies for honing your nonverbal skills:

- Smile genuinely. A fake smile is obvious because the timing is not right and the wrinkles don't follow.
- Be aware that people may give false nonverbal cues.
- Keep appropriate distance and use physical contact only when appropriate.

- Respect status with your eye contact.
- Adopt a handshake that matches your personality and intention.

Remember, few gestures which convey meaning in and about themselves have to be interpreted in clusters, and they should reinforce your words. It should be remembered that the above outlined strategies should be used with appropriateness and with relevance.

IMPROVING YOUR ORAL COMMUNICATION SKILLS

Speaking and listening are the communication skills people use most. Given a choice, people would rather talk to each other than write to each other. Talking requires less time and needs no composing, keyboarding, rewriting, duplicating, or distributing. More importantly, oral communication provides the opportunity for feedback. When people communicate orally, they can ask questions and test their understanding of the message; they can share ideas and work together to solve problems. Talking things over helps people in organizations build the morale and establish a group identity. In addition to this, oral communication satisfies our common need to be part of the human community, and it makes us feel good.

Whether you are using the telephone, engaging in a quick face-to-face conversation with a colleague, or attending a meeting, oral communication is the vehicle you use to get your message across. When communicating orally, make it your goal to work in improving two key skills of speaking and listening.

Speaking

Speaking is such an ingrained activity, that we tend to do it without much thought, but that casual approach can be a problem in academic or business setting. You have far less opportunity to revise your spoken words than to revise your written words. If you let your attention wander while someone else is speaking, you miss the point. You either have to get along without knowing what the other person said, or admit that you were daydreaming and ask the person to repeat the comment.

Another problem is that people tend to confuse your spoken message with you as an individual. They are likely to judge the content of what you say, by your appearance and style of delivery.

To improve your speaking skills, be aware of using speech as a tool for accomplishing your objectives. To do this, break the habit of talking spontaneously, without planning what you are going to say or how you are going to say it. Before you speak, think about your purpose, your main idea, and your audience. Organize your thoughts, decide on a style that suits the occasion (for example, formal or informal, lecture or conversation) and your audience (supervisor or assistant, client, or colleague), and edit your remarks mentally. Perhaps the most important thing you can do is to remember the 'you' attitude, earning other people's attention and goodwill by focusing on them. Try to predict how the other person will react and organize the message accordingly. Your audience may not react the way you expect, so have alternative approaches ready. As you speak, watch the other person, judging from verbal and nonverbal feedback whether your message is making the desired impression. If it is not, revise it and try again.

Listening

Speaking is, of course, only one side of the oral communication story. In fact, you spend over half your communication time listening. Generally, miscommunications stem from a failure to listen to and understand the needs of the others.

Listening is a routined, everyday activity and only few people think of developing their listening skills. Yet, unlike hearing, listening demands total concentration; it is an active search for meaning. 'Many people confuse hearing with active listening,' notes one communication consultant. 'Hearing is an automatic, physical function. Because you heard the words doesn't necessarily mean you were listening to the message.' It is not that we do not mean to listen with our full minds in gear. It is just that most of us have so many things pulling at our brain cells at once that we often do not give our full attention. You must have learned a great deal about listening skills in your spoken English chapter.

The Seven Dos of Good Listening

i. Listen caringly.
ii. Listen with your body.
iii. Listen with your eyes.
iv. Listen with your ears.
v. Listen with your heart.
vi. Listen with your mouth closed.
vii. Validate and confirm the message.

The Seven Don'ts of Good Listening

i. Don't interrupt.
ii. Don't contradict. (May do it politely, but only after the speaker completes his/her statement.)

iii. Don't criticize or lecture about past behaviour.
iv. Don't nod your head constantly to hurry them along.
v. Don't assume that what they are talking about is the total content of their message.
vi. Don't interrogate.
vii. Don't use the occasion for self-aggrandizement.

Table 8.2 Active Listening Skills

Skills	Examples
Attending skills	
• Appropriate nonverbal skills	• Open posture/inclining body forward/ appropriate distance/effective eye contact
• Providing an appropriate environment	• Careful regard to seating/light/sound/ non-interruptions
Following skills	
• Appropriate cues to help the other to begin talking	• Non-advice giving/no false reassurances/ open and honest invitation to talk/ emphasis upon exploring the problem non-defensive/attending skills
• Appropriate cues to help the other continue talking	• Minimal encouragers /little questioning/ open questioning/silence
Reflective listening	
• Clarification	• Requesting confirmation of what has been said
• Reflective Responses	• Responses which summarize the feeling and factual content of the other's responses
• Paraphrasing	• Concise, specific and concrete responses which include essential elements of the other's position and interests
• Summarizing	• A brief restatement or synthesis of the other's statement/s

STRENGTHEN YOUR COMMUNICATION SKILLS

Recognizing the importance of efficient communication, many academic institutions and companies today train employees in communication skills. Some companies organize seminars and workshops on handling common oral communication situations (such as dealing with customers, managing subordinates, and getting along with co-workers).

Mastering communication skills is an essential component for teachers. Perhaps the best place to begin is with an honest assessment of where you stand. In the next few days, watch how you handle the communication situations that arise. Try to figure out what you are doing right or wrong. In the months ensuing ahead, try to focus on building your competence in areas where you need to work the most.

One way to improve your skills is to practice. Lack of experience in writing or speaking can prevent you from developing effective messages. Perhaps you have a limited vocabulary or are uncertain about questions of grammar, punctuation, and style. Perhaps you are simply frightened by the idea of writing something or of appearing before a group. People aren't 'born' writers or speakers. Their skills improve the more they speak and write. Someone who has written ten reports is usually better at it than someone who has written only two reports. You learn from experience, and some of the most important lessons are learned through failure.

TEN COMMANDMENTS OF GOOD COMMUNICATION

The American Management Association has given excellent essentials of good communication. They are popularly called Ten Commandments of good communication, they are as follows:

i. Clarify ideas before communicating: by systematically thinking through the message and considering who will be receiving and/or affected by it, the manager overcomes one of the basic pitfalls of communication—failure to properly plan the *communiqué*. The more systematically a message is analysed, the more clearly it can be communicated.

ii. Examine the true purposes of communication: the manager has to determine what he or she really wants to accomplish with the message. Once this objective is identified, the *communiqué* can be properly designed.

iii. Take the entire environment, physical and human into consideration: questions such as what is said, to whom, and when will all affect the success of communication. The physical setting, the social climate, and past communication practices should be examined in adapting the message to the environment.

iv. When to obtain valuable advice from others in planning *communiqués*—consulting with others can be a useful method of obtaining additional insights regarding how to handle the communication. In addition, those who help to formulate it usually give it active support.

v. Beware of the overtones as well as the basic content of the message: the listener will be affected by not only what is said but also how it is said. Voice, tone, facial expression, and choice of language, all influence the listener's reaction to the *communiqué*.

vi. When possible, convey useful information—people remember things that are beneficial to them. If the manager wants subordinates to read the message, he or she should phrase it so that it takes into consideration their interests and ends as well as the company's.

vii. Follow up on communication—the manager must solicit feedback in ascertaining whether the subordinate understands the *communiqué*, is willing to comply with it, and then takes appropriate action.

viii. Communicate with the future as well as the present in mind: most communications are designed to meet the demands of the current situation. However, they should be in accord with the long-term goals as well. For example, *communiqués* designed to improve performance or morale is valuable in handling present problems. Yet, they also serve a useful purpose in promoting long-run organizational efficiency.

ix. Support words with deeds: when managers contradict themselves by saving one thing and doing another, they undermine their own directives. For example, an executive who issues a notice reminding everyone to be in the building by 8.30 a.m., while he or she continues to show up at 9.15 a.m. should not expect anyone to take the notice seriously. Subordinates are always cognizant of such managerial behaviour and quickly discount such directions.

x. Be a good listener—by concentrating on the speaker's explicit and implicit meanings, the manager can obtain a much better understanding of what is being said.

SUMMARY

- Communication is essential for the psychological survival of the human beings. It is the emotional sine qua non of human beings.
- There are several barriers to effective communication such as criticizing, labelling, diagnosing, ordering etc. These barriers function as a blockade to communication which results in problems in communication.

- Successful communicators share five common traits such as accurate perception, being precise, credible, controllability on their emotions, and congeniality.
- Fostering an open communication climate, committing to ethical communication, adopting an audience-centred approach to communication, creating and processing your messages effectively and efficiently are the four central themes of communication.
- Our voice influences people's first impressions of us and the message they ultimately receive. Hence, it is important to remember how you say it is what counts.
- Listening is an integral aspect of communication. True listening is done with our heart and eyes as well as our ears. It is about self-discipline, the responses we make, the questions we ask and our body language. With high-quality listening, we can understand people in a better way.
- Good communication skills are fundamental to all relationships and one can learn these skills through practice.

REFERENCES

McKenna, Colleen, 2003, *Powerful Communication Skills*, Viva Books.

Cole, Kris, 2000, *Crystal Clear Communication*, East West Books.

Monippally, Matthukutty M., 2001, *Business Communication Strategies*, Tata McGraw-Hill.

9

Communication: Spoken English

After reading this chapter, you will be familiar with:

- Listening skills
- Articulation skills
- Presentation skills
- Interviewing skills

LISTENING SKILLS

Introduction

Most languages on earth are associated with four basic skills. They are generally referred to as LSRW (listening, speaking, reading, and writing). These skills are like tools. The more you use them with the right technique, the more adept and effective you will be in the use of language.

Listening is a remarkably sensitive skill that makes interpersonal communication truly effective and rewarding. You must realize that listening is not a passive skill. In fact, it is surprising to know that it is not only active but requires a good deal of hard work which is often accompanied by a slightly increased heartbeat indicating that there is increased activity in the body.

If you want to be a good and attentive listener you must put in a great deal of effort and self-discipline. You must not only understand the content of the message, but also the feeling and intention conveyed by the speaker. A poor listener can render ineffective or even completely ruin the speaker's desire to talk and devastate his confidence in his ability to communicate. Poor listening can result in a complete breakdown in communication.

Listening is the most important of all the skills that one has to master in order to be successful in a career. The higher the position in an organization, the greater is the responsibility involved in listening.

Did you know that listening, which is so extremely critical in our daily lives, is neither taught nor studied as much as the other three skills (speaking, reading, and writing) of communication? The skill of effective listening can be improved by understanding the steps involved in the process of listening.

The Four Steps of Listening

- Hearing
- Interpretation
- Evaluation
- Response

Hearing

It is the first step of listening. If you are able to repeat the speaker's utterances, then it can be said that the message has been heard.

Interpretation

It is the second step to effective listening. Interpretation of the message depends on your knowledge, vocabulary, attitude, experience, culture, and background. You must also be able to interpret the speaker's body language.

Evaluation

This is the stage where you choose to believe or disbelieve the speaker. The discernment made at this stage is crucial to the listening process.

Response

The response, whether verbal or nonverbal, is the final step in the listening process. It is at this stage that the speaker knows if at all you have understood the message right. Inefficient listening affects interpersonal relationship as well as decision-making. Effective listening reduces verbal conflict and improves discussion.

Physical Listening

Listening involves giving physical attention to the speaker. Listening with the whole body shows your interest in what is being said. You can be a better listener when you have face and eye contact and incline your body towards the speaker. Position yourself appropriately. Too much distance may be interpreted as indifference or rejection and too close proximity may make the speaker feel uncomfortable.

You must then react to the speaker with certain nonverbal signals. Your face must move and your expressions must indicate that you are following what the speaker has to say.

It is an arduous task to receive information when your mouth is reading information out at the same time. A good listener will stop talking and use receptive language like, 'I see.........', 'un hunh', 'oh... really.....', instead.

A good listener must also note the discrepancies between what people say and their expression. For example, if they say they are happy, they must also look so and not appear to the contrary.

Reflective Listening

Reflective listening restates the feeling and content that the speaker communicated and demonstrates that you understand and accept the speaker's message.

Reflective listening requires observation of nonverbal communication and helps you to focus on the central points of the issue. It encourages the speaker to disclose his feelings, thereby helping him understand his emotions and move towards a solution to the problem. It is not easy to listen actively all the time. Our concentration lasts only for about 15–20 minutes. All of us get distracted at times. But the good listener gets back on track and asks clarifying questions when things aren't clear. Above all we must guard against prejudices, close-minded opinions, defensive remarks, and fears of being wrong which prevent us from believing what is said.

A good listener must respond, allowing the speaker to know that he/she was understood. Empathic listening is more complex than just listening. An empathic listener focuses on the speaker's feelings.

Benefits of Effective Listening

Listening is an intellectual activity; our faculties function in different ways according to the kind of listening required by the occasion. Listening to presentations, lectures, and instructions requires attention so that the information and ideas are understood and stored in the memory. Listening to political speeches, sales talks, or judging of elocution contests requires evaluative critical listening.

Effective listening offers numerous benefits. Some of them are listed below:

- Can obtain more information.
- Can get acquainted with people and perceive how their minds work.

- Can improve good relationship with people.
- Can raise people's morale.
- Can obtain suggestions and new ideas.
- Can know why people perform as well as or as poorly as they do.
- Can solve problems and face situations that present perplexity with a composed state of mind.

Improving Listening Skills

Some positive habits can be cultivated to improve listening. First of all, you must pay full attention to the speaker. This concentration is helped by alertness of the mind and the body. If you are determined to pay attention, you can train and discipline your mind and body to get into the listening mode.

Training for good listening is largely a personal responsibility and can be achieved with personal effort. Listening skills can be improved by following some of the strategies given below.

Maintain Eye Contact

Eye contact helps the listener to remain focused and helps to feel involved.

Interpret the Speaker's Nonverbal Signs

The ears are not enough to listen to the message completely. We need the eyes as well. The speaker's body language can tell a lot about the state of his/her mind. Facial expressions, gestures and posture, tone and pitch of the voice help the listener to have an idea about the enthusiasm, excitement, anger or fear, nervousness, or impatience of the speaker.

Avoid Interrupting the Speaker

It is not possible to listen effectively while talking.

Ask Questions

If you are not sure of what the speaker is saying, ask. But do not ask questions randomly. Ask at suitable moments to get a clear perception. It is quite acceptable to ask 'Do you mean…?'

Avoid Being Judgemental

Keep an open mind; do not jump to conclusions. Avoid making any judgment until the speaker has completed speaking.

Listening: Vital to Teaching

Effective listening is of enormous importance to teaching. It is not only the students but also the teachers who have to practise listening skills.

In a teaching-learning process, it is generally believed that the student is at the listening end and the teacher at the talking. But this is a wrong notion. The teacher is not always at the authoritative talking end. The teacher is also a friend and a facilitator. There are a number of occasions where a teacher needs to listen, not just give an indifferent hearing, but a patient, empathic listening to the students' problems. He understands the problems of the students and perhaps even solve them.

Listening is not a subject taught at school like reading and writing. Many of us seem to feel that it comes naturally. The latest studies reveal that listening is a very large part of school learning and is one of our primary means of interacting with people on a personal basis. It is estimated that between 50 to 75 per cent of students' classroom time is spent listening to the teacher, to other students or to audio media.

In a classroom the students need to listen attentively to the lectures. Students must consider listening skills to be an art that should be used effectively for accomplishing the set goals. Listening skills must be consciously improved by following some strategies.

Some Listening Strategies for the Student

i. **Concentrate on content:** Do not pay too much importance to the style of delivery and the teacher's idiosyncrasies. If you are doing so, you are not focussing on the content of the lesson.

ii. **Avoid emotional involvement:** Do not be readily affected with or stirred by emotion. If you are emotionally involved, then you tend to become selectively receptive. You listen to what you want to but not to what is being said.

iii. **Maintain eye contact:** You will, of course, have to look into your books at times, but eye contact with the speaker keeps you focused on the subject at hand and keeps you involved in the lecture.

iv. **Expel distractions:** Don't let your mind wander and be distracted by any noise around you. Try to find a solution for any discomfort due to a bad seat or bad weather.

v. **Consider listening to Be a stimulating mental task:** Listening to an academic lecture is not a passive act. You need to concentrate on what is said so that you can comprehend and process the information.

vi. **You can ask yourself some questions as you listen:** 'What is the key point the professor is making?', 'How does this fit with what I know from previous lectures?', etc.

vii. **Be focused:** All the above suggestions will help you keep your mind occupied and focused on what is being said. You can actually begin to anticipate what the professor is going to say as a way to keep your mind from straying. Your mind does have the capacity to listen, think, write and ponder at the same time, but it does take practice.

Some Listening Strategies for the Teacher

A teacher must concentrate on what the student is saying, and have an open mind to receive and listen to information. The teacher needs to understand the students' background and let them know that he/she understands how they feel strongly about the issues being discussed. Their intense emotions must be acknowledged and affirmed before serious solutions can be discussed.

The teacher should encourage the students to 'let off steam' and explain their concerns by using certain phrases such as: 'I see', 'I understand', 'Yes, I know'

Some Listening Strategies That Can Be Followed by the Teachers

- Demonstrate that they are listening by
  - body language
  - making eye contact
  - echoing words
  - nodding of the head
  - leaning toward the speaker.
- Some students need an invitation to talk. The teacher needs to patiently elicit a response and gradually draw the student into a conversation discussion.
- Students can tell whether they have a teacher's interest and attention by the way the teacher replies or does not reply. Avoid cutting students off before they have finished speaking. It is easy to form an opinion or reject student's views before they finish what they have to say. It may be difficult to listen respectfully and not correct misconceptions, but respect their right to have and express their opinions.
- Listen to nonverbal messages that are often communicated by students. The tone of their voice, their facial expressions, their energy level, their posture, or changes in their behaviour patterns can often

tell, more than what is actually verbally said. When a student comes in obviously upset, be sure to find a quiet time then or sometime later to help explore those feelings.

- Be interested in and ask about the student's ideas and opinions regularly. If you show your students that you are really interested in what they think, what they feel and what their opinions are, they will become comfortable about expressing their thoughts to you.
- Avoid dead-end questions (that require a yes or no answer). They put an end to the interaction rather than extending it. Students should be asked to describe, explain or share ideas to extend the conversation.
- One of the most important skills good teachers must have is to listen to and have the ability to put themselves in the shoes of the students and empathize with them by attempting to understand their thoughts and feeling. As you listen, try to make the students feelings clear by stating them in your own words. Your empathic listening can help students express themselves clearly and accurately and give them a deeper understanding of words and inner thoughts.

ARTICULATION SKILLS

Introduction

Communication is a means of conveying our ideas, thoughts, emotions etc. However, it is quite possible to communicate without using any language. Just as animals do with each other. For e.g., let us consider the bee dance. The speed with and angle in which one bee dances conveys the distance and direction in which the nectar is found by all other bees. Interspecies communication occurs when some communication takes place between animals belonging to two different species. A dog barking to convey to its master an approaching stranger can be said to be interspecies communication. Human communication can be both linguistic and non-linguistic. Non-linguistic communication includes communicating through facial expressions, gestures etc. Linguistic communication is the use of language to communicate.

Language, a social phenomenon is a system of communication through speech, and written language is only an attempt to represent the spoken language by visual symbols. The British brought the English language to India more than 150 years ago and ever since it has been enjoying a very privileged position. It has been institutionalized in India. It is not only being studied as a subject but also being used as a medium of instruction. In fact all higher education is imparted only through the English language. English is the library language and is practically indispensable in all spheres of life.

Today, to be able to communicate effectively in English is the most powerful resource for success in both professional and personal life.

In India the standard Indian English is a non-native variety. There are also a number of regional varieties of Indian English. This is because of the multilingual set up that is present in India and because we Indians tend to learn the English language based on the rules of our respective mother tongues. We need to wean ourselves from the interferences of our mother tongues so that our English sounds intelligible.

The English language does not maintain the correspondence between the written form and the spoken form. There is absolutely no one-to-one correspondence between sound and symbol. English is a non-phonetic language. Therefore it is necessary for Indian students to make a systematic study of the English sound system known as the Phonetics of English, and avoid any prejudices arising out of their study of written English.

The Sounds of the English Language

The English language has 26 letters but 44 sounds. Therefore, obviously some letters must account for more than one sound.

For example:

The letter C corresponds to two sounds /k/ and /s/.

c	/k/	curtain
	/s/	certain

The letter S corresponds to the following sounds.

	/s/	soon
s	/z/	house
	/ʒ/	measure
	/ʃ/	censure

The letter E corresponds to the following sounds.

	/e/	egg
	/I/	repeat
e	/iː/	complete
	/ɪə/	serious
	/aI/	eye

The letter I corresponds to the following sounds.

	/aI/	survive
i	/ɪ/	glitter
	/ɜː/	bird

The letter **O** corresponds to the following sounds.

	/ɒ/	cot
	/ɔː/	story
o	/ʊ/	book
	/uː/	food
	/ʌ/	come
	/əʊ/	go, no

The letter **U** corresponds to the following sounds.

	/ʊ/	pull
	/uː/	crude
u	/jʊ/	cucumber
	/juː/	music
	/ʌ/	hut
	/ɜː/	burn

Some letter combinations too correspond to more than one sound.

	/k/	character
ch	/tʃ/	church
	/ʃ/	machine
	/əʊ/	though
	/ʌf/	rough
ough	/ɒf/	cough
	/uː/	through
	/ɔː/	bought

Now let us study the sound system of the English language in detail. As mentioned earlier English has 44 sounds all of which are produced by the egressive pulmonic air stream mechanism, (i.e., the air that is moving out of the lungs is modified at several regions in the vocal tract to produce the different sounds).

The organs involved in the production of speech are: the trachea, the larynx containing the vocal cords, the glottis, the pharynx, the tongue, the lips, the roof of the mouth which includes the alveolar ridge, the hard palate, the soft palate or velum, and the uvula.

The sounds that are produced when the air stream moves out freely and continuously, without any obstruction, are termed vowels. There are 20 vowel sounds in English. Twelve of them are called monophthongs or pure vowels where the tongue takes a single position to produce them. The other

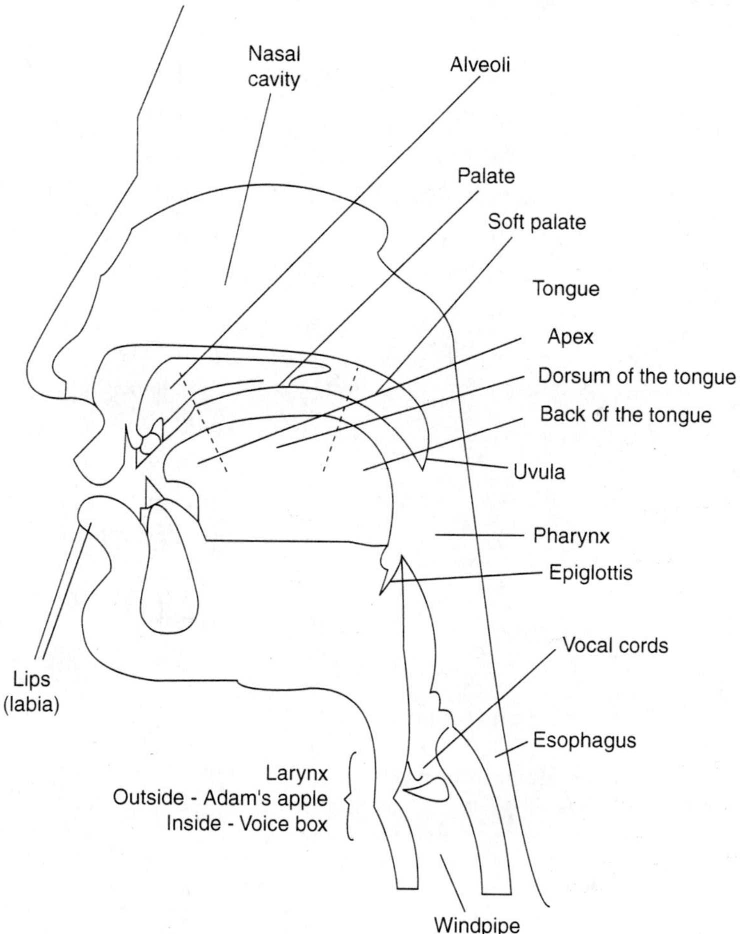

Figure 9.1
Diagram of the speech organs

eight are called diphthongs or vowel glides. These are produced when the tongue shifts positions. The tongue takes two positions in order to produce these sounds. Try saying the words 'see' and 'sky'. You will notice that, while you articulate the vowel sounds in these words, the tongue takes just one position for the first word (/iː/ in see) but takes two positions for the second (/aɪ/ in sky).

The sounds that are produced when the air stream that is moving out of the lungs is obstructed at some point or the other before being released to the exterior are called consonants. There are 24 consonant sounds in the English language.

It is convenient to use the phonetic symbols suggested by the International Phonetic Association to represent the sounds of speech. Let us first list out the consonant sounds.

English Phonetic Symbols for Consonant Sounds

/p/	as in pen	/b/	as in back
/t/	as in tea	/d/	as in day
/k/	as in key	/g/	as in get
/tʃ/	as in church	/dʒ/	as in judge
/f/	as in fat	/v/	as in view
/θ/	as in thank	/ð/	as in this
/s/	as in soon	/z/	zero
/ʃ/	as in ship	/ʒ/	as in pleasure
/h/	as in hot	/l/	as in light
		/r/	as in right
		/m/	as in more
		/n/	as in nice
		/ŋ/	as in ring
		/j/	as in yet
		/w/	as in wet

English Phonetic Symbols for Vowel Sounds

Vowels–Monophthongs

/iː/	as in bean
/e/	as in pet
/uː/	as in boon
/ɔː/	as in born
/aː/	as in barn
/ʒː/	as in burn
/i/	as in pit
/æ/	as in pat
/ʊ/	as in put
/þ/	as in pot
/Λ/	as in but
/ɔ/	as in another

Diphthongs

/ei/	as in bay
/al/	as in buy
/ɔi/	as in boy
/lə/	as in peer

/ʊə/	as in poor
/eə/	as in pair
/əʊ/	as in no
/aʊ/	as in now

Voiced and Voiceless Sounds

Speech sounds are described on the basis of the nature of the air stream, the state of the vocal cords and the position of the soft palate, the tongue and the lips.

The air from the lungs has to come out through the windpipe and the larynx. In the larynx are situated a pair of lip-like structures called the vocal cords. These are placed horizontally from front to back and attached in front but can be separated at the back. The opening between the cords is called the glottis. When the two cords come very close to each other the glottis is shut completely. This is the position of the vocal cords when we eat or drink to prevent food or water from entering the lungs. When the glottis is wide open the air stream moves out without vibrating the cords producing voiceless sounds (p, t, κ, tʃ, f, s, ʃ, θ, h are voiceless sounds). When the vocal cords are loosely held together the pressure of the air from the lungs makes them open and close rapidly. This vibration of the vocal cords produces voiced sounds. All vowels and the remaining consonants are called voiced sounds.

Now let us look at the correct distribution of /s/ and /z/ sounds in inflexional suffixes (i.e. in the plural and possessive forms of nouns and the present simple third person singular forms of verbs).

The inflectional suffix -s or –es is pronounced as /s/ after voiceless consonants except /tʃ/, /s/ and /ʃ/.

admit

appoint

drop

heap

book

brick

remark

week

months

laugh

The inflectional suffix is realized as /z/ after voiced sounds except /dʒ/, /z/ and /ʒ/.

dog

bag

bird

call

breath

cave

combine

cousin

dam

defend

join

pull

tell

lady

enter

good

For those words which end in the following sounds /tʃ/, /dʒ/, /s/, /z/, /ʃ/ and /ʒ/ the –s/-es inflection is realized as /iz/.

church

catch

judge

damage

office

pass

noise

compose

wash

dish

garage

The past tense morpheme –d/-ed too is realized differently depending on the final sound of the word. For words that end in a voiceless sound except /t/ the –d/ed morpheme is articulated as /t/.

scrape

scratch

laugh

polish

push

wash

escape

ice

place

race

Words that end in a voiced sound except /d/ the –d/ed suffix is realized as /d/.

call

anger

gain

behave

measure

describe

apply

In words that end in the /t/ or /d/ sounds the –d/-ed inflection is articulated as /ɪd/.

scold

import

guard

sort

record

support

wait

The Syllable

The unit that is next in hierarchy to the individual speech sound is called the syllable.

The syllable is a combination of two or more sounds. However there are a few syllables that have just a single sound, eg. ah! -/aː/, oh! -/ əʊ/ and sh -/ʃ/

The presence of a deep resonating sound (which is generally a vowel sound) is mandatory in every syllable. There are certain exceptions which we shall discuss later.

The structure of a syllable could be any one of the following:

V	–	ah!, oh! /aː/, /əʊ/
CV	–	boy, tea /bɔɪ/, /tiː/
VC	–	oil, up /ɔIl/, /ʌp/
CVC	–	girl, toil /gɜːl/, /tɔIl/

(V stands for vowel and C stands for consonant sounds) Words may be monosyllabic, disyllabic, tri-syllabic or polysyllabic. Examples of monosyllabic words:

/ gɜːl /	/ muːv /	/ tiː /
CVC	CVC	CV

Examples of disyllabic words

/ tiːtʃɔ /	/ dɒktə /
CV-CV	CVC-CV

Tri-syllabic words:

/ rɪmembə /	/ kjʊkəmbə /
CV-CVC-CV	CCV-CVC-CV

Polysyllabic words

/ Igzæmlneɪʃn /	/ æplikerʃn /
VC-CV-CV-CV-CV	VC-CV-CV-CV

There are certain syllables which do not have a vowel sound in them. In such syllables a consonant sound takes the role of the nucleus of that syllable. Such consonants are called syllabic consonants.

e.g. /n/ and /l/

e.g:

/ bɒtl/	-	CV-CV
/metl/	-	CV-CV
/b^tn/	-	CV-CV
/m^tn/	-	CV-CV
/setl/	-	CV-CV

Two or more consonants can occur in succession. They are called consonant clusters. Consonant clusters can occur with the word initially placed or word finally placed. The maximum numbers of consonants that can be present in word initial consonant clusters are three.

For example:

/spl–/	splash, spleen
/spr–/	spring, sprain

/spj-/	spurious
/str-/	strain, strike
/stj-/	stupid, student
/skr-/	screen, scratch
/skl-/	sclerosis

There can be a maximum of four consonants in the final clusters.

For example:

/-mpts/	prompts
/-mpst/	glimpsed
/-lpts/	sculpts
/-lfθs/	twelfths
/-ksts/	texts

Word Accent

We have just examined the nature and structure of the syllable. Let us now see what a word and word accent are.

A word may be defined as a linguistic entity that consists of one or more syllables. A word with more than one syllable is not just a simple addition of syllables that constitute it. It combines them into a certain relationship of interdependence i.e., the syllables so combined are uttered with varying degree of prominence.

The accentual pattern of English words is fixed as well as free. It is fixed in the sense that the main accent always falls on a particular syllable of any given word and free in the sense the main accent is not tied up to a particular syllable for all the words in the language. For example, the stress is always on the first syllable in 'Czech', the last syllable in French, and the penultimate syllable in Polish.

In words having more than one syllable there is one syllable or occasionally two that stand out more prominently than the others. Word accent is therefore a relative degree of prominence with which the different syllables of a word are pronounced.

Therefore monosyllabic words pronounced in isolation (i.e., not in connected speech) can be said to have 'no accent' that is why accent of monosyllabic words is not marked in dictionaries.

Prominence may be due to stress (greater breath force) higher pitch, length or quality of the vowel sound.

We have just seen that one or two syllables are more prominent than the others in longer words. But both the syllables do not show the same degree of prominence. One of them is more prominent than the other. It is said to be carrying the primary accent. The other syllable that shows less prominence than the syllable carrying the primary accent is said to be carrying the secondary accent. Secondary accent is generally to the left of the primary accent and is taken up by the syllable carrying the primary accent in the un-derived form of the word

For example:

/ ɪgzæmɪncɪʃn / examination

/ æplɪkeɪʃn/ application

Word accent in English is not unpredictable. In fact, words belonging to certain patterns are accented on a particular syllable. There are a set of rules, which help to place the accent on the right syllable. Some of the rules are given in Table 9.1.

Table 9.1

	Pattern	Stressed Syllable	Examples
1.	Weak prefixes	accented on the root	a′ broad
2.	Words ending in –ion	accented on the penultimate syllable	appli′ cation culti′ vation
3.	Words ending in –ic –ical and –ically	accented on the syllable preceding the suffix	e′ lectric gram′ matical po′ litically
4.	Words ending in –ity	accented on the antepenultimate syllable	ac′ tivity ne′ cessity e′ quality
5.	Words ending in –ate with more than two syllables	accented on two syllables before the suffix	′complicate par′ ticipate
6.	Disyllabic verbs ending in –ate	accented on the 2nd syllable	mi′ grate nar′ rate
7a.	Inflectional suffixes –ed, –es and –ing	do not affect accent	recom′ mended ′ focuses ad′ vancing
7b.	Derivational suffixes –age , –ance , –en , –er, –ess , –ful, –hood , –ice, –ish , –ive , –less, –ly , –ment, –ness , –or, –ship, –ter, ure and –zen	do not normally affect the word accent	′ childhood ap′ pearance ′ friendship
8.	Words with the Suffixes –ian , –iance , –ious , –ity	accented on the syllable preceding the suffix	ci′ vilian mu′ sician ′ brilliance am′ bitious uni′ versity millio′ naire

(*Continued*)

Table 9.1 (Continued)

	Pattern	Stressed Syllable	Examples
9.	Words ending in –aire, –eer, –ental, –entail, –esce, –escence, –esque, –ique, –it is, –ean, –een , –eum, –ee, –ental		u′ nique gro′ tesque funda′ mental ca′ reer euro′ pean mu′ seum can′ teen employ′ ee
10.	Words ending in –cracy, –gamy, –graphy, –gyny, –logy, –metry, –nomy, –phony, –scopy and –sophy	accented on the syllable preceding this ending	de′ mocracy mo[1] nogamy bi′ ography e′ conomy
11a.	Disyllabic verbs ending in –ize or –ise. An important exception being 'realize'	accented on the second syllable	bap′ tize cap′ size
11b.	Verbs consisting of 3 or 4 syllables and ending in –ize or –ise.	accented on the third syllable from the end	′ agonize ′ criticize a′ natomize ac′ climatize ′ characterize

Shift in Stress

Sometimes variations in word accent in English are associated with the morphological structure of words, i.e., the way words are formed from their stems, prefixes and suffixes. Accent shifts from the first syllable to the second, third, or the fourth syllable as longer words are derived from smaller words. Given below are examples of derivations (with a common stem) in which we find a shift in accent.

i. 'democrat	de′ mocracy	demo′ cratic
ii. ′ photograph	pho′ tographer	photo′ graphic
iii. ′ politics	po′ litical	poli′ tician
iv. a′ cademy	aca′ demic	acade′ mician
v. indi′ vidual	individu′ ality	individua′ listic

Distinctive Word Accentual Patterns

The accentual pattern of a word establishes the contrastive relationship of its parts; it may also have a distinctive function in that it opposes words of comparable sound (and identical spelling). Such word oppositions may or may not involve phonemic changes of quality.

A relatively small number of words exhibit oppositions of accentual patterns, which are manifested mainly by a shift of pitch or stress prominence, with slight variations of quantity. Pitch prominence is on the first element for nouns, and on the second element for verbs.

	Noun/Adjective	Verb
i. abstract	/'æbstrækt/	/ɔb'strækt/
ii. digest	/'daɪd3est/	/Id'd3est/
iii. torment	/tɔːmənt/	/tɔː'mənt/

More commonly, the change in accentual pattern is manifested mainly by a shift in pitch prominence together with a related variation of quality. The qualitative change takes the form of a reduction of the unaccented vowel of the first element of the verbal form.

	Noun/Adjective	Verb
i. absent	/æbsənt/	/əb'sent/
ii. conduct	/'kþndʌkt/	/kən'dʌkt/
iii. perfect	/p3ːfikt	/pə'fekt/
iv. Object	/þbd3ɪkt/	/əb'd3ekt/
v. record	/rekɔːd/	/ri'kɔːd/

Some exceptions like 'limit, 'order, re 'mark, 'visit, etc are accented on the same syllable whether used as nouns or verbs.

Accent in Compound Words

Compound words are made up of two words written as one word with or without a hyphen. Most compound words have the primary accent on the first element.

i. ' black board
ii. ' book case
iii. ' bull dog
iv. ' card board
v. ' knee-cap
vi. ' mail-bag
vii. ' tail-coat
viii. ' gas-mask

Compound words *with fore, up, under and out* as the first element are accented as follows:

a. If the second element is a noun then the accent is on the first element.

    i. ′ forenoon
    ii. ′ upward
    iii. ′ underclothes
    iv. ′ outdoor

b. If the second element is a verb then the accent is on the second element.

    i. fore′ see
    ii. up′ hold
    iii. under′ take
    iv. out′ look

Compound words having here, there, where, over and self as the first element, irrespective of the status of the second element (i.e., whether it is a noun or a verb) have the accent on the second element.

a.

    i. here'in
    ii. here'to
    iii. here′th
    iv. here

b.

    i. there′ after
    ii. there′ in
    iii. There′ of
    iv. there′ upon

c.

    i. where′ as
    ii. where′ by
    iii. where′ in
    iv. where′ ever

d.

i. over′ whelm

ii. over′ flow

iii. over′ hear

iv. over′ night

e.

i. selfab′ use

ii. selfes′ teem

iii. selfde′ fence

iv. self′ confident

When *self* and *ever* are the second element the primary accent is always on the second element.

a.

i. her′self

ii. him′self

iii. my′self

iv. them′ selves

b.

i. how′ ever

ii. what′ ever

iii. where′ ever

iv. who′ ever

Stress and Rhythm in Connected Speech

Connected Speech is an utterance made up of several words. In English connected speech we can find accentual features that are similar to the accentual features of polysyllabic words said in isolation.

For example,
'Meet me at 'ten.
I 'lost my 'bunch of 'keys.

In normal speech, content or lexical words are more likely to receive accent than the form or structure or grammatical words. Content words are nouns, adjectives, adverbs, main verbs and demonstrative and interrogative pronouns. Form words are auxiliary or helping verbs, prepositions, articles, conjunctions, personal pronouns and relative pronouns.

In utterances said without any special emphasis, content words receive the accent and form words do not.

For example,

The 'boy has 'gone to 'school.

Form words are accented only when you wish to convey emphasis.

For example,

a. 'She is 'coming
b. No, 'she is not 'coming
c. She 'is' coming.

Rhythm

The English language is said to be having a stress-timed rhythm. This means that in an English utterance, the prominent or stressed syllables tend to occur at regular intervals of time, irrespective of the number of weak or unaccented syllable between any two accented syllables.

Consider the following sentences:

a. 'Tom has 'just re'turned from London.
b. My 'friend has ar'ranged for my re'turn trip.

Sentence (a) has eight syllables; there is one unaccented syllable between any two accented syllables and therefore it is quite easy for a speaker to speak in such a way that the accented syllables occur at regular intervals of time. Sentence (b) has ten syllables, four of which receive accent. The 1st two accented syllables have two unaccented syllables between them, the next two have three and the last two have none. The time interval between **ranged** of arranged and **turn** of return will be approximately the same as between **turn** of return and trip though there are three unaccented syllables between **ranged** and **turn** and none at all between **turn** and **trip.** This is a very important feature of English connected speech and if it is neglected, the characteristic rhythm of the language is lost. To achieve this regularity of occurrence of accented syllables, unaccented syllables, if they are too many are pronounced rapidly. The use of weak forms of structure words and contractions too contribute to maintaining the rhythm of the language.

Weak Forms

There are some words in English that have two or more qualitative and quantitative patterns. These words are accented in isolation and their strong forms are used. When not accented and used in connected speech their weak forms are used. Weak forms exhibit reductions of the length of sounds, weakening of the vowels in them, (many of them are pronounced with /ə/ or /ɪ/ in their weak forms) and also in the elision of vowels and consonants.

Some of the strong and weak forms of words are given below.

Articles	Strong form	Weak form	
a	/eɪ/	/ə/	
an	/æn/	/ən/	
the	/ðiː/	/ðɪ/	before a vowel
		/ðə/	before a consonant
Auxiliaries			
am	/æm/	/əm/	
are	/ɑː/	/ə/	
can	/kæn/	/kən/	
does	/dΛz/	/dəz/	
have	/hæv/	/həv/	
shall	/ʃæl/	/ʃəl/	
will	/wɪl/	/ɪl/	
would	/wud/	/əd/	
is	/ɪz/	/z/	
Prepositions			
at	/æt/	/ət/	
for	/fɔː/	/fɔ/	
from	/frɔːm/	/frɔm/	
of	/þv/	/əv/, /v/	
to	/tuː/	/tɔ/ more before a vowel	
		/to/ more before a consonant	
Conjunctions			
and	/ænd/	/ɔnd/, /ɔn/	
as	/æz/	/ɔz/	
than	/ðæn/	/ðən/	
that	/ðæt/	/ðət/	
but	/bΛt/	/bət/	
Others			
been	/biːn/	/bɪn/	
he	/hiː/	/hɪ/, /ɪ/	
him	/hɪm/	/ɪm/	
some	/sΛm/	/səm/	
because	/bɪkɔːz/	/bɪkəz/	
		/kɔz/	

Weak forms of prepositions are not used when they occur finally.

For example:
Where has he gone to?
Where did you come from?
to and from are pronounced as /tuː/ and /frɔːm/ and not /tɔ/ and /frɔm/

Contractions

Contractions are of two kinds

- Auxiliary + Negation
- Pronoun + Auxiliary

1. Examples of the first category are:

does + not	–	doesn't
has + not	–	has n't
can + not	–	can't
would + not	–	wouldn't
should + not	–	shouldn't
will + not	–	won't
do + not	–	don't

2. Examples of the second category are:

she + will	–	she'll
he + is	–	he's
they + will	–	they'll
they + are	–	they're
he + was	–	he's
It + is	–	It's

The use of such contractions also helps to maintain the rhythm of the language to a large extent.

Intonation

Intonation is a feature of the spoken language. It consists of the continuous changing of the pitch of a speaker's voice to express meanings. People can mean different things by using the same group of words, arranged in the same order, but saying them in different ways. For many, the use of spoken English will be closely tied up with particular professional interests. For instance, the need to make oral reports in connection with work, to present seminar papers in English, to participate in social conversations in English and to feel more confident about one's ability to speak and perform.

The speaker presents speech not as separate words, but as chunks of utterances known as tone groups. Tone groups are the building blocks out of which all spoken communication is constructed. The meaning to be conveyed depends on the choice of the nucleus and the nature of pitch variations within these tone groups. The overall pitch treatment of an utterance will carry a significant component of indexical information. An increase in anxiety, anger or physical discomfort might result in a gradual rise in the general pitch of the voice. A hearer might, in a given situation, derive a great deal of information of this kind from the variations that are superimposed on the segmental composition of the utterance, (sentences with the same words, arranged in the same order). Impersonation and similar devices can result in a speaker deliberately adopting a pitch level or pitch range that is not his/her usual one and the effect is part of the total 'meaning' of his/her present behaviour.

Intonation is a network of three systemic variables: tonality, tonicity, and tone.

1. **Tonality** is the distribution into tone groups—the number and location of the tone group boundaries. Tonality is concerned with division of long utterances into smaller groups while speaking. We pause here and there in the middle of an utterance. The stretch of speech between any two pauses constitutes a tone group. Tone groups are also called, sense groups or breath groups. Pauses separate these groups and they can be marked by a vertical bar in writing.

   For example:

   // Hello, Mr John/ How are you?//

2. The number of tone groups in a sentence also sometimes changes the meaning.

   For example:

   (a) *// she dressed and fed the baby //*

   (b) *// she dressed / and fed the baby //*

3. In (a) it is the baby she dressed and fed, while in (b) she only fed the baby after she dressed herself.

4. **Tonicity** is the location in each tone group of the pre-tonic and tonic sections. The location of the tonic syllable within a tone group is 'tonicity'. The tonic syllable is the syllable on which the speaker initiates the pitch movement.

5. For example, in a sentence like

   // 'Put it on the 'table //

6. The first syllable of *table* is the tonic syllable. Tonic prominence marks the culmination of what is new in the particular information unit. Anything after the tonic, but still in the same tone group is thereby signalled as given. What comes before the tonic may be all new or may start with something given; so that the total formula of the information unit is (G) N (G)—Obligatory new element. Optionally preceded and / or followed by something given.

   For example, in a sentence like

   // You want me to come / I won't come //

7. In the second tone group the tonic syllable is located on *won't* since it is the 'new' information as compared to *come* which has already been mentioned and in fact is located as the tonic syllable in the first tone group. Within a tone group, the choice of the nucleus is determined by the meaning that the speaker wants to convey. Only that syllable carries the nuclear tone, which the speaker wishes to make most prominent. Consider, for example, the following sentences:

   a. *// John generally leaves at seven in the 'morning //*

      (John leaves at seven in the morning and not in the evening).

   b. *// John generally leaves at 'seven in the morning //*

      (Not earlier or later than seven).

   c. *// John generally leaves at seven in the morning //*

      (John leaves at seven, not gets up at seven)

   d. *// John 'generally leaves at seven in the morning //*

      (There may be occasions when John fails to leave at seven).

   e. *// 'John generally leaves at seven in the morning //*

      (Not Peter or Paul)

8. **Tone:** Choice of tone. Every utterance has one or more than one tone group and every tone group has its own pattern or contour of pitch variation. This pattern depends on the number of accented syllables in a particular tone group, the location of the tonic syllable in it and the nature of the change of pitch direction on the tonic syllable.

9. Nuclear tone, which is also known as the kinetic tone, is carried by the tonic syllable. This changing pitch or tone is of different kinds, the most important of which are

Falling	[\]
Rising tone	[/]
Falling rising tone	[ˇ]
Rising falling tone	[ˬ]

Functions of Intonation

No sentence, however carefully constructed grammatically, can convey the desired message unless it is said with the appropriate intonation. In the organization and communication of meaning, intonation is complementary to grammar. In all the three functions it performs, grammatical, attitudinal and accentual, it conveys meaning in one sense or another.

i. **Grammatical function**

Intonation distinguishes different types of sentences. The difference between the following two pairs of sentences, which are grammatically identical, is only one of intonation.

- He is ˋlate. (statement) (Falling Tone)
- He is, late. (question) (Rising Tone)
- Shut the ˋdoor. (command) (Falling Tone)
- Shut the, door. (request) (Rising Tone)

Intonation also helps the speaker divide longer utterances into smaller, grammatically relevant word groups (tone groups) each carrying a different pattern of pitch changes and indicating for the listener whether a particular tone group is a complete or incomplete utterance.

The following example will illustrate this.

//when you come here, (incomplete/ I'll get you what you want (complete)

ii. **Attitudinal function**

Intonation is perhaps the chief means by which the speaker conveys his attitudes and emotions. The grammar of an utterance does not reveal in any noticeable way whether the speaker's attitude is one of politeness, assertiveness concern, incredulity etc.

Intonation makes distinctions of attitudinal nuances to which grammar most often gives no structural clues. The following pairs of sentences show how intonation signals the speaker attitudes and emotions.

a. When can you ˋcome? (neither polite nor impolite)
b. When can you, come ? (expresses politeness)

a. He is very ′good, (plain statement)
b. He is very ˇgood, (reservation on the part of the speaker)

a. Thank ,you (genuine gratitude)
b. Thank ˋyou (casual)

a. He'll ˋfall (uninterested)

b. He'll ˇfall (concern)

iii. **Accentual function**

Accentual function enables the speaker to make any part of his utterance prominent in accordance with the meaning he/she would like to convey. Any part of an utterance can be specially emphasized or focussed by choosing the appropriate nucleus. The following sentences will illustrate this.

a. You want, ′tea? (I thought you wanted coffee)

b. You, ˏwant tea? (I didn't think you wanted it)

c. ˏYou want tea? (I thought somebody else wanted it)

Accentual function also helps distinguish between the 'new' and the 'given' information and thereby enables the speaker to determine the choice of the tonic syllable.

The following example will illustrate this.

a. I went to the ˋoffice.

b. ˏWhich office?

c. To the en, quiry office.

Uses of Tones

i. **Falling tone**

A falling tone is generally used for:

1. Statements

   The postman was looking for ˋyou.

2. Wh-questions

   When will she ˋcome?

3. Tag questions

   It's a lovely ˋday / ′isn't it?

4. Commands

   Shut the ˋdoor.

5. Exclamations

   How sur ˋprising!

ii. **Rising tone**

A rising tone is used for:

1. Incomplete statements.

   It is not very ˏgood...

2. Yes–No type of questions

   Is he, looking?

   Do you have a, pen?

3. Tag questions intending to ask for information.

   He didn't ˋdo it / ˏdid he?

4. Requests

   Shut the ˏdoor

5. Expressing surprise/disbelief.

   She ˏwould?

iii. **Falling rising tone**

1. Reproach

   I saw you at the ˇcinema (you said you had to study physics)

2. Sarcasm

   She is ˇbeautiful (but not intelligent)

3. Concern

   ˇCareful (otherwise you will fall)

iv. **Rising falling tone**

1. Enthusiastic agreement (Do you agree) ^Yes!

2. Suspicious interest

   But is her son in the ^picture?

By now you must have realized that syntax and intonation make significant contributions to the overall interpretation of the composite message. You must make use of the right intonation patterns because the meaning conveyed by intonation is beyond the bare words and grammatical constructions. This will help you wipe away the imprecision and ambiguities in speech, which are most likely to creep in with tunes used by mistake, and which do not faithfully reflect your intention.

Because your attitude is conveyed through intonation, you may be responsible for what your tone 'seems' to say. When you say something with the wrong intonation pattern, there are chances that your listener may not understand you. It would be worse still if you are misunderstood.

The intonation of a foreign language is an extremely difficult aspect of the language to master. It is perhaps necessary to listen extensively to the standard pattern of the language and also practise for a considerable length of time to gain mastery over this complex aspect of spoken English.

Pronunciation Improvement Strategies

If you are really motivated to learn the English language in all its complexities, with special reference to pronunciation, there are a number of other aids besides the teacher. Some of them are;

a. English Pronouncing Dictionary
b. Language Laboratory
c. Digital Dictionary

English Pronouncing Dictionary

The English pronouncing dictionaries describe the type of pronunciation recorded as 'Received Pronunciation' (R.P). The type of speech that had for centuries been regarded as a kind of standard has its base in the educated pronunciation of London and the Home Counties. The R.P. continues to have wide intelligibility throughout Britain. This is one of the reasons why this type of pronunciation was originally adopted by the BBC for use by its newsreaders. The English Pronouncing Dictionaries (EPDs) are particularly relevant to foreign teachers and learners of English. The notation used in these dictionaries is basically phonemic and the symbolization of the vowel and consonant sounds is based on the system, approved by the International Phonetic Association (IPA). Once the student gets acquainted with the symbols and the sounds that they correspond to, it becomes very easy to pick up the standard variety of pronunciation. When the student becomes adept in the use of the EPD, he/ she need not go to anybody for help in pronunciation. It is a perfect self-learning strategy.

Language Laboratory

Language laboratories provide the right resources, facilities and support for language instruction. In an English language lab, students have a great deal of exposure to the standard variety of English through audio and video material. There is special double track audio recording, which plays an audio file and also simultaneously records (the student's voice). This way the student is able to play back the recording and compare his/her speech patterns with those of the teacher and immediately check on the mistakes. The lab also facilitates high quality audio and video production and duplication. There are also multi media language labs that serve the same purpose, the only difference being that everything happens through the computer. You can also access any 'on-line' language lab provided you register or subscribe for it.

Digital Dictionary

The digital dictionary is a reliable reference source for words belonging to any system or province of knowledge. All you have to do is to key in the word, if you don't find the information you are looking for, and then look up the root form of the word. For example, if you look up *forensics* you will find a definition but no etymology. Try *forensic* for the complete entry. Also, try removing common prefixes and suffixes and looking up each part separately.

When you look up a word at Dictionary.com, you are actually looking it up in several dictionaries at once. If the first definition doesn't make sense in context do not forget to scroll and see the definitions further down.

Use the tab key: In most browsers, a hit on the tab will put the cursor in the search box; that way you don't have to use the mouse. It will also highlight any text already in the box so that you can begin typing a new word immediately without having to erase the old. Hit tab again to go to the next search box (if any).

Download CleverKeys: CleverKeys is a free programme that allows you to look up words at Dictionary.com and Thesaurus.com (and more) from almost any application, without having to type or copy and paste.

Fast, uncluttered access to the world's most popular online dictionary and thesaurus, Dicrionary.com and Thesaurus.com with premium features is available only to subscribers.

You can sign up and get:

- Advertising-free access to Dictionary.com and Thesaurus.com
- Audio pronunciations
- Colour illustrations
- Crossword puzzle dictionary
- Legal dictionary
- Medical dictionary
- More word games

Once you have signed up for an account, you log in with your name and password. Now you have instant access to all premium features on both Dictionary.com and Thesaurus.com, no matter where you are.

All you have to do in order to subscribe is to simply sign up with a major credit card (Visa, MasterCard, American Express, or Discover).

PRESENTATION SKILLS

Introduction

Presentations are a way of communicating information and ideas to a group of people. It is a potentially effective means of bringing people together to plan, raise issues, present problems, monitor, and review the progress of any project on hand. In many ways they are like reports, except that they are delivered in person rather than on paper.

A presentation has a logical beginning, middle and end that are well sequenced and structured so that there is absolute clarity in communication to the audience. Reports have footnotes and appendices. The reader has the opportunity to read and re-read till every aspect is clear. But in an oral presentation the audience is completely at the mercy of the presenter. We can say that one of the major components of any presentation is the speaker himself/herself who is the source of the message. Therefore, the speaker's motivation, credibility as a speaker and style of delivery matter a great deal to make a good presentation.

If the audience too is motivated and inspired, it is much easier to influence, prevail over and convince them. It also encourages them to ask questions and initiate a discussion. In such a situation the audience could also help to provide valuable input to your decision-making at the end of the presentation.

The Objective

The very first step to be taken care of before you plan, research or organize a presentation is to determine the precise objective of the presentation. You must have a very clear and focused objective before you begin. In order to decide on your objective you need to ponder about:

a. Why you are giving this presentation

You should at the very beginning be absolutely clear about the purpose of the presentation. Is it to convince the audience of a particular idea, or is it to bring people together to plan and review the progress of a particular project or are you seeking approval for a new project and emphasizing on its innovative aspects.

b. Who is it aimed at

Then you should consider who it is aimed at. You must have a fair idea of the intellectual level of the audience and accordingly structure the presentation. It is indeed a task to consider the audience to determine how best to achieve your objectives in the context of these people During the presentation, you must be able to identify their aims and somehow convince them that they are achieving their aims while you are achieving yours at the same time.

c. When and where it will happen

When you are sure about the place and the timing of the presentation, plan the way you would like to interact with the audience. If you can win them over in the first minute then they would be with you till the end. It is a good idea to try and meet them before the presentation. You can have a chat with them over a cup of tea. This will help to build a rapport and thereby establish a special relationship. You may be presenting yourself as a friend, an expert, or an evaluator. Whatever be the role you choose, you must establish it at the very beginning.

d. The subject of the presentation

Once the subject, on which you are going to speak is decided upon, structure or format the talk so that it becomes easy for the audience to comprehend what is being said. There should be a careful and deliberate sequential and hierarchical arrangement of thoughts. However, too much attention to structuring may get in the way of the main message.

e. The goal that outlines the purpose of the presentation

If you are not sure at the outset about what you are trying to do, it is unlikely that your plan will achieve it. Different objectives cannot be achieved at the same time. It is far more productive to achieve one goal than to clutter it with several. The best approach is to isolate the most essential one and remain focused. Being Focused is the key to a successful presentation. Without focus, you will end up in utter confusion and disorder.

The Audience

After having worked towards a focused and precise objective, the next task is to analyse the audience.

You must determine as to how the objective can be achieved in the context of the particular diverse composition of audience. You must identify the aims and objectives as well. The whole preparation and content of a presentation should be directed towards them.

The audience analysis might include consideration like age, sex, career, education, geographic location etc. A well-prepared presentation that is ill suited for the audience can fail miserably. Proper audience analysis is extremely essential to understand their background, needs and expectations, their knowledge about the concerned topic etc.

The whole process of transmission would be an utter failure if there is no proper reception. The audience needs to understand and be persuaded by the ideas that you put across. Quite often the first few minutes are lost while people adjust themselves in their seats, finish off with either the coffee or the conversation that they were having with the one next to them. From the very beginning, try to influence their attention.

Do anything to capture their attention and make a lasting impression upon them. You can try drawing a sign, a picture, say something very catchy or perhaps crack a good joke. But then take care that it is apt and not rude and offensive. If you are not too sure then you better avoid jokes completely. Amusing asides are useful not only to catch the attention of the audience but also to relieve the tension of making a speech. However, you must make use of this strategy only if humour comes to you naturally; otherwise it would prove to be disastrous.

You must also watch out for nonverbal clues from the audience and be sensitive enough to understand them and make sensible modifications to bring a change in the audience's reactions and responses.

The Subject

After making a preliminary outline of the presentation the main idea has to be taken care of. The subject that conveys this main idea forms the crux of the entire presentation. You should research the subject well. This research plays a vital role in the success of the presentation. Because it lists out the results of the previous surveys, the latest developments in the area concerned etc. it is important to keep in mind the time factor before you develop on the content matter. The structure of the subject also has to be organized into

- Introduction
- Body
- Conclusion

The introduction should be very carefully planned. It must be impressive and must grab the attention of the audience. The opening remarks must imply a solution to the problem at hand. The ideas and thoughts should be perfectly ordered so that the audience can easily follow them. You should also give them an agenda and the main purpose of the presentation. The body must establish the theme and also have something concrete to hold firm the attention of the audience. The main points and ideas must support the main message.

The conclusion must summarize the main points, but implicitly. Never explicitly state that the main points are going to be summarized. The final impression is almost as important as the first impression. Therefore careful planning of the conclusion can be worth the trouble. If possible, time should be allotted for a question and answer session.

The Delivery

The presenter remains the focus of the audience's attention from start to end. Therefore the presenter is completely responsible to keep the audiences motivated and inspired and not let them get distracted or diverted. If delivered clumsily without the necessary skill and grace even the best structured message can fall flat. But its worth can be enhanced a hundred times if it is delivered in a crisp manner.

What is being said is important. But how it is being said is just as important as well.

Apart from the message itself a number of other factors have to be taken care of for a perfect delivery. They are:

- Facial expression
- Eye contact
- Gestures
- Posture
- Voice

Facial Expression

Your facial expression should be pleasant because the audience watch the face most of the time. If you are listless and distracted or lost, the expression would also spread among the audience like an epidemic. You have to try hard to wipe away all nervousness and keep a smile on and be as natural as possible.

Eye Contact

Intensity and duration of eye contact is of utmost importance to build a rapport with the audience. In fact it is through the eyes that you can convince people of your honesty, integrity and truthfulness.

You can also show your confidence in the objectives of your presentation.

While, eye contact is terribly important and can really make a difference in your presentation, it can also have a ruining effect if it is improperly done. If the gaze is fixed on a particular person/or only a section of the audience, it can make them feel very uncomfortable and perhaps even intimidated. Eye contact with every member of the audience for five to six seconds at a time would be very ideal.

Gestures

Effective gestures are an integral part of a dynamic speaker. Gestures are generally motivated by the content of the presentation. Every gesture must be purposeful and faithfully reflective of your words. They must be smooth, well timed, spontaneous and in perfect harmony with speech. They must never overpower the content of the message. When too much attention is given to gesturing by either the presenter or the audience, they tend to drift away from the more important aspects of the presentation. The best way to learn smooth gesture or unlearn overpowering gesture is to use a camcorder while speaking. Watch yourself and identify and eliminate the oddities. There should be no discrepancy or disparity between words and gestures.

Posture

The stance and posture of a presenter tells a lot about his/her personality. You must use your posture as a dynamic tool to reinforce your rapport with the audience. You must not stand in a position where you obscure the screen. Avoid pacing up and down the place. Do not fiddle with a pen, juggle keys or change in the pocket. Make meaningful gestures that are in complete agreement with what you are saying.

Voice

The voice is probably the most valuable tool of the presenter. As mentioned earlier, it is not only important for you to say the right thing but also important to say it the right way. Clarity of speech is essential to comprehend of the message. Depending on the acoustics of the room, the pitch and loudness of the voice have to be adjusted.

Do not rush or be deliberately slow. Maintain an optimum tempo so that the audience does not miss out on important points in the message.

You have to be very careful about the volume, pitch, tone and tempo of the voice while presenting.

The volume should be loud enough to reach the last row of the audience, but you should not shout in order to be heard. Good speakers lower their voice to draw the attention of the audience and make it louder to emphasize the point.

The tone of your voice carries your attitude. You must make a careful and judicious use of the falling, rising and falling-rising tones. Pitch of the voice too conveys the emotional state of the speaker. Fear, anger or anxiety are reflected in a high pitched voice.

Tempo of the voice too must be optimum. Too fast or too slow would result in gabbling and mumbling. Avoid hesitations and pauses. If you use such non-linguistic material like 'umm-----and er----' the continuity of the presentation would be affected.

The best method of improving your voice is to LISTEN to it. Record your voice and play it back to listen to and wean yourself away from all those features that contribute to a bad voice.

Visual Aids

Visual aids significantly improve the quality of a presentation. However, they must be relevant, and only support what is being orally said. They must add impact and clarity to the point you are making and enhance the verbal message. You should be sure that the audience benefits from these visual aids

Some of the visual aids that can be used are:

- A black board
- Charts and real objects that can be passed around
- Video, film, and 35 mm slides
- Computer projection (Powerpoint, applications such as Excel, etc)
- Overhead projection transparencies (OHPs)

Visual aids should be very prudently used. Unnecessary and improper use of these aids may end up in confusing the audience and worse still if you are yourself confused. Before beginning, make sure you know when to and more importantly how to operate the equipment.

Too much information on slides and OHPs should be avoided as it tends to distract the audience's attention from what is being said.

The Over Head Projector

The advantage of using an OHP is that while using it, you can still have face to face contact with the audience. You can also modify the transparencies during the presentations and store them in folders.

The transparency material is not very expensive. At the same time, there are a few disadvantages of using OHPs. The OHP is too heavy to transport and the transparencies though not expensive, are difficult to store. OHP is considered to be 'less professional' than slides in a formal setting.

The Slide Projector

Slide projectors are considered to be 'more professional' than the OHP. Many kinds of materials (photography, video frame, slide scanner, etc.) can be captured or copied. However, there is also the disadvantage of having no face-to-face contact with the audience, since the projector is placed at the back of the room. Another drawback is that the room has to be darkened.

Visual aids when used properly can enhance the audience's interest and contribute significantly to the success of a presentation.

Computer Projection

Computer Projection is best suited to all types of presentations. The date can be convieniently carried in laptops which in turn can be attached to an

LCD projector. At the same time it has an advantage of having face-to-face contact with the audience. The projector does not binder the view as it can be mounted on the ceiling.

Question-answer Session

After the presentation, enough time must be allotted for questions and discussion. It is vital since they contribute to the presenter's decision making and in developing further the project at hand (concerning which the presentation had been given).

You should generally ask open-ended questions that stimulate thinking and churn out new ideas which in turn elicit discussions. Closed questions which ask for a one-word answer (like yes or no) close the doors for a discussion.

While asking questions, keep in mind that they have to be clear, concise and challenging enough to provoke thought. Do not ask rambling ambiguous questions covering multiple issues. You could direct questions either to a group or to an individual.

INTERVIEWING SKILLS

Introduction

The interview is the most important component of job search. It is a formal meeting in which the interviewer/s and interviewee ask questions, gather information, evaluate and form an opinion about each other. The interviewer assesses the interviewee's personality, his knowledge, qualifications, skills, accomplishments and enthusiasm. The interviewee too forms an intuitive impression, based on which he/she would decide whether or not to join that particular organization. Therefore, it is not only the interviewee but also the interviewer/s who have to prepare for an interview.

Techniques of Interviewing

Interviewers adopt different kinds of techniques. Some of them are listed below.

- Behavioural interview
- Traditional interview
- Serial interview
- Panel interview
- Stress interview

Behavioural Interview

This technique is largely adopted for 'on campus' recruiting. It is based on the assumption that the most satisfactory way to predict future behaviour is to ascertain and evaluate behaviour of the past.

The desired behaviour like taking the initiative, planning, motivation, flexibility etc are assessed based on questions regarding a past situation. The questions that might be asked are: 'What did you do', 'What did you say', 'What was the action taken', 'What was the result'.

Traditional Interview

This is the most prevalent technique of interviewing where the interviewee, besides responding to questions is also expected to ask/articulate, well-formed questions. An excellent way to prepare for this type of an interview is to research the employer and organization.

Serial Interview

This technique involves a series of sequential interviews with a number of different interviewers. Each of them plays a key role in the decision-making process.

Panel Interview

This technique involves a panel of three to ten interviewers, interviewing at the same time. Each of them is assigned to evaluate a particular area. The interviewee should be tactful enough to show equal eye contact and attention to every individual.

Stress Interview

This technique is rarely and deliberately used to test the candidate's ability to be poised and expressive under pressing compelling or constraining situations.

Types of Interviews

Interviews are held for reasons other than just selection for employment. Based on the purpose for which they are held, interviews can be classified as

- Promotion interview
- Assessment interview
- Exit interview
- Problem interview
- Employment interview

Promotion Interview

This type of interview is held when people are due for their promotion. It is an informal one and introduces the candidate to the new responsibilities and persons he/she would have to interact with. Clarifications about the job title, nature of duties, responsibilities and expectations are made clear during a promotion interview. This type of an interview is held whether there is competition or not.

Assessment Interview

It is a method of assessing the employee at regular intervals of time. This interview is more a discussion than a question-answer session. Here attention is paid to the career development of the employee. Strengths and weaknesses, shortcomings and improvement strategies are generally discussed here.

Exit Interview

Such an interview is conducted at the time of resignation. Here the employer gets a chance to find out the reason for the employee's decision to leave, to get a feedback from the employee about the organization, check all information regarding personal file, cheques, payments and other benefits.

Problem Interview

This type of interview is conducted to alleviate the problems that are either being created by or being faced by an employee. This interview suggests solutions after discussion with the employee about the problems.

Employment Interview

This is the most conventional type of an interview where people are assessed on their employability skills. Both the interviewer and the interviewee have to make important decisions (whether to employ and whether to take up the employment).

Interviewer's Preparation

The interviewer must at the outset have a transparent idea of the nature of the job for which the interviews are being held. He must also have a clear perception of the job description, the personal qualities that are required in the candidate to fill in the post. The interviewer must assess the candidate based on his/her

- Qualification/training
- Experience
- Appearance and self confidence
- Communication skills
- Motivation

Careful preparation and planning much in advance would really help to keep out of chaos. The applications received must be sorted out and scrutinized and deserving candidates must be called for the interview.

The interviewer must be an experienced person who can do a quick personality sketch of each interviewee in the limited time period of 15–30 minutes. And if the number of deserving candidates is larger making the choice difficult, he/she should be able to do the elimination process by careful examination and re-assessing the candidates before the final ranking is done.

The interviewer must be highly proficient in social and interpersonal skills. He/she must be able to make the interviewee feel comfortable. The questions asked should have clarity of perception and be lucid and intelligible.

He must also have a deep insight, intuition and knowledge of the subject in which the candidate is being interviewed. The way he asks questions is very important. He must take care not to sound sarcastic, contemptuous or disdainful and make the candidate feel unworthy.

Interviewee's Preparation

The interviewee must be very well prepared physically, intellectually as well as psychologically because it is not just his knowledge of the subject but his entire personality which will be assessed.

Physical Preparation

The interviewee must be well groomed and must essentially follow a conventional form/mode of dress. He must be meticulous about neat hair style, nails, foot wear, etc. The briefcase or handbag and the folder containing all the important documents should be handled gracefully. Awkward or clumsy handling would leave a bad impression. Never drag the chair you are asked to sit on. And take utmost care of the body language. Before leaving you are expected to shake hands only if you are offered. Otherwise just leave the room with a 'thank you'.

Mental Preparation

It is extremely important that you revise well the subject of your study with special reference to the area of specialization. General knowledge too is equally important. Brush up your knowledge of current affairs—both national and international. Reading extensively and watching news channels on television do help a lot. You must also be prepared to give a few personal views and opinions about certain issues.

The candidate should also be prepared to ask the interviewer certain questions and seek clarification about the organization based on the information already obtained.

Psychological Preparation

A good night's sleep prior to the interview is a must. This would help alleviate any undue stress. Arrive at the place at least 10 minutes before the scheduled time. This would serve to keep you in a calm, tranquil and composed state of mind.

Avoid nervous mannerisms like biting nails, clicking the pen, twisting hair or juggling change in your pockets. Control these abrupt urges and inclinations. Everyone is nervous, but you must learn to control these impelling forces within you and appear to be calm, composed and collected. Be affirmative. Display a certain and positive attitude. Do not be explicitly doubtful; at the same time do not show an overconfident and dogmatic attitude. Be ardently absorbed in the discussion and show that you can be extremely zealous and committed. Be honest while you are answering questions related both to information and knowledge as well as personal qualities, attitude to work, etc. Dishonesty often surfaces and creates a bad impression. Once the good impression is lost it becomes a stupendous' task to survive the rest of the interview. The interviewee is not supposed to only answer questions. He/she could also ask questions related to the working conditions, prospects of career growth, etc.

After the interview is wrapped up, leave the room gracefully with a pleasant smile after thanking the interviewers.

Questions Commonly Asked in Interviews

i. What made you choose this profession?

ii. What are your long-term career plans?

iii. What do you know about our institution?

iv. In what way do you think you can make a worthwhile contribution to our company/institution?

v. Why are you leaving your current job?

vi. Tell us about your accomplishments.

vii. Why did you choose this course/area of specialization?

viii. How do you evaluate yourself?
ix. What are your major strengths?
x. What are your major weaknesses?
xi. Are you comfortable working individually or as a team?
xii. Tell us about yourself.
xiii. How do you handle pressure?
xiv. What do you see yourself doing after five years?
xv. How long do you expect to work here?

POINTS TO REMEMBER

Listening Skills

- Listening is a remarkably sensitive skill that makes interpersonal communication extremely effective and rewarding.
- Hearing, Interpretation, Evaluation, and Response are the four stages of listening.
- Listening involves giving physical attention to the speaker.
- Reflective listening restates the feeling and content of the speaker's message and demonstrates that you understand and accept it. An empathic listener focuses on the speaker's feelings.
- Listening is an intellectual activity and offers a number of benefits if you train yourself to be attentive, evaluative and critical while listening.
- Training for good listening is largely a personal initiative responsibility.
- Effective listening is of enormous importance in the area of teaching and has to be practised by both the students and the teachers.

Articulation Skills

- The English language does not consistently maintain the correspondence between the written form and the spoken form.
- The English language has 26 letters but 44 sounds. Therefore some letters must account for more than one sound.
- Of these 44 sounds, 20 are vowel sounds and 24 are consonant sounds.

- The plural and past tense morphemes have different phonetic realizations depending on the final sound of the word.
- The unit that is next in hierarchy to the individual speech sound is called the syllable.
- Depending on the number of syllables, words can be classified as mono, di, tri, and polysyllabic words.
- Word accent in English is not unpredictable. Words belonging to certain patterns are accented on a particular syllable. There are a set of rules, which help to place the accent on the right syllable.
- Incorrect accentual patterns lead to unintelligible speech.
- The English language is said to be having a stress-timed rhythm, where the prominent or stressed syllables tend to occur at regular intervals of time, irrespective of the number of weak or unaccented syllables between any two accented syllables.
- The use of weak forms and contractions helps to a large extent to maintain the rhythm of the language.
- Intonation is a feature of the spoken language.
- No sentence, however carefully constructed grammatically, can convey the desired message unless it is said with the appropriate intonation. In the organization and communication of meaning, intonation is complementary to grammar. In all the three functions it performs, grammatical, attitudinal, and accentual, it conveys meaning in one sense or another.
- Syntax and intonation make significant contributions to the overall interpretation of the composite message.
- The following are some of the aids that help learn the English language in all its complexities, with special reference to pronunciation:

  a. English Pronouncing Dictionary

  b. Language Laboratory and

  c. Digital Dictionary

Presentation Skills

- Presentation is a way of communicating information and ideas to a group of people.
- The determination of the precise objective of a presentation should precede its plan, research or organization.

- The next task is to analyse the audience. You must determine as to how the objective can be achieved in the context of the particular diverse composition of audience and also identify the aims and objectives of the audience.
- The subject that conveys the main idea is the crux of the entire presentation. You should research the subject well because it lists out the results of the previous surveys and the latest developments in the area concerned. The structure of the subject also has to be organized into an introduction, body, and a conclusion.
- The worth of the message can be enhanced a hundred times if it is delivered in a crisp manner, with the right facial expression, eye contact, gestures, posture, and voice.
- Visual aids significantly improve the quality of a presentation. Some of the visual aids that can be used are:
  a. A black board
  b. Charts and real objects that can be passed around
  c. Video, film, and 35 mm slides
  d. Computer projection
  e. Overhead projection, transparencies
- After the presentation, enough time must be allotted for questions and discussion. You should generally ask open-ended questions that stimulate thinking and churn out new ideas, which in turn elicit discussions. Closed questions which ask for a one-word answer (like Yes or No) close the doors for discussions.
- Do not ask rambling ambiguous questions covering multiple issues. You could direct questions that are clear, concise, and challenging either to a group or to an individual.

Interviewing Skills

- The interview is the most important component of job search. It is a formal meeting in which the interviewer/s and interviewee ask questions, gather information, evaluate, and form an opinion about each other
- Interviewers adopt different kinds of techniques such as behavioural interview, traditional interview, serial interview, panel interview, and the stress interview.

- Interviews are held for reasons other than just selection for employment. Based on the purpose for which they are held, interviews can be classified as:

    a. Promotion interview

    b. Assessment interview

    c. Exit interview

    d. Problem interview and

    e. Employment interview

- It is not only the interviewee but also the interviewer(s) who has/have to prepare for an interview.

10

Communication: Written English

After reading this chapter, you will be familiar with:

- Aspects of writing as a communication skill
- Basics of grammar
- Vocabulary building and punctuation as sub-skills of writing as a communication skill
- The use of these sub-skills to structure academic writing

INTRODUCTION TO WRITING AS A COMMUNICATION SKILL

'Reading maketh a full man, conference a ready man, and writing an exact man', opined Francis Bacon in his famous essay entitled *Of Studies*. This axiom is indeed the motto currently. In the Internet era today when words rule the virtual space as well, the Hamlet like exasperation—'words! words! words!'—is no longer valid. In fact, your writing skills speak a lot about you these days.

Defining Writing

In other words, despite the entire contemporary visual and/or oral-aural distractions-knowing how to write and how to write well is the need of the hour, howeverboring and dull the staid skill may appear.

Apparently writing may appear 'dull' and/or difficult because, unlike speaking or listening (the skills you are to learn more about in the next chapter), it is not an innate or natural skill. Speaking or listening is inborn to the human species excluding those who are hearing disabled. In the case of the rest of us, as we grow older, we merely need to refine these skills. Writing, on the contrary, is a skill that is not inborn. We need to consciously learn it, beginning with the alphabet and proceeding through orthography, vocabulary, semantics, and syntax, till we finally reach the structuring of our message in to communicable units that begin with a paragraph, and end with a coherent and cohesive discourse. In this sense writing is a secondary skill.

As a mode of communication, writing has yet another interesting facet. We start communicating through writing at a much later stage of our intellectual development. The best empirical proof of this facet of writing would be observing a growing baby. The phenomenon would prove to you undeniably that writing occurs at a much later stage of human development. A cursory glance at the history of pedagogy from Rousseau to Piaget, too, proves to us that writing was neither the method nor the mode of transmitting knowledge. Despite the rare handcrafted manuscripts, the primary mode of production and reproduction of knowledge has always, everywhere been the oral-aural method, at least until Caxton popularized printing.

It is noteworthy that writing becomes a mode of communication only when a child enters the social sphere beyond the immediate family, that is, the school. Interesting it is hence to note that both these processes of socialization: schooling, and consequently writing, enter a child's life at the same time

So let us recapture the definition of writing. Writing, we must remember, is a unique tool of communication that is neither innate nor natural, and this secondary type of skill is acquired at a much later stage of development. Unlike speaking or listening it is a more complex tool of communication. The coordination of mental processes and physical organs involved in the actual execution of this skill is more elaborate than an action like listening. Moreover, it has to be more precise than speaking. The formality/informality binary that writing employs is far more precise than speaking.

Such a difference is more marked because, unlike speaking as a tool of communication, writing is not temporary. Communication through speaking happens and then vanishes in to thin air literally. The written mode of communication, on the contrary, is ever lasting, permanently available across the barriers of time and space. So we have to be more specific about its sub-skills that are listed below:

i. presenting ideas logically and coherently through organization and structuring of ideas;

ii. connecting sentences in a cohesive manner; and

iii. being able to communicate effectively to perform different functions of writing that range from entertainment to information.

Elements of Writing

A better understanding of these sub-skills of writing emerges once we look at the elements of writing. Writing operates at three levels; namely, word level, sentence level, and the discourse level.

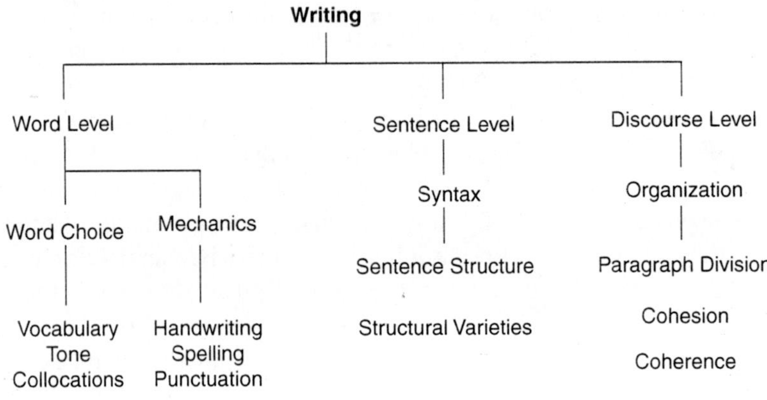

Figure 10.1
Writing Skills

These three levels are inter-related interestingly. When we communicate through writing, our choice of word is determined by the sentence construction and by the larger discourse. In fact, discourse, the largest unit of meaning, communicates the author's intention to the reader and determines the tone and the tenor of the communication. The way you would write your science textbook, for example, is totally different from the way you would pen a letter to the educational authorities for further grants. The discourses are different.

In the science textbook, for example, you would use more of the passive while you may use more of conditionals in your 'grant' letter. Your words in the science textbook may be technical while your 'grant' letter would use more business-oriented vocabulary. It is, thus, that the discourse defines communicative strategies at all the levels of writing.

Let us represent the skill of writing diagrammatically.

In other words, right from the most fundamental level, that is, the word, communicating through writing involves making choices that jell at the sentential and the discourse level, so as to enable us to convey ideas clearly and logically to our decoders.

Types of Writing

Now that we know the basic elements of writing as a communication skill, let us look at the types of writing that we use to communicate through writing. Through its tone, writing can be sub-divided as formal and informal. In the earlier section, we have already referred to this division. Let us define it properly here.

Formal writing refers to communication used in official contexts, especially when you are addressing colleagues, rank-wise higher than you in the hierarchy. Similarly, in the personal context, your writing will be formal when you are writing to decoders distantly related to you and/or decoders older than you.

Informal writing, on the contrary, is in the personal domain and is used while communicating with decoders you are close to or with decoders who are your age. Rarely used in the official context, it could be used, if at all, while communicating with colleagues you are close to.

Writing can also be sub-divided as fictional and non-fictional. Fictional writing refers to writing of novels, short stories, and poems. Non-fictional writing is what most communicators need. It consists for example of CVs, letters of application, reports, brochures, schedules, articles, or advertisements.

Non-fictional writing can be further sub-divided into five types:

i. descriptive: *describes* things/places/persons/processes

ii. expository: *explains* processes/scientific subjects/professions/functioning of institutions, industries

iii. narrative: *narrates* (that is, describes in a sequential and causal order) events/a series of events/natural phenomenon and disasters/accidents/journeys/legends/biographies

iv. reflective: *discusses* issues/abstract ideas/provides pros and cons of a debate.

v. imaginative: the encoder tries to *identify* with situations/things/people/events which (s)he might not have experienced.

You use the descriptive type while writing reports, the expository type while preparing workbooks introducing stem cell research to your students, the narrative while explaining schedules to your colleagues and/or learners, the reflective while submitting an article to a research journal, and the imaginative while making your learners explore and express possibilities.

Unique Qualities of Writing As a Communication Skill

Whichever may be the type of writing you use, writing is a special communication skill. Let us now understand the unique qualities of writing as a communication skill.

i. Let us begin with the division academia generally prefers. During your B.Ed. days, you must have learnt how to teach the four LSRW skills. In this context you must have learnt that writing is an active skill of communication. In other words, when we communicate through writing we are an agent or initiator of the act of communicating. We are not mere recipients as in reading.

ii. Reading, the passive counterpart of writing has, nevertheless, a unique role to play in refining an encoder's written message. For effective communication through writing, the encoder has to be an efficient reader. Such reading skills as previewing, skimming and scanning, and effectively using a library help a reader. In the final analysis, the encoder, who reads more, communicates better through writing. You would agree that the more you read the better is your written communication in your capacity as a teacher and as an administrator.

iii. Now let us look at the communication chain to understand yet another unique quality of writing. Communication, as you have already learnt in your earlier chapters, is a process wherein an encoder sends a message to a decoder. The encoder uses a medium via which he conveys message. Writing is unusual as a communication skill because it uses many different means to communicate this message. In addition to language an author can use visuals and graphics–diagrams, charts, graphs, and tables—to communicate well. Secondary means such as these enhance the communicative possibilities of writing. We have to remember though that these effects are often not integral to the conveying of the message. Language is primarily responsible in conveying the meaning of the written communication. The content of your message and the style you use are much more important than such visual designing which is often accused of diverting the decoder's attention—a fact we should keep in mind when we communicate as academics. It should not make us forget that of all the communication skills writing alone enjoys such a simultaneous multiplicity of media.

iv. As a communication skill writing is unusual in yet another way. When an encoder communicates through writing, we must remember that his decoder is not physically present. Yet any form of writing is clearly decoder-oriented. A reader determines the way a writer writes. When you are writing a textbook for the pre-primary kids, your content and style would radically differ from the way you would write while preparing a handbook for management trainees. The way you would write a memo to your junior colleagues would differ from the official correspondence you share with the HRD Ministry. In all these instances, the absent decoder determines the contours of your communication. Your textbook for the nursery kids, for example, would be heavy on visual effects while your handbook for the management trainees would be rich in ideas and more formal in tone.

v. Interestingly, moreover, as a communication skill, writing mixes the private and the public domains uniquely. As a communication event it exists for the eyes of the decoder only. Your learner alone is reacting in total privacy to the content you have generated but the concerns you, thus, share with him deal with the rest of the world.

vi. Such a double bind makes writing a very effective tool of communication. It is not in vain that traditional wisdom maintains that 'the pen is mightier than the sword'. A book by Fidel Castro, for example, read in the privacy of the decoder's reading environment has a more radical effect than Castro thundering on in a public meeting. In the field of academics, for example, we can refer to Paulo Freire's literacy primers to understand how writing radicalizes its decoder. In this resistant sense, writing is the only communication skill that makes, mars, and changes its decoder's personality.

Writing As an Essential Skill for an M.Ed. Trainee

As writing, thus, communicates profoundly you need to understand its relevance to communicate well in your roles as a teacher and as an administrator the duties you are going to take up in a more professional way once you are a trained teacher.

Your professional duties, both as a classroom teacher and as an able administrator, require that you write well, precisely and effectively. Hence this chapter explains to you the basics of grammatical usage, vocabulary building, punctuation, and other such mechanics of writing as well as the technicalities of writing research paper. Moreover, you will get to know how to use these sub-skills to structure lesson plans and prepare handbooks and workbooks, manage various reports, acquire strategies for reviewing projects, and produce policy statements and agendas.

GRAMMAR

Let us start at the beginning of effective and efficient writing, that is, with an overview of grammar. Grammar defines our identities linguistically. The following anecdote can prove this assertion the best.

> It was pitch dark. St. Peter was guarding the Pearly Gates to the Heaven. Past the midnight he decided to steal a wink. His conscientious daily duties denied him. A certain knock woke him up rudely. 'Who is it?' was St. Peter's usual query, albeit a bit weary. 'It is I', echoed the reply. 'Go to hell', snapped St. Peter, 'You are a teacher of English'.

In other words, effective and exact grammar (the precise pronoun 'I' instead of the colloquial 'me' in this anecdote) in its own place can make hell of a heaven. This chapter helps you to avoid such pitfalls.

Sentence Construction in English

Simple, complex, and compound are the three varieties of sentence construction in English. The basic sentence construction in English, also known in the grammar books as the simple sentence, is a very defined and rigid structure. Unlike our mother tongues English does not have case markers to define the grammatical functions of a unit of a sentence. An English sentence, hence, always has to begin with a subject, immediately followed by a verb. At times, if the verb is intransitive, the sentence may consist of only these two units ('it rains' or 'it snows' or 'all animals, even of the human species, die' are a few examples). If the verb so requires, the sentence acquires other such elements as an object, a subject complement, an adjective and an adverb. Let us look at a few examples of each of these varieties. The Glossary at the end of the book will provide you further details about these grammatical terms.

i. Subject-verb-object

   e.g., All of us need English.
   Teachers help students.
   Teachers explain grammar to students.

ii. Subject-verb-subject complement

   e.g., Dr Kalam is the President of India.
   Mr Naidu is the chief guest of the function today.

iii. Subject-verb-adjective

   e.g., Hyderabad is beautiful.
   English appears difficult.
   Duties of a school principal seem heavy.

iv. Subject-verb-adverb

   e.g., The school opens at 8 a.m.
   The students study chemistry in the laboratory.
   The teacher explains mathematics effectively.
   Students often bunk classes.

Good written communication is marked by an abundance of such simple sentences in all their varieties. An effective writer uses the required sentence structure (s-v or s-v-o) and alternates it with the other types (s-v-adj or s-v-adv) without sacrificing sense or meaning in any way. In fact, simple sentences give your writing a sense of clarity and immediacy. This is the sentence construction you should prefer in the classroom or when you are writing the teachers' handbook(s) or students' workbook(s).

Your reports, reviews, or research papers, however, need complex and compound sentences as well. A repetitive use of simple sentences alone may give such extracurricular documents a less professional look. If compound sentences help you list required details or provide alternatives or indicate the caveats to your assertions, complex sentences can enrich your professional writing with subtlety. The following examples will help you understand these statements

A compound sentence (all the three varieties) may be used in a policy statement, for example:

i. The government should introduce English at the primary stage or the learners in our state may suffer later when they compete with candidates from other states (providing an alternative).

ii. The concerned authorities may provide language laboratories in the rural areas and our students are sure to overcome their pronunciation problems (adding on details).

iii. Teachers may use all possible measures to improve the learners' written communication but they cannot ensure a total success, given the limitations, human and/or technological (indicating caveats to your assertion).

Different types of complex sentences may be used in an annual report, for example:

i. The school donated handsomely when the earthquake destroyed the normal life in Gujarat.

ii. Whenever a science exhibition is organized within the twin cities, our brilliant and enthusiastic students participate in it to win a few more laurels for us.

iii. If we strive hard, we are sure to win.

The other sentence construction that you may need is the 'empty it' or the 'empty there' construction. The grammatical subject in such a sentence is a dummy subject. Hence, it is known as the 'empty' construction. It is very useful to objectively present information or opinions. Let us look at some examples that you may use in your reports.

> It is appreciable that our students are taking up water conservation projects.
> It is a worthy experiment. There is a need to encourage it.

In addition, a good writer at times uses infinitival and gerundive constructions as well as such transformations as passive or conditionals or so-that or not only-but also to add variety to his writing. A word of caution, however, is that an excessive use of passive, though Indians use it rather fondly, is a stylistic blemish. In fact, passive is preferably used for certain such registers as science, commerce, banking, and management.

Object–Verb Concord

Whichever sentence type you may choose to use, the subject–verb concord is very essential to good written English. Such sentences as 'you know it very well' or 'they goes home early too often', or 'he ready to work late' are just not permissible in good written English. Hence let us briefly look at the major principles of subject–verb concord.

i. Basically, if the subject (a noun/a pronoun) is singular, the verb has to be singular. If the subject is plural, the verb, too, must be plural.

   e.g., A student performs well if his teachers teach sincerely.

ii. A verb agrees with the subject, not its complement.

   e.g., During the journey at night in those deserts, our only guide was the stars.

   The stars were our only guide at night.

iii. When two singular nouns used together refer to the same person or thing or are practically synonymous or jointly express a single idea, the verb is singular.

   e.g., Dr Kalam, the President and scientist, is an ideal of the youngsters today. His power and influence is very great. Idli and sambar is his favourite breakfast.

iv. If a collective noun used as a subject shows some internal division, use the plural form of the verb; otherwise, the singular.

   e.g., The School committee is divided in their opinion on the issue of capitation fee.

   The Indian cricket team at times actually plays professionally.

v. If a plural noun indicates a specific quality or amount considered as a unit, the verb is singular.

   e.g., Ten thousand rupees per annum is not a large sum to pay if you want to join our school.

   Three parts of the chapter is almost complete.

   Two kilometers is not a long distance marathon.

vi. In 'not-only-but-also' construction, the verb agrees with the noun immediately preceding it.

   e.g., Not only the teacher but also all the students were irritated with his boorish behaviour.

Not only the students but also the teacher was laughing at him.

vii. (N)either-(n)or requires a singular verb though the noun nearest to the verb defies its number, that is, whether it should be singular or plural.

e.g., Either a car or an auto is passing by. The racket it is making is unbelievable.

Neither the principal nor his colleagues in the committee are ready to help you.

Either he or I am in the wrong.

Neither you nor your friends come on time.

viii. 'Each' and 'every' require a singular verb.

e.g., Each of our students is an unpolished gem.

Every teacher in our school is sincere.

ix. 'None' is singular but is followed by a plural verb if plurality is implied.

e.g., None (but fools) have ever believed this pet nonsense.

None ill-treat her worse than her teachers.

x. 'Many a' + singular noun + singular verb is the correct sentence construction.

e.g., Many a gem of purest ray serene is lost.

xi. The verb is plural if you wish to express a wish or a supposition.

e.g., If wishes were horses, many Indian students would ride away to America.

I wish I were the principal.

These are some of the basic principles of the very necessary subject–verb concord that is central to good communication in English, whether written or spoken. But the S–V concord, or the lack thereof, can make or mar the impression of written English.

Using Articles Correctly

As important as the S–V concord are the articles. As our mother tongues lack an explicit surface level realization of articles we often forget them in English also. Such a mistake is unpardonable though. Hence let us look at the basic principles of article usage.

i. Use 'a' for every common, countable, singular noun.

e.g., A teacher helps a student maintain a yearly register.

ii. Use 'an' for a common, countable, singular noun if it begins with a vowel sound.

e.g., Let me give you an example.

iii. Use 'the'

a. with a common, countable, singular noun if it has a specific reference.

e.g., The student in the corner is not paying attention.

b. with uncountable nouns, if specific.

e.g., The Camlin ink is the best.

c. with plural nouns, if specific.

e.g., The students in the morning session are very committed.

d. with unique phenomena.

e.g., the sun, the moon, the earth, the Taj Mahal

e. with abbreviations.

e.g., the USA, the UNICEF

f. with superlative forms of adjectives/adverbs.

e.g., The nicest student in my class is the one most harassed.

iv. Whenever words such as school, college, hospital, temple, church, mosque, market, prison, or bed are used in their primary sense, do not use any article.

e.g., My son goes to school early in the morning.

v. Use a/an when you mean one.

e.g., I have a son and a daughter.

vi. Do not use any article when you refer to materials.

e.g., Glass is brittle.

Wood is expensive.

vii. Use 'the' with musical instruments.

e.g., Many South Indians play the violin very well.

Mastering these principles would make your written English appear faultless though it would benefit you to look up for more practice.

Prepositions

Prepositions are tiny but they pose mighty problems when Indians attempt speaking or writing in English. They are the Waterloo of many an Indian writer. Basically, prepositions show relationships of space, time, relation, or direction. Here we can consider only a few examples, given the space constraints though actually prepositions are a vast subject-area.

i. 'On' indicates a specific day. (e.g., On Sunday he celebrates his birthday.)
ii. 'In' indicates a period of time. (e.g., In 1999 he was in the States.)
iii. 'During' indicates a period of time defined by precise boundaries, (e.g., Cell phones are not allowed during the exam.)
iv. 'At' indicates a specific point of time. (e.g., The lecture starts at 7 a.m.)
v. 'On time' refers to the exact hour, on the dot. (e.g., The English always arrive on time.)
vi. 'In time' means before the specific activity ends. (e.g,. You must join the school prayer on time and not in time.)
vii. 'In good time' means sooner or later, (e.g., He will improve in good time.)

These very prepositions mean differently in the spatial context. Let us look at how their meaning changes in the spatial context.

i. 'In' indicates volume, (e.g., in the classroom, in your lunch box)
ii. 'On' indicates a surface, (e.g., Our teacher loved to jump on the table whenever his explanation reached a frenzied pitch.)
iii. 'At' indicates in the vicinity of (e.g., They met at the gate and chatted a little.)

Endless is the list of such usage. Space constraints limit us from exploring this vast area. You must remember though that you must never ever use the vincorrect expression 'at the backside (of)'. Use instead 'behind' or 'at the back of.

Remember always that 'between' refers to two co-ordinates while 'among' refers to more than two. (e.g., Between the morning prayers and the lunch, students get a small break. Among all the sciences, Maths appears the most difficult to school children.)

Never ever forget the 'since'/'for' difference. 'Since' is used if the reference is to a specific point in past while 'for' refers to some undefined period,

(e.g., Since 1999, our school has been winning this trophy. For ten years our students have topped the SSC merit list.)

Prepositional or phrasal verb is another area you must practise well. Prepositional verbs are made of a verb and a preposition. For example, 'call up' is a prepositional verb and is made of two elements, the verb 'call' and the preposition 'up'. Its unique meaning (make a telephone call) goes beyond the individual meanings of each of its constituents. Such verbs add a smart look to you English, especially the spoken variety.

For example, 'You can telephone me' sounds pompous but 'you can ring me up' appears far friendlier. Similarly, instead of 'extinguishing the tube light', it is better to 'switch it off and then 'switch it on' when you need it.

Oxford Advanced Learners' Dictionary (OALD) is your best guide to such verb usage. Along with the verb entry itself, the OALD provides you with each of its phrasal variants. The actual examples, abundantly provided, make it easy for you to remember the list.

In fact, one of your projects for your senior students could deal with specific phrasal alias prepositional verbs, preferably needed for a specific theme. For example, your students can make a list of such verbs needed in the lab. Such an exercise is sure to hone your students' use of prepositions as well.

Modals

If prepositions give your English a 'propah' look, modals make it 'pukka' professional. Modals are auxiliary (that is, helping) verbs that indicate the mood of a speaker, e.g., 'Can I come in' is more informal, but 'May I come in?' is very formal.

Similarly, 'it may rain' indicates a strong possibility but 'there could be water on Mars' indicates a dim chance about which the writer is not very sure.

These different shades of meaning are conveyed through the use of such modals as 'may', 'can', 'could', etc. Effective use of modals, in brief, is essential for efficient written communication.

Given the constraints of space here, we can look at the basic modals, though we suggest that you should consult the books listed in the bibliography to acquire a good command over use of modals in your communication, both written and/or oral.

Here is a tabular representation that would help you remember the modals. Do remember, please, that when we use the modals as auxiliaries, the main verb should be in its basic, dictionary form. For example,

i. He can teach German and Japanese.
ii. The PM might grace the occasion of our school anniversary.
iii. The managing committee could grant two more appointments.

Here the main verb, 'teach', 'grace', or 'grant', does not change, if you have noticed it. Do keep this grammatical axiom in mind while using modals. Box 10.1 below will help you gain an overview of modals.

Box 10.1: Overview of Modals

Can

i. have the ability
   She can teach the sciences as well as English.
ii. permission
   You can't go out this evening.
iii. possibility
   The student can improve if he works hard.
iv. request
   Can l come in?

Could

i. past ability
   Raman could tackle any difficult sum by the time he was ten years old.
ii. polite request
   Could you attend the meeting please?
iii. dim possibility
   Our student could top the merit list next year.

Be able to ability in the present ('be' changes to 'am', 'is', 'are') or past ('be' becomes 'was', 'were') or future ('will be', 'shall be')
The child was able to adjust to the school within a week.
We are able to provide a computer per student .
They will be able to lift the elocution trophy this year.
Please remember:
Never write 'can able to. It is wrong and must be avoided.

Must indicates compulsion.
You must attend the lectures regularly

(Continued)

Box 10.1 (Continued)

Have to	indicates compulsion, but it is less obligatory. You have to stand up and greet the Dean when he enters the classroom.'
Should	indicates a moral duty. You should intimate the office if you are going on leave.
Ought to	indicates an ethical oblication You ought to treat your teachers with respect

May

i. indicates giving and asking for permission in a formal way.

   You may leave now.

   May I come in?

ii. a possibility.

   The Principal may attend me important meeting tomorrow.

This list, please remember, is by no means complete and we earnestly request you to consult the books listed in the bibliography.

Miscellaneous Errors

We have so far looked at the aspects of grammar that have been with us ever since we started learning English. However, beyond such usage and grammar rules we have to be aware of some subtle niceties of usage and grammar that, otherwise, can make our writing appear to be a very inefficient communication. In this unit, we are going to look at few of such miscellaneous errors. Once again we suggest strongly that you should consult H.W. Fowler's 'A Dictionary of Modem English Usage', in addition to the books listed in the Bibliography, if you want your written communication to be truly effective. Given the limitations of space, here we can collate only a few.

i. Use 'apostrophe's' (boy's) only for animate nouns, especially human beings.

   e.g., Never say 'The book's cover is nice'.

ii. With inanimate things, use the 'of' form.

   e.g., The cover of the book is nice.

   The diagram of the wheel is neatly labelled.

iii. Never use 'according to me'. Instead write 'in my opinion'. In fact, avoid the 'I' reference. Instead use the 'let us' or 'one feels' format. In written communication excessive use of 'I' can make your communication sound pompous.

iv. Remember, please, your students never 'give an examination'! They 'take an examination' or they 'appear for an examination'.

v. Remember you 'reply to' a person and/or a letter but you 'answer' a telephone call or a letter.

vi. If you 'speak to' your colleagues it would imply that you are doing all the speaking. If you 'speak with' them, it means you believe in a dialogue; you prefer a conversation to a monologue that could be admonishing in nature.

vii. Similarly, you never 'write the Minister of Education'. Rather, you 'write to the Minister of Education'.

viii. Remember please that 'a book comprises five chapters' but it 'consists of five chapters'.

ix. Use 'say' to refer to a person's actual words or in an indirect sentence.

e.g., The President said, 'Children must dream'.

But use 'tell' when the indirect sentence has an indirect object.

e.g., The Principal told the striking students to disperse immediately.

Remember the Table 10.1 for idiomatic usage of 'say' versus 'tell'.

e.g., Never write to a publisher: 'say us the price of the volume'. Write instead, 'tell us the price of the volume', or better still, 'let us know the price of the volume'.

x. 'Make' refers to constructing or manufacturing something while 'do' suggests accomplishing a thing. So you cannot 'make exercise', please. Similarly, your students do not 'do noise'. Rather they 'make noise' in the classroom. Table 10.2 once again lists the common usage of 'make' and 'do'.

Table 10.1 The Idiomatic Usage of 'Say' Versus 'Tell'

Say	Tell
say one's prayers	tell the truth/a lie
say so	tell a story
say no more	tell the time
say a good word for	tell a secret
	tell the price
	tell one's name

Table 10.2 Common Usages of 'Make' and 'Do'

Make	Do
make a mistake	do good
make a speech	do one's best
make a promise	do one a favour
make an excuse	do wrong
make haste	do a lesson
make fun of	do a problem
make progress	do business
make an experiment	do exercises

Such minor errors can ruin your written communication. Given the constraints of space, here we have collated only the 'top ten'. But if you avoid these, remarkably clear would be your written communication.

Sentence Clarity: Mistakes to Avoid

For good written communication, grammar alone does not help though. Grammar can help you with parts of speech, their usage, and so on. What you need in addition is appropriate communication. Hence, here we collate a brief discussion of factors that affect sentence clarity. If you follow these principles, your written communication would be able to convey clearly your message to its receiver, that is, your decoder.

i. Avoid incomplete sentences.

   Sentence fragments suit the advertising discourse alone. If your written communication has too many of these, it will not be effective either for your learners or for your colleagues.

ii. Do not pack into a sentence two or more unrelated ideas.

   e.g., His brother was a sturdy fellow, and he was a good sprinter.

   Who is a good sprinter here? The brother? He? Avoid such confusion.

iii. Avoid choppy sentences.

   e.g., 'Naidu read our invitation. He visited our school. He saw for himself the efficacy of the Froebel method. He praised us to skies.' Such chopped and cut-n-dried sentences make reading a tedious job. Avoid them. Instead write, 'As per our invitation, Naidu visited our school and praised our efforts to introduce the Froebel method of education'.

iv. Avoid rambling sentences that are put together with umpteen 'and's', 'or's', 'if s', 'but's', 'not only but also's' and never end!

v. Use parallel grammatical forms for parallel ideas. Pair nouns with nouns; adjectives with adjectives; and phrases with phrases, etc..

e.g., Do not write a sentence such as 'the new textbook offers ease of classroom interaction, less costly and it is easily available'. Rather write, 'the new textbook offers easy classroom interaction, pocket-friendly price and ready availability'. In this sentence, we have consistently used 'adj + noun' to list on details.

Please remember that this principle makes your writing precise and appropriate.

vi. Please remember that a modifier must immediately precede the word it modifies. Otherwise, it can cause unintended mirth!

e.g., 'My first wife's job' is not the same as 'My wife's first job'.

vii. Avoid split infinitives, please.

Never write as follows:

'We tried to quickly and economically issue the needed laboratory material.'

Here, between the 'to' and the 'verb', there are unnecessary insertions. Avoid such a usage. Very rarely it gets used to emphasize an idea.

viii. Avoid wordy expressions.

Don't say, 'I have been wondering if you have found yourself in a position to consider our request'.

Say instead, 'Please consider our request'.

Here are some wordy expressions often used and the preferred parallel expressions.

Table 10.3 Verbose and Preferred Expressions

Wordy/Verbose	Preferred
I would appreciate it if	Pleased…
In the month of June...	In June…
It has come to our attention that	–
It is interesting to note that	–
In the event that	If
At the present time	Now
On condition that	If
Are of the opinion that	Believe that
In as much as	For/since

ix. Why use repetitive expressions? Why say, for example, 'It is audible to the ear' or 'completely unanimous', or 'more better', or 'totally perfect', or 'join together', or 'this afternoon at 3 p.m.', or 'most unique'? It is sheer sloppy writing and must be avoided.

x. Arrange your sentences in such a way that the initial idea gets your reader's least attraction and your sentence progresses to the most important final idea.

e.g., 'Some of my professors have been bad, some excellent, some indifferent, some fair' should be re-written as 'Some of my professors have been bad, some indifferent, some fair, and some excellent'.

VOCABULARY

In the last example, you must have noticed that the word power seemed to control the sentence construction. Often words are the lords of all they survey in a sentence. Hence, vocabulary is like a diamond mine. The more you cut and polish your unshaped jewels, the brighter they would be. Hence in this unit, let us '*better*' understand words.

Principles of Word Making

Words are the backbone of communication. Especially our written communication can never be precise unless our vocabulary, that is, our word power is well-stocked, yet fresh.

To make newer, more effective words for precise writing:

1. Often two or simple words are compounded/joined together.

   e.g., 'nonetheless', 'undertake', 'quicksilver', 'blackboard', 'green house', 'hot house', 'cut-throat', 'dare-devil'.

2. Often prefixes are attached to the root to form words.

   e.g., ante (before) + date = antedate

   a (indifferent to) + theist = atheist

   arch (main) + bishop = archbishop

3. Similarly suffixes can be placed after the base of the word to get new derived usages.

   e.g., demon → demonic → demonically → demonize

   With one singular noun 'demon', we, thus, get an adjective (demonic), an adverb (demonically) and a verb (demonize).

4. Often words came into existence through acronyms

   e.g., The UNICEF helps disadvantaged learners.

5. Sometimes two words merge to form a new vocabulary item.

   e.g., breakfast + lunch = brunch

   teleprinter + exchange = telex

Such procedures help us understand our learners addicted to the SMS lingo! Any good grammar book, such as the ones listed in the Bibliography, would give you more examples. So look up these books to make your written communication smarter. Table 10.4 gives a list of useful prefixes

Table 10.4 Some Useful Prefixes

ambi – both	trans – across
ante – before	intra – inside
anti – against	inter – among
contra – against	in – not
post – after	

Synonyms

For your immediate reference though, make it a habit to consult Roget's *Thesaurus* often. This volume gives you synonyms that are listed as per a concept. Moreover, Roget also provides derivation-based variants of his synonyms. Incidentally, MS-Word-based or 'compu' dictionaries (known as digital dictionaries) is yet another source to locate the exact word. If your learners are computer savvy, do insist on their using such a technological tool so that they write the exact word precisely, without any bombast.

Synonyms indeed help our written communication. They show our control over subtlety of expression because very few languages has two exactly similar words. So if we know a lot of synonyms, we can choose the right one to indicate precisely our meaning as well as our prejudices/opinions.

e.g., 'It is a thin volume' and 'it is a slim volume' indicate two different attitudes to the volume. 'Thin' indicates distaste, while its synonym 'slim' is more positive in implication.

Do use synonyms intelligently. That will add poise and grace to your precise writing. But do not indulge in malapropism in the process, please. Malapropism refers to misusing big-sounding words. For example, saying 'destruct' instead of 'deduct' is malapropism. Please avoid such usage.

Antonyms

The table entitled 'Some Useful Prefixes' listed some prefixes. Now look at the following two words:

Sym + pathy
Anti + pathy

These two words are antonyms. See the way they are formed. It might help you prepare on your very own list of antonyms. 'Family Word Finder' published by the Reader's Digest is a rich resource, in addition to the OALD or its digital variant, to understand and use antonyms. Such reference books stocked in your school library would make your own as well as your learners' written communication more effective. An interesting way to make your learners, thus, take interest in their vocabulary growth would be to ask them prepare lists of specialized terms, relating to 'mania', 'phobias', different '-ologies' and '-graphies' so as to make them understand the value (and the wealth of) of a precise word.

As you must know, we have two types of vocabulary—'active' and 'passive'. 'Active' vocabulary is the limited repertoire for our ready usage. 'Passive' vocabulary forms the deep resources that we can tap if we truly want to communicate well through writing.

Antonyms (words with opposite meanings) mostly form a part of our passive vocabulary. Truly, most human beings love to criticize others and the more powerful they are, the merrier they are while indulging in such an activity. The comments we, as teachers, write on our helpless learners' notebooks/answer sheets, the nasty nothings we, as administrators, uncharitably express about our colleagues' (especially the junior ones) work show how much we need antonyms.

In English, we have certain antonyms which are formed at the root level itself, e.g., 'bad', 'evil'. Often, though, an antonym is formed through prefixing. 'Dis' (disrespectful), 'anti' (antipathy), and 'a' (atheist) are some of the examples of this process.

For effective communication through writing, it helps to have a good repertoire of antonyms. One of the assignments we can give to our learners is asking them to make a list of negative prefixes (for example, 'un', 'in', 'im') with some examples of words they can be affixed to. Such an assignment will help them understand how English is an interesting language when it comes to the pronunciation–spelling mismatch.

Homonyms

Homonyms form one such unit of the English language exhibiting the pronunciation–spelling mismatch

A homonym is a word identical with another word as far as the spelling and pronunciation go. It differs though from the other word in origin and meaning. In fact, you can, thus, help your learners note the etymological growth and development of words.

e.g., Our three words 'synonym', 'antonym' and 'homonym' have 'nym' as the root to which prefixes ('syn', 'anti' as 'anto' and 'homo') are affixed to create new words.

Homonyms provide us many examples of such vocabulary processes. Here is a list of some homonyms, which you would immediately notice, often perform two different grammatical functions.

E.g.,

i. bear (n) = an animal
ii. bear (v) = carry, endure
iii. or bar (n) = a rod
iv. bar (v) = to prevent
v. or cross (n) = the Christian symbol of piety
vi. cross (v) = to go across

Table 10.5 Homonyms: Some Examples

fere (n)	= passage money	
fare (n)	= eatables	
light (n)	= natural radiation making things visible	
light (adj)	= not heavy	
light (v)	= to strike a match to get fire.	
Here are a few more homonyms. Understand how they differ in form and function and meanings.		
saw (n) (v)	practice (n) (v)	table (n) (v)
plant (n) (v)	march (n) (v)	part (h) (v)

Words Often Confused

Given the mismatch between spellings and pronunciation English words suffer from further confusion due to the same vocabulary item performing many grammatical functions, often novitiate writers tend to confuse words.

'Whether'–'weather' is a famous pair that exemplifies such a pitfall. Another such notorious example is 'principle'–'principal'. In this pair, the second item, if you notice it, performs two grammatical functions as a noun and an adjective.

Hence, for effective writing, we need to prepare for ourselves such lists which often are a blind spot for every communicator. Here we provide a few examples. Add your own favourites to form a list of words often (not to be) confused.

Table 10.6 Noun–Adjective Pairs

Herd/heard	Plane/plain
Piece/peace	Allowed/aloud
Counsel/council	Sight/site
Fair/fare	Brake/break
Birth/berth	Prey/pray
Week/weak	Hole/whole
Floor/flour	Taste/test
Weak/week/wick	Pure/pour/poor
Heir/hair/hare	Later/letter/latter
Wonder/Wander	Patrol/petrol
Advice/advise	Bath/bathe
Leave/live	Use/use (n/v)
Quite/quiet	Princes/princess
Price/prise	Compliment/complement
Lose/loose	Medal/meddle
Affect/effect	Prophesy/prophecy
Stationary/stationery	Dependent/dependant
Licence/license	Disease/decease
Difference/deference	Assent/ascent
Illicit/eliicit	Eminent/imminent
Illusion/allusion	President/precedent
Resource/recourse	Disquisition/inquisition

You must have wondered why we have gone into such details of vocabulary acquisition and vocabulary cognition. Use of effective vocabulary makes our written communication precise and moreover, it gets the right tone; formal or informal friendly or distant, approving or disapproving. In other words, if our vocabulary is proper, we never have to regret to the effect 'what was well-thought but never well-taught or well-expressed'.

In addition, it helps us while preparing study material. For example, when we prepare vocabulary exercises we can grade them, we can explain them (including the origin of the woed and/or the change in the meaning of a word over time) better if we know some basic principles of vocabulary acquisition.

In our own academic writing, moreover, we can choose the right density of vocabulary, thereby making our written communication effective. If we know vocabulary acquisition rules, we would tend to use:

1. the right amount of content words (noun, adjective, adverb, verb);

2. the precise density of structural/functional words (for example articles or prepositions) for making the sentence grammatically complete;
3. active words that help our decoders immediately grasp the idea.

In brief, we so adopt and select words that we choose words that communicate and we prefer words that help our decoder visualize the content. Our communication, thus, becoming less and less ambiguous, our writing becomes a pleasure for our decoders.

PUNCTUATION

Now that we know how to string effective words together meaningfully, let us look at the mechanics of writing that make our communication further easier to grasp for our decoders.

Punctuation indeed plays a major part in making writing easy to grasp. In his book, entitled *Spoken and Written English* (Oxford University Press, 1989), the great linguist M.A.K. Halliday maintains that punctuation, or the mechanics of writing, has the following functions:

i. Marking the boundary, e.g., a comma marks off a phrase, a list, etc.
ii. Marking the status, e.g., a full-stop or an exclamation mark at the end of a sentence decides its status as a statement or an exclamation.
iii. Marking relationship, e.g., a hyphen suggests that a word is a compound word or the apostrophe's' explains what belongs to whom.

In other words, punctuation as the mechanics of writing gives our writing a spoken clarity and intonation/stress effect. Hence, let us try to understand here the major punctuation marks and their basic usage. Do look up the books in the Bibliography for more details.

Capitalization

i. Capitalize the first alphabet of the word after a full stop.

   e.g., She was happy. Her happiness reflected itself in her very being.
ii. Always capitalize 'I'.
iii. Acronyms are often capitalized.

   e.g., The UNICEF helps disadvantaged children.
iv. Capitalize proper nouns, that is, the names of places, people, countries, for example.

Full Stop

Use a full stop

i. at the end of a statement.

e.g., He answered your call. You must call back.

ii. in abbreviations.

e.g., 'Feb.', 'e.g.', 'p.m.'

iii. in internet based e-mail addresses.

e.g., www.yahoo.com

Comma

Use a Comma

i. to separate words in a list. But never use a comma when you end your list with 'and...'

e.g., I read Dickens, Hardy, Trilling, and Chekov.

ii. to separate phases or clauses.

e.g., If you work hard, you are sure to win.

iii. before and after a phrase or a clause that gives additional, non-essential information about the noun it describes.

e.g. The Abids shopping area, which is very expensive, is beautiful at night, what with its neon lights.

iv. to separate an introductory word or phrase or an adverbial phrase defining the word sentence.

e.g., As it happens, however, I have never met the president.

v. to separate a tag question.

e.g., She works sincerely, doesn't she?

vi. before a short quotation.

Shakespeare wrote, 'Frailty, thy name is woman.'

Colon

Use a colon

i. to introduce a list of items.

We have four possibilities: win-win, win-lose, lose-win, and lose-lose.

ii. in formal writing, use it before a clause or a phrase that gives more information the main clause. Often a full stop is used in such a context instead of a colon.

e.g., 'The repatriation issue has been neglected for a long time; it has got blown out of proportion, and has become dangerous.'

iii. to introduce a longer quotation that needs indenting.

e.g., As Wordsworth writes:

'I wondered lonely as a cloud/that floats on hills..........'

Question Marks

Use this punctuation mark

i. at the end of a direct question.

e.g., What is your name?

ii. Never use a question mark at the end of an indirect question.

e.g., I asked him if he needed my help.

iii. Never use it at the end of a statement. That would mean your own statement is getting questioned as a valid statement.

iv. Use a question, in other words, if you are doubtful about facts.

e.g., Geoffrey Chaucer (1453–?)

Exclamation Mark

Use this punctuation mark

i. at the end of a sentence that expresses a strong emotion.

e.g., Wow! What a lovely evening!

ii. in informal writing, use it before a question mark to show strong doubt.

e.g., 'Triplets!?' (The implication here is that it is impossible.)

Apostrophe

Use 's' to indicate

i. possession by animate beings, especially human beings.

e.g., the king's orders

ii. in short forms to show that same letters (or numbers) in between have been omitted

e.g., it's = it is.

I'm = I am

the summer at '42 = the summer of 1942

iii. to indicate with an 's' the plural of letter, a figure or an abbreviation.

e.g., mind your p's and q's, during the 1990's.

Quotation Marks

Use quotation marks

i. to indicate that the words following or preceding form direct speech.

e.g., 'Why did you come late?', he asked.

She answered, 'I was held up in the traffic'.

ii. to show that a certain expression is special.

e.g., 'National security' is quoted whenever cross-border terrorism gets discussed.

iii. to indicate titles of literary works.

e.g., Keats' 'Ode to Autumn'

Italics

Use Italics

i. to show emphasis.

e.g., *You* are answerable; not I.

ii. to indicate titles of books, newspapers.

e.g., I read *The Times* daily

iii. to indicate non-English words.

e.g., The poor can now build a *pukka* house.

iv. to indicate your creatively concocted words, jargon et al.

e.g., Her *in-between*'s made the meeting lively.

CLASSROOM-ORIENTED WRITTEN COMMUNICATION

Now that we have looked at the basic factors underlying written communication and are aware of the necessary details regarding its mechanics, let us look at how we can channelize this data towards writing that is academics-oriented.

In your future career you will have to write certain academic and/or official documents. In the remaining part of the chapter, we are going to explain how to communicate effectively through writing.

Let us begin with the basics. Please remember that good, effective communication through writing pre-supposes clear thinking. Only if you have thought through an issue to its last details, you can write effectively. Otherwise, your writing tends to lack coherence and appears very jumpy and illogical.

Next, good written communication requires thorough research. While speaking we can get away with a casual approach to the issue but when we put it in black and white, the lack of sincere research shows very glaringly.

Hence, often it is argued that for good writing, you require a six-point programme:

i. **Brain storming** to arrive at a precise definition and a statement of the theme to be dealt with. You can do this kind of exercise of mapping out points on loose sheets of paper by yourself.

ii. **Collecting data** through research.

iii. **Planning** the actual document, its lay-out and final shape.

iv. **Putting** the pen to paper.

v. **Editing** your draft for grammar punctuation, spelling, and consistency.

vi. **Revising,** it necessary.

Good communicators use every draft as a stage in the process of writing and not as a final or finished product. It indeed helps to determine in advance the length of your written communication because you can arrange and organize and explain your points accordingly.

Basically, good written communication requires a unity of effect. We can achieve it if our writing has a clear progression of the beginning—middle—end variety.

It has been observed that an effective beginning, made attractive through a quote/ an anecdote/ a process provides the 'get set, go' effect, a crisp start, is precisely the need of good communication.

The middle part of the communication should contain all the solid data that is coherently stated through cohesive devices such as 'therefore', 'so,' 'here', 'as a result' (to indicate cause-effect relationship), 'moreover', 'in addition' (to show adding of supplementary details), 'or', 'on the contrary', 'on the other hand', 'nevertheless', (to show contrast) and 'on the whole', 'in brief' (to sum up), etc.

Your conclusion should summarize the writing and indicate future possibilities, if any. Please remember that you can start your argument in the middle. In other words, you need not always begin with the beginning.

For example, you may want to state a case history, analyse it in detail, and then come to your theme statement that you would have otherwise stated in the beginning.

In other words, good writing shuttles back and forth through analysis on the basis of its certain premises. In other words, you can write deductively or inductively. Deductive writing would indicate an analysis of facts, data, and case histories to arrive at a conclusion while inductive writing means you state an axiom and exemplify it in the rest of your argument. Use either of these styles. You can even blend them for effect.

Please remember that your argument should be structured in paragraphs that a reader can manage comfortably. Solid chunks of information bound together into a monolit, terrorize more than an atom bomb. Every paragraph should have a theme statement and its relationship with the theme statements of other paragraphs should feed into the overall argument of the entire piece of writing.

Precise vocabulary and a gentle tone with a firm purpose (with a dash of humour, if possible) make your communication a delight for your decoder.

Please remember that in good formal writing, a sentence should never begin with 'and', 'but', 'for example', 'or', 'moreover', etc. These days with times that are a-changing such rules of usage are getting lax, but a good writer prefers not to abandon them.

Now that we have looked at the basic principles of good written communication, let us briefly deal with some classroom-oriented written communication that is sure to form part of your academic career. Here we can provide mere suggestions given the spatial limitations. Try to develop these through looking up the books listed in the Bibliography. Try and write out, at least as first drafts, each of the items we are going to talk about. Practice makes man perfect when it comes to written communication.

Box 10.2: Tips for Effective Writing

- Be direct and explicit. Remember, nobody has the time to unravel the relevance and significance of your jig-saw puzzles.
- Do not waste too many lines 'introducing' yourself.
- Before writing you should have outlined the entire structure of your writing. Stick to it.

(Continued)

Box 10.2 (Continued)

- Deal with one relevant issue per paragraph. Don't cram in too many ideas in a paragraph.
- Don't provide too many appendices and/or footnotes. Build all this information into your writing.
- Your presentation should be effective. The page should present a neat, clean legible look.
- Write several versions if necessary, of your material. *Revision* helps.
- Copyedit your writing to avoid spelling, punctuation, and grammatical mistakes.

Structuring Lesson Plans

Whether you are sketching an outline or jotting down points for a content subject (for example, history, geography, mathematics) or a skill subject (for example, language studies), effective teaching needs a lesson plan.

It helps to think of the lesson plan as a planned audio-visual presentation. It is useful hence to divide the information into three stages:

i. **Pre-teaching** activities that make the learner curious and oriented towards the main topic or the actual lesson he/she deals with. Often, these activities consist of a quick-fire round of question-answer series. You should write out at the planning stage all possible questions and all probable answers.

   At times, pre-teaching consists of activities that are framed as leads. In such a case, you have to plan the lesson in such a way that either you yourself as the teacher (or the learners' reactions) lead to the main argument. You could tell half the story, for example, and ask your learners to complete it and then start your teaching working through these reactions.

ii. During the **actual teaching**, it is necessary to plan in such a way that the multiplicity of media that we talked of in Chapter 5 is used to the utmost advantage. Please see to it that the entire data is dealt with through stages that you cohesively link though markers such as 'now my next point is', 'my third observation deals with', and so on. The learners, thus, understand the progression of the argument. It is the teacher's duty to plan these activities in such an ordered way during the structuring of the lesson plan.

iii. During the **post-teaching interaction,** sum up and further open up to questioning, the data presented in the lesson.

In brief, the structure of a lesson plan should look as follows:

Table 10.7 Structure of a Lesson Plan

	Stage	Time Required	Activities Involved	Audio-visual Aids
i.	Pre-teaching	20 minutes	1. question-answer 2. reading by learners	flash cards black board
ii.	Teaching	25 minutes	1. reading by teacher	textbook, slides
iii.	Post-teaching	5 minutes	1. summing up through question-answers	cue cards

Please remember that this is a rough outline and you can individuate it as you like it; but it does help preparing a lesson plan in this fashion. During your B.Ed. training, you must have undertaken assignments during which you wrote out each and every individual question-answer. Once you are good at it, you need not go to such lengths. However much your experience be, it is necessary, nevertheless, to structure your lecture in advance.

It is a good practice, moreover, to maintain a diary in which you evaluate yourself against every detail. Such a process helps you find at your lacunae, work on them, and improve your performance as a teacher.

Such diary entries are often written out as bullet points as elucidated in Table 10.8:

Table 10.8 Planning a Diary Entry

Date:	pre-teaching time was not sufficient.
Time:	students did not get the hang of the idea.
Topic:	questions appeared superfluous to them; they took too much time re-arranging themselves into groups.

Preparing Teacher's Handbooks/Students' Workbooks

The contemporary models of teaching believe that a textbook, often prepared by a board that may not have the requisite academic leaning/qualifications/interests, may not be sufficient as a teaching/learning aid. Hence, often teacher's handbooks and students' workbooks are prepared as additional teaching/learning aids. The proliferation of 'special purpose' courses further necessitates such a move.

The *Teacher's Handbook* gives tips to the teacher for effective teaching. When you are scripting such a teacher's handbook, see to it that it is self-sufficient. A teacher without any further training (which is welcome, if possible) should manage to use this extra resource.

It is necessary, hence, to provide clear indications in a teacher's handbook about how to use it, about how it should supplement, and how to extend the textbook.

It is essential to provide numerous graded activities listed out in detail. These should make both teaching and reading enjoyable for the experimenting teacher.

Your handbook should have clear indications regarding how to go about the graded activities and how actually to use them.

Your units should not be too lengthy and should address a given point through every possible related activity, e.g., if your handbook deals with 'hotel management English', there could be a unit on 'taking calls'. List out all possible responses; create situations to give your learners to actually try them out.

Your handbook, which covers all related skills, should structure each unit into 'teaching points', 'expressions to learn', 'structures to practice', 'activities', for example.

It helps your reader if you provide an answer key as well. Your handbook, thus, becomes a self-instructional material.

Make your handbook very communicative and try to grade activities, specifying the level and the stage when it should be introduced and how.

In other words, your fellow teacher staying miles away from you should find in your handbook a friend, a guide, and a philosopher who encourages him to think and experiment more, and on his own.

Students' Workbooks are visually more effective. Often they are clearly situation-oriented, even for content subjects. They provide a series of activities mostly with a key. As an author you are supposed to explain difficult vocabulary, concepts, and structures as the pre-lesson preparation. Most importantly of all, your student's workbook must be photo-copiable. Students require this kind of freedom. A big, fat bound book may terrorize them and will dissuade them into thinking that it is yet another textbook. Content-rich but entertaining is the nutshell definition of a students' workbook that often has many grids, tables as fill-in-the-blank activities.

Essentially a supplement to the course book, it reduces knowledge bits into simple, suitable bytes. So make your instructions very clear and precise. Give extra information, but as entertaining tricks of the trade.

Visually to be very appealing your workbook should have 'multiple choice' type of exercises that are non-threatening in nature.

Structuring Reports for Different Academic Domains

If handbooks and/or workbooks are more narrative/imaginative types of writing, reports, projects, agendas, and policy statements are more descriptive in nature.

A report or a policy statement is unique in nature. It has a clear, defined reader profile but this reader is multiple as the same report, policy statement, etc., may get used in multiple committees.

Hence, reports for different academic domains (sciences, humanities, or applied sciences) essentially need to be focused. They have to be very orderly. To make them credible, they have to be objective, evaluative but non-judgmental. They are a written communication that is made of factual information and/or data. Your opinion, if any, has to be supported by this irrefutable data.

So it helps to clearly determine its purpose. Next, it is necessary to state a clear theme statement. Once your preliminary research work is through, you should think of its presentation that provides to your reader your hypothesis through identifiable topics and sub-topics.

Your outline should clearly have an introductory unit, a concluding unit, and a summary. If a summary collects all your points the concluding unit can chart out the new directions you may possibly foresee.

The length of your report should be neither too brief (appears very casual) nor too long. Your report should directly come to the point as your possible future reader—an official, for example, or a bureaucrat may not have the time or the patience to go through it. So be precise, please.

Append visual aids wherever necessary. The layout arrangement, the headers/ footers, numbering, constructing of title (underlining/bolding it), placement of titles, and the use of illustrations (pie charts, line charts, and computer graphics) make your visual aids which should never attract attention to themselves.

In brief, the report should succinctly and clearly give a neat picture of the activities it encompasses.

Any report should be arranged in three parts according to our reference books.

They are front matter, main body; and back matter.

Table 10.9 Front Matter, Main Body and Back Matter

Front Matter	Main Body	Back Matter
• Cover (tide, number, date, whether confidential) • Title page (author's name, designation) • Copyright notice • Forwarding letter, if necessary • Preface • Acknowledgements • Table of contents • List of illustrations • Abstract	• Introduction • Discussion/Analysis • Conclusions • Recommendations	• Appendices • References • Bibliography • Glossary • Index

Structuring Annual Reports

School/college annual reports need not be very content-rich. They are more a quantitative statement with a warm note to give their clientele, that is, the students and their parents, a feel-good effect.

Essentially, the tone is friendlier and warmer. The facts are kept to a minimum and are presented in a tabular format and a very colourful way designed for easy access.

As a read-it-and-throw-it-away presentation, such reports hove a glossy newspaper like feel. Often reports provide many snaps.

While structuring them you have to pay more attention to the visual presentation. Give the minimum matter through bullet points. All the financial details should be presented in a tabular format. Use simple and easily accessible English.

Reviewing a Project

This kind of written communication in a project differs from a report in two ways:

i. It includes a report but it goes beyond it through comments
ii. It is very formal in nature. So the vocabulary and tone, unlike an annual report, reflect this aspect.

You can visualize it in the following way:

Table 10.10 Reviewing a Project

Sender's address	
Date	
For the attention of:	
Sub: Review of..........	
Contents:	i. the report ii. critical comments iii. recommendations
Signature and designation of the sender	

Please remember that your reader is not going to have too much time on hand. So 'embolden' the important points.

It could look as follows:

Box 10.3: Water Conservation Strategies Progress Review

Aims

- Increasing ground water level
- Storing monsoon water

Plans as stated in report

- Awareness raising
- Central Government funding

Limitations

- Appears expensive
- Lacks popular support

Recommendations and suggestions

- NGO participation necessary

Just like your report, your review, too, should identify the problem, its causes, the relative importance of each, and the possible solutions along with your opinions and recommendations.

Preparing Policy Statements

A policy statement is also a kind of a report. So it should also begin with an overview of the past achievements, facts, and data.

It should be followed by the need for a new policy. A thorough, well-documented and research-backed data, supported by needs analysis, should supplement and strengthen your statement.

Mention the policy change and its aim succinctly. Discuss its advantages and indicate possible difficulties and ways to overcome them.

Agendas for Staff Meeting

An agenda is essentially an official list of activities to be looked at, discussed, and dealt with in a particular meeting.

Hence it should indicate the importance, the urgency, and hence the ordering of items. It should be time sensitive.

It should place routine items at the beginning. It should be followed by matters arising from the previous meeting(s).

The new items for consideration are placed next. An agenda, thus, maintains a proper order for a meeting, minimizes discussion, and preserves continuity in the proceeding of the meeting. In brief, it professionally prepares the staff for the issue under discussion. For instance, a good agenda makes taking down minutes very easy.

Technicalities of Writing a Research Paper

A research paper essentially requires collating material, taking notes, compiling a bibliography, and documenting the sources to analyse a given topic.

It, thus, helps to select a subject that interests you and does not extend too much the time and space limitations.

Write a precise theme statement. Arrange the collated material into a structured argument that consists of definition, classification, analysis, comparison, and contrast. Your detailed outline with thus emerge.

Then try a first draft with a clear beginning-body-conclusion structure. Evaluate it critically and improve on it though self-check editing.

You would say, 'all these points do not differ from the earlier forms of written communication.' What differentiates a research paper is its documenting of the secondary material.

Given the spatial constraints, here let us quickly remind ourselves to use reference cards for note-making and note-taking, whatever our source may be- dictionaries, encyclopedias, yearbooks, microfiche or vertical files, and/or dissertation abstracts.

While compiling a bibliography, follow the basic format given below:

Box 10.4: Format for Referencing

Author's surname, name. The title of the book (underlined). Place of publication: Publication house, Year of publication.

Look up the MLA Style Sheet for further, finer details. The Chicago Manual, mostly used for social science research, is another source book,

Since websites are often used these days as a reference source, here we give the technicalities of quoting from a website in Box 10.4:

Box 10.5: Writing a Website Reference

Author's first name, surname, title of document in inverted commas, title of complete work in italics, date of last revision, the complete URL in angled brackets, the date of access in parenthesis.

e.g. Natalie Winsten, 'Horrle Page', *Red Herring,* Aug. 11, 2000
http://www.yahoo.com/naralie (Jan 10, 2003).

LETTER WRITING

In the following two units we are briefly going to talk of official letters. The main point to remember, in addition to the introductory remarks discussed is that the tone matters a lot here. It has to be clearly formal.

Official Letters Within the Organization

Mostly these letters would consist of notices, memos, and minutes. These are essentially formal and precise and to the point.

A notice is often an invitation to a meeting. So clearly state the notice period, the day, date, time, venue of the meeting, the purpose of the meeting, and the actual business to be carried out. Here is an example.

Box 10.6: Format for a Notice

Hyderabad Private School
Banjara Hills, Hyderabad – 16
February 29, 2000
Notice

A meeting of the Executive Committee will be held in the committee room at 11.30 a.m. on March 10, 2000.

The agenda is:

1.
2.
3.

Signature
Designation

To
All Members of the Executive Committee

A memo is written almost the same way. Instead of 'Notice', you write 'Memorandum'. Next follows 'To'. On the next line, you have the name(s) and designation(s) of your addressee(s). Then provide the actual matter of the memo.

Minutes are the official record of the business carried out during a meeting. Essentially mnemonic, they guide further action. So minutes should have, in addition to the name of the department/unit, a mention of the date/time/venue. Next, minutes should list the names of chairperson(s), members, special invitees etc. The minutes should include an item-wise record of the discussion and finally, the signature of the authority.

Other Official Letters

These include letters of recommendation, letters to educational authorities, letters of appreciation, etc. You have studied formal letter writing since the days of your higher secondary days. Here we point out some details regarding mechanics. Please note:

1. Mostly the Americanized, left-aligned style is preferred today.
2. The sender's address is either on top left-hand side of the page, or at the bottom left.
3. Just below is the date, separated by single space.
4. Spacing is very important in such writing.
5. The receiver's address is two spaces below.
6. Next is the addressee's name and designation.
7. Next follows the attention column.
8. It is followed by the body of the letter that consists of salutation, subject, content, complimentary close, sender's signature, and designation.

Please remember that often these days MS-Word takes care of all such details. It is necessary hence to consistently use either the Americanized or the British spelling, as the computer mostly prefers the American spelling as well as spacing. Your formal letter should look as follows:

Box 10.7: Specimen of a Formal Letter

Letterhead:	HPS School, Jubilee Hills, Hyderabad
Sender's Address:	The Principal, HPS School, Hyderabad

(Continued)

Box 10.7 (Continued)

Date:	June 30, 2001
Address's Designation:	To
Official Address:	The Hon. Minister, Dept. of Education, A.P.
Attention: Addressee's Name:	Shri GVSR Reddy
Salutation:	Respected Sir,
Sub:	Regarding **Educational**
Body	**Grants**
Complimentary Close:	Yours faithfully/truly,
Sender's Signature and Designation	

CONCLUSION

In this chapter, we have looked at the different aspects of writing as a communication skill. We have understood that content matters, and so does presentation. In other words, it is as important to write legibly, with proper margins on all sides, as it is to write clearly, concisely, and precisely

Now a days, most people use word-process. In case you belong to this growing tribe, use double-spacing and a decent-sized font. Go in for a spell-check Do touch up your grammar, if necessary.

As you realize in today's era of smart computer programmes, thus, completing half our work, the truth-value of your material is what matters most. In other words, the credibility of your material is of utmost importance. So write precisely without any ambiguity. Provide all the documentation necessary.

Similarly, in today's equal and democratic days, it is necessary to be sensitive to people challenged in various ways, be it, physical, mental, gender, or race. Our writing would be a sensitive communication if it does not offend the others in any humiliating way.

SUMMARY

In this chapter, you learnt the techniques of grammar and vocabulary acquisition, in addition to mechanics of writing. Initial discussion of writing as a communication skill helped you understand such acquisition within the context of communication strategies. The chapter ended with outlines and brief suggestions about various types of academic writings.

11

Emotional Skills

After reading this chapter, you will be familiar with:

- What emotion is
- How emotions can be controlled and monitored
- How students can be provided with emotional support
- How to help students develop positive emotions

EMOTION AND COMMUNICATION

Emotion serves many functions in human behaviour and relationships. In this chapter we shall see what are the three components of emotions? What are the basic emotions? And, what is the relationship between emotion and communication?

Emotion can be defined as a psychological state involving three distinct components: subjective experience, physical arousal, and a behavioural or expressive response. Let us take a simple example to understand how these three components interact to produce a familiar emotional state; your friend borrowed your car to go for shopping. After a while you get a phone call saying that your friend has met with an accident on a highway fifty kilometers from the city; the car is smashed but your friend escaped slightly injured. First, you would probably experience a sense of relief that your friend was not injured, but you would also respond with anger. Your heart would pound, your face would turn red you would most probably utter unpleasant words or throw things around. This emotional response displays all the three distinct components of emotion. First, you experience a subjective conscious state that you label as anger. Secondly, you experience distinct physical changes in this case physiological arousal. And thirdly, you express the emotion in some sort of behaviour—your words, actions, or facial expressions. In addition to their subjective and physiological components, emotion usually involves an expressive, behavioural component. When we experience an emotion, we often express it in some fashion- we talk about how we are feeling, hug someone or slam the door—all these communicating our behavioural state. We also express our emotion by our nonverbal behaviour such as our gestures, changes in postures, and most importantly, facial expressions. A facial expression can display a single intense emotion, such as, anger or disgust, but it can also communicate the subtleties involved in mixed or complex emotions. Facial emotions are powerful in nonverbal communication.

Freud observed, 'Mortals can keep no secret. If their lips are silent, they gossip with their finger tips'. Betrayal forces its way through every pore. The nervous fidgeting of a teacher belies his or her dead-pan expression. Being able to pick up on such emotional cues is one of the most interesting and important skill in communication. Sensing what others feel without their saying so, captures the essence of empathy. Others rarely tell us in words what they feel; instead they tell us in their tone of voice, facial expression, or other nonverbal ways. The ability to sense this subtle communication requires more basic competencies, particularly self-awareness and self-control.

Being emotionally tone-deaf leads to social awkwardness, whether from misconstruing feelings or through a mechanical out-of-the bluntness, or indifference, that destroy rapport, which in turn affects our relationships and may also lead to responding to other people as stereotypes, rather than as the unique individuals they are.

Simply put, empathy requires being able to read another's emotions, it means sensing and responding to a person's unspoken concern and feelings. At the highest level, empathy is to understand the issues or concerns that lie behind another's feelings. The key to knowing other's emotional terrain requires an intimate familiarity with own. To be tuned to others' emotional cues, we need to put aside our own emotional agendas for the time being. This competency is especially important for teachers and counselors. Among counselors for instance, the most effective and empathetic were best able to tune into their body's own signals emotions essential for any job where empathy matters, from teaching to sales.

Although our nervous system is automatically tuned to this emotional empathy, but how we use this capacity is largely a learned ability that depends on motivation. Our first lesson in empathy begins in infancy when we are held in u our mothers' or fathers' arms. The extent to which we master this emotional curriculum determines our level of social competence.

Empathy represents the foundation skill for all the social competencies important in every performance especially in teaching. These include:

- **Understanding others:** Sensing others' feelings and perspectives, and taking an active interest in their concerns.

- **Service orientation:** Anticipating, recognizing, and fulfilling institutional needs.
- **Developing others:** Seeking students' development needs and bolstering their attitudes.
- **Leveraging diversity:** Cultivating opportunities through diverse people.
- **Awareness:** Being aware of the social, political, and emotional currents in the institutions/organizations.

Two most important competencies required in teaching are emotional or supportive communication, and the art of listening. We have discussed in detail what supportive communication is.

We do much better in our profession when we listen well and empathize. A finely tuned ear is at the heart of empathy. Listening well is essential to success at work and those who cannot, or do not listen, come across as indifferent or uncaring, which in turn makes others less communicative. Listening is also an art, and the first step is to make the others aware that one is open to listening. Teachers with an 'open door' policy, who appear approachable or go out of their way to hear what people have to say, 'Embody this competence'. Naturally then, who seem easy to talk to are those who get to hear more.

Emotional competence is a learned capability based on emotional intelligence that results in outstanding performance at work. Our emotional intelligence determines our potential for learning the practical skills that are based on its five elements: self-awareness, motivation, self-regulation, empathy, and adeptness in relationships. Our emotional competence shows how much of that potential we have translated into on-the-job capabilities. For instance, being a caring and understanding teacher is an emotional competence based on empathy. Likewise, trustworthiness is a competence based on self-regulation or handling impulses and emotions well.

Emotional competencies are categorized into groups, each based on a common underlying emotional intelligence capacity. The underlying emotional intelligence capacities are vital, if people are to successful in learning the competencies necessary to succeed in the work place. If they are deficient in social skills, for instance, they will be inept at persuading or improving others, at leading the team, or catalyzing change. If they have little self-awareness they will be oblivious to their own weakness and lack self-confidence that comes from the certainty about their strength.

There are four dimensions of emotional intelligence and the twenty-five emotional competences. None of us is perfect; we inevitably have a profile of strengths and limits. But as we shall see, the ingredients for outstanding performance require only the fact that we have strengths in a given number of the competencies, typically, least six or so, in order for the strengths be spread across all four areas of emotional intelligence. These emotional intelligence capacities are:

- **Independent:** Each draws emotions to some extent from certain others' will exhibiting many strong interactions.
- **Hierarchical:** The emotional intelligence competitiveness builds up on another factor. For example, self-awareness is crucial for self-regulation of empathy; self-regulation and self-awareness contribute to motivation; all the first four are at work in social skills.
- **Necessary, but not sufficient:** Having underlying emotional intelligence ability does not guarantee the people who will develop or display the associated competencies. Factors such as climate of the institution or a person interacting in his or her job, will also determine whether the competence manifest itself.
- **Generic:** The general list is applicable to some extent for all jobs. However different jobs make differing competence demand.

EMOTIONAL COMPETENCE

Emotional competence is the awareness of the emotions one has. People with emotional competence will know which emotion they are feeling and why. They realize the links between their feelings and what they think, do, and say. They realize how their feelings affect their performance. They have a guiding awareness of their values and goals.

The Emotional Competence Framework

Personal Competence

These competencies determine how we manage ourselves. People with this competence are attentive to emotional cues and listen well. They show sensitivity and understand others' perspectives. They help out the situation based on understanding of other peoples' needs and feelings. Their self-awareness will help them in knowing one's internal states, preference, resources, and institutions. Their emotional awareness gives them the ability in recognizing their own emotions and their effects.

Self-regulations

Self-regulation means proper management of one's internal states, impulses, and resources. It implies self-control and keeping disruptive emotion and impulse in check. It helps to develop trustworthiness to maintain standards of honesty and integrity. It gives consciousness to take responsibility for personal performance. It gives the capacity of adaptability and flexibility in handling change. One develops innovation and becomes comfortable with novel ideas, approaches, and new information through self-regulation.

Motivation

Emotional tendencies that guide or facilitate reaching goals:

- **Achievement drive:** Striving to improve or meet a standard of excellence.
- **Commitment:** Siding with the goals of the group or organization/institution.
- **Initiative:** Readiness to act on opportunities.
- **Optimism:** Resistance in pursuing goals, dispute obstacles and setbacks.

Social Competence

This competence determines how we handle relationships. It gives us an awareness of other's feelings, needs, and concerns. Social competence helps in understanding others, sensing others' feelings perspective, and taking an active interest in their concerns. This competence helps in the development of others. It is possible through seeking others' developmental needs and bolstering their aptitudes.

This competence gives rise to service orientation. It helps in anticipating, recognizing, and meeting customers' needs. This helps in the possibilities of leveraging diversity and cultivating opportunities through different kinds of people. It brings political awareness and the ability in reading a group's emotional currents and power relationships.

Handling Difficult People and Tense Situation with Diplomacy and Tact

Spot potential conflict, bring disagreements into the open and help to de-escalate. Debate and open discussions always help. Orchestrate and win the solution. If you can lead that will help in inspiring and guiding individuals and groups. Change the catalyst, initiate, and manage change. Help to build new bonds. Nurture instrumental relationships. In working with others toward shared goals, one should collaborate and co-operate to the maximum extent. In order to achieve the collective goals one should be able to develop team capabilities.

Technique of Emotional Display

The art of inspiring others is to make tactical use of emotional displays by showing our emotions and feelings for effect and clarifying that we are using them in a tactical and planned manner. The emotions one displays for effect can be negative or positive. Appropriate emotional displays give a boost to effective teaching characteristic. The following techniques will help you to make good use of display of emotions and feelings:

- Save emotional displays for rare occasion, otherwise you will appear to be emotionally volatile and perhaps unfit for your designated role.
- Be explicit about your feelings. Make statements such as, 'I am so happy that all of my student are capable and behave so well' or, 'I feel disappointed that some of you could not make the grade'.
- Concentrate on your nervous system which must match your emotions. For example, if your eyes widen and blood rushes to your skins when you are screaming, you will be more effective than if you don't feel angry inside.
- Practice showing positive and negative emotions even when you don't feel that way inside. An inspirational teacher can flip and switch for emotional displays as needed.

SUMMARY

In this chapter, we have learned about emotions and its relation to communications. We learned about the negative as well as positive emotions. We learned about how we can make use of emotions. We also learned how to handle difficult situations.

12

Interpersonal Effectiveness

After reading this chapter, you will be familiar with:

- Goals of interpersonal effectiveness
- Essential concepts of interpersonal effectiveness
- Qualities that demonstrate interpersonal effectiveness

INTRODUCTION

Interpersonal effectiveness is learning to communicate with others, whether in intimate relationships, friendship, bosses or coworkers as in all walks of life we communicate with one another. Interpersonal effectiveness is the result of many disciplines, mainly those involving the communication process. One can improve one's interpersonal effectiveness by building skills in five of the most challenging areas that exist in today's personal, professional, and social domain: conflict and negotiation, assertion, communication, persuasion, and cooperation. The person who possesses interpersonal skills displays empathy, supports others, and possesses effective communication skills.

QUALITIES THAT DEMONSTRATE INTERPERSONAL EFFECTIVENESS

Qualities, which demonstrate interpersonal effectiveness, are as follows:

- Builds and sustains positive relationships
- Handles conflicts and negotiations effectively
- Builds and sustains trust and respect
- Collaborates and works well with others
- Shows sensitivity and compassion for others

- Encourages shared decision-making
- Recognizes and uses ideas of others
- Communicates clearly, both orally and in writing
- Listens actively to others
- Honours commitments and promises

Interpersonal effectiveness starts with two things. First, understanding yourself; it is essential to understand what drives your behaviour, and knowing your strengths, weaknesses, and triggers. Secondly, understanding the impact you have on others, and how they see you. Interpersonal effectiveness is about understanding ourselves in order to understand people.

ESSENTIAL CONCEPTS OF INTERPERSONAL EFFECTIVENESS

- A key concept in interpersonal effectiveness is mental fitness. This starts with developing a passionate purpose, whether in your personal or professional life, and it is the development of this passionate purpose that lets you simplify, focus, be result-oriented, and engage in meaningful relationship.
- You need to understand what motivates you and develop a set of good questions to figure out what motivates other people. In order to motivate people we need to motivate ourselves. Self-motivation is of utmost importance. In processes such as decision-making, problem-solving, etc., you must be transparent, and then people will be loyal to whatever decision has been taken if there has been a fair hearing.
- Feedback is one of the key elements. There are two types of feedback: supportive feedback and corrective feedback. The golden rule is three times more supportive feedback than corrective feedback. When giving a corrective feedback, first invite the recipient to give a self-appraisal, and then state the facts as you see them, and listen actively to the response. This creates a feeling in the other person that he is understood and encourages a willingness to listen and make changes. Next, you develop action plans together, but that is not enough. Every time you have somebody's commitment you express your support so that the person is motivated to do a better job, then you follow it up with a positive or supportive feedback every time that person does something that was agreed. If you take this for granted it will go away.

- The use of constructive language is important in interpersonal effectiveness.There are three no-nonsense tips for people to follow. First, avoid questionsthat start with the word 'why'. The reason for this is that questions startingwith 'why' often put people on the defensive. Typically, these are questionsfor justification, not clarification. Second, avoid the words 'yes' and but'. It isbetter to replace the word 'but' with 'if', 'and', or nothing at all. And thirdly, it is no use saying 'I disagree', because you then enter yourself into anunnecessary debate or discussion. Of course, you are entitled to disagree, buta much better approach is to change how you formulate your words.
- It is important to appreciate the other person, not despite her or his differences, but because of them; and to understand differences and where they come from. There's nothing more unequal as treating different people equally and you have to understand that different people will work in different ways. It is also about really listening to the other person in order to better understand her or him. And it is about creating environment for people where they have the freedom to be themselves; it is to do with realizing that we need to avoid the temptation of turning the other person into a copy of us. It is about enabling people to excel and accepting that they achieve excellent results in different ways.
- Another important element is being able to understand the complexity of the communication processes. The biggest problem with communication is the illusion that it has already been accomplished. Hence, it is much better to start from the conviction that when you communicate you are misunderstanding and you are being misunderstood. When you start from this you become much more focused on checking your understanding, and you give the other person the true feeling that she or he is being understood - and that helps in relationships with people.
- You need to learn how to deal with resistance to change and have a constructive attitude when looking at problems and making suggestions for improvements. If you try to force people in their ways of working you are basically making them work against the grain, and nobody is effective when doing this. Another point is about embracing conflict and seeing conflict as a source of energy. There are many positive outcomes of conflict and so it is not about avoiding conflict but about embracing it. Finally, it is about being obsessed with learning - learning about you and learning about others. Relentless self-renewal is critical.

GOALS OF INTERPERSONAL EFFECTIVENESS

Interpersonal effectiveness is quite essential for individuals to achieve both personnel and organizational goals. Some of the proven behavioural actions that can generate effective interpersonal relations are as follows:

- Standing up for your rights in such a way that they are taken seriously.
- Requesting others to do something in such a way that they want to.
- Refusing unwanted or unreasonable requests (learning to say no).
- Resolving interpersonal conflict.
- Getting your opinion or point of view taken seriously.
- Acting in a way that makes the other person actually want to give you what you are asking for.
- Balancing immediate goals with the good of the long-term relationship.
- Golden Rule: treating others, as you want to be treated.
- Maintaining or developing the good feeling about yourself, respecting your own values and beliefs.
- Acting in ways that fit your sense of morality.
- Acting in competent ways.
- Expressing thoughts, ideas, and concern clearly.
- Giving courteous, accurate and complete response.
- Listening attentively to others without interruption.
- Keeping commitments.
- Seeking accurate information (avoid jumping to conclusions).
- Treating all employees with respect regardless of their level, personality, culture, or background.

To sum up this interpersonal effectiveness imparts conflict management and negotiation skills, assertiveness skills, communication skills and team-building skills.

DIMENSIONS OF INTERPERSONAL EFFECTIVENESS

Self-understanding and Acceptance

We all have goals and in order to reach to those goals, we must have relationships with other people. Usually these relationships include shared goals. When people become involved in shared goals in a relationship, it becomes important to coordinate behaviour to build the relationship so that each person can achieve these goals. This happens to students in every aspect of their lives from living in shared accommodation to team projects in the classroom.

Self-disclosure

The first step in developing relationships involves self-disclosure. This means being able to share how you feel about events that have just occurred with another person. This does not mean revealing intimate details of your past life. People get to know you by learning how you react, not by what happened in your past history. Past history only helps if it clarifies why you are reacting in a certain way. People, who self-disclose too much, can scare others away.

Development and Maintenance of Trust

Trust can take many years to build, but can be ruined by one destructive act. The key to being trustworthy is to be accepting and supporting. When you achieve this, others will be more willing to disclose their thoughts, ideas, theories, conclusions, feelings and reactions to you. The more trustworthy you are in response to such disclosures, the deeper and more personal will be the thoughts a person will share with you.

Managing Feelings

Students should manage feelings. You can't avoid stress. How you manage stress has a great influence on your ability to reach out to other people, build relationships, and maintain it over a long period of time.

SUMMARY

- Interpersonal effectiveness is about relationships. Getting what you want (e.g., asking for what you need, learning to say no, setting limits and boundaries); keeping relationships; and keeping your self-respect.
- Interpersonal effectiveness does not occur in isolation. This is an umbrella-term, which encompasses several concepts such as assertiveness, conflict-management, negotiation skills, communication skills, time management and team-building skills.
- There are several qualities, which demonstrate interpersonal effectiveness. Among many building and sustaining positive relationships,

handling conflicts and negotiations effectively, being assertive, and communicating well are the essential qualities.

- Interpersonal effectiveness starts with understanding self and then moves on to interpersonal situation such as understanding others or reaching out to other people.

13

Assertiveness Skills

After reading this chapter, you will be familiar with:

- Behavioural aspects of assertive, aggressive, and non-assertive responses
- Verbal and non-verbal aspects of assertive, aggressive, and non-assertive responses
- Assertive/responsive model
- Advantages of assertiveness
- Strategies to overcome non-assertive behaviour

INTRODUCTION

Many people have difficulty speaking up in conflict situations. Others may feel intimidated by intimidating people, or have low self-esteem and regularly put aside their own desires in favour of what others want. This can result in a lack of assertiveness, low self-esteem, and helplessness. Lack of assertiveness makes you feel powerless. Sometimes, if we feel our rights are being violated, we need to stand up for ourselves in order to be treated fairly. This means expressing our needs, opinions, and feelings in a tactful and effective manner. Psychologists call this self-assertion and distinguish it from aggression, which is generally an expression of hostility.

Some of us want to be 'nice' and 'not cause trouble', and, thus, we suffer in silence, turning the other cheek, and feeling helpless to repair offensive situations. We understand that most people appreciate those who accommodate others' needs before their own. Whenever a 'nice' person permits a dominant person to take advantage of him or her, however, the passive person is not only cheating him or herself but is also rewarding unfair, exploitive behaviour in the aggressor.

BEHAVIOURAL RESPONSES

When animals are confronted with a problematic situation, they come up with two responses such as flight or fight. Whereas when human beings are confronted with a situation, three behavioural responses are possible, namely assertive, aggressive, and nonassertive.

The main characteristics of assertive, aggressive, and non-assertive behaviour are as follows:

- **Assertive**: stating clearly what we would like to happen, but without a demand that it should.
- **Aggressive**: making sure that we do get what we want, no matter what the other person feels.
- **Non-assertive**: doing nothing and hoping, or trying to get what we want in a roundabout way.

ADVANTAGES OF BEING ASSERTIVE

By employing assertive behaviour you will know how to refuse unreasonable requests from others, how to assert your rights in a non-aggressive manner, and how to negotiate to get what you want in your relationship with others.

Assertiveness requires a change in attitude as well as a change in behaviour. We interact with others based on a set of beliefs about status (who is better or more important), about how we should behave in social situations, and about what consequences we expect from our behaviour. Non-assertive people worry about making a bad impression on everyone (including those who treat them badly). They also worry about looking foolish in front of others, and are fearful of negative consequences all of the time.

Making a good impression, avoiding public embarrassment, and protecting yourself are all important traits, but non-assertive people take them too far. They always give in to others. Training in assertiveness helps you learn how to judge when it is reasonable and appropriate to stand your ground, rather than giving in to others. It is not about being intimidating or aggressive.

Becoming more assertiveness helps people to overcome fear, shyness, passivity, and even anger and depression. There is an astonishingly wide range of situations in which this type of training is appropriate. Some of these situations are enumerated as follows:

- To speak up, make requests, ask for favours and generally insist that your rights be respected as a significant, equal human being.
- To overcome the fears and self-deprecation that keeps you from doing these things.

- To express negative emotions (complaints, resentment, criticism, disagreement, and the desire to be left alone).
- To refuse requests.
- To show positive emotions (joy, pride, liking someone, attraction) and to give and receive compliments.
- To ask questions, including questioning authority or tradition.
- To assume responsibility for asserting your share of control of the situation and to make things better for you.
- To initiate, carry on, change, and terminate conversations comfortably. Share your feelings, opinions, and experiences with others.
- To deal with minor irritations before your anger builds into intense resentment and explosive aggression.

ASSERTIVE/RESPONSIVE MODEL

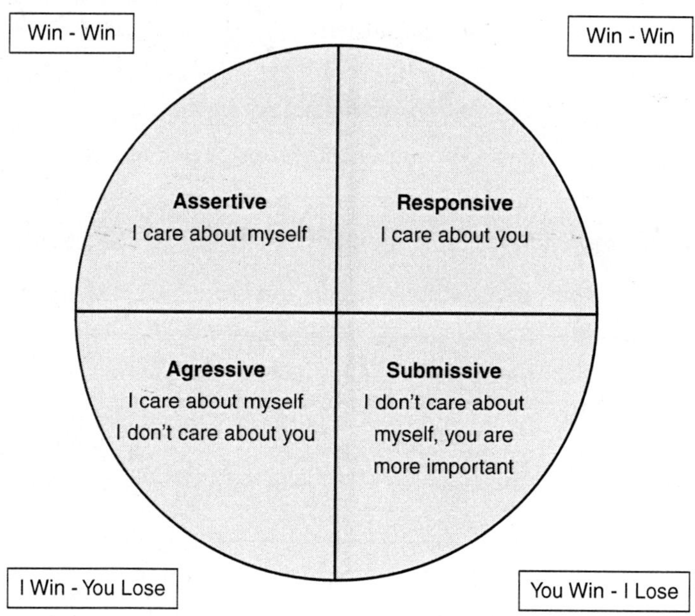

Figure 13.1
Assertive–Responsive Model

Assertion

Assertion refers to a behaviour that involves the following:

- Standing up for your own rights in such a way that you do not violate another person's rights.

- Expressing your needs, wants, opinions, feelings, and beliefs in direct, honest, and appropriate ways.

So, assertiveness is based on beliefs that in any situation:

- You have needs to be met.
- The other people have needs to be met.
- You have rights, and so do others.
- You have something to contribute, and so do others.

The aim of assertion is to satisfy the needs and wants of both parties in the situation (known as 'Win/Win').

Non-assertion

Non-assertion refers to a behaviour that involves the following:

- Failing to stand up for your rights or doing so in such a way that others can easily disregard them.
- Expressing your needs, wants, opinions, feelings, and beliefs in apologetic, diffident, or self-effacing ways.
- Failing to express honestly your needs, wants, opinions, feelings, and beliefs.

Non-assertion is based upon the beliefs that in any situation:

- The other person's needs and wants are more important than your own.
- The other person has rights but you do not.
- You have little or nothing to contribute; the other person has a great deal to contribute.

The aim of non-assertion is to avoid conflict and to please others.

Aggression

Aggression refers to a behaviour that involves the following:

- Standing up for your own rights, but doing so in such a way that you violate the rights of other people.
- Ignoring or dismissing the needs, wants, opinions, feelings, or beliefs of others.
- Expressing your own needs, wants, and opinions (which may be honest or dishonest) in inappropriate ways.

Aggressive behaviour is based on the belief that:

- Your own needs, wants, and opinions are more important than other people's.
- You have rights but other people do not
- You have something to contribute; others have little or nothing to contribute.

The aim of aggression is to win, if necessary, at the expense of others.

Examples of the three different behaviours are as follows:

Situation: Taking an unsatisfactory letter back to the person who produced it.

Assertion: 'Sarita, I'd like you to re-do this letter as there are several mistakes in it.'

Non-assertion: You find an excuse not to take the letter back, or you say. 'I know it is .... any chance at all you could find a spare minute to — just change one or two small things on this letter for me.'

Aggression: 'I don't know how you've got the nerve to give me this sort of stuff for signing. It is full of mistakes.'

Verbal Aspects of Aggression, Assertion, and Non-assertion

The following table discusses the various verbal aspects of aggressive, assertive, and non-assertive behaviours:

Table 13.1 Verbal Aspects of Aggressive, Assertive, and Non-assertive Behaviours

Non-assertive	Assertive	Aggressive
Long, rambling statements	Statements that are brief, clear, and to the point	Excess of 'I' statements
Fill in words (e.g., may be)	'I' statements: 'I' would like	Boastfulness: 'my'
Frequent justifications	Distinctions between fact and opinion	Threatening questions
Apologies and permission seekers	Suggestions not weighed with advice	Requests as instructions or threats
Few 'I' statements	No 'shoulds' or 'oughts'	Heavily weighed advice in the form of should and ought
Self put-downs ('I am hopeless')	Questions to find out the thoughts, opinions and wants of others	Assumptions
Phrases that dismiss own needs (for example, 'not important really')	Constructive criticism without blame or assumptions	Blame put on others

Non-verbal Aspects of Aggression, Assertion, and Non-assertion

Non-verbal behaviour refers to all the observable aspects of behaviour that accompany speech, apart from the words themselves. These are:

Voice: The tone: sarcastic or sincere; warm or cold; rich and expressive or dull and flat.

Volume: shouting; barely audible; or medium volume

Speech pattern: Slow, hesitant, fast, jerky, abrupt or steady even pace

Facial expression:

Brow: wrinkled or smooth

Eyebrows: wrinkled or smooth

Jaw: set firm or relaxed

Eye contact: Whether the speaker looks at other people or the surroundings and for how long

Body movement:

Movement with individual parts of the body (for example, head and hands)

Movement and position of the whole body

The following table discusses the various non-verbal aspects of aggressive, assertive, and non-assertive behaviours:

Table 13.2 Non-verbal Aspects of Aggressive, Assertive, and Non-assertive Behaviours

	Non-assertive	Assertive	Aggressive
Voice	Sometimes 'wobbly'. Tone may be 'singsong or whining'. Over-soft or over-warm. Often dull and in monotone. Quiet, often drops away at end.	Steady and firm. Tone is middle range, rich and warm. Sincere and clear. Not over-loud or quiet.	Very firm. Tone is sarcastic and sometimes 'cold'. Hard and sharp. Strident, maybe shouting, rises at end.
Speech pattern	Hesitant and filled with pauses. Sometimes jerks from fast to slow. Frequent throat clearing.	Fluent, few awkward hesitancies. Emphasizes key Words. Steady, even paced.	Fluent, few awkward hesitancies Often abrupt, 'clipped'. Emphasizes blaming words. Often fast.
Facial expression	'Ghost' smiles when expressing anger, or being criticized. Eyebrows raised in anticipation (for example, of rebuke).	Smiles when pleased. Frowns when angry, otherwise 'open'. Features steady, not 'wobbling' and jaw relaxed.	Smile may become 'wry'. Scowls when angry. Eyebrows raised in amazement/disbelief. Jaw set firm. Chin thrust forward.

(Continued)

Table 13.2 (Continued)

	Non-assertive	Assertive	Aggressive
Eye contact	Evasive. Looking down.	Firm, but not staring 'down'	Tries to 'stare down' and dominate.
Body movements	Hand-wringing. Hunching shoulders. Stepping back. Covering mouth with hand. Nervous movements which detract (for example, shrugs and shuffles). Arms crossed law for protection.	Open hand movements (inviting to speak). 'Measured pace hand movements'. Sits upright or relaxed (not slouching or cowering). Stands with head held up.	Finger pointing. Fist thumping. Sits upright or leans forward. Stands upright, head held high. Strides around (impatiently). Arms crossed high (unapproachable).

RIGHTS WITHIN THE AREA OF ASSERTIVENESS

These derive from various humanistic beliefs such as 'all people are equal' or 'all people are entitled to freedom'. They are similar to the statements underpinning the constitutions of many countries and the universal declaration of human rights.

All People Are Equal

This is not to say that all people are the same, but rather that, regardless of race, colour, creed, background, or behaviour, all people are of equal value as human beings. Thus, your colleague may put forward ideas that are different from yours (some might say 'better ideas'). This does not mean that he/she is a better, or a more valuable person person than you; it merely means that he is different.

All People Are Entitled to Freedom

This is to say, all people are free to do and be what they like provided they do not affect others, taking away their freedom of choice. So, for instance, you are free to listen to your transistor on the beach provided you do not inflict that choice on others who prefer not to listen.

As with any belief system, an assertive belief system affects the rights you give yourself and to others, which in the run affects your behaviour.

The following list contains some of the general rights that are available to you under 'assertiveness'. They are important if you want to behave assertively in many situations in your life.

- I have the right to have and express opinions, views and ideas which may or may not be different from others—and so do you.

- I have the right to have these opinions, views, and ideas listened to and respected (not necessarily agreed with or put on a 'pedestal', but accepted as being valid for you)—and so do you.
- I have the right to have needs and wants that may be different from others—and so do you.
- I have the right to ask (not demand) that others respond to your needs and wants—and so do you.
- I have the right to refuse a request without feeling guilty or selfish—and so do you.
- I have the right to have feelings and to express them assertively if I so choose—and so do you.
- I have the right to be 'human', e.g., to be wrong sometimes—and so do you
- I have the right to decide not to assert myself (e.g., to choose not to raise a particular issue)—and so do you.
- I have the right to be true to my own self; this may be the same as, or different from, what others would like me to be (it includes choosing friends, interests, etc.)—and so do you.
- I have the right to have others respect my rights—and so do you.

STRATEGIES TO OVERCOME NON-ASSERTIVE BEHAVIOUR

The following steps can be considered to overcome non-assertive behaviour:

Realize Where Changes Are Needed and Believe in Your Rights

Many people recognize that they are being taken advantage of and/or have difficulty saying 'no'. Others do not see themselves as unassertive but do feel depressed or unfulfilled, have numerous physical ailments, have complaints about work but assume that the boss or teacher has the right to demand whatever he/she wants, etc. Nothing will change until the victim recognizes his/her rights are being denied and he/she decides to correct the situation. Keeping a diary may help you assess how intimidated, compliant, passive, or timid you are or how demanding, whiny, bitchy, or aggressive others are.

Almost everyone can cite instances in which he/she has been outspoken or aggressive. These instances may be used to deny that we are unassertive in any way. However, many of us are weak in some ways—we cannot say 'no' to a friend asking for a favour, we cannnot give or take a compliment, we let a spouse or children control our lives, we won't speak up in class or disagree with others in a public meeting, we are ashamed to ask for help, we are afraid of offending others, and so on. Ask yourself if you want to continue being weak.

Consider where your values—your 'should'—come from. Children are bombarded with rules: Don't be selfish, don't make mistakes, don't be emotional, don't tell people if you don't like them, don't be so unreasonable, don't question people, don't interrupt, don't trouble others with your problems, don't complain, don't upset others, don't brag, don't be anti-social, do what people ask you to do, help people who need help, and on and on. Do any of these instructions sound familiar? They help produce submissive children and adults. There are probably good reasons for many of these rules-for-kids but as adults we need not blindly follow rules. Indeed, each of these injunctions should be broken under certain conditions: You have a right to be first (sometimes), to make mistakes, to be emotional, to express your feelings, to have your own reasons, to stop others and ask questions, to ask for help, to ask for reasonable changes, to have your work acknowledged, to be alone, to say 'no' or 'I don't have time', and so on. The old feelings deep inside of us may still have powerful control over us. We can change.

Besides recognizing that we have outgrown our unthinking submissiveness, we can further reduce our ambivalence about being assertive by recognizing the following harmful effects that result due to unassertiveness:

i. You cheat yourself and lose your self-respect because you are dominated and can't change things.
ii. You are forced to be dishonest, concealing your true feelings.
iii. Inequality and submissiveness threatens, if not destroys, love and respect.
iv. A relationship based on your being a doormat, a slave, a 'yes-person', a cute show piece, or a source of income is oppressive and immoral.
v. Since you must hide your true feeling, you may resort to subtle manipulation to get what you want and this creates resentment.
vi. Your compliance rewards your oppressor.

On the positive side, assertiveness leads to more self-respect and happiness. Build up your courage by reviewing all the reasons for changing.

Finally, there are obviously situations in which demanding immediate justice may not be wise, e.g., if you can get fired, if it would cause an unwanted divorce, if you might be assaulted, etc. Even in these more extreme cases, perhaps well planned or very gradual changes would be tolerated. Under any circumstances, discuss the reasons for becoming assertive with the other people involved so they will understand and approve (if possible) or at least respect you for being considerate of them, others, and yourself.

Figure Out Appropriate Ways of Asserting Yourself in Each Specific Situation that Concerns You

There are many ways to devise effective, tactful, and fair assertive responses. Watch a good model. Discuss the problem situation with a friend, a parent, a supervisor, a counselor, or any other person. Carefully note how others respond to situations similar to yours and consider if they are being unassertive, assertive, or aggressive. Most assertiveness trainers recommend that an effective assertive response contain several parts:

i. Describe (to the other person involved) the troublesome situation as you see it. Be very specific about time and actions; don't make general accusations like 'You are always hostile...upset...busy'. Be objective; don't suggest the other person is a total jerk. Focus on his/her behaviour, not on his/her apparent motives.

ii. Describe your feelings, using an 'I' statement, which shows that you take responsibility for your feelings. Be firm and strong, look at them, be sure of yourself, and don't get emotional. Focus on positive feelings related to your goals if you can, and not on your resentment of the other person. Sometimes it is helpful to explain why you feel, as you do, so your statement becomes 'I feel_______because____'.

iii. Describe the changes you would like to make. Be specific about what action should stop and what should start. Be sure the requested changes are reasonable; consider the other person's needs too, and be willing to make changes yourself in return.

Practise Giving Assertive Responses

Using the responses you have just developed, role-play the problem situations with a friend or, if that isn't possible, simply imagine interacting assertively. Start with real life easy-to-handle situations and work up to more challenging ones expected in the future.

You will quickly discover if your friend plays the role realistically, that you need to do more than simply rehearse the assertiveness responses. You will realize that no matter how calm and tactful you are, how much you use 'I' statements, and how much you play down a desire for change, it will still sometimes come out smelling like a personal assault to the other person. The other person may not be aggressive (since you have been tactful) but you should realize that strong reactions are possible, e.g., getting mad and calling you names, counter-attacking and criticizing you, seeking revenge, becoming threatening or ill, or suddenly being contrite and overly apologetic or submissive. Your friend helping you by role-playing can act out the more likely reactions.

When we are criticized, there are various ways of attacking back. We may be sarcastic, get mad, or criticize back. We assume 'I count, you don't'. That is being aggressive. We may cry, be quiet, or get away. We imply 'You count, I don't'. That is being passive. We may pretend to forget but get even by procrastinating, being late or slow, being silent or whiny, bad mouthing the critic, or doing any thing that drives him/her up a wall ('Oh, I didn't know that was bothering you'). That is being passive-aggressive. Instead of these kinds of reactions to criticism, use one of these approaches reflecting a 'We both count equally' attitude:

Acknowledge that the criticism is true, if it is. Don't make flimsy excuses but do give honest explanations (if you have a valid one). For example, 'Yes, I have put off doing the report' or 'Yes, I was late this morning but my car wouldn't start'.

Even if you don't agree with most of the criticism, you can single out some part that you do agree with and indicate where you agree, disregarding all the disagreements. For example, 'You could be right about...', 'I understand how you feel about...' or 'This is really ducking the issue but that may be what you want to do'.

Listen carefully and ask for clarification until the person's views are understood. Focus on his/her main point and ask, 'What is it that bothers you about...?'

Finally, assertiveness is used to confront difficult situations and people. Some people just won't take 'no' for an answer, some kids continue arguing; some people don't realize how determined you are until you repeat the message many times. One technique is called the broken record: you calmly and firmly repeat a short, clear statement over and over until the other person gets the message. For example, 'I want you to be home by midnight', 'I don't like the product and I want my money back', or 'No, I don't want to go drinking, I want to study'. Repeat the same statement in exactly the same way until the other person 'gets off your back', regardless of the excuses, diversions, or arguments given by the other person.

Try Being Assertive in Real Life Situations

Start with the easier, less stressful situations. Build some confidence. Make adjustments in your approach as needed. Look for or devise ways of sharpening your assertiveness skills. For example, ask a friend to lend you a piece of clothing, a record album, or a book. Ask a stranger for directions. Ask a store manager to reduce the price of a soiled or slightly damaged article, to demonstrate a product, or exchange a purchase. Ask an instructor to help you understand a point, find extra reading, or go over items you missed on an exam. Practise speaking and making small talk, give compliments to friends and strangers, call up a city official when you see something unreasonable or inefficient, praise others when they have done well, tell friends or co-workers about the experiences you have had, and so on. Keep a diary of your interactions.

'I' MESSAGES

Another effective way of overcoming non-assertive behaviour is giving 'I' messages. The following aspects will explain the same.

'I' messages are used for expressing feelings and accepting responsibility for your feelings. This is one of the most important skills you can acquire. A good rule of thumb is: 'If you have a problem, make an 'I' statement. If you are helping someone with a problem, make empathy responses'. An 'I' statement consists of a description of how you feel and an indication of the conditions under which you feel that way. It takes this form: 'I feel (your emotions) when (under what conditions)'. It will be helpful if you recognize how many decisions you have made in the process of becoming emotional or upset.

Regardless of the etiology of feelings, suppressing, or denying our feelings may lead to several problems: (1) increased irritability and conflicts with others, (2) difficulty resolving interpersonal problems (being 'logical' doesn't mean ignoring feelings, but dealing with them), (3) distorted perception and blind spots (like seeing only the bad parts of a person we are mad at) in a relationship, and (4) other people may suspect we have feelings and ask us to be honest with them (which is hard to do if we are being dishonest with ourselves or unaware). These are good reasons for expressing our feelings, in a tactful, constructive manner. 'I' statements serve this purpose.

'I' statements do not judge, blame, threaten, put down or try to control others; they simply report how you feel, which is rarely challengeable by anyone else. When you make an 'I' statement, you are taking responsibility for yon emotions 'I' statements inform others about your feelings and, thus, may lead to change, but they do not demand change or direct others. They leave the other person responsible and free to decide if he/she will change to accommodate your needs.

Consider using 'I' statements:

- Any time you want to share your feelings or desires in a frank, unthreatening, undemanding way. When you are trying to disclose more about yourself to build a relationship.
- Any time stress is experienced in a relationship, especially if you are feeling angry or dissatisfied or if the other person is resistive to changing in response to your requests or demands.

- If both parties have problems, i.e., both of you can take turns giving 'I' statements and giving empathy responses.
- If the other person is using a lot of 'you' (blaming, critical) statements, try to translate them into 'I' statements and empathize with the accuser's feelings.

Understand When to Use and How to Use 'I' Statements in Place of 'You' Statements and Other Perilous Statements

In order to communicate our feelings clearly to others, we must, of course, be aware of or be comfortable or at least acknowledge them, and able to accurately express the feelings to them in words. When we lack this awareness, acceptance, or verbal skill, our feelings are likely to be expressed indirectly and ineffectively, as shown in Table 13.3.

Table 13.3 'You' and 'I' Statements

'You' Statements	'I' Statements
Blaming: 'You make me so mad.'	'I feel angry when you..' or, 'I have chosen to let it bother me when you ______.'
Judging or labelling: 'You are an inconsiderate, hostile, arrogant creep.'	'I feel betrayed when you criticize me in front of others.'
Accusing: 'You don't give a damn about me!'	'I feel neglected when you avoid me.'
Ordering: 'You shut up!'	'I feel annoyed when you call me names and make fun of me.'
Questioning: 'Are you always this flirtatious?', or 'Why did you do that? I feel like slapping your face.'	'I really feel insecure about our relationship when you flirt.'
Arguing: 'You don't know what you are talking about.'	'I feel convinced it is this way.'
Sarcasm: 'Of course, you are an expert!'	'I would like you a lot more if you were a bit more humble.'
Approving: 'You are wonderful', or 'You are attractive.'	'I really am impressed with your and besides I like you, I am attracted to you.'
Disapproval: 'You are terrible.'	'I feel crushed when you seem only interested in spending my money.'
Threatening: 'You had better …'	'I'd like it if you'd …'
Moralizing: 'You ought to …'	'I think it would be fair for you to …'
Treating: 'You need to rest and …'	'I'd like to be helpful to you.'
Supporting: 'It will get better.'	'I' m sorry you feel …'
Analyzing: 'You can't stand to leave your mother!'	'I'm disappointed that you are so reluctant to leave …'

Note that many of the 'you' statements are intended to exert power, to control, to intimidate, or to put down the other person. They are not statements made by non-judgmental, mutually respecting equals. They are authoritarian statements made by manipulators. Hence 'I' statements arerecommended to parents when talking to children. Watch out for 'you' statements.

Personal responsibility is avoided in other ways too: we use 'we', 'it' or 'they' when we are trying to depersonalize our comment and/or vaguely conceal our feelings or opinions. Sometimes we use 'we' when trying to make it sound like a lot of people agree with us, while in reality no one has authorized us to speak for them. We should take responsibility for expressing our own opinions or feelings.

Table 13.4 exhibits certain examples.

Table 13.4 'We' and 'I' Statements

'We', 'it', 'they' statements	'I' statements
'Most people would have an affair if they wouldn't get caught.'	'I would have an affair if…'
'The group isn't interested in…'	'I don't think the group cares...'
'The glass slipped out of my hand.'	'I dropped the glass.'
'People have a hard time with math.'	'I am ashamed of my math score.'
'The group is trying to help you.'	'I want to understand you but I'm having a hard time.'
'This weather is depressing.'	'I feel depressed.'
'This class is boring.'	'I feel bored.'

The last example above shows how our language also causes us problems. It is important to be aware that personal opinions sound like facts when one uses a form of 'am' or 'is', such as 'you are…', 'I am...', 'it is...', and so on.

When personal opinions are stated as facts, it is no wonder that arguments arise. Note the use of 'is' in this example:

Person A: 'This class is a lot of work but it contains useful information.'
Person B: 'This class is a complete waste of time.'

These two people could debate the merits and faults of the class for an hour. It could degenerate into a personal conflict, like 'You are the teacher's pet' and 'You wouldn't like anything that required a brain' and continue with the argument. On the other hand, if both A and B had made 'I' statements there would have been no argument.

Person A: 'I really like the self-help class, especially the group.'
Person B: 'I'm disappointed in that class because I'm not getting anything out of my group, or those ridiculously long readings.'

In this case, A and B can see that they have responded very differently to the same class. There can be no argument about that. The class is not inevitably great or terrible; it meets many peoples' needs but not everyone's. After the 'I' statements, A and B could discuss their differences and learn more about themselves, each other, their groups, and the class.

To summarize,

- An 'I' statement may have 2 to 4 parts: (a) it is a self-disclosure, referring to 'I', 'me', or 'my'; (b) it expresses a feeling, urge or impulse; (c) it may describe the other person's behaviour which is related to your feelings; and (d) it may indicate what you would like to see changed, much like an assertive statement.
- Assume responsibility for your feelings and opinions, and don't hide behind the 'it' or the editorial 'we'.
- Avoid stating personal opinions as facts and avoid the over-generalizations sometimes implied by forms of the verb 'to be', like 'are', 'is', 'am', and so on.
- Clearly, giving an 'I' statement is more constructive than giving an order, an accusation, a moral judgment, and so on. However, this is not an easy concept to grasp. The pronoun 'you' is used all the time, many uses are not bad. Try to become aware of the undesirable ways you use 'you'.

Look for Opportunities to Use 'I' Statements

Review the examples of 'you' and 'we' statements above and see if any remind you of possible situations in your life. If so, make some notes on how you could handle such situations differently in the future and perhaps plan to arrange an opportunity to try out 'I' statements.

Pay special attention to stressful relationships or when you want to communicate in sensitive, areas, such as sex, anger, submissiveness and others.

Practise Giving 'I' Messages in Your Daily Conversations

Most of us find it hard to change our speech patterns. We feel awkward. 'I' statements seem counter to what we have been taught in English classes, 'Don't say I, I, I'. We are self-conscious about focusing on ourselves. It takes practise to get comfortable with 'I' statements. Role-playing may be a good way to start seeing how well they work.

Keep watching for opportunities in casual conversations to express a feeling or an opinion tactfully. Act quickly, as soon as you are aware of a feeling say, 'I am feeling…'. Most people are interested in genuine feelings, especially if the feelings involve them. It is nourishment for growing friendships.

Tell yourself that one of the best ways to resolve a conflict is for all relevant factors to be considered in arriving at a 'no-lose' solution. Your feelings, needs, and preferences are important factors! So are the other person's. Feelings have to be shared, diplomatically.

'I' statements are more likely to improve a relationship, certainly better than demanding, whining, asking accusatory questions, manipulating, accusing, and criticizing will do. There are no known dangers.

SUMMARY

- Assertiveness and the skills associated with it are increasing in popularity because it empowers people who use it and improve the psychological well being.
- Assertiveness is a skill that can be learned and it is useful with everyone with whom you come into contact. One can learn this skill with good communication, implementing broken record method, using 'I' statements.
- When people learn how to be assertive, they experience benefits such as feeling less stressed, having greater self-confidence, being more tactful.
- Employing assertive behaviour helps resisting other people's attempts to manipulate them through bullying, emotional blackmail, flattery etc.
- An assertive person is not just concerned about his own rights but always encourages and promotes assertiveness in others.

REFERENCES

Lindenfield, Gael, 1986, *Assert yourself*, New Delhi: Harper Collins.

Paterson, J. Randy, 2000, *The Assertiveness Book*, Mumbai: Magna Publishing.

Gillen, Terry, 1995, *Assertiveness*, Hyderabad: University Press India Ltd.

Claire, Walmesley, 1991, *Assertiveness: the right to be you*, London: BBC Books.

14

Conflict Management and Negotiation Skills

After reading this chapter, you will be familiar with:

- The nature of conflict
- Various conflict resolution styles
- Purpose of conflict resolution
- The collaborative versus the coercive conflict
- Conflict management skills
- Principles of 'win-win' negotiation

INTRODUCTION

Conflict is an inevitable part of any relationship. Conflict takes place between parent and child, wife and husband, teacher and student. Conflict is a very normal phenomenon. However, conflicts do not have to end with some one losing and with both parties hating each other. Unfortunately, we have many wars, political fights, divorces, lawsuits, business break-ups, strikes, effort-, time- and money-wasting arguments at work, etc. Wise individuals are able to resolve disagreements with both parties satisfied and respecting each other. Hence, learning to resolve conflict, which yields a positive outcome, is a real skill.

Each of us has his/her own way of dealing with conflicts in our lives. Knowing our own style and motives of the other person with whom we are in conflict will help us to handle situation. Also, it is obvious that self-serving and hostile underlying emotions are often the cause of disputes. The conflict may be power struggle, a need to prove you are right, a superior attitude, a desire to hurt, or some other motive.

DEFINITION

Conflict is defined as a form of relating or interacting where we find ourselves (either as individuals or groups) under some sort of perceived threat to our personal or collective goals. These goals are usually to do with our interpersonal wants. These perceived threats might be either real or imagined. (Condliffe 1987, 78).

This definition has three elements which are helpful in explaining the nature of conflict. Firstly, conflict is seen as involving a perceived threat. 'Perceived' is an important word here as the basis of the conflict may be 'false' or indirect in the sense that there is no real clash of interests or goals between the parties, but the parties nevertheless perceive, and therefore experience conflict. Secondly, conflict is experienced at the interpersonal level that is in our interactions with people. Thirdly, the dimensions of conflict, relating to our interpersonal wants, are helpful in linking conflict to the idea of personal and social aspirants. All of these elements are useful to understand the nature of conflict.

CONFLICT RESOLUTION STYLES

Psychologists have identified the following conflict resolution styles:

- **Avoiding** or denying the **conflict:** Assuming that the person involved in the conflict will give in and move away is quite unusual. Hence, this is not a desired approach. This kind of resolution style does not help the individual.
- Many prefer to **give in** rather than fight. The reason may sometimes be such that they are being a martyr, sometimes they are scared, or sometimes they seek appreciation, etc. In any case, this is another undesirable approach, because it is unfair, and it generates no creative solutions, and usually such an accommodator remains very unhappy.
- Some people **get mad and blame** the other person. 'You ignored my authority' or 'You are totally unfair' or 'You've hurt me' etc. are some such utterances in a state of blaming others. Such a conflict becomes an unpleasant battle in which they must 'get their way' and win at any cost (like in a divorce settlement). This is also a terrible approach because it stops all constructive thinking, is unfair (deceitful, threatening, chauvinistic), and produces lasting hostility.
- Other people appear to seek a **compromise**, i.e. find some 'workable agreement'. It would be wonderful, if it were entirely true, but

sometimes a part of this approach is subtle but skilfully trying to win more ground than your opponent. The objective becomes an effort of trying to prove you are clever. Thus, political or social pressure, misrepresentation, threats-with-a-smile, and so on may slip in, rather than simply seeking an optimal solution for both sides.

- A few people can control their anger, competitive instincts, and 'I-give-up' feelings and genuinely seek an innovative, fair, optimal solution for both parties. This is a creative and an integrative approach that one can opt for. However, this requires skill and ability to exercise wisdom in the trying times of conflict.

'Win-win' negotiating is complex process for resolving conflicts, a way of fairly settling a disagreement. It isn't getting the best for me; it is finding the best solution for us. The conflict could involve a lover, your own children, a parent, a friend, a co-worker, a teacher, a boss, or almost anyone. This involves respectfully discussing as equals the general situation with the other person, so that you can understand his/her situation and interests. You must suspend your judgement and needs; you must 'hold your fire' and listen to the other side; you must see their viewpoint and know their needs. Both parties must view the conflict as a problem to be solved by them in the best way possible, not just fairly but optimally, and even creatively. Both should be open and honest, and not be deceptive and manipulative. Trust must be built.

If an attempt to find a co-operative, integrative solution fails, you could seek professional help with the mediation, as in marital mediation. In some cases, you will have no choice except to confront an aggressive opponent. Win-win solutions (integrative) are fair, optimal solutions between reasonable people; tough bargaining occurs with an untrustworthy, self-serving opponent. In some cases, perhaps win-win negotiating can be combined with tough bargaining methods, but most of the time they are very different processes. It is probably important to know both methods, however, and to be willing to get tough (or empathic) if the situation calls for it.

PURPOSE OF CONFLICT RESOLUTION

Resolving disagreements as fairly and peacefully as possible is the purpose of conflict resolution. This may involve parent-child, teacher-student or marital conflicts, disagreements at work, business transactions and many other situations. Resolving conflict in a peaceful way will enhance the psychological well-being of both the parties and it helps both the parties.

THE COLLABORATIVE VERSUS THE COERCIVE APPROACH

In conflicts we experience and observe, we witness the inability of parties to be open and co-operative. They treat each other like nations at war. Sometimes, however, the parties are able to engage in open and well-regulated approaches. In other words the issue or the problem is dealt with in a collaborative way so as to serve the interests of all the parties in the best possible way. Roger Fisher and Cot Brown have provided a seven-point summary contrasting a collaborative approach with what they term a coercive approach (Fisher and Brown 1989). This approach to conflict management is often termed as 'win-win' or integrative negotiation.

- **Attacking the individual vs attacking the problem:** Instead of criticizing the other concentrate on the problem. It is better to be hard on the problem and soft on the people. A simple technique to help this is to be by the side rather than being head on.
- **Winning a contest vs solving a problem:** Making an assumption that we are in a contest immediately leads us to conclude that someone is going to win and someone lose. It is better to treat negotiation as a joint problem-solving effort.
- **Making an early commitment vs remaining open:** The often-used tactic of locking oneself into a particular solution so as to try to force the other to negotiate on one's own terms sometimes works but may be disadvantageous in the long-term. People often resent such tactics. It is usually better to remain open to persuading and alternative solutions.
- **Focus on positions vs exploring interests:** Instead of trying to settle the matter too early by stating a position, it is better to try to understand the issue. Instead of trying to find a solution by bargaining over respective positions, concentrating on interests can bring the parties closer together.
- **Worsening their outcomes vs improving ours:** Instead of concentrating on threatening, hurtful, or 'either/or' outcomes, it i s better to think about one's 'Best Alternative to a Negotiated Agreement' (BATNA) which is what one could achieve or get if the negotiation fails.

CONFLICT MANAGEMENT SKILLS IN PRACTICE

Attitudinal change, having clear communication, being empathetic, brain storming, negotiating, and working out the agreeable and best compromise are the basic strategies one can use to resolve the conflict. One may follow the below outlined guidelines to effectively manage the conflict.

Start with the Right Frame of Mind

As Thomas Gordon (1975) emphasizes, referring to parents in conflict with children, it is better to view the situation as 'two equals trying together to solve our problems' than to think 'you will do it my way because I say so'. Being in conflict doesn't necessarily mean being mad at each other. It can mean an opportunity to show your wisdom, to create a better situation, to help both of you be winners. Having a negative, distrustful attitude is detrimental to this process; believing you must 'win' the argument or otherwise you lose face is a bad attitude; feeling superior or being 'hard-nosed' and feeling inferior or being a 'soft-touch' are both problems. Start by seeing your opponent as a decent, reasonable person who wants to arrive at a fair solution (until proven otherwise).

Deal with him/her with respect. Just as you would separate the person from his/her behaviour, separate the person from the conflict.

In this fair and co-operative spirit, invite the other person to sit down and talk it over with you. Even with warring spouses, marriage mediation has proven to be far superior to settling disputes in divorce courts. Lawyers in court do not take a co-operative, integrative problem-solving approach; they take an adversarial, 'get all you can', 'let's-prove-who's-wrong' approach. If we can control our emotions just a little, however, we can usually work out good solutions. The co-operative, integrative solution approach is not appropriate in all cases.

Have a Discussion to Understand the Problem of Both Sides. Be Empathic.

It is an important to make the first meeting as cordial as possible while being honest and open. Persuading the other person to take the 'win-win' approach may take time, especially if the other person is angry. Admit there is a conflict; acknowledge that both of you have legitimate needs and goals. Be respectful and, empathize as much as possible, with each other. Indicate that you are willing to be flexible and open-minded; ask them to be so and if both are willing to make a sincere effort to work out an optimal solution, recognizing that neither can have everything he/she wants, an amicable resolution can be designed. It always makes sense to take the necessary to understand both the sides.

Start by clarifying to each other exactly what the conflict or problem involves. Find out what they want. Get all the information the other person has to offer. Ask for all the additional information you need. Do not try to offer solutions right away. First, just listen to their side, get all the facts, and give the situation some thought (solutions come next time). Keep on maintaining a good relationship, talk over coffee or take a walk together. Be as understanding, empathic, and sympathetic as you can be (considering that you may be viewed as the villain).

It is important to use 'I' statements and avoid blaming 'you' statements. Be especially aware of offensive language or attitude, e.g. don't assume that union's only care about pay increases, don't use offensive language, don't act as if all females are secretaries, etc. When describing your hopes for the future, don't just express the benefits you want, describe the benefits you hope the other person (or other side) receives too.

Special attention must be given to the causes (try to avoid blaming) of the conflict, as seen by both people. List the things each of you do that has not helped to resolve the conflict. Consider what attempts have been made to resolve the issue before. Also, very specific behavioural descriptions of the desired outcomes should be gotten from both people. At the end of this discussion, both people should understand the exact nature of the disagreements. Be sure you do much more listening than defending or 'explaining'. Do not, at this point, disagree with the other person's ideas and certainly don't attack or insult them.

Suppose an employee asks for a higher salary (his/her 'position') but the company can't pay it. If you found out that the employee liked the job but his/her 'interest' was primarily to get some transportation for his/her family, the company may be able to find extra work or a vehicle for the employee. Suppose a principal wanted to fire a poor teacher ('position') but couldn't because of tenure. If the principal's 'interest' (and the poor teacher's goal) was to improve the instruction in the teacher's classroom, there may be many solutions, such as hiring a skilful teacher's assistant to help out, co-teaching with a superior teacher, helping the teacher get more training, transferring the teacher to another kind of work, etc. Stating different demands or 'positions' does not mean that your basic 'interest' is irreconcilable.

Recognize that there are probably many possible solutions that would meet the interests of both the parties. Talk about your shared interests. It helps you avoid thinking you will accept only one solution. Also, avoid feeling competitive and that you must come out on top or get some concession to save face. All of this takes time.

Gather All the Additional Information You Need and Think of Several Options or Plans for Resolving the Conflict and Satisfying Shared Interests. Try Brainstorming.

Drawing upon the things you both agree on and upon your shared goals and interests, draft some plans for changing things and for greater co-operation which will maximize the desired outcome for both of you. Have several plans or ideas (to demonstrate your flexibility).

One person, say a parent or child, may simply ask the other to join in a rational, adult-like effort to resolve a difficulty between them. They are respectful of each other as equals; both contribute to the solution. There is no force, no threats, no crying or whining or other pressure to get one's way. You should possess logic, respect, and consideration of each other. Both accept in advance that the final 'solution' must be acceptable to both. No one is drawn; everyone wins as much as possible.

If you are negotiating for a promotion or trying to sell an idea, obviously you must amass all the evidence supporting your points. For the promotions, list all of the strengths you bring to the company, what extra responsibilities you will shoulder, how your salary can be made contingent on your productivity, how much support you have from colleagues, etc. Put together your best arguments and present them well. Don't just assume the decision-makers will 'consider your merits', even if you say nothing.

If you can't think of good solutions to the conflict, try brainstorming with friends, colleagues, or with person with whom you are in conflict. Both of you are looking ways you both can win. Do some reading. Try to be creative.

Both of You Present Your Plans for Resolving the Conflict: Try to Integrate the Best of Both Plans. Or, Make a Fair Offer or Express a Request. Negotiate the Differences.

Don't present your ideas as the 'ideal solution'; be tentative and honestly welcome different or better ideas. Nevertheless, clearly state the logical reasons for the plans or offer you are proposing. Make it obvious that you have considered the other person's needs and preferences.

It may be wise to present two of your best alternatives and then ask other person which he/she likes the most or if he/she can see ways to improve on your proposals. This shows your flexibility. If the other person seems unhappy with your suggestions, ask: 'What would you do if were in my shoes?' or 'What don't you like about my suggestion?'. These kinds of discussion may disclose the other person's interests and motives, which can perhaps be integrated.

It is often to your advantage to consider what your alternatives are if you do not get your 'interests' met through this negotiation process. If you have other acceptable options (besides the one you are negotiating for), that gives you some security and some power because you can always walk away from these negotiations. Also, you might not always but sometimes be wise to reveal to the other person that you have other choices. If you do not have good alternative (like another job opportunity), present your best case, appeal to the other person's sense of fairness, and use the opinion or factual information to support your proposals.

Normally, the other person will have his/her own plan or will make a counter-proposal. Do not attack the plan immediately. Instead, earnestly ask 'why' and 'how' these changes will help them and you (you are looking for a mutually beneficial solution); this discussion will uncover his/her basic 'interests'. Give the other person support and encouragement when he/she proposes solutions that address your shared interests. Then the best of both plans can be integrated, while the remaining disagreements can be discussed and compromises sought.

Watch Out for These Common Pitfalls in Negotiations

One of the most common mistakes is assuming that one proposal (usually yours) will solve all the problems. So, forget about finding 'the best single answer'. In most situations, a good compromise is made up of several changes that benefit you the most (and the person. So, don't argue over every proposal made; the task is to find the best combination of changes. This is why *brainstorming* is so helpful.

Perhaps the most serious pitfall is failing to agree about how to make decisions. If this is left unclear, people will naturally start using all the power they have to get their way, including threats, power, withdrawal, crying, personal attacks, amassing personal support from friends, saying, 'Take it or leave it', and so on- a process that is destructive. In 'win-win', the two people must agree on the basis for deciding, e.g., the proposed change is fair, it hurts no one else, it is reasonable, it is likely to produce the desired outcome (meet our 'interests'), etc. Use reason, not emotions (such as a determination to get one's way). Thus, decisions are based on principles of justice and logic, and on rational expectations about effectiveness, if that is what both parties agree on.

Occasionally, you may misjudge the type of person you are dealing with, for example, you may assume the opponent is a congenial, dependable person willing to participate in a 'win-win' negotiation but find out in the final stages that he/she is really a determined, hostile barracuda, posing a potential risk. However, win-win negotiation is based on the assumption that most people will see the wisdom of being fair and seeking an optional solution for both sides. It certainly would be a mistake to assume that every adversary will be inconsiderate, unyielding, and hostile. Sometimes, though, tough and even mean negotiation can't be avoided.

Max Bazerman describes five common mistakes while trying to resolve more competitive negotiation:

i. Believing the person must lose for you to win.
ii. Discovering too late that more information was needed, e.g. 'I should have had valves checked before I bought the car'.
iii. Making extreme demands, investing too much in getting your way, and thus, becoming reluctant to back (and, at the end, not getting the promotion or the improved relationship). It should be a warning sign

to you when you start to use anger or try to make your opponent look bad or weak.

iv. There is a consistent human tendency to believe that we are right and are being reasonable. Much more often than we realize, other people disagree with what we think is fair. Therefore, get an unbiased outside opinion. Negotiators, who are realistic and willing to see the other views of justice, are more successful compromisers.

v. If you are thinking mostly in terms of what you could lose, you are likely to hold out for more – and lose everything. We hate to lose, even by a little. The wise negotiator facing big losses may quickly 'cut his/her losses'. However, when you have accepted a small loss, emphasize to your opponent what he/she has to gain by your co-cooperativeness.

vi. Lastly, watch out for deceptive, mean, and selfish techniques.

What to Do if and when the Going Gets Tough

Keep in mind a saying- 'The relationship is much more important than the conflict'. Stress to the other person the importance of a positive future. Look for the opponent's real reasons. Ask him/her why he/she resists giving in on some issue. May be the other person will start person will start talking about his/her needs ('interests') and reveal his/her underlying motives. If it is a martial conflict, perhaps the histories of both partners need to be considered.

If the opponent attacks your position or you personally, listen politely and then try to divert his/her into the constructive development of a workable option by saying, 'That's interesting! What other ideas do you have that would improve this plan'. Stick with the win-win philosophy.

On the other hand, it would be foolish not to even consider the possibility that the negotiations might fail to produce a wonderful solution. Make sure that you do all that you can to plan or even develop good alternatives for your life in case this effort is disappointing.

When the discussion continues to be heated and opponents seem impossibly at odds, it may be helpful to take a break. If there is a stalemate, it may be fruitful to call in a mediator. In marriage counselling and divorce settlements, mediators are especially helpful. Labour disputes profit from a negotiator. When the animosity is so intense that it blocks all progress, someone else has to intervene.

Agree upon the Best Compromise Solution Available. Try it Out.

Consider the pros and cons of each possible solution, based on the criteria you have agreed to use. Do this co-operatively without either person dominating the decision-making process. No solution is possible that will completely satisfy both parties but both parties can be equally satisfied. It takes time to achieve this balance and still have a solution that both parties see as a definite 'win', not over the opponent but over the problems.

Work out the details of how to carry out the solution. Who does? What? When? Be specific. What responsibilities does each person have? Decide how to determine if the agreement is working well. Try out the solution for a week or so, and then re-evaluate it. Set a date to discuss your progress. Praise each other for making contributions to the solution. Make more changes as needed.

Any method, which reduces the animosity and stress in a conflict situation, is worthwhile. One danger is not taking the time to negotiate well. Another danger is the outbreak of animosity, regardless of how well win-win negotiation is attempted.

NEGOTIATION

Negotiation is one of the most common forms of conflict management. Everyday we negotiate with something. We negotiate with our colleagues over where to go for lunch, with our co-teacher as to whether she/he can take our class when applied for leave. We also negotiate with ourselves about how to keep certain commitments like a diet or stopping a specific bad habit. It has been widely acknowledged that 'win-win' negotiation is the best kind of negotiation. There are four steps to win-win negotiation that almost anyone can perform with ease. These steps include plans, relationships, agreements, and maintenance.

Establishing Win-win Plans Is Simple

You need only to set your own goals before you. Therefore, you must be able to anticipate goals of the other party in advance, determine areas of probable agreement between the goals of the others, and your goals. Develop win-win solutions to reconcile areas of probable disagreement.

Developing a Win-win Relationship Is Easy

You have to plan the activities in such way to allow a positive personal relationship to develop. Cultivate a sense of mutual trust with others. Allow the relationship to fully develop before discussing business in earnest.

Forming Win-win Agreements Is Easy

In order to enter into an agreement with others, you have to confirm the other party's goals. You must verify areas of agreement between your goals and others' purpose, and consider win-win to reconcile areas of disagreements jointly resolve any remaining differences.

Performing Win-win Maintenance Is Simple

You nee only to

- maintain commitment by:
  a. providing meaningful feedback, based on performance.
  b. holding up your end of the agreement
- maintain the relationship by:
  a. keeping in contact
  b. reaffirming trust

SUMMARY

- Conflict is an unavoidable and arises in many spheres including in educational institutions. Learning to resolve conflict yields a positive outcome to both the parties in a conflict situation.
- The conflict may be a power struggle, a need to prove you are right, a superior attitude, a desire to hurt or some other motive.
- Conflict is defined as a form of relating or interacting where we find ourselves (either as individuals or groups) under some sort of perceived threat to our personal or collective goals. These goals are usually to do with our interpersonal wants. These perceived threats might be either real or imagined.
- There are five identified conflict resolution styles and 'win-win' method of negotiating is considered to be an advantages conflict resolution method.
- Attitudinal change, having clear communication, being empathetic, brainstorming, negotiating, and working out the agreeable and best compromise are the basic strategies one can use to resolve the conflict.

REFERENCES

Codiffe, Peter, 1995, *Conflict Management: A practical guide*, Malaysia: Buisness Information Press.

Fisher, R. and S. Brown, 1989, *Getting together*, London: Business books.

Gordon, Thomas, 1979, *Conflict and conflict management in Handbook of industrial and Organizational Psychology*, Chicago.

15

Team-building Skills

After reading this chapter, you will be familiar with:

- Characteristics of well-functioning teams
- Team roles
- Characteristics of good team-building
- Guidelines for team effectiveness

INTRODUCTION

Individuals do not work in isolation. Students, teachers, doctors, scholars, and everybody, irrespective of their professional background, work in teams. Team-working is the ability of a group of individuals to form into a cohesive unit to achieve a common goal. Teams have significant advantages over disorganized individuals in many work situations, such as (i) distribute workload evenly and co-ordinate effort, as long as everyone on the team contributes fully; (ii) shared responsibility for problem-solving, testing ideas and decision-making; and (iii) better motivation and support through building rapport between colleagues.

However, building a successful team takes effort. To be successful, a team needs to be united in the pursuit of a goal, with an agreed process to achieve the goal. However, in addition to focusing on the goal and meeting deadlines, the needs of the team members should also be taken into consideration. When working in a team, it is important to remember to treat colleagues as you would your customers. You can use customer-service-skills (attitude, active listening, assertiveness, negotiation, questioning, conflict resolution, communication, and so on) to manage your relationships within the team.

TEAM

'A group of people, working together, reporting to one boss, flexibility, co-operation, having one aim, synergy, whole is greater than sum of its parts' are the terms and phrases that are used to describe 'a team'. Some of these terms are the features of good teams. For example, 'whole > sum' is a feature of a team that is working well together, but there are some teams whose collective performance falls short of what you might expect given the quality of individuals. The Apollo Syndrome is a good example–where a team composed of highly intelligent people often performs worse than teams made of up 'mess-able' members.

The term 'reporting to one boss' can be misleading. In a well-designed organizational structure, people reporting to one boss do often form 'teams'. But reporting lines are frequently designed within the constraints of grading structures. There is often a compromise between pay structures or traditional reporting lines, and grouping people together who are a team, out of sheer necessity. In reality, team structures are often complicated, and people can be members of several teams, as a team is a group of people working together for a common goal.

Characteristics of Well-functioning Teams

- **Purpose:** Members proudly share a sense of why the team exists and are invested in accomplishing its mission and goals.
- **Priorities:** Members know what needs to be done next, by whom, and by when to achieve team goals.
- **Roles:** Members know their roles in getting tasks done and when to allow a more skillful member to do a certain task.
- **Decisions:** Authority and decision-making lines are clearly understood.
- **Conflict:** Conflict is dealt with openly and is considered important to decision-making and personal growth.
- **Personal traits:** Members feel their unique personalities are appreciated and well-utilized.
- **Norms:** Group norms for working together are set and seen as standards for every one in the groups.
- **Effectiveness:** Members find team meetings efficient and productive, and look forward to this time together.
- **Success:** Members know clearly when the team has met with success and share in this equally and with pride.
- **Training:** Opportunities for feedback and updating skills are provided and taken advantage of by team members.

Team Roles

According to Dr Meredith Belbin's analysis of how teams work, as well as the job functions they perform, each team member can take on a role within the team. Teams require the following basic roles to succeed:

- Creators: to originate and discover ideas
- Leaders: to organize, manage, and direct the team
- Implementers: to build and support the team and find practical applications of ideas
- Completers: to evaluate and test ideas critically and in detail.

Working in a Team

It is important for each member of the team to understand and accept their role and responsibility in contributing to the group effort. Ideally, the team should contain people capable of balancing these different roles. People are generally naturally suited to one role more than others, though they may have to take on other roles in order to sympathize with and balance the team. Members of a team should take their responsibilities seriously, or they risk generating resentment from other team members. Team workers should:

- Maintain their customer service attitude, to treat their colleagues with respect
- Contribute fully to the team, while remaining open to others' ideas
- Be prompt when attending meetings and meeting deadlines.

When working in a team, it must be realized that your own failures or poor behaviour will affect everyone else in the team. It is important for team members to be aware of the roles and tasks that other people are playing. This can be achieved by maintaining proper documentation of tasks and progress and by mentoring (one-to-one instruction). This contributes to the rapport within the team, and in a practical sense, allows someone to takeover in the case where a critical team member is ill or on vacation. It also helps to induct new members into the team, allowing them to contribute to the group effort more quickly.

TEAM-BUILDING

A team is a group of people working towards a common goal. *Team-building is the process of enabling that group of people to reach their goal.* In its simplest terms, the stages involved in team-building are:

- To clarify the team goals.
- To identify those issues which inhibit the team from reaching their goals.

- To address those issues, remove the inhibitors and enable the goals to be achieved.

The primary skills in this process are recognizing the right issues, and tackling them in an appropriate way and an appropriate order. Team-building can also take a different form depending on the size and the nature of the team. In a project environment, where team composition is continually changing, the emphasis must be on developing the skills in individuals to be effective team members.

Team-building is an effort in which a team studies its own process of working together and acts to create a climate that encourages and values the contributions of team members. Their energies are directed toward problem solving, task effectiveness, and maximizing the use of all members' resources to achieve the team's purpose. Sound team-building recognizes that it is not possible to fully separate one's performance from those of others.

Characteristics of Good Team-building

Team-building works best when the following conditions are met (Francis and Young 1979).

i. There is a high level of interdependence among team members. The team is working on important tasks in which each team member has a commitment and teamwork is critical for achieving the desired results.
ii. The team leader has good people-skills, is committed to developing a team approach, and allocates time to team-building activities. Team management is seen as a shared function, and team members are given the opportunity to exercise leadership when their experiences and skills are appropriate to the needs of the team.
iii. Each team member is capable and willing to contribute information, skills, and experiences that provide an appropriate mix for achieving the team's purpose.
iv. The team develops a climate in which people feel relaxed and are able to be direct and open in their communications.
v. Team members develop a mutual trust for each other and believe that other team members have skills and capabilities to contribute to the team.
vi. Both the team and individual members are prepared to take risks and are allowed to develop their abilities and skills.
vii. The team is clear about its important goals and establishes performance targets that cause stretching but are achievable.

viii. Team member roles are defined, and effective ways to solve problems and communicate are developed and supported by all team members.

ix. Team members know how to examine team and individual errors and weaknesses without making personal attacks, which enables the group to learn from its experiences.

x. Team efforts are devoted to the achievement of results, and team performance is frequently evaluated to see where improvements can be made.

xi. The team has the capacity to create new ideas through group interaction and the influence of outside people. Good ideas are followed up, and people are rewarded for innovative risk-taking.

xii. Each member of the team knows that he or she can influence the team agenda. There is a feeling of trust and equal influence among the team members that facilitates open and honest communication.

Part of building the winning team is having some group meetings. Meetings, or even parties or celebrations, with as many people as possible from the entire organization, help to build a feeling of solidarity throughout the organization. But it is also important to have everyone participate in smaller group meetings where some work is done or some decisions are made. This makes people feel that they aren't just part of some big group, but that they are an active, important part of a team. For key managers, or people in your work group, you should have an interactive meeting once per week; not a meeting where you just make announcements and summarize the work that has been done and needs to be done, but a meeting where everyone has an opportunity to give their feedback on substantive issues.

Team Destroyers

Some of the problems can rip the team-building process apart.

- **Jealousy:** Be on guard for jealousy. It is essential to smoothly work out on the aspect of jealousy. Start appreciating their work and slowly work out the differences.
- **Cynicism:** Some people are just negative by nature. They are to be handled with great care.
- **Lack of confidence:** Some people lack confidence in themselves and view attacks on their opinions as attacks on themselves, responding with statements like, 'Are you telling me my fifteen years of experience doesn't matter?'. Stop any discussion like this immediately and, patiently point out the defensive behaviour in a private one-to-one meeting.

You Do Not Have to Be Best Friends to Make a Team

There is no question that the personal relationships we develop on our team make a big difference in how we feel about our work and our workplace, as well as our team. But, contrary to popular belief, you don't have to be best friends to be an effective team. Best friends do not necessarily make a best team; best team-mates make a best team. Being a best team-mate is all about thoughtful behaviour. In a sense, it is about treating a team-mate as if, he or she were your best friend. It does not include socializing outside of work, or sharing personal feelings; what it does include is every kind of behaviour you can think of that conveys respect.

Think about the ways you demonstrate respect for your best friend. Do you offer help to your best friend when she needs it? Do you listen to your best friend without prejudging his ideas or opinions? Are you sensitive toward your best friend when he is experiencing personal problems? Do you accept your best friend's idiosyncrasies? Do you arrive on time for engagements with your best friend when you know it will benefit her? Do you share in your best friend's excitement and praise when he has achieved something? The answer can be 'yes' to all of the above questions. You can think of many more ways in which you show respect to your best friends. That is what it takes to be a best team-mate.

Being a Valuable Team Member

Taking responsibility is a key criterion towards being a valuable team member. Although the team leader is held accountable for establishing and monitoring team performance measurements, all team members are responsible for their team's success. If your prior experience was as a member of a work group, your contribution was to get your work done, your contribution as a team member goes far beyond the work itself. The notes in this reading provide you with advice about how you can interact with the people on your team more productively and offer you tips on how you, as an individual team member, can facilitate constructive team dynamics.

Your team meeting *is* your meeting and therefore it *is* your responsibility to do whatever is called for to make it effective. Team meetings are not something that happen to you; they are something that you make happen. Your team leader, as a participating member, has a piece of the action but he is not solely responsible. If your team has established a role called 'meeting facilitator', the concerned person might take the lead in reserving the meeting room, distributing the advance agenda, or similar tasks, but he is not totally responsible. Every single team member is responsible.

This is a drastic change in role definition for most team members and for team leaders as well. As a team member you can no longer afford to sit back and be an attendee, spectator, or complainer. You must be a full-time participant/observer, actively contributing to the content of the meeting and at the same time observing team dynamics and intervening when team members are behaving in dysfunctional ways. It is not an easy job but it must definitely be a part of your responsibility as a team member.

If you view meetings as an event that someone else plans and leads, and that you attend, it will not be an easy adjustment to make. And if your team leader is accustomed to being in charge of the meeting, the adjustment will be even more difficult. The first step in making the transition to this new role of participant/observer requires a major shift in mind-set by all. To behave responsibly, you must feel responsible. And your team leader must also be willing to share the responsibility.

Talk about how your meetings are structured, who decides what the agenda will be, what behaviours are inhibiting the team from accomplishing its intended tasks, and how the team feels at the end of the meeting and why. Then make some decisions collectively about what you can do to improve it.

Don't expect to feel comfortable right away with this added responsibility. It is like becoming a parent for the first time. There's so much to pay attention to. You cannot sit back and expect others to make it happen. It is a hard job and it takes an incredible amount of energy.

Your team meeting has two major focal points that require your attention—content and process. Content is what your team is working on; process is how your team members are working together. If I asked you to tell me how your last meeting went and you said, 'We discussed the consolidation project, put together a plan for year-end closing, and decided to set up a meeting with quality team to discuss error rates', you would have reported on the content of your meeting. Content sounds like those items which you would summarize in your meeting minutes.

There may be times during a team meeting when you feel you cannot participate because you are not conversant with the topic being discussed. Just because you cannot contribute to the content does not mean you cannot contribute at all. You are in a perfect position to observe and facilitate the team's process - and that's where teams need most help. Teams generally do fine with content; they usually have the right items on the agenda and enough contributing experts. Ineffective meetings are usually the result of dysfunctional teams' dynamics or process. The entire team is responsible for the success of your meeting and hence, all members should play an active role in facilitating healthy dynamics. When you are not engrossed in the meeting content, you have an advantage of perspective; you can concentrate solely on process.

How do you know whether a team's process is functional or dysfunctional? If the team strikes a balance between satisfying both its task and relationship needs, it has a healthy, functional process going, it marks an efficient team. Members behave in ways that facilitate getting the job done and at the same time make members feel valued, respected, included, and energized. Members leave the meeting saying, 'We were very productive and I surely like being a member of this team'. When there is an imbalance between task and relationship needs satisfaction, or not enough attention paid to either, the team's process is dysfunctional. If you hear members saying, 'We got a lot of things accomplished, but I can't stand the way members treat each other', it is an obvious sign that the team has not paid enough attention to its relationship needs. And if you hear, 'We are so cohesive; just like a family. But we sure didn't get much done', the team has slipped on the task side. And if ever you should hear, 'Another waste of two hours - nothing accomplished. Why can't people at least be civil to each other?', you know there is much work to be done on both the task and relationship sides of the equation.

Learning how to observe your team's process and intervene appropriately takes time and practice. If you randomly try to watch everything, you will see nothing. The key is to train your eyes and ears so that you can focus your observations. A good way to start focusing is to become acquainted with a few specific team facilitation roles, also known as intervention behaviours. Then look for the appropriate situations during your meeting to apply them. In other words, first learn what the helping behaviours are, and why and how they help.

'Take SOFI HAGE to your meeting. Put her to work and I guarantee she will make a significant contribution to your team's progress and success.' Exhibit 1 introduces SOFI HAGE. The name comes from the first letter of each of the task and relationship roles.

Exhibit 15.1

Team Facilitation Roles

Task	Relationship
Summarizer	Harmonizer
Orienter	Analyser
Gatekeeper	Fact Seeker
Encourager	Initiator

It is important that all team members understand and employ each of the four task and relationship roles listed in the exhibit.

The *Summarizer* urges the group to acknowledge consensus and reach a decision. When team members are wound up like the Energizer Bunny, the Summarizer breaks in with, 'It seems like we're all in agreement with the parts of the programme that need to be changed; can we move off that topic and discuss specific changes to be proposed?'. By asking for verbal agreement with the summary, the Summarizer helps the team get past one decision and onto the next decision point.

The *Orienter* prevents the team from wandering too far from the topic at hand; he or she brings them back and focuses them again when they do stray. This redirecting should not be done abruptly as in, 'Hey, we're way off here; let's get back on track', or 'David, you just took us off the topic again', because you don't want to introduce a negative effect into the relationship side of the equation. A useful and neutral way to intervene is with the question, 'Are we off topic right now?'.

The *Fact Seeker* tests reality to make sure the decision the team is about to make is doable. This team member always wants more information and is quick to point out the difference between a fact and an opinion. The Fact Seeker is also very helpful in pointing out when a team does not have all the information it needs to make a good decision. The Fact Seeker will suggest that the team get more data before proceeding. He or she is also good at checking the decision-making boundaries of the team, asking, 'Do we have the authority to make this decision?'.

The *Initiator* gets the team started on the right foot by always beginning discussions with the question, 'How should we approach this task?'. Getting agreement on a game plan before starting to work on the task itself is crucial to team effectiveness and is the distinguishing characteristic of the Initiator.

When you plan the Summarizer, Orienter, Fact Seeker and Initiator roles, you contribute to your team's productivity by moving the task along towards completion. Play the following relationship roles to ensure that the team members feel valued and respected, and you will make a major contribution to your team's cohesiveness.

The *Harmonizer* realizes that conflict is inevitable and that if left unresolved, they are the biggest barrier to a team's achieviement of health and success. The Harmonizer calls the team's attention to a conflict (especially if team members have not wanted to acknowledge it), by saying something like, 'Let's be honest: we've got some strong conflicting feelings about this issue. What steps can we take to resolve our differences?'. The Harmonizer is also able to focus discussion on meeting-specific needs as a way of mediating conflict. More help on mediation is given in some of the sections which follow: *When you reach an impasse, talk about needs* and *Hey, no Problem.*

The *Analyser* watches for changes in the vital signs of the team and brings these changes to the attention of the team. The Analyser, as the team member, is most likely to ask, 'How is everyone feeling about how we're working together?', or 'It seems we've lost our energy; what is happening?'.

The *Gatekeeper* is concerned primarily with team communication and participation. This member makes sure that all team members are actively listening to each other and understanding each other's messages. The Gatekeeper paraphrases message to make sure that everyone is on the same wavelength, and that every idea is understood by the group before being discredited or discarded. The *Gatekeeper* invites quieter members to participate and makes sure that more active members do not dominate.

The *Encourager* builds and sustains team energy by showing support for people's efforts, ideas, and achievements. If the *Gatekeeper* focuses on making sure that the content of the team members' ideas is clearly understood by all, the *Encourager* emphasizes members' participation by giving verbal approval: 'Good point—that's a great idea.' This is another role that helps people to feel valued.

It is extremely important that every member be ready and able to intervene as a facilitator. If you were an eight-member team and each person had a delegated responsibility to wear one of the SOFI HAGE hats and intervene appropriately, you would see a significant increase in your effectiveness. But you can do better than that by having each member wear all the hats and, thus, provide maximum facilitation coverage.

Learning the eight different roles may seem at first like an overwhelming challenge to you and your team-mates, but you will probably be surprised to find that some team members are natural at orienting or encouraging, or that some easily assume the role of summarizers and gatekeepers. To have all eight roles covered may just be a matter of learning a few more facilitation behaviours. I know you can do it and as a team you'll be glad you did.

Guidelines for Effective Team Membership

- Contribute ideas and solutions
- Recognize and respect differences in others
- Value the ideas and contributions of others
- Listen and share information
- Ask questions and get clarification
- Participate fully and keep your commitments
- Be flexible and respect the partnership created by a team—strive towards the 'win-win'
- Care about the team and the outcomes.

Team Leadership

Leadership is inspiring a group of people to achieve an objective. A combination of most or all of the following qualities may be considered:

- Form and organize a well-balanced and productive team, recognizing the different skills, abilities, and roles that other people can bring to the team.

- Encourage the best qualities in others so that they contribute fully to the team.
- Maintain a balance between the team members in group situations to ensure that everyone makes a useful contribution.
- Deal with difficult team members and get them 'back on track'.
- Organize team members and delegate responsibilities.
- Take responsibility for the completion of a project and the successful achievement of the goal.

TEAM EFFECTIVENESS

When evaluating how well team members are working together, the following statements can be used as a guide:

- **Team goals** are developed through a group process of team interaction and agreement in which, each team member is willing to work towards achieving these goals.
- **Participation** is actively shown by all team members and roles are shared to facilitate the accomplishment of tasks and feelings of group togetherness.
- **Feedback** is asked for by members and freely given as a way of evaluating the team's performance and clarifying both feelings and interests of the team members. When feedback is given it is done with a desire to help the other person.
- **Team decision-making** involves a process that encourages active participation by all members.
- **Leadership** is distributed and shared among team members and individuals willingly contribute their resources as needed.
- **Problem solving,** discussing team issues, and critiquing team effectiveness are encouraged by all team members.
- **Conflict** is not suppressed. Team members are allowed to express negative feelings and confrontation within the team which is managed and dealt with by team members. Dealing with and managing conflict is seen as a way to improve team performance.
- **Team member resources,** talents, skills, knowledge, and experiences are fully identified, recognized, and used whenever appropriate.
- **Risk-taking and creativity** are encouraged. When mistakes are made, they are treated as a source of learning rather than reasons for punishment.

After evaluating team performance against the above guidelines, determine those areas in which the team members need to improve and develop a strategy for doing so.

The team leader should be the liaison between the team and upper management. The team leader needs to know and work with upper management to obtain a full commitment from them in support of the team's programme.

However, when this happens, team members must realize that they have a major responsibility to make maximum use of the resources and support provided.

The team leader can encourage team member growth, and should be willing to take some risk by having members, whose resources are relevant to the immediate task, provide the leadership.

The team leader should be fair, supportive, and recognized by team members as one who can make final judgments, work with upper management, and give direction to the team as needed.

To assist the team leader in evaluating the level of team development, have each team member answer the twelve questions outlined. This should be followed by a discussion of the questions to determine where and how changes should be made to help facilitate the development of a strong team.

As team members build commitment, trust, and support for one another, it will allow them to develop and accomplish desired results. This commitment, trust, and self-determination by each team member are critical in achieving a sustained high level of performance. Team members will learn to appreciate and enjoy one another for which they are and will help keep one another on track. The team will have developed its working methods so that they become an informal set of guidelines.

SUMMARY

- A team is a group of people working towards a common goal.
- Team-building is a process of enabling the team to achieve that goal.
- The stages involved in team-building including clarifying the goal, identifying the inhibitors, and removing them.
- Team-building will occur more easily when all team members work jointly on a task of mutual importance.
- The team leader should be fair, supportive, and recognized by team members as one who can make final judgments and give directions to the team as needed.

REFERENCES

Adams, John D., 1988, 'The Role of the Creative Outlook In Team Building', in W. Brendan Reddy and Kaleel Jamison, eds, *Team Building*, Virginia: Institute for Applied Behavioral Science and San Diego; California: University Associates, Inc., pp. 98–106.

Francis, Dave and Don Young, 1979, *Improving Work Groups: A Practical Manual for Team Building*, San Diego, California: University Associates, Inc.

Eales-White, Rupert, 1995, *Building your team*, Kogan Page Ltd.

16

Time-management Skills

After reading this chapter, you will be familiar with:

- Common problems due to ineffective time management
- Purpose of time management
- Effective time management principles
- First things first

INTRODUCTION

According to Alan Lakein (1973), if you control your time you can control your life. Time is a precious commodity; everyone gets an equal share but we use it very differently. We also look at time very differently. About 57 per cent of us are present- and future-oriented, 33 per cent are mainly future-oriented, 9 per cent are present-oriented and only 1 per cent focuses on the past. Societies have different attitudes toward time. Some are rushed and punctual, others are relaxed and disregard the clock. Successful managers, professionals, and students are future goal-oriented. Productive people have set their priorities and scheduled their time accordingly. Unsuccessful, unskilled workers and procrastinating students are present-oriented and unorganized, fatalistic, and hedonistic. When current needs demand your attention, whether that is because the family must be fed or you 'must' have a good time with friends, it becomes harder to carefully plan for the future. Our situation and needs influence our orientation of time, but our time orientation (and needs) can be changed, leading to more success in life.

SCHEDULING TIME

Actually, once a time-utilization problem is admitted, scheduling your time may not be as difficult as you might think since several hours are already 'filled' with sleeping, eating, showering, working or classes, and other essentials. You only have to schedule the 'unfilled', available hours (for college students that's about 10 hours per day). If you don't plan how to use those hours, it is easy to be lulled into watching TV, talking with friends, etc. The idea is to decide, 'what is the best use of my time?'. Make a list of what you need to do each week and then, based on the time available, make a daily 'to-be-done list' for working on your high priority tasks.

COMMON PROBLEMS DUE TO INEFFECTIVE MANAGEMENT OF TIME

Since a lot of people waste time there must be a lot of problems managing time. First of all, many people have little experience organizing their lives, because parents, teachers, bosses, and friends have done it for them. They don't see the need for a schedule. Also, many people resent any barrier that interferes with their doing whatever they feel like doing at the moment. Thus, a schedule is seen as stifling by some and resisted. Planning their time is too time-consuming for others.

Secondly, some of us are pushed by pressing needs—a need for love and attention, a need to avoid responsibility and work, a need to believe the future will take care of itself (So, I can do whatever I want to right now), a need to escape real life by listening to music, watching TV, or reading a novel, and so on. In some cases, a new determination to schedule your time will get you going. In other cases, greater self-awareness (honestly looking at how you really waste your time) is needed. In still other cases, it seems to be almost impossible to become more controlled until some of the above mentioned basic psychological needs have been satisfied or, more likely, until we realize we are headed for failure, i.e., our life isn't working out as we had hoped. Many college students don't get motivated until they flunk out and have to work in a miserable job for a year or two.

Thirdly, as Covey, Merrill and Merrill (1994) point out, many of us spend our days handling what appears to be 'urgent' problems, such as answering the phone or mail, beating deadlines for never-read reports, attending meetings, impressing the boss, etc. which are not in a broader sense very important or useful. If your schedule is filled with unimportant urgencies, you won't have time to learn new things, to do long range planning, to be creative and original, to do research, to exchange ideas with others, to re-think your major objectives, to invent new opportunities, to try to prevent future problems, to help others, and so on. These latter activities result in greater productivity and more benefits to everyone; they are the essence of a thoughtful life. It is said, that 'the person who concentrates entirely on sawing wood, is likely to forget to sharpen the saw'. As aptly stated by Covey, Merrill and Merrill, our goals should be selected with care.

Fourthly, some people make their daily schedules too rigid and overly demanding. Your schedule should make you feel as if you have 'got it together', not like a failure or an incompetent. It would be foolish to plan every minute of every day. An opportunity—a chance to talk with the boss, a chance to become involved in a project, or a chance to meet someone—may appear at any moment. You must be ready to explore any good opportunity; otherwise, life can become a drag. Priorities and assignments and deadlines change every day; thus, the use of your 'tree' time every day must change a little, too.

PURPOSE OF TIME MANAGEMENT

It is essential to make better use of your time, both in terms of devoting time to high priority activities and to avoiding wasting of time or spending your time on less important things. It is also required to be time effective, not necessarily time efficient, by selecting the best thing to do at this moment from among the infinite possibilities. Effective time management principles will help you to do this.

EFFECTIVE TIME MANAGEMENT PRINCIPLES

There are several steps which outline the effective time management principles. They are outlined below:

Set Your Priorities. List Your Major Goals for the Next Few Months. Rate Each Goal. Ask 'What Are the Most Important Things for Me to Do?'

At least every month or so, reconsider your goals of life, your purpose in life, and/or your organization's mission. In this context, it will also be helpful to think of the important roles you would play, such as a son, a student, a part-time worker, a fraternity member, a teacher and an employee, or perhaps you are a husband, father, Head of the Department. Make a list of major goals which you consider are really important to accomplish in each of your roles—at work or school, in relationships, in organizations, and, of course, in personal growth. Now, go through the list and rate each goal as being the 'top' priority, 'second' priority or 'low' priority. We can't do everything which we'd like to do. However, we can guard against spending too much time on second or low priority activities. And we can avoid spending all our time in one area, e.g,. working desperately to be successful in our career while neglecting our family.

List What Needs to Be Done This Week in Order to Reach Your Top Priority Goals. Rate Each Activity:

It is very beneficial to review your situation each week, giving a few minutes of serious thought to what actually needs to be done to achieve your goals. For example, what would be especially appreciated by loved ones? What would improve my physical or emotional health? What can I learn that would help me do my work better or improve my relationships with others? What future problems can I avoid or prevent? What school or work assignments are due and most important? What kinds of things could I do that would really thrill me or inspire me or turn me on, or would leave a legacy to others? What tasks must be done to successfully achieve my major goals? You are now translating your major purpose in life—your aspirations—into concrete actions.

Based on your rather wide-ranging thoughts and feelings, make a realistic list of the learning and work that seems to be required to reach your 'top' priority goals. Be creative and realistic. Don't confuse goals with activities. Getting into M.Ed. course at ICFAI is a goal; activities leading to that goal are studying 4 to 6 hours every day, doing well in every semester, preparing for the examinations and projects for 5 hours every week or for 3 or 4 months, and so on. You will surely list many more activities than can possibly be done. Hence again rank the importance of each activity as 'top', 'second', and 'low'. This helps you decide what needs to be done to reach your important goals. If you don't know how to reach your goals, i.e., where you want to go, talk to people who have made it (or read their histories and advice). It is vitally important that your actions actually lead you to your goals. This knowledge of what leads to what comes from science, experience, and wisdom.

Observe How You Spend Your Time

It could be an eye-opening experience to simply record how you spend your 168 hours per week. Note how you waste time, spend time on low priority tasks, have trouble getting started, or tend to be inefficient. Also notice when you have most of the energy for exercising or hard work, when you are alert mentally, when you get tired or irritable, and what distracts you from high priority activities. This information may be useful in setting up a daily schedule so you will stay on task.

Make a Master Schedule of Fixed Activities for the Week

A master schedule for the week tells you how time is 'committed', i.e., time periods that you have already scheduled. It includes sleeping, dressing, eating, travel time, meetings or classes, housekeeping chores, time with loved ones, friends or children, and some leisure-relaxation-exercise time. This is your fixed schedule. It includes the things you must do. Your master schedule is pretty stable week after week. You need to write it down only once, and then make occasional changes as needed. The master schedule identifies the hours that are 'free', and that you have control over.

Keep a Running List of Assignments You Need to Get Done This Week

You have to keep track of what needs to be done soon, e.g., get a report written. Note any due dates, the time required (remember many things take twice as much time as we expected), and the importance of the task.

Make a 'To-Be-Done List' for Every Day

Considering your list of major long-range goals, your list of important goal-directed activities, your inefficient use of time, your already scheduled time, and your assignments due this week, you need to decide on your priorities for each day of the week. Then start scheduling activities in your 'free' time, giving priority to the most important ones. Some activities must be done at a specific time, e.g., an appointment to talk to an advisor. Other activities need to be done but can be done at any available time.

Do this scheduling early in the day (or the night before) and at the same time every day, so that it becomes a habit. This is the crux of wise time management. Do first things first. If possible, don't let yourself get inundated with 'urgent matters' that may not actually be as important as having time to think, to learn new skills, to plan better ways of doing the job, etc. Don't try to do a lot of little tasks first ('clear your desk') so you will be free to do important work later. That wastes prime time. It is important to avoid, whenever possible, doing low priority tasks, which can often be put off, perhaps forever. However, it is wise to include time in your schedule, say half an hour, for handling unexpected chores and another half an hour for 'catching up'. Don't feel guilty if you don't get everything done; you can do it tomorrow, if it is important. Make your daily schedule (to-be-done list) fairly specific indicating when during your 'free' time you will do certain tasks. Work on your more difficult or important tasks when you are most alert. Don't use your peak performance time for easy assignments or for socializing and playing.

Follow Your Daily 'To-Be-Done List'. Reward Yourself.

Learn to make your daily schedule realistic. You have to be flexible; new things will come up each day that requires attention. But the basic point is simple: work on your highest priority activities during most of your 'free' time each day. However, as Lakein (1973) points out, many of us procrastinate when faced with long and difficult or unpleasant tasks, even though they are quite important to us. What are the solutions?

The best is to recognize the tendency to 'put it off and, instead, do it now!'. Another approach to finishing the overwhelming job is called the 'Swiss cheese method'. You poke holes in a big project by finding short tasks to do whenever you have a few minutes that will contribute to the completion of the lengthy project. You can get some required information or a book. Or else you can at least write the first paragraph.

If you are avoiding an unpleasant task, perhaps you can get started by telling yourself, 'I'll quit in 5 minutes if it is really terrible'. It might not be as bad as you imagined. Recognize that putting off an inevitable chore just generates more stress and embarrassment. If nothing else works, take 15 to 20 minutes to do nothing! Don't fudge, do absolutely nothing. By the end of 20 minutes, you will be so bored and so anxious to 'get on with it' that you will start working on the difficult task immediately.

Being organized and productive in the areas that are important to you will be rewarding, but you need more rewards. Consider these suggestions: build into your daily schedule rest breaks or friendly interaction, give yourself 15 minutes for exercise or relaxing or light reading, mix pleasure with work, at the end of the day take time to review with pride what you have done, and so on.

Put First Things First

Covey identifies four generations of time management, after extensive survey he carried out. They are as follows:

i. Notes and checklists
ii. Calendars and appointment books
iii. Prioritization, clarifying values, and comparing the relative of worth of activities
iv. Preserving and enhancing relationships and accomplishing results

The first generation exemplifies the effort to give some semblance of recognition and inclusiveness to the numerous demands that consume our time and energy. The second generation reflects an attempt to look ahead, and to schedule events and activities in the future. The third generation adds to those preceding generations the important idea of prioritization, of clarifying values, and of comparing the relative worth of activities based on their relationship to those values. In addition it focuses on setting goals, daily planning, etc. However, as against time management, the fourth generation talks about managing ourselves. Rather than focusing on things and time, the fourth generation focuses on preserving and enhancing relationships and accomplishing results.

Table 16.1 The Time Management Matrix

	Urgent	Not Urgent
Important	QUADRANT I Crises, Pressing problems, Deadline-driven projects	QUADRANT II Prevention, Production capability activities, Relationship building, Recognizing new Opportunities, Planning, Recreation.
Not important	QUADRANT III Interruptions, Some calls, Some mail, Some reports, Some meetings, Popular activities	QUADRANT IV Trivia, Busy work, Some mail, Some phone calls time wasters, Pleasant activities

Every activity we perform during the day can be put in one of four quadrants:

i. **Quadrant I: Urgent and important**

This quadrant includes those items that represent true crises (for example, your mother has a stroke and you need to take her to the hospital), deadline driven projects (for example, a paper that has a deadline that cannot be moved and represents a substantial part of your grade), and other such truly important and pressing items.

ii. **Quadrant II: Not urgent but important**

This quadrant includes items that are truly important in our lives (preparation, relationships, relaxation, self-renewal, etc.) that we truly need to do to maintain our production capability abilities. Unfortunately, since they are not urgent ('Oh, I can put that off!') we tend not to do them. We procrastinate because they are not urgent. Unfortunately, if we do this long enough, this tends to create highly urgent crises which then force us back into Quadrant I and gives us less time doing quality activities. Upon reflection, most of us would conclude that our first things fall in Quadrant II. Hence although we ignore things, we are set up conditions so that we will have even less time to devote to these vitally important activities. If you don't take the time to plan for your paper and manage your time on that project you will find yourself having to stay up all night to get it done.

- Urgent matters are usually visible; they insist on action, and they are easy and fun to do.
- Important matters contribute to our mission.
- Effective people stay out of Quadrants III and IV.
- Quadrant II is the heart of effective personal management.

Answer this question: What one thing could you do in your personal and professional life that, if you did on a regular basis, would make a tremendous positive difference in your life? Chances are that it is a Quadrant II activity. Effective, proactive people spend most of their time in Quadrant II. Suggest Quadrant II activities instead.

iii. **Quadrant III: Urgent but not important**

This quadrant contains those activities which appear to be urgent (or at least seem to demand our attention as such) but are really not that important. Examples include: needless interruptions, multiple phone calls, and other people's minor issues (which they invariably seek to make major ones because they like to live in this quadrant!) among others. A good example is that of phone calls during your study time. Most of us are 'phone addicted' and find ourselves unable to resist a ringing phone. If you really take notice, you will find that most phone calls are not important. If it is important the person will call you back! This is a quadrant we tend to fall into when we become 'urgently addicted'. We get a nice rush from the pressures of Quadrant I and the success we have in solving these issues. Unfortunately, we then begin to fall into the habit of mistaking urgent matters in Quadrant III which are not important as being important. Hence our precious time tends to drift into Quadrant III (since there are more of these items hitting in on our daily lives than any other) and we end up dealing with not very important matters most of the time. As a result our PC abilities begin to erode and hence our productivity rapidly falls off as well. This is the sure path to personal failure. The message is clear. Our 'first things first' planning should aim at spending less time in Quadrant II and moving that time to Quadrant III activities. This planner, along with the planning instructional materials, is designed to help you move in this direction!

iv. **Quadrant IV: Not urgent and not important**

Here we find items such as excessive TV watching, means of time wasting, busy work, some phone calls, 'escape' activities, and others. Obviously we don't want to do these things in excess. The key is 'in excess'. Reading escapist literature (Romance) is not bad in and of it self, but when taken to extremes (i.e., we spend all week finishing off that novel instead of going over our notes) the danger should be clear. All the activities enlisted here have a valued place as once-in-a-while rewards, if not used excessively!

In summary, spending less time in Quadrant III and IV will give us more time to spend in Quadrant II, so that we can put first things first, with the added benefit that we will also be finding ourselves dealing with fewer Quadrant I crises.

The only place to get time for Quadrant II in the beginning is Quadrants III and IV. If you were to fault yourself in one of three areas, which would it be?

- The inability to prioritize.
- The inability or desire to organize around those priorities.
- The lack of discipline to execute around them.

To be effective, you need to stay out of Quadrants III and IV. To do this, you need to tell yourself and other people 'no' to activities, which lie in these areas.

The advances of the fourth generation are:

i. Principle-centred
ii. Conscience-directed
iii. Defines your unique mission
iv. Helps balance your life by identifying roles
v. Gives greater context through weekly organizing. The practical thread running through all five of these advances is a primary focus on relationships and results a secondary focus on time.

EFFECTIVENESS AND ADVANTAGES

Making the master schedule should only take a few minutes. Changes can be added quickly. It takes a few minutes to keep a continuously updated list of assignments and chores to be done. Making the to-be-done List for each day requires careful thought and may take 10 to 15 minutes. It is time well spent. A planned and organized day is more fruitful than one lived whimsically without any carefully considered goals. If you can avoid getting trapped into doing unimportant, unnecessary chores, the dangers of living an intelligently planned life are minimal compared to the risks of wasting time if you don't use to-be-done Lists. The advantage is that you have at least given your brain (and your values) a chance to influence your life.

SUMMARY

- Time is a precious category and controlling and utilizing time is required to be effective and successful.
- Lack of organization, planning, and inaccurate priorities are some of the common problems, which would result in ineffective management of time.

- It is essential to make better use of your time, both in terms of devoting time to high priority activities and avoiding wasting time or spending your time on less important things.
- Putting first things first is the cardinal principle of time management.
- Spending less time in Quadrant III and IV will give us more time to spend in Quadrant II so that we can put first things first, with the added benefit that we will also be finding ourselves dealing with fewer Quadrant-I crises.

REFERENCES

Culp, S., 1986, *How to get organized when you don't have the time*, Cincinnati, OH: Writer's Digest Books.

Mayer, J. J., 1991, *If you haven't got the time to do it right, when will you find the time to do it over?*, New York: Simon & Schuster.

Covey, Stephen R., A. Roger Merrill and Rebecca R. Merrill, 1994, *First things first*, Simon & Schuster.

Model Question Papers

Model Question Paper I

Time: 3 hours **Total Points: 100**

SECTION – A (40 POINTS)

Answer any two out of four.

1. a. Outline the conflict resolution styles with examples.
   b. Define soft skills and hard skills.
   c. Mention the functions of communication.

(10 + 6 + 4 = 20 points)

2. a. Discuss the time management matrix.
   b. What are the benefits of effective listening?
   c. Enumerate the major barriers to communication.

(10 + 6 + 4 = 20 points)

3. a. What are the channels of communication and its attributes?
   b. Our learners today are addicted to the SMS lingo that curtails and creates words interestingly. If we, as teachers, want to understand such learners enslaved by telephonic messages, we, the responsible teachers, should be aware of the principles of word making. List the five major principles of vocabulary construction. Give an example of each.
   c. Distinguish between communication context and communication intent.

(10 + 4 + 6 = 20 points)

4. a. What do you understand by models of communication? What are its purposes and functions?
   b. What is Apollo syndrome?
   c. Explain the importance of feedback in communication.

(10 + 4 + 6 = 20 points)

SECTION – B (20 POINTS)

Answer any two out of three.

5. a. What are the components of paralinguistic communication?
   b. Elucidate the ten commandments of good communication?

(5 + 5 = 10 points)

6. a. Explain the levels of communication.
   b. What are the desirable qualities of a good teacher?

(5 + 5 = 10 points)

7. a. Explain meta communication.
   b. What are the goals of interpersonal effectiveness?

(5 + 5 = 10 points)

SECTION – C (40 POINTS)

Answer any two out of four.

8. What are the characteristics of nonverbal communication? Give its functional importance.

(20 points)

9. Explain the role of 'I' messages in being assertive?

(20 points)

10. Discuss the unique qualities of writing as a communication skill that justifies the opinion that even in today's era of audio-visual explosion, writing well is the need of the hour.

(20 points)

11. Enumerate the characteristics of good team building.

(20 points)

SUGGESTED ANSWERS

Section – A

1. a. Conflict is part and parcel of life. It is essential to resolve conflicts, and researchers have identified five different kinds of conflict resolution styles. They are as follows:

i. Avoiding or denying the conflict

Some people deny or avoid the conflicts. Such people hope that the problem will recede. Usually it doesn't. So, this is a bad approach. This kind of resolution style does not help the individual. Ram has a conflict with Sudhakar. Ram, instead of resolving the conflict, is hopeful that the problem will vanish on its own in the due course of time. He does not do anything actively to deal with the problem. Ram's approach will only end up in sending wrong signals to Sudhakar. Hence, avoiding or denying the conflict does not take anybody anywhere.

ii. Giving in

Many individuals prefer to give in rather than fight. Sometimes people are being a martyr, scared, or seeking appreciation, etc. In any case, this is another bad approach, because it is unfair, it generates no creative solutions, and usually such an accommodator remains very unhappy. Whenever Radha is confronted with a problem with her husband, she has a tendency to give in instead of staying in a dialogue or resolving. She keeps brooding over the issue and spoils her psychological health and gets into depression. Hence, giving in is equally a bad approach to resolve the conflict.

iii. Blaming others

Some people get mad and blame the other person. They say, 'You ignored my authority', or 'You are totally unfair', or 'You've hurt me' etc. Such a conflict becomes an unpleasant battle in which they must 'get their way' and win at any cost (like in a divorce settlement). This is also a terrible approach because it stops all constructive thinking; it is unfair (deceitful, threatening, and chauvinistic), and produces lasting hostility. Mr. Rao has had problem with his subordinate and he expects his subordinate to listen to him and abide by his words at any cost. He does not communicate his ideas and is not transparent. He holds an illogical view that his subordinate should get things done without his explaining. He ends up in blaming his subordinate most of the time. This kind of resolution style is detrimental to the human relationship.

iv. Compromise

Some people appear to seek a compromise, i.e., find some middle ground and 'work out an agreement'. Sometimes a part of this approach is subtle but skillfully trying to win more ground than your opponent. The objective becomes trying to prove that one is clever. Thus, political or social pressure, misrepresentation, and so on may slip in, rather than simply seeking an optimal solution for both sides. Subbarao and Ramarao have an ongoing land dispute for several years. Instead of looking at win-win solution, each of them would like to win at the expense of other party. Hence, compromise is a better alternative in this kind of situations.

v. Win-win approach

'Win-win' negotiating is a complex process for resolving conflicts, a way of fairly settling a disagreement. It isn't getting the best deal for me; it is finding the best solution for us.

The conflict could involve a child, a parent, a friend, a co-worker, a teacher, a boss, or anyone. This involves respectfully discussing as equals the general situation with the other person, so that one can understand his/her situation and interests. Integrative solutions require both sides to carefully identify how their preferences are different and how they are similar. Then a solution is built on the similarities—similar ways of doing things, similar values, and similar desired outcomes. Both parties must view the conflict as a problem to be solved by them in the best way possible, not just fairly but optimally, even creatively. Both parties should be open and honest, not deceptive and manipulative. Trust must be built. Both parties work hard together to develop a wise, workable, 'win-win' solution.

b. Hard skills and soft skills can be defined as follows:

Hard skills

Hard skills are the technical competencies that an individual possesses, skills gained through educational learning, and practical hands-on application. Hard skills are quantitative in nature and can be measured. Raja, a 10th standard student can do any complicated sum in mathematics within no time. Padma, a 10th standard student has a very good grasp of science concepts. She can do even complex problems in science, very easily. Raja's and Padma's skill in mathematics and science drives them to choose engineering and medicine respectively. In the due course of time, Raja completes his B.Tech. from the Indian Institute of Technology and Padma completes her M.B.B.S. from the All India Institute of Medical Sciences. Both their skills in engineering and medicine can be called as hard skills, which they have learned through learning over a period of time. Their skills are quantitative, which means that their skills can be seen in terms of grades and percentages. Their skills are also comparable. In other words hard skills are essentially the technical abilities required to do a particular job or perform a specialized task. For example, a machinist must have the skills- the knowledge and know-how-to read technical diagrams and to shape metal to exacting specifications using a variety of equipment. A degree, diploma, or a certificate confirms that the relevant abilities necessary to perform a particular job have been sufficiently mastered. Hard skills are vital to get into employment. However, hard skills alone might not suffice to survive successfully. Soft skills are important in addition to hard skills. While the term hard skills, or technical skills, is a relatively straightforward concept, soft skills is somewhat more difficult to pin down, referring as it does to a very diverse range of abilities.

Soft skills

In contrast to hard skills, soft skills are generally interpersonal competencies and are more difficult to define due to their subjectivity, which consequently makes them difficult to measure. Typically, included in the ambit of the soft skills domain are the following things:

- Listening skills
- Communication skills
- Team-building skills
- Leadership skills
- Problem-solving skills
- Time management skills
- Persuasion skills
- Negotiation skills
- Analytical thinking skills
- Conflict management skills
- Assertiveness skills
- Feedback skills
- Counseling skills
- Presentation skills
- Mentoring
- Flexibility
- Self-awareness

The above list of soft skills are the skills relating to people's issues. Soft skills, in other words is the human capital. Raja, a B.Tech. graduate, from the Indian Institute of Technology has problem in being assertive and his friends generally bulldoze him. While Padma's professional skills are far more superior, she has difficulty in managing her time. Raja's non-assertiveness and Padma's inefficient management of her time can be regarded as lack of soft skills. Lack of such a skill is detrimental to the professional and personal success. Soft skills are as important, and often, even more important than technological skills to the success of an individual. One can achieve synergy if one has the combination of both hard and soft skills.

c. Communication is always purposeful. We engage in communication to achieve something functional. Communication serves different purposes at different times and different settings. Some of the major functions of communication are:

   i. Instrumental function – to achieve, or obtain something
   ii. Control function – to get someone to behave in a particular way
   iii. Information function – to express feelings

iv. Social function – for interaction and social contact
v. Alleviation of anxiety function – to sort out or to ease worry
vi. Stimulation function – to create interest
vii. Role-related function – to fulfill role expected behaviour
viii. Motivation function – the stimulation of personal choice and aspirations
ix. Educational function transmission function
x. Cultural function – to reinforce culturalties
xi. Entertainment function – to provide leisure time activity and
xii. Integration function – to bring about greater cohesion between social groups.

2. a. Stephen R. Covey has put forth the concept of time management matrix. After extensive survey in the said area, he has come up with an innovative way of looking at the concept of time.

The Time Management Matrix

He holds the view that the time management matrix has four quadrants and he explains the same as follows:

	Urgent	**Not Urgent**
Important	QUADRANT I crises, pressing problems, deadline-driven projects	QUADRANT II prevention, production capability activities, relationship building, recognizing new opportunities, planning, recreation
Not important	QUADRANT III interruptions, some calls, some mail, some reports, some meetings, popular activities	QUADRANT IV busy work, some mail, some phone calls, time wasters, pleasant activities

Every activity we do during the day can be put in one of four quadrants:

Quadrant I: Urgent and important. This quadrant includes those items that represent true crises (your mother has a stroke and you need to bring her to the hospital), deadline driven projects (a paper that has a deadline that can not be moved, and represents a substantial part of your grade) and other such truly important and pressing items.

Quadrant II: Not urgent but important. This quadrant includes items that are truly important in our lives (preparation, relationships, relaxation, self-renewal, etc.) that we truly need to do to maintain our production capabilities. Unfortunately, since they are not urgent we tend not to do them. We procrastinate because they are not urgent. Unfortunately, if we do this long enough, this tends to create highly urgent crises which then force us back into Quadrant I and gives us less time doing quality activities. Upon reflection, most of us would conclude that our First things fall in Quadrant II.

- Urgent matters are usually visible; they insist on action, they are easy and fun to do.
- Important matters contribute to our mission of life.
- Effective people stay out of Quadrants III and IV.
- Quadrant II is the heart of effective personal management.

Quadrant III: Urgent but not important. This quadrant contains those activities, which appear to be urgent (or at least seem to demand our attention as such) but are really not that important. Examples include: needless interruptions, many phone calls, other people's minor issues (which they invariably seek to make major ones because they like to live in this quadrant!), among others. A good example is that of phone calls during your study time. Most of us are 'phone addicted' and find ourselves unable to resist a ringing phone. If one really observes, one will find that most phone calls are not important. If it is important the person will call you back!

Quadrant IV: Not urgent and not important. Here items such as excessive TV watching, time wasters, busy work, some phone calls, 'escape' activities and others are found. Obviously one doesn't want to do these things in excess. The key is 'in excess'. Reading escapist literature (Romance) is not bad in it self, but when taken to extremes (i.e. one spends all week finishing off that novel instead of going over our notes) the danger should be clear. The activities here all have a valued place as once-in-a-while rewards, if not used excessively!

In summary, spending less time in Quadrant III and IV will give us more time to spend in Quadrant II so that we can put first things first, with the added benefit that we will also be finding ourselves dealing with fewer Quadrant I crises. Stephen R. Covey's approach is novel and is based on principle-centred paradigm.

b. Listening is an intellectual activity, our faculties function in different ways according to the kind of listening required by the occasion.

There are a number of benefits that you can get if you train yourself to listen effectively. Some of them are listed below:

- Can obtain more information.
- Can get acquainted with people and perceive how their minds work.
- Can improve good relationship with people.
- Can raise people's morale.
- Can obtain suggestions and new ideas.
- Can know why people perform as well as or as poorly as they do.
- Can solve problems and face situations that present perplexity with a composed state of mind.

c. Transmission of information, ideas, and feelings are the primary functions of communication. Effectiveness of communication depends upon the ability of the speaker to convey information to the audience clearly, accurately, and in a manner that will hold interest and attention. At times the process of communication is distorted because of the barriers that come between the communicator and the receiver.

Some of the major barriers are:

i. Filtering – a deliberate or unintentional selection of information.
ii. Distortion – selecting what suits us and our values.
iii. Communication overload – channel capacity can retain only a certain amount of information, overloading the system leads to mental fuse and shut down the communication process.
iv. Absence of redundancy – problem of grasping or appreciating anything new communicated.
v. Psychological conditions – all behaviours have a psychological base, the two important psychological factors that affect learning are, learning and motivation.

3. a. Communication channels are the means through which a source conveys a message to a receiver. Channels can be thought of as the path or the vehicles that carry messages from an originating point to a destination.

All communication can be broadly categorized as either interpersonal or mass media. This helps one to analyze the effects in the communication process. Communication through word of mouth as in face-to-face interaction between two or more persons can be classified as interpersonal. The channel in the interpersonal situation becomes the individual through whom the message is flowing. Mass media channels are those means of transmitting messages that involve a mechanism to reach a wide and often non-contiguous audience, e.g., newspaper magazines, films, radio, television, etc. Another important channel of communication is nonverbal communication. According to Ruesh and Gregory Bateson, nonverbal communication falls into three categories, sign language, action language and object language. Sign language is the way of codifying meaning. Action language is transitory and the most universal kind of language, e.g., the deaf depend upon the interpretation of lip reading. Action language is the principal way in which emotions are expressed, e.g., a person slams his fist upon the table. Symbolic information, tactile information a sin Braille—a language for blind in signs and words, like the creative arts, dance ballet, etc.

Channel attributes

Communication channels differ with regard to the effectiveness and efficiency with which they handle different topics of information. Channels vary with regard to

- the speed with which they transmit signals
- the ability to separate their own signals from those of other channels

- the accuracy with which meanings are conveyed
- the effectiveness with which channels communicate emotional information
- the effectiveness with which the channel communicates factual information.

b. Words are the backbone of communication. Especially our written communication can never be precise unless our vocabulary, that is, our word power is well stocked, yet fresh.

To make newer, more effective words for precise writing:

i. Often two or more simple words are compounded/joined together.
E.g., nonetheless, undertake, quicksilver, blackboard, green house, hothouse, cut-throat, and daredevil.

ii. Often prefixes are attached to the root to form words.
E.g., ante (before) + date = antedate
a (indifferent to) + theist = atheist
arch (main) + bishop = archbishop

iii. Similarly suffixes can be placed after the base of the word to get new derived usages.
E.g., demon → demonic → demonically → demonize
With one singular noun 'demon', we, thus, get an adjective (demonic), an adverb (demonically) and a verb (demonize).

iv. Often words come into existence through acronyms.
E.g., The UNICEF helps disadvantaged learners.

v. Sometimes two words merge to form a new vocabulary item.
E.g., breakfast + lunch = brunch
teleprinter + exchange = telex

c. A context or situation is a specific type of environment that produces specific requirements for successful communication. Some of the typical communication contexts are, interpersonal communication, public communication, group communication, and communication in career settings. Every day of our life we find ourselves in hundreds of situations requiring communication—all these situations are called context of communication. The context of communication influences the kind and type of communication.

Communication intent: communication is always carried out with a purpose. We acquire the skills of communication so that we can convey our messages appropriately; we try our best to communicate our intentions accurately to the intended receiver. This process is called communication intent. Both verbal and nonverbal communication plays a very significant role in intentional communication. However, in non-intentional interactions the nonverbal communication aspects are more important.

4. a. Communication process or a system is like a tool for explanation and analysis often in diagrammatic form, to show how the various elements of a situation being studied relate to each other.

Communication models are visualizations of the communication process. They are explanations of the basic theories concerning these elements of communication and how these elements operate and interact.

According to Devito (1978), communication models serve to organize the various elements and processes of the communication act. No model can organize all the data pertaining to communication, but we can expect a reasonably good model to organize at least some of the data into meaningful and interesting way. These models aid in the discovery of new facts about communication. Thus, they serve a heuristic function. These models enable us to make predictions concerning communication—what will happen under certain conditions. The models to a great extent can provide a means of measuring the elements and processes involved in communication.

The most important function of model is to assist in the development of more precise theories. Such functions can be enumerated as:

Descriptive function: A model is constructed to describe a particular form of behaviour of which either no theory exists or the theory is grossly inadequate. The model supplies more precision and specificity.

Explicative function: Models explain important but poorly developed concept in an existing theory and define more rigoursly a concept central to relatively well developed theory thereby rendering theory more testable.

Simulative function: Models simulate functional or process relations among concepts. An essential property is that, components be given values, relations among components be specified clearly and

b. Apollo Syndrome is a term that describes a team consisting of highly talented or qualified members who, however cannot function effectively as a team. 'A group of people, working together, reporting to one boss, flexibility, co-operation, having one aim, synergy, whole is greater than sum of its parts' are the terms and phrases that are used to describe 'a team'. For example, 'whole > sum' is a feature of a team that is working well together—but there are some teams whose collective performance falls short of what you might expect given the quality of individuals. The Apollo Syndrome is a good example of this—where a team composed of highly intelligent people often performs worse than teams made of up 'less-able' members.

c. Feedback refers to those messages sent by listeners and received by speaker, which enable speaker to gauge their effect on their receiver. Without feedback, we have no precise measure of how well the others are functioning in the communication system. Both positive and negative feedback can provide with valuable information as to the current qualitative state of communication in the group or between two individuals.

Positive feedback increases the magnitude and frequency of the communication.

Hence, behaviour can have beneficial effects when it follows desirable communication. Conversely, positive feedback is that which follows undesirable communication.

Behaviour can have undesirable effects on the quality of communication.

Negative feedback is particularly important in groups or individuals experiencing communication problems or where the quality of communication is not up to the mark. Positive feedback reinforces undesirable communication behaviour and negative feedback extinguishes undesirable communication behaviour. Feedback may be given in both verbal and nonverbal responses.

Section – B

5. a. In any context of communication, certain nonverbal cues are resorted to aid and reinforce the content of the verbal communication. These cues have rationale and are based on certain behavioural factors and are communicator specific. That could be speech modifiers or variations in speech delivery.

   The four important components of paralinguistic communication are: (i) rate – this refers to the tempo of speech, too fast or too slow (ii) pitch – this refers to the range of the voice-too high or too low (iii) volume – a good volume is one which can be comfortably heard by the listener. Effective communication requires suitable changing of volume (iv) appropriateness – speech delivery must be tailored for the speaking occasion. Communication can be effective only when it is appropriate.

   b. The American Management Association has given essentials of good communication. They are popularly called Ten Commandments of good communication, and are as follows:

      i. Clarify ideas before communicating: By systematically thinking through the message and considering who will be receiving and/or affected by it, the manager overcomes one of the basic pitfalls of communication—failure to properly plan the *communiqué*. The more systematically a message is analyzed, the more clearly it can be communicated.

      ii. Examine the true purposes of communication: The manager has to determine what he or she really wants to accomplish with the message. Once this objective is identified, the communiqué can be properly designed.

      iii. Take the entire environment, physical and human into consideration: Questions such as what is said, to whom, and when will all affect the success of communication. The physical setting, the social climate, and past communication practices should be examined in adapting the message to the environment.

      iv. When valuable obtain advice from others in planning communiqués: Consulting with others can be a useful method of obtaining additional insights regarding how to handle the communication. In addition, those who help to formulate it usually give it active support.

      v. Beware of the overtones as well as the basic content of the message: The listener will be affected by not only what is said but also how it is said. Voice, tone, facial expression, and choice of language, all influence the listener's reaction to the *communiqué*.

vi. When possible, convey useful information: People remember things that are beneficial to them. If the Manager wants subordinates to read the message, he or she should phrase it so that it takes into consideration their interests and ends as well as the company's.

vii. Follow up on Communication: The manager must solicit feedback in ascertaining whether the subordinate understands the communique, is willing to comply with it, and then takes appropriate action.

viii. Communicate with the future as well as the present in mind: Most communications are designed to meet the demands of the current situation. However, they should be in accord with the long-range goals as well. For example, communiqués designed to improve performance or morale is valuable in handling present problems. Yet, they also serve a useful future purpose promoting long-run organizational efficiency.

ix. Support words with deeds: When managers contradict themselves by saving one thing and doing another, they undermine their own directives. For example, an executive who issues a notice reminding everyone to be in the building by 8.30 A.M. while he or she continues to show up at 9.15 A.M. should not expect anyone to take the notice seriously. Subordinates are always cognizant of such managerial behaviour and quickly discount such directions.

x. Be a good listener: By concentrating on the speaker's explicit and implicit meanings, the manager can obtain a much better understanding of what is being said.

6. a. There are two levels of communication-intrapersonal and interpersonal. Intrapersonal communication is the process where we become the sender and/receiver of messages and then we evaluate, label, analyze or talk to ourselves. This process takes place within the self (intrapersonal) rather than between separate individuals. We receive stimuli either through the brain in the form of electrical impulses. At this point we make a determination about the relevance of the stimuli and either discard the thought or continue dealing with it. Dreams are a form of interpersonal communication. It is the most important level of human communication. Interpersonal communication means interaction between two individuals. The underlying reason for interpersonal communication is mainly for establishing meaningful relationships, changing attitude and behaviour, passing information, personal discovery etc. for effective interpersonal communication five qualities are essential—openness, empathy, supportiveness, positivity and equality.

b. A teacher has to be a good communicator. He should be cooperative and understanding, besides being involved in the education. A teacher should, besides having complete knowledge about his subject, have the following qualities:

i. He must possess a good and pleasing personality.

ii. His voice should be clear and understandable.

iii. He should make adequate preparations to present his subject.

iv. He should make a lively presentation that will instill and sustain the interest of the students.

The teacher should be well informed, well aware of his subject, having good personality, and should be interested in the profession. Desirable features to develop good communication are:

- Good physical health and personality.
- Above average intelligence.
- Creativity, imagination and resourcefulness.
- Good grooming, poise, refinement in voice and action.
- Courtesy, kindness, sympathy and tact.
- Patience.
- Sincerity and honesty.
- Firmness.
- Promptness, efficiency and ability to organize.
- Positive and encouraging attitude.
- Democratic leadership.
- Professional status.

7. a. Both verbal and nonverbal communication can be meta-communicational. The anthropologist Gregory Bateson (1972) pointed out that every communication must simultaneously communicate two messages, the basic message and the meta-message. The meta-message is encoded and superimposed upon the basic, which indicates how one wants another to take the basic message. The word 'meta' is derived from the Greek word and means higher or more. According to John Gumprez, each successful message carries with it a second meta-message, which tells the listener how to interpret the basic message. A basic message by itself cannot be interpreted without the help of the meta-message. Meta communication can simply be called communication about communication.

   b. The interpersonal effectiveness is for individuals wanting and willing to learn how to apply interpersonal skills to modify aversive environments and to obtain their goals in interpersonal encounters. Behaviours individuals will learn to increase include:

   - Standing up for your rights in such a way that they are taken seriously.
   - Requesting others to do something in such a way that they want to.
   - Refusing unwanted or unreasonable requests (learning to say no).
   - Resolving interpersonal conflict.
   - Getting your opinion or point of view taken seriously.
   - Acting in a way that makes the other person actually want to give you what you are asking for.

- Balancing immediate goals with the good of the long-term relationship.
- Golden rule: treating others, as you want to be treated.
- Maintaining or developing the good feelings about yourself, and respecting your own values and beliefs.
- Acting in ways that fit your sense of morality.
- Acting in competent ways.
- Expressing thoughts, ideas, and concerns clearly.
- Giving courteous, accurate, and complete responses.
- Listening attentively to others without interruption.
- Keeping commitments.
- Seeking accurate information (avoids jumping to conclusions).
- Treating all employees with respect regardless of their level, personality, culture, or background.

Section - C

8. According to Devito (1978) all nonverbal behaviour in an interactional situation is communicative. Nonverbal communication is inevitably contextual and is meta-communicational.

   Nonverbal behaviour whether of the hands, the eyes or the muscle tone of the entire body, are normally accompanied by other nonverbal behaviours that reinforce and support each other. Nonverbal communication can occur in packaged forms, we do not express fear in our eyes when we are smiling. Rather the entire body expresses that particular emotion. In fact it is difficult to express widely different or contradictory emotions with different parts of the body.

   The functional importance of nonverbal communication includes:

   - Nonverbal factors are the major determinants of meaning in the interpersonal context.
   - Feeling and emotion are more accurately exchanged by nonverbal communication.
   - The nonverbal characteristics of communication convey meanings and intentions that are relatively free of deception, distortion or confusion.
   - Nonverbal cues represent a much more effective means of communication than verbal cues.
   - Nonverbal cues serve meta-communicative function that is indispensable in attaining high quality communication.
   - Nonverbal cues represent the most suitable means for suggestion. We most frequently and accurately communicate our true feelings and emotions by nonverbal means.

9. Effective way of overcoming non-assertive behaviour is giving 'I' messages. The following aspects will explain the same.

   'I' messages denote accepting responsibility for our feelings. This is one of the most important skills you can acquire. A good rule of thumb is: 'If you have a problem, make an "I" statement. If you are helping someone with a problem, make empathy responses.' An 'I' statement consists of a description of how you feel and an indication of the conditions under which you feel that way. It takes this form: 'I feel (your emotions) when (under what conditions)'. It will be helpful if you recognize how many decisions you have made in the process of becoming emotional or upset.

   How we handle our feelings is based on our perceptions, our attributions, our understanding of what we are feeling, and our intentions, we are responsible for our feelings, because we have chosen to feel whatever we feel (no matter how miserable), so we must 'own' our feelings. In short, no one can make us feel any way; we decide.

   Regardless of the etiology of feelings, suppressing or denying our feelings may lead to several problems: (i) increased irritability and conflicts with others, (ii) difficulty resolving interpersonal problems (being 'logical' doesn't mean ignoring feelings, but dealing with them), (iii) distorted perception and blind spots (like seeing only the bad parts of a person we are mad at) in a relationship, and (iv) other people may suspect we have feelings and ask us to be honest with them (which is hard to do if we are being dishonest with ourselves or unaware). These are good reasons for expressing our feelings in a tactful, constructive manner. 'I' statements serve this purpose.

   'I' statements do not judge, blame, threaten, put down or try to control others; they simply report how you feel, which is rarely challengeable by anyone else.

   One can consider using 'I' statements:

   - Any time one wants to share one's feelings or desires in a frank, unthreatening, undemanding way. When one is trying to disclose more about oneself to build a relationship.
   - Any time stress is experienced in a relationship, especially if one is feeling angry or dissatisfied or if the other person is resistive to changing in response to the requests or demands.
   - If both parties have problems, i.e., both can take turns giving 'I' statements and giving empathy responses.
   - If the other person is using a lot of 'you' (blaming, critical) statements, try to translate them into 'I' statements and empathize with the accuser's feelings.

'You' statements	'I' statements
Blaming: 'You make me so mad'.	'I feel angry when you ___.' Or, 'I have chosen to let it bother me when you___.'
Judging or labelling: 'You are an inconsiderate, hostile, arrogant creep.'	'I feel betrayed when you criticize me in front of others.'

Accusing: 'You don't give a damn about me!'	'I feel neglected when you avoid me.'
Ordering: 'You shut up!'	'I feel annoyed when you call me by names and make fun of me.'
Questioning: 'Are yon always this flirtatious?' or 'Why did you do that? I feel like slapping your face.'	'I really feel insecure about our relationship when you flirt.'
Arguing: 'You don't know what you are talking about.'	'I feel convinced it is this way.'
Sarcasm: 'Of course, you are an expert!'	'I would like you a lot more if you were a bit more humble.'
Approving: 'You are wonderful', or 'You are-attractive'.	'I really am impressed with your ______ and besides I like you. I am attracted to you.'
Disapproval: 'You are terrible'.	'I feel crushed when you seem only interested in spending my money.'
Threatening: 'You had better ...'	'I'd like it if you'd ...'
Moralizing: 'You ought to ...'	'I think it would be fair for you to...'
Treating: 'You need to rest and...'	'I'd like to be helpful to you.'
Supporting: 'It will get better'.	'I'm sorry you feel ...'
Analyzing: 'You can't stand to leave your mother!'	'I'm disappointed that you are so reluctant to leave...'

Many of the 'you' statements are intended to exert power, to control, to intimidate, or to put down the other person. They are not statements made by non-judgmental, mutually respecting equals. They are authoritarian statements made by manipulators. That's why it is recommended 'I' statements to parents when talking to children.

'We', 'it', 'they' statements	'I' statement
'Most people would have an affair if they wouldn't get caught.'	'I would have an affair if...'
'The group isn't interested in...'	'I don't think the group cares...'
'The glass slipped out of my hand.'	'I dropped the glass.'
'People have a hard time with math.'	'I am ashamed of my math score.'
'The group is trying to help you.'	'I want to understand you but I'm having a hard time.'
'This weather is depressing.'	'I feel depressed.'
'This class is boring.'	'I feel bored.'

In summary

- An 'I' statement may have 2 to 4 parts: (a) it is a self-disclosure, referring to 'I', 'me', or 'my', (b) it expresses a feeling, urge or impulse, (c) it may describe the other person's behaviour which is related to your feelings, and (d) it may indicate what you would like to see changed, much like an assertive statement.

- Assume responsibility for your feelings and opinions, don't hide behind the 'it' or the editorial 'we'.
- Avoid stating personal opinions as facts and avoid the over-generalizations sometimes implied by forms of the verb 'to be', like 'are', 'is', 'am', and so on.
- Clearly, giving an 'I' statement is more constructive than giving an order, an accusation, a moral judgment, and so on. However, this is not an easy concept to grasp. The pronoun 'you' is used all the time, many uses are not bad. Try to become aware of the undesirable ways you use 'you.'

10. Writing is a special communication skill. Let us understand the unique qualities of writing as a communication skill.

    i. Let us begin with the division academia generally prefers. While studying the B.Ed., we have already learnt that of all the four LSRW skills, writing (of course, in addition to speaking) is an active skill of communication. In other words, when we communicate through writing, we are an agent or an initiator of the act of communicating. We are not mere recipients as in reading.

    ii. Reading, the passive counterpart of writing, has, nevertheless, a unique role to play in refining an encoder's written message. For effective communication through writing, the encoder has to be an efficient reader; such reading skills as pre-viewing, skimming and scanning, and using a library effectively to help a reader. In the final analysis, the encoder who reads more communicates better through writing.

    iii. Now let us look at the communication chain to understand yet another unique quality of writing. Communication is a process wherein an encoder sends a message to a decoder. The encoder uses a via media to convey his message. Writing is unusual as a communication skill because it uses very many different means to communicate this message. In addition to language, an author can use visuals and graphics—diagrams, charts, graphs, and tables—to communicate well. Secondary means such as these enhance the communicative possibilities of writing. We have to remember though that these effects are often not integral to the conveying of the message. Language is primarily responsible in conveying the meaning of the written communication. The content of the message and the style used are much more important than such visual designing which is often accused of diverting the decoder's attention. This possible problem should not conceal the fact that of all the communication skills, writing alone enjoys such a simultaneous multiplicity of media.

    iv. As a communication skill, writing is unusual in yet another way. When an encoder communicates through writing, his decoder is not physically present. Yet any form of writing is clearly decoder-oriented. A reader determines the way a writer writes. While writing a textbook for the pre-primary kids, our content and style would radically differ from the way we would write while preparing a handbook for management trainees. The way we would write a memo to our junior colleagues would differ from the official correspondence we share with the HRD Ministry. In all these instances, the absent decoder determines the contours of your communication. The textbook for the nursery kids, for example, would be heavy on visual effects while the handbook for the management trainees would be idea rich and more formal in tone.

v. Interestingly, moreover, as a communication skill, writing mixes the private and the public domains uniquely. As a communication event, it is for the eyes of the decoder only. The decoder is reading in total privacy, and all by himself, the content the encoder has generated but the concerns the encoder thereby shares with him deal with the rest of the world.

vi. Such a double bind makes writing a very effective tool of communication. It is not in vain that traditional wisdom maintains that 'the pen is mightier than the sword'. A book by Fidel Castro, for example, read in the privacy of the decoder's reading environment has a more radical effect than Castro thundering on in a public meeting. In the field of academics, for example, we can refer to Paulo Freire's literacy primers to understand how writing radicalizes its decoder. In this resistant sense, writing is the only communication skill that makes, mars, and changes its decoder's personality. Hence, it can very well be claimed that even in today's era of audio-visual explosion, writing well is the need of the hour.

11. Team building works best when the following conditions are met.

    i. There is a high level of interdependence among team members. The team is working on important tasks in which each team member has a commitment and teamwork is critical for achieving the desired results.

    ii. The team leader has good people skills, is committed to developing a team approach, and allocates time to team-building activities. Team management is seen as a shared function, and team members are given the opportunity to exercise leadership when their experiences and skills are appropriate to the needs of the team.

    iii. Each team member is capable and willing to contribute information, skills, and experiences that provide an appropriate mix for achieving the team's purpose.

    iv. The team develops a climate in which people feel relaxed and are able to be direct and open in their communications.

    v. Team members develop a mutual trust for each other and believe that the other team members have skills and capabilities to contribute to the team.

    vi. Both the team and individual members are prepared to take risks and are allowed to develop their abilities and skills.

    vii. The roles of the team member are defined, and effective ways to solve problems and communicate are developed and supported by all team members.

    viii. Team members know how to examine team and individual errors and weaknesses without making personal attacks, which enables the group to learn from its experiences.

    ix. Team efforts are devoted to the achievement of results, and team performance is frequently evaluated to see where improvements can be made.

x. The team has the capacity to create new ideas through group interaction.

xi. Each member of the team knows that he or she can influence the team agenda. There is a feeling of trust and equal influence among team members that facilitates open and honest communication.

Part of building the winning team is having some group meetings. Meetings, or even parties or celebrations, with as many people as possible from the entire organization, help build a feeling of solidarity throughout the organization. However, it is also important to have everyone participate in smaller group meetings where some work is done or some decisions are made. This makes people feel that they aren't just part of some big group, but that they are an active, important part of a team.

Model Question Paper II

Time: 3 hours **Total Points: 100**

SECTION – A (40 POINTS)

Answer any two out of four.

1. a. Distinguish between verbal and nonverbal communication.
   b. What is functional accent? Give examples.
   c. How important is gestural communication with reference to groups?

   (10 + 6 + 4 = 20 points)

2. a. Explain briefly kinesis and proxemies.
   b. Elucidate with examples two strategies to overcome non-assertive behaviour.
   c. What is entropy in communication?

   (10+ 6 + 4 = 20 points)

3. a. What are the principles of interpersonal context of person-perception?
   b. What are the dimensions of interpersonal effectiveness?
   c. Explain relational communication.

   (10 + 6 + 4 = 20 points)

4. a. Highlight the importance of soft skills in an educational setting.
   b. Explain the cognitive model of impression formation.
   c. What do you understand by the term 'communication apprehension'?

   (10 + 6 + 4 = 20 points)

SECTION – B (20 POINTS)

Answer any two out of three.

5. a. Explain briefly communication disposition and communication apprehension.
   b. Discuss with examples the functions that M.A.K. Halliday assigns to punctuation. You should give at least two examples per function. It would be interesting if you could explain these functions through the example of a letter you have to write to your school principal. It could be a leave application, for example.

   (5 + 5 = 10 points)

6. a. Self-esteem has clear correlation with a variety of communication-related outcomes. Explain.

   b. Outline the criteria of quadrant II organizer with respect to prime management.

(5 + 5 = 10 points)

7. a. What is emotional intelligence?

   b. Describe the common mistakes people make while resolving conflicts.

(5 + 5 = 10 points)

SECTION – C (40 POINTS)

Answer any two out of four.

8. What are the verbal patterns of persons with low self-concept?

(20 points)

9. What is physical and reflective listening? Is effective listening vital to teaching? List some strategies for effective listening that should be followed by students as well as teachers.

(20 points)

10. How important is the 'self' in communication?

(20 points)

11. What are the predominant traits that are shared by successful communicators? Outline the guidelines for improving communication.

(20 points)

SUGGESTED ANSWERS

Section – A

1. a. Language is called the vehicle of expression. There are three known forms of language—the sign (picture) language, vocal (spoken) language, and the symbolic (written language).

   Verbal language can be defined as a system of orderly vocal sounds and combinations of sounds manipulated by one individual (sender) to form a message which will facilitate the creation of meaning in the mind of a receiving individual (receiver). Language is essentially a system of interrelated parts working together as a whole communication but served when all the parts work together as a whole.

   Nonverbal communication according to Ruesh and Gregory Bateson falls into three categories: sign language, action language, and object language. Sign language is the way of codifying meaning where words or numbers are replaced by gestures languages such as the language of the deaf or dumb. We can also assimilate symbolic information by touch as in the case of Braille.

b. The same word is stressed differently depending on its grammatical status i.e., whether it is being used as a noun/adjective or a verb. For a noun/adjective the stress is on the first syllable and for a verb it is on the second. The change in accentual pattern is manifested mainly by a shift in pitch prominence together with a related variation of quality. The qualitative change takes the form of a reduction of the unaccented vowel of the first element of the verbal form.

	Noun/Adjective	**Verb**
i.	-absent	ab-sent
ii.	-conduct	con-duct
iii.	-perfect	per-fect
iv.	-object	ob-ject
v.	-record	re-cord

Some exceptions like 'limit', 'order', re'mark', 'visit', etc are accented on the same syllable whether used as nouns or verbs.

c. Gestures represent a form of nonverbal communication. In human communication, a communicator's gestures are reliable indicators as to be the intensity of his or her feelings. Gestures serve two functions:

   i. They are reliable cues as to a communicator's behavioural predispositions, whether cooperative, defensive or hostile.

   ii. They function to regulate interaction among group members. There are a number of important types of gestures that communicate the communicator's attitudes and feelings at the moment of the gesture. Of the major types of gestures, the following are particularly important: openness, evaluation, confidence, self-control, defensiveness, suspicion, secretiveness, and nervousness. The first four types of gestures might be viewed as positive and the last three as negative gestures.

2. a. Kinesis means the specific meanings attached to nonverbal behaviour. Even in universal human action of smiling and laughter, there are basic differences in the meaning attached to such actions and the situations that causes them. For example, when two persons meet in the west, the first thing they do is to shake hands as a matter of social courtesy. In Asia when two persons meet, they embrace each other, or say *namaste.* If the meaning attached to these nonverbal signs are not understood the very same action can lead to misinterpretation and barriers in communication.

   Kinesis can be divided into three major areas; prekinesis, microkinesis, and social-kinesis. Prekinesis is concerned with the physiological aspects of bodily movements.

Microkinesis is concerned with bodily emotions that communicate different meanings. Social kinesis is concerned with the role and meaning of different bodily movements.

Proxemies refers to the interpersonal distance that individuals maintain when they interact with one another. The usual face to face distance in ordinary conversation is four to five feet, and variations of even a few inches may create feelings of discomfort. In different parts of the world, people belonging to different cultures have their own sense of a comfortable distance between them and the person they are talking to. Effective communication can take place, if one knows and respects these differences in nonverbal signs in intercultural communication.

b. The two strategies considered for overlapping non-assertive behaviour are broken record and fogging.

Broken record: When a record gets stuck it plays the same thing over and over again. So, in broken record all you have to do is to repeat yourself again and again and again, until the person gives in or concedes to your demands.

Children are masters at being broken records, but somehow during adolescence we lose the skill. It is observed most people capitulate after you repeat yourself three times.

Broken record is particularly useful when:

- Dealing with those in authority, or when you feel that the other person has more expertise than you.
- You think you are not getting what you are entitled to.
- You are dealing with people brighter or more fluent that you.
- The other person is likely to use put-downs, or attack you verbally.

Example

You: 'I' m not satisfied with the service, I would like to see the manager.'
Reply: 'He is busy right now.'
You: 'I'm sure he is, but I would still like to see him.'
Reply: 'He doesn't usually get involved in these matters.'
Your: 'I can understand that, but I want to see him.'
Reply: 'You will have to make an appointment and write in.'
You: 'That may be your procedure, but I want to see him now.'
Reply: 'Well, if you would like to wait for an hour I'll see what I can do.'
You: 'Thank you but I want to see him now.'

Fogging: Fogging is useful when someone is putting pressure on you to do something that is really not in your best interest, and you would rather not do it. Thus, your response to the request is to put up a god. Listen to what the person says, and decide whether or not you wish to comply. If not, then using their words, or similar, acknowledge their need but state your case. In this way you show the person that you have understood their request, but that you are not going to comply. This method is a very polite method of saying 'No'.

Request	**Response**
'I want it now'	'I can see why you would want that but my priority is….'
'You should help me'	'Perhaps I should but right now I have other priorities.'
'This is important'	'Of course it is important but not as important….'
'I need this'	'I am sure you do but it is just not possible now.'

By using this technique you are less likely to be manipulated into doing something you would rather not and yet you cannot be accused of recognizing the other person's need.

c. Entropy means a tendency towards disorder, randomness and confusion in communication. An epochal break through was made by Shannon and Weaver (1949), in identifying noise in communication and entropy as opposed to information in signals. The second law of thermodynamics says that, confusion is more probable than order and even if there is a decrease of entropy in some parts of the universe, this will be more than compensated by a larger increase in some other parts. But human beings has an uncanny ability to decode information, use feed back intelligently, organize itself and his capacity to temporarily defeat entropy locally in spite of the total increase entropy globally. The value of studying entropic communication is to identify it early. Great empires simply, collapsed and were thrown into oblivion just because they were unable to cope with the increasing entropy in communication.

3. a. Person perception is the process through which we seek to understand other persons. We engage in Social perception in every social situation we encounter. The 'other person' remains always a mystery; they say and do things which we do not understand, they have motives which we don't understand, and behave in certain ways that we cannot comprehend. Because it plays such an important role, in inter-personal behaviour and interaction, and is of utmost social importance.

- The process of nonverbal communication.
- Attribution.
- Impression formation.
- Impression management.

Person perception refers to the mental processes we use to form judgment and draw conclusions about the characteristic of others. Person perception is an active and subjective process that always occurs in some interpersonal context. Every interpersonal context has three key components:

- The characteristics of the individual we are trying to sum up.
- Our own characteristics as a perceiver.

The specific situation in which the process occurs. Person perception follows some basic principles.

Principle – 1 – our reaction to others are determined by our perception of them, not by whom or what they really are.
Principle – 2 – one goal in a particular situation determines the amount and kind of information one collects about others.
Principle – 3 – in every situation, we evaluate people partly in terms of how.

b. **Self Understanding and Acceptance**

We all have goals, and to reach those goals, we must have relationships with other people. Usually these relationships include shared goals. When people become involved in shared goals in a relationship, it becomes important to coordinate behaviour to build the relationship so that each person can achieve these goals. This happens to students in every aspect of their lives from living in share accommodation to team projects in the classroom.

Self-disclosure

The first step in developing relationships involves self-disclosure. This means being able to share how you feel about events that have just occurred with another person. This does not mean revealing intimate details of your past life. People get to know you by learning how you react, not by what happened in your past history. Past history only helps if it clarifies why you are reacting in a certain way. People who self disclose too much can scare others away. Likewise, not enough closes you off to new relationships. Getting the balance right is important rather than being ruined by one destructive act. The key to being trustworthy is to be accepting and supporting. When you achieve this, others will be more willing to disclose their thoughts, ideas, theories, conclusions, feelings and reactions to you. The more trustworthy you are in response to such disclosures, the deeper and more personal will be the thoughts a. person will share with you.

Managing feelings

The most important for students is to understand the various aspects of anger, stress, and managing feelings. You can't avoid stress. How you manage stress has a great influence on your ability to reach out to other people, build relationships, and maintain it over a long period of time.

c. Relational communication, impression management and identity have close resemblance with regard to specific nonverbal cues used to signal evaluation and self-images. Relational communication is distinct in three aspects.

- Relational communication follows a participant as opposed to an observer perspective.
- A relational message is directed toward a specific target as opposed to a generalized audience.
- Relational communication typically focuses on dyadic interaction between sender and receiver and may use the dyad as the unit of analysis.

4 a. Soft skills are important to students for various reasons. Some of them are outlined below:

- To handle interpersonal relations.
- To choose career and make appropriate decisions.
- To communicate effectively.

An investment in student's soft skills ultimately affects the bottom line by building new knowledge in the student. Relationships play a vital role in human life. One of the keys to successful relationships is to develop soft skills. In today's fast changing pace of technology, hard skills are continuously in need of being updated. A technologist's hard skills and his or her related state-of-the-art knowledge require continuous regeneration. Similarly, the importance of having soft skills in students needs an emphasis. A student who has interpersonal problem and another who has difficulty in making a choice about his career suffers from lack of soft skills. Hence, a continuous renewal of soft skills in terms of teaching and training to students is called for. This will facilitate their being effective and successful.

According to Daniel Coleman, emotional intelligence, or EQ—referring to a combination of competencies that contribute to a person's ability to manage his or herself and relate to other people—matters twice as much as IQ or technical skills in job success. Not only does it create happier and more successful employees, according to the psychologist, but it also helps create more successful companies. The results of one study on the opinion of the importance of soft skills indicated that the single most important soft skill for a job candidate to possess was interpersonal skills, followed by written or verbal communication skills, and the ability to work under pressure. Technical skills and knowledge were at the bottom of the list—this may be due to the fact that technical competency for the job is assumed. It is interesting to note that another larger survey done in the US in 1998 indicates, that more than two thirds (68 per cent) interviewed, rated soft skills as very important, compared to less than half (46 per cent) rating soft skills as very important in 1996. It is clear then that there are forces at play, which are changing the face of the working environment.

b. According to this model, impression of others' involves two major components: concrete examples of behaviours that are consistent with a given trait-exemplars of this trait; and mental summaries that are abstracted from repeated observations of others' behaviour-abstractions, as they are usually termed. Some models of information formation stress the role of behaviour exemplars. These models suggest that, when we make judgments about others, we recall examples of their behaviour and base our judgments and our impressions based on these. For example, you meet a person for the first time, and he or she smiles warmly at you and comes running to help you when you drop your books—all these actions are examples of the trait of kindness, so we include this trait of kindness in our first impression of this individual.

In contrast, other models stress the role of abstractions—such views suggest that, when we make judgments about others, we simply bring our previously formed abstractions to mind and use these as the basis for our impression and our decisions. A growing body of evidences suggests that, both exemplar and mental abstractions play a role in impression formation. In fact, it appears that the nature of impressions may shift as we gain increasing experience with others. At first, our impression of someone we have just met consists of largely of exemplars (concrete examples of behaviour they have performed) later, as our experience with this person increases, our impression comes to consist mainly of mental abstractions derived from many observations of the person's behaviour.

c. The most studied individual difference in the field of interpersonal communication has been communication apprehension. Communication apprehension is more interpersonally oriented it is also known as unwilling to communicate/and social-communicative anxiety.

Behaviourally, people with high levels of communication apprehension are less likely to talk in social settings, and when they do participate they engage in mostly acknowledgements and confirmation. They also engage in less eye contact and are more self-protective and less disclosure. Perceptually, they are seen less positively by others in variety of settings, such as interviews and social interactions.

Apprehensive people are less assertive or argumentative, less conversationally sensitive, less independent and more interdependent. They have lower self-esteem, are more insecure, not willing to take risk, and has inferiority complex. Not surprisingly, such individuals suffer from more social isolation and more emotional and psychosomatic health problems, related to academic achievement and cognitive performance, Occupationally, this disposition affects career development and career choices, and apprehensive individuals are less likely to be successful the harmful effects of this disposition be reduced through the use of a variety of behavioural techniques. The most common of these are systematic desensitization, cognitive restructuring and visualization.

Section – B

4. a. Individuals have certain dispositions in communication. One is argumentativeness and the other verbal aggressiveness. Argumentativeness is considered to be constructive, as it involves an individuals' willingness to attack another's arguments while defending his or her positions. Highly argumentative individuals are better decision makers and are more interesting than less argumentative individuals. They are also more dynamic, competent and credible. They do not withdraw from conflicting situations.

Communication apprehensions are an important area of study in communication and are more interpersonally oriented. Communication apprehension means an unwillingness to communicate and social-communicative anxiety; individual with communication apprehensions are less likely to talk in social settings, and when they do, they are less assertive. They also engage in less eye contact, are more defensive and less self-disclosure. They are seen less positively by others in a variety of settings, such as interviews and social interactions.

b. Punctuation indeed plays a major part in making writing easy to grasp. In his book entitled, *Spoken and Written English* (Oxford University Press, 1989), the great linguist M.A.K. Halliday maintains that punctuation, the mechanics of writing, has the following functions:

   i. Marking the boundary, e.g., a comma marks off a phrase, a list etc.

   ii. Marking the status, e.g., a full stop or an exclamation mark at the end of a sentence decides its status as a statement or an exclamation.

   iii. Marking relationship, e.g., a hyphen suggests that a word is a compound word or the apostrophe 's' explains what belongs to whom.

   In other words, punctuation as mechanics of writing gives our writing a spoken clarity and intonation/stress effect.

   Let us understand these functions of punctuation through a letter we often tend to use. It is a leave-application. In every leave-application, we begin with the salutation that ends with a comma (Dear Madam,) or we indicate the subject of the letter with a colon (sub: leave application). These two examples show how punctuation 'marks boundary'.

   At the end of our letter, we write 'this is to request you to do the needful at your earliest' and finally we add a full-stop, but we continue with, 'Can I expect your response at your earliest', and end it with a question mark. This process exemplifies the second function Halliday assigns to punctuation.

   In our letter, we may write, 'I shall not be able to attend to my duties as I have to take my sister-in-law to hospital. Her doctor's advice...' The hyphens or the apostrophes used here establish the third function of punctuation.

6. a. Who we think we are, is confirmed or denied by the responses others make to our communication with them. Unless we get clear and supportive messages, we are not likely to have effective communication experiences. We learn early in life to give and receive responses which have effect on our feelings and self-esteem, as well as, how we accomplish our work without support for our activities, we cannot accomplish what we want to accomplish. Much of the development of our self-esteem is intimately related to our work, and roles we learn in the formal organizations where we participate. Much of our sense of our inner-worth comes from performing the roles that society provides, and we always try to measure up to it. Not being able to do so, leads to the loss of our self-esteem.

In the process of developing self-esteem, we develop certain images of ourselves and we look for confirmation or disconfirmation of those images, and when we get that confirmation, we feel that we are entitled to that self-image. Self-esteem is the feeling we get, when what we do and think, matches our self-image and when that particular image approximate an idealized version of what we wish we were like, this validation increases the feeling our self-worth and hence our self-esteem.

b. A Quadrant II organizer will meet six criteria:

- Coherence: Harmony, unity, and integrity between vision and mission, priorities and plans, and desires and discipline.
- Balance: Success in the various roles of our life.
- Quadrant II focus: Organize your life on a weekly basis. Schedule your priorities don't prioritize what's on your schedule.
- A 'People' Dimension: Focus on people not just the schedule.
- Flexibility: The planning tool should be tailored to you.
- Portability: You should be able to carry your tool with you.

7. a. In recent years, researchers have paid significant attention to a construct called emotional intelligence. Daniel Goleman suggested that, Emotional intelligence consists of five basic emotional competences. They are: self-awareness, motivation, self-regulation, empathy and adeptness in relationships. For instance, being caring and understanding teacher is an emotional competence based on empathy. Likewise, trust worthiness is a competence based on self-regulation or handling ones emotions well. Emotional intelligence is emotional quotient (EQ) that is the amount of positive emotion one is capable of expressing. Salovy and Mayer (1990), have defined emotional intelligence as the ability of people to monitor their own emotions, discriminate among them, and use the information to guide their thinking and action.

b. Max Bazerman describes five common mistakes while trying to resolve more competitive negotiations:

1. Believing the other person must lose for you to win.
2. Discovering too late that more information was needed, e.g., 'I should have had the valves checked before I bought the car'.
3. Making extreme demands, investing too much in getting your way, and, thus, becoming reluctant to back down (and, in the end, not getting the promotion or the improved relationship). It should be a warning sign to you when you start to use anger or try to make your opponent look bad or weak.
4. There is a consistent human tendency to believe that we are right and are being reasonable. Much more often than we realize, other people disagree with what we think is fair. Therefore, get an unbiased outside opinion. Negotiators, who are realistic and willing to see other views of justice, are more successful compromisers.

5. If you are thinking mostly in terms of what you could lose, you are likely to hold out for more and lose everything. For some reason, most people will take a sure small gain over a risky greater gain but not a sure small loss over a possible larger loss. We hate to lose, even by a little. The wise negotiator facing big losses may quickly 'cut his/her losses'. However, when you have accepted a small loss, emphasize to your opponent what he/she has to gain by your cooperativeness.

Section - C

8. Our self concept develops through interpersonal communication. It is also maintained and changed through communication. Each person and experience we encounter, changes our view about the world and others, as well as ourselves through the process of confirmation and disconfirmation. A study of the verbal patterns of persons with low self-concept and high self-concept, shows some tendencies which can be identified. Self-concept may vary with situation or people with whom one is communicating. The way people see themselves in relation to others has a great effect on the changing patterns of communication. The following are some verbal patterns which may characterize low self-concept:
   - Frequent use of cliched phrases or a few words which are used not so much to help identify something in common with others, because the person with low self-concept.
   - A need to talk about self in terms of criticism, weaknesses and difficult experiences which help to explain why he or she is not better.
   - Inability to accept praise gracefully.
   - Defensiveness about blame to the degree that the person may be more anxious about who gets credit or blame.
   - A cynicism about accomplishment or possessions a hypercritical attitude about others.
   - A persistently whining or sneering tone of voice, or posture as assumed in relation to one's own or others' success.
   - A pessimistic attitude expressed about competition.
9. Listening is the most important skill of all the skills of a language that one has to master in order to be successful in a career. This extremely critical skill is neither taught nor studied as much as the other three skills (speaking, reading and writing) of communication. Therefore, if one wants to be a good listener one must put in a great deal of effort and self-discipline to listen attentively.

Physical listening

Listening involves giving physical attention to the speaker. Listening with the whole body shows ones interest in what is being said. Good listeners must have face and eye contact and incline their body towards the speaker. It is important to position oneself appropriately. Too much distance may be interpreted as indifference or rejection and too close proximity may make the speaker feel uncomfortable.

The listener must react to the speaker with certain nonverbal signals. His/her face must move and the expressions must indicate that the speaker is being followed.

A good listener will stop talking and use receptive language.

Reflective listening

Reflective listening restates the feeling and content that the speaker communicated and demonstrates that listener understands and accepts the speaker's message. It is not only to understand the content of the message, but also the feeling and intention conveyed by the speaker.

Reflective listening requires observation of nonverbal communication and helps you to focus on the central points of the issue. It encourages the speaker to disclose his feelings, thereby listeners must guard against prejudices, closed minded opinions, defenses and fears of being wrong which prevent us from believing what is said.

He/she must respond, letting the speaker know that he/she was understood. Empathic listening is more complex than just listening. An Empathic listener focuses on the speaker's feelings.

Listening is extremely vital to teaching

Effective listening is of enormous importance in the area of teaching. It is not only the students but also the teachers who have to practise listening skills.

In a teaching-learning process, it is generally believed that the student is at the listening end and the teacher at the talking. But this is a wrong notion. The teacher is not always at the authoritative talking end. The teacher is also a friend and a facilitator. There are a number of occasions where a teacher needs to listen, not just give an indifferent hearing, but a patient, empathic listening to their problems. Understand and perhaps even solve them.

Listening is not a school subject like reading and writing. It does not come naturally although we feel so. Listening is a very large part of school learning and is one of the primary means of interacting with people on a personal basis. It is estimated that between 50 to 75 percent of students' classroom time is spent listening to the teacher, to other students or to audio media.

In a classroom the students need to listen attentively to the lectures. Students must consider listening skills to be an art that should be used effectively in order to accomplish the set goals. Listening skills must be consciously improved by following some strategies.

Some listening strategies for the student

i. **Focus on content:** Do not pay too much importance to the style of delivery and the teacher's idiosyncrasies. If you are doing so, you are not focusing on the content of the lesson.

ii. **Avoid emotional involvement:** Do not be readily affected with or stirred by emotion. If you are emotionally involved, then you tend to become selectively receptive. You listen to what you want to but not what is being said.

iii. **Maintain eye contact:** You will, of course, have to look into your books, but eye contact keeps you focused on the subject at hand and keeps you involved in the lecture.

iv. **Expel distraction:** Do not let you mind wander and be distracted by any noise around you. Try to find a solution for any kind of discomfort due to a bad seat or bad weather etc.

v. **Consider listening to be a stimulating mental task:** Listening to an academic lecure is not a passive act. You need to concentrate on what is said so that you can comprehend and process the information.

   You can ask yourself some questions as you listen: 'What key point is the professor making?', 'How does this fit with what I know from previous lectures?', etc.

vi. **Be focused:** All the above suggestions will help you keep your mind occupied and focused on what is being said. You can actually begin to anticipate what the professor is going to say as a way to keep your mind from straying. Your mind does have the capacity to listen, think, write and ponder at the same time, but it does take practice.

Some listening strategies for the teacher

A teacher must concentrate on what the student is saying, and have an open mind to receive and listen to information. The teacher needs to understand the students' background and let them know that he/she understands how they feel strongly about the issues being discussed. Their intense emotions must be acknowledged and affirmed before serious solutions can be discussed.

The teacher should encourage the students to 'let off steam' and explain their concerns by using certain phrases such as, 'I see', 'I understand', 'Yes, I know'.

Some listening strategies that can be followed by me teachers are:

i. Demonstrate that they are listening by
   - body language
   - making eye contact
   - echoing words
   - nods of the head
   - leaning toward the speaker.

ii. Some students need an invitation to talking. The teacher needs to elicit patiently and gradually draw the student into a conversation.

iii. Students can tell whether they have a teacher's interest and attention by the way the teacher replies or does not reply. Avoid cutting students off before they have finished speaking. It is easy to form an opinion or reject student's views before they finish what they have to say. It may be difficult to listen respectfully and not correct misconceptions, but respect their right to have and express their opinions.

iv. Listen to nonverbal messages that are often communicated by students. The tone of their voice, their facial expressions their energy level, their posture, or changes in their behaviour patterns can often tell, more than what is actually verbally said. When a student comes in obviously upset be sure to fine a quiet time then or sometime later to help explore those feelings.

v. Be interested in and ask about the student's ideas and opinions regularly. If you show your students that you are really interested in what they think, what they feel and what their opinions are, they will become comfortable about expressing their thoughts to you.

vi. Avoid dead-end questions (that require a yes or no answer) they put an end to the interaction rather than extending it. Students should be asked to describe, explain or share ideas to extend the conversation.

vii. One of the most important skills, good teachers must have is to listen to and have the ability to put themselves in the shoes of the students and empathize with them by attempting to understand their thoughts and feelings. As you listen try to make the students feelings clear by stating them in your own words. Your empathic listening can help students express themselves clearly and accurately and give them a deeper understanding of words and inner thoughts.

10. The self is the most important agent in the process of communication. Who we are and how we see ourselves as well as, how others sees us, what roles we play for the various audience, what we need and value—all these are very important in interpersonal communication. Who we are is to a large degree determined by responses we get from others to our behaviours. These responses shape in many ways how we see ourselves, and so we are in an ongoing, spiraling, transactional process called communication'. In short, self concept is learned, maintained and changed through interpersonal communication. See how others see us. Cooley for example, developed the concept of the 'looking glass self', as the process of imagining how the self appears to be for another person. The concept of self is a reflection from the mind of others. All these develop because of our interactions with people and on their interpretation of our behaviour. The entire cycle frequently turns into a self-fulfilling prophesy.

11. Successful communicators share predominantly five traits. They are as follows:

    i. Perception: They are able to predict how you will receive their message. They anticipate your reaction and shape the message accordingly. They read your response correctly and constantly adjust to correct any misunderstanding.

    ii. Precision: They create a 'meeting of the minds'. When they finish expressing themselves, you share the same mental picture.

    iii. Credibility: They are believable. You have faith in the substance of their message. You trust their information and their intentions.

    iv. Control: They shape your response. Depending on their purpose, they can make you laugh or cry, calm down, change your mind, or take action.

v. Congeniality: They maintain friendly, pleasant relations with you. Regardless of whether you agree with them, good communicators command your respect and goodwill. You are willing to work with them again, despite your differences.

Effective communicators work hard at perfecting the messages they deliver. When they make mistakes, they learn from them. If a poorly written memo does not get the response they hoped for, they change their approach the next time around. If a meeting they are running gets out of control or becomes unproductive, they do things differently at the next one. If they find themselves having to explain themselves over and over again, they reevaluate their choice of communication medium or rework their message.

It is essential to understand what it means to communicate effectively. Four themes emerge as effective guidelines for overcoming barriers and improving your communication skills:

i. Fostering an open communication climate.
ii. Committing to ethical communication,
iii. Adopting an audience-centred approach to communication.

Fostering an open communication climate

An organization's or educational institute's communication climate is a reflection of its culture: the mixture of values, traditions, and habits that give a place to its atmosphere or personality. Some academic institution's tend to block off the upward flow of communication, believing that debate is time consuming and unproductive. Some other institutions, work to maintain an open communication climate. They encourage openness and honesty, and their employees feel free to confess their mistakes, to disagree with the superiors, and to express their opinions.

Committing to ethical communication

The second guideline for effective communication is a commitment to ethics, the principles of conduct that govern a person or a group. Unethical people are essentially selfish and unscrupulous, saying or doing whatever it takes to achieve an end. Ethical people are generally trustworthy, fair, and impartial, respecting the rights of others and concerned about the impact of their actions on society. Former Supreme Court Justice Mr. Venkata Chalamaiah defined ethics as 'knowing the difference between what you have a right to do and what is the right thing to do'.

Ethics plays a crucial role in communication. Language itself is made up of words that carry values. So merely by saying things a certain way, you influence how others perceive your message, and you shape expectations and behaviours. Ethical communication includes all relevant information, is true in every sense, and is not deceptive in any way.

When sending an ethical message, you are accurate and sincere. You avoid language that manipulates, discriminates, or exaggerates. You do not hide negative information behind an optimistic attitude, you don't state opinions as facts, and you portray graphic data fairly. You are honest with employers, co-workers, and clients, never seeking personal gain by making others look better or worse than they are. You don't allow personal preferences to influence your perception or the perception of others, and you act in good faith. On the surface, such ethical practices appear fairly easy to recognize. But deciding what is ethical can be quite complex. Recognizing ethical choices, making ethical choices is one of the pertinent aspects of committing to ethical communication.

Adopting an audience-centred approach to communication

The third guideline contributing to effective communication is adopting an audience-centred approach, or keeping your audience in mind at all times during the process of communication. Because you care about your audience, you take every step possible to get your message across in a way that is meaningful to your audience. In fact, empathizing with and being sensitive to your audience's feelings is the best way to overcome such communication barriers as differences in perception and emotional interference. If you are aware of others' feelings, you'll be able to choose neutral words, understand their views, and perhaps empathize with their position by trying to view the situation through their eyes.

Creating and processing your messages effectively and efficiently

Creating an effective message is difficult if you are unfamiliar with your audience or if you don't know how your message will be used. For example, if you are writing a report and you don't know the purpose of the report, it is hard to know what to say. What is the content, what aspects are to be covered, what are issues to be viewed with caution, how long should the report be, should it provide conclusions and recommendations or simply facts and figures, are the dimensions to be taken care of? Unless you know why the report is needed, you can't really answer those questions intelligently, so you are forced to create a very general document, one that covers a little bit of everything.

Likewise, you need to know something about the biases, education, age, status, and style of your receiver in order to create an effective message. If you are addressing strangers, try to find out more about them; if that's impossible, try to project yourself into their position by using your common sense and imagination. Whatever the tactic, the point is to write and speak from your audience's point of view.

The best way to create messages carefully is to adapt your message to your audience so that you can help them understand and accept it. If you are writing for a specialist in your field, for example, you can use technical terms that might be unfamiliar to a layperson. On the other hand, if you are communicating to someone who might not share your understanding of a topic or someone who might not have your wealth of experience, you can minimize language barriers by using specific and accurate words–once your audience will understand. Decisions about the content, organization, style, and tone of your message all depend, at least to some extent, on the relationship between you and your audience. If you don't know your audience, you will be forced to make these decisions in the dark, and at least part of your message may miss the mark.

Deciding what to say is the first hurdle in the communication process. Many people make the mistake of trying to convey everything they know about a subject. Unfortunately, when a message contains too much information, it is difficult to absorb. As you decide what to include and what to leave out, keep in mind that if you try to explain something without first giving the receiver adequate background, you'll create confusion. Likewise, if you recommend actions without first explaining why they are justified, your message may provoke an emotional response that inhibits understanding.

It is also important to make written messages visually appealing and easy to understand by balancing general concepts with specific illustrations. When you come to an important point, say so. Use specific details such as numbers, tables, and figures, and try using memorable words such as colours, objects, scents, sounds, and tastes to create a picture in your audience's mind. You can also call attention to an idea visually by using headlines, bold type, and indented lists and by using charts, graphs maps, diagrams, and illustrations. Furthermore, be sure to show how new ideas are related to concepts that already exist in the minds of your audience. Such connections help make the new concepts acceptable.

Finally, keep your messages as brief and as clean as possible. With few exceptions, one page is easier to absorb than two. However, because it is important to develop each main idea adequately, you are better off covering three points thoroughly rather than skimming through eight points superficially. Remember, by highlighting and summarizing your key points, you help your audience understand and remember the message.

Model Question Paper III

Time: 3 hours **Total Points: 100**

SECTION – A (40 POINTS)

Answer any two out of four.

1. a. Define the term 'impression management'. What are the techniques of impression management?

   b. How do you improve nonverbal communication?

   c. Explain briefly the favourable and unfavourable influences of mass communication.

   (10 + 6 + 4 = 20 points)

2. a. Explain assertive/responsive model in detail.

   b. What is the attitudinal function of intonation?

   c. What are the factors that influence communication?

   (10 + 6 + 4 = 20 points)

3. a. How important, according to various research findings, is individual differences in communication?

   b. 'Models make your communication real precise' is the opinion of linguists and grammarians. Imagine you are a secondary school teacher. Do you agree with this statement? Support your reactions to this statement through examples drawn from your daily teacher-like duties/contexts.

   c. What is cognitive complexity?

   (10 + 6 + 4 = 20 points)

4. a. How are needs related to communication?

   b. Explain the steps involved in skill acquisition.

   c. Give the characteristics of confirming responses.

   (10 + 6 + 4 = 20 points)

SECTION – B (20 POINTS)

Answer any two out of three.

5. a. The need for affection is closely related to communication. Discuss.

   b. Explain the importance of having a precise and focused objective before you give a presentation.

(5 + 5 = 10 points)

6. a. Discuss the role of listening in communication.

   b. What are the characteristics of well-functioning teams?

(5 + 5 = 10 points)

7. a. What are the qualities that demonstrate interpersonal effectiveness?

   b. Choose any model and explain the process of communication.

(5 + 5 = 10 points)

SECTION – C (40 POINTS)

Answer any two out of four.

8. 'Communication is a two-way sharing process, not a movement along a one-way track. To communicate is to make an idea common to two or more persons.' Examine this statement.

(20 points)

9. What are the principles involved in conflict management?

(20 points)

10. Explain the basic principles of good written communication.

(20 points)

11. List all the 44 symbols for the vowel and consonant sounds of the English language. Give examples to show the sound that each symbol corresponds to.

(20 points)

SUGGESTED ANSWERS

Section – A

1. a. Impression management is the art of looking and appearing good. Most of us do our best to look good to others when we meet them for the first time. The desire to make a favourable impression on others is a strong one. Social psychologists use the term, impression management or appropriate self-presentation. People, who are good in

impression management, often gain important advantage in many situations. The tactics an individual uses for impression management is known as techniques of impression management.

- The technique of self-enhancement.
- Describing oneself in positive terms.
- Other enhancement techniques.
- Appropriate emotional cues.

b. Nonverbal communication can be improved by paying more attention to the kinds of signals they send. It is particularly important to avoid giving others conflicting signals. It is important to be as honest as possible in communicating emotions. The following are some strategies for honing nonverbal skills.

1. Smile genuinely: A fake smile is obvious because the timing isn't right and the wrinkles don't follow.
2. Be aware that people may give false nonverbal cues.
3. Keep appropriate distance and use touch only when appropriate.
4. Respect status with your eye contact.
5. Adopt a handshake that matches your personality and intention.

A few gestures convey meaning in and of themselves; they have to be interpreted in clusters, and they should reinforce your words. It should be remembered that the above outlined strategies should be used with appropriateness and with relevance.

More than any specific strategies per se, it is essential to follow some golden and time-tested rules (showing empathy, unconditional positive regard, non-judgmental attitude). Nonverbally communicating one's empathy towards another person through gestures such as by nodding head, communicating unconditional positive regard, acceptance to others is essential. To sum up, being aware of one's own and others non-verbal cues and regulating these cues through practice are the strategies to improve nonverbal communication.

c. In the current context each member of society is directly or indirectly influenced by the elements of mass communication.

Unfavourable influences

1. Lowering public cultural taste.
2. Increasing rates of delinquency.
3. Contributing to general moral deterioration.
4. Lulling the masses into political superficiality.
5. Suppressing creativity.

Favourable influences

1. Exposing sin and corruption.
2. Acting as guardian of free speech.
3. Giving entertainment to millions of people.
4. Exposing to culture.
5. Providing information and knowledge to many.
6. Improving the standards of living.

2. a. Assertive/responsive model

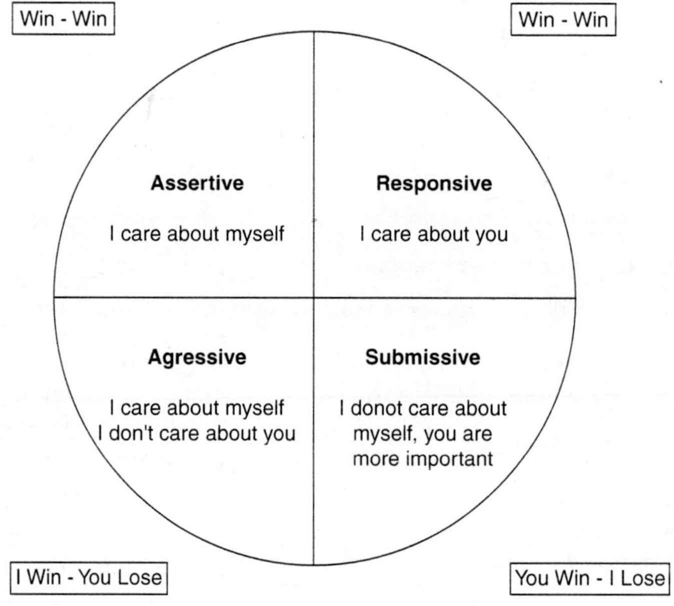

Figure M.1

Assertion refers to behaviour that involves:

- Standing up for your own rights in such a way that you do not violate another person's rights.
- Expressing your needs, wants, opinions, feelings and beliefs in direct, honest and appropriate ways.

So, assertiveness is based on *beliefs* that in any situation:

- You have needs to be met.
- The other people have needs to be met.
- You have rights, so do others.
- You have something to contribute, so do others.

The *aim* of assertion is to satisfy the needs and wants of both parties in the situation (known as 'win-win').

Non-assertion refers to behaviour which involves the following:

- Failing to stand up for your rights or doing so in such a way that others can easily disregard them.
- Expressing your needs, wants, opinions, feelings and beliefs in apologetic, diffident or self-effacing ways.
- Failing to express honestly your needs, wants, opinions, feelings and beliefs.

Non-assertion is based upon the *beliefs* that in any situation:

- The other person's needs and wants are more important than your own.
- The other person has rights but you do not.
- You have little or nothing to contribute; the other person has a great deal to contribute.

The *aim* of non-assertion is to avoid conflict and to please others.

Aggression refers to behaviour that consists of the following:

- Standing up for your own rights, but doing so in such a way that you violate the rights of other people.
- Ignoring or dismissing the needs, wants, opinions, feelings or beliefs of others.
- Expressing your own needs, wants and opinions (which may be honest or dishonest) in inappropriate ways.

Aggressive behaviour is based on the *belief* that:

- Your own needs, wants and opinions are more important than other people's.
- You have rights but other people do not.
- You have something to contribute; others have little or nothing to contribute.

The *aim* of aggression is to win, if necessary, at the expense of others.

Example of the three different behaviours situation

Taking an unsatisfactory letter back to the person who produced it.

Assertion

'Sarita, I would like you to re-do this letter as there are several mistakes in it.'

Non-assertion

You find an excuse not to take the letter back, or you say: 'I know it is .... any chance at all you could find a spare minute to—just change one or two small things in this letter for me'.

Aggression

'I don't know how you've got the nerve to give me this sort of stuff for signing. It is full of mistakes.'

b. Intonation is perhaps the chief means by which the speaker conveys his attitudes and emotions. The grammar of an utterance does not reveal in any noticeable way whether the speaker's attitude is one of politeness, assertiveness, concern, incredulity, etc.

Intonation makes distinctions of attitudinal nuances to which grammar most often gives no structural clues. The following pairs of sentences show how intonation signals the speaker attitudes and emotions.

c. There should be a common experience between two or more people for an effective communication. Several factors, which influence the process of communication, are as follows:

1. Age factor (we are young or old)
2. Sex factor (we are men or women)
3. Economic factor (we are rich or poor)
4. Location factor (we are rich or poor)
5. Mental factor (we are bright, slow or average)
6. Education factor (we are graduates or illiterate)
7. Organization factor (we are of this institution party or that institution)
8. Vocation factor (we are teachers or farmers)
9. Social factor (we are in the middle income group or in low income group)
10. Racial factor (we belong or do not belong to a minority ethnic group)

The above mentioned are some of the factors, which influence communication. There are several others but the above list includes only the major factors.

3. a. A number of communication related behaviours have been identified by researchers, most of which are inherited, e.g., sociability, public speaking, assertiveness, etc. Other researchers like Beatley, Mc Crosky and Hiesel, (1996), found genetic predispositions and communication, such as communication apprehension. Krants and Price (1976), gives the explanation of personality variables such as reinforcement, social norms and modeling. Each of these alternative explanations is, to some degree relevant to the development of various communica-

tion related predispositions. The notion behind these alternative approaches is that, genetics may predispose a person to certain traits, but environment factors increases or reduces the development of these traits. For example, in the case of social—communicative anxiety, evidences exists that, individual's anxiety may be shaped by the kind of reinforcements they received for communicating with children, the level of social skills they were taught and the adequacy of the models of communication to which they were exposed. Besides the heredity factors, differences in culture is also responsible for individual differences in communication. The cultural construal decides how skilled individuals are in communication. The cultural differences in communication skill are known as the intercultural communication competence. People with higher levels of intercultural communication competence interact more effectively with people from different cultures.

b. If prepositions give our English a 'propah'. Modals are auxiliary (that is, helping) verbs that indicate the mood of a speaker, e.g.,'Can I come in?' is more informal, but 'May I come in?' is very formal.

Similarly, 'it may rain' indicates a strong possibility but 'there could be water on the Mars' indicates a dim chance about which the writer is not very sure.

These different shades of meaning are conveyed through the use of such modals as 'may', 'can', 'could', etc. Effective use of modals, in brief, is essential for efficient written communication.

Let us look at some examples of use of modals. All these examples relate to the academic context.

'Can' means

i. have the ability
'She can teach the sciences as well as English.'
ii. permission you can't go out this evening
iii. possibility
'The student can improve if he works hard.'
iv. request
'Can I come in?'

'Could' means

i. past ability
'Raman could tackle any difficult sum by the time he was ten years old.'
ii. polite request
'Could you attend the meeting please.'
iii. dim possibility
'Our student could top the merit list nest year.'

'Be able to' means

Ability in the present ('be' changes to 'am', 'is', 'are') or past ('be' becomes 'was', 'were') or future ('will be', 'shall be') The child was able to adjust to the school within a week. We are able to provide a computer per student 'They will be able to lift the elocution trophy this year.'

'Must' means

Indicates compulsion.
'You must attend the lectures regularly.'

Have to' means

Indicates compulsion, but it is less obligatory.
'You have to stand up and greet the Dean when he enters the classroom.'

"Should' means	Indicates a moral duty. 'You should intimate the office if you are going on leave.'
'Ought to' means	Indicates an ethical obligation. 'You ought to treat your teachers with respect'.
'May' means	i. indicates giving and asking for permission in a formal way. 'You may leave now. May I come in? ' ii. a possibility 'The Principal may attend the important meeting tomorrow.'

c. Cognitive disposition means the communication style and characteristics of an individual, one such can be called cognitive complexity. Cognitive complexity may be defined as the number of different constructs an individual has to describe others (differentiation), the degree to which these constructs cohere (integration), and the level of abstraction of the constructs (abstractness) Individuals who are cognitively more complex, offer more person-centred responses whether in terms of comforting, persuading or the use of regulative messages. The reason for this appears to be that, cognitively complex individuals are better able to perform a variety of tasks related to communication, such as recognizing affect, decoding nonverbal behaviours, integrating information etc.

4. a. Much of our behaviour can be explained by our needs. William Schutz has identified three basic interpersonal needs which underline most of our behaviour around other people. These needs can be best represented as dimensions or continuum along which most people fall. Schutz calls these interpersonal needs the 'need for inclusion', the 'need for control', and the 'need for affection'.

According to Schutz, 'the need for inclusion' is the need to be recognized as an individual distinct from others. Such a person likes to be in the spot light, to be singled out, to be noticed. They feel to be punished is better to be ignored. On the other hand, a person with a low inclusion tendency, prefers not to stand out, would rather not receive too much attention, does not like to be prominent in the public eye.

The need for inclusion has some influence on the process of interpersonal communication. In a situation in which two or more individuals are equally high on the need for attention, get together to plan something. Much of the energy they are going to spend in that interpersonal context will be spent establishing in the group a position from which they will get the recognition they need. However, if all members are recognition seekers, chances are that, they will have a difficult time securing attention from one another. A group composed of a reasonable balance of people high and low on inclusion will probably function in a smoother fashion and have effective communication.

b. Soft skills come naturally for some people, or they can be taught, and then applied in practice. Let us examine the process of skill acquisition. Guthrie (1952) defines a skill as the ability to bring about some end result with maximum certainty and minimum outlay of energy or of time and energy. Skill acquisition is an essential component of any learning system. An understanding of the basic principles of skill acquisition can enhance all teaching and coaching. The development of a skill, from playing basketball to resolving a conflict, will progress in levels of achievement. An individual will begin by struggling through attempts to perform the skill. In time, success and improved confidence will take place. With enough practice, a person can become an expert in the performance of the desired skill. It has been described that this progression occurs through four steps. From the raw beginning, through to mastery, a person will move from:

Unconsciously Incompetent

to

Consciously Incompetent

to

Consciously Competent

to

Unconsciously Competent

Described further, a person can begin the learning of a skill with no concept about it, and no ability to perform it. With some teaching and/or practice, the individual becomes aware of skill and its goal, but still cannot perform the skill with any significant success. With more teaching and practice, the skill is acquired and can be performed well, with high levels of concentration. More practice brings the person to the highest level of function in which the skill can be performed with great success and without the need to concentrate intently. At this point the skill has become very repetitious. There are a great number of examples to illustrate the point. A young child learning how to walk is an obvious case. At the earliest stages, the child will rise to their feet, soon to tall with the first attempt to move. They do not know how to perform the skill, and have no knowledge of what to do to improve. They are unconsciously incompetent. With more attempts, the child begins to realize to potential to walk or move, but is unable to perform the skill to any significant extent. With still more practice, the child can move about, but only with significant concentration. If they are distracted from their intent, they will quickly topple over. In time, the skill becomes second nature to them and can be performed without conscious intent. They have become unconsciously competent. New skills are added in progressions. The child will begin to run only to be met with a new series of challenges. Over the course of skill acquisition, the child will learn to run while catching and throwing, followed by more and more complex skills. At the highest level, very skilled athletes perform seemingly impossible tasks with relative ease. Just like learning to walk, training the thinking system to resolve conflict, to overcome non-assertiveness, to improve communication requires time, patience, and many thousands of repetitions. One school of thought vehemently argues that soft skills are innate and cannot be learned. The other school of thought holds the view that soft skills can be learned. It is important to take a balanced view that the by product of the two schools of thought. Irrespective of these controversies, it is has to be remembered that acquiring soft skills needs tremendous effort on the part of learner.

c. The characteristics of confirming responses are:

   1. Direct acknowledgement, when we respond directly to another person's message and, thus, indicate that we heard what was said and that the other person is included in our perceptual world.
   2. Agreement about content when we reinforce or support that the opinions are included in our perceptual world.
   3. Supportive response—when we give assurances, express understanding, or somehow attempt to make the other person feel better or encouraged.
   4. Clarifying responses, when we try to get the other person to express more, to describe feelings or information, to seek repetitions or make past remark clearer.
   5. Expression of positive feelings, when we share positive feelings about what the other person has done or said.

Section – B

5. a. The need for affection has to do with how close people want to be to one another, some individuals are high on the need for affection. Affection is closely related to disclosing behaviour, which greatly influences our interpersonal relations and communication.

   Interpersonal communication is satisfying when one manage to satisfy ones' needs. In the case of interpersonal needs, one depends solely on others for their satisfaction, for example, giving recognition, able to influence, close intimate feeling etc. We feel satisfied, and we seek the company of such individuals. We tend to avoid that type of interpersonal communication situations, where our needs are generally thwarted. An understanding of interpersonal need is essential in understanding communication.

b. The first step to be taken care of before you plan, research or organize a presentation is to determine the precise objective of the presentation. You must have a very clear and focused objective before you begin. In order to decide on your objective you need to ponder over:

   i. Why you are giving this presentation: You should at the very beginning be absolutely clear about the purpose of the presentation. Is it to convince the audience of a particular idea, or it is to bring people together to plan and review the progress of a particular project or are you seeking approval for a new project and emphasize on its innovative aspects.
   ii. Who is it aimed at: Then you should consider who it is aimed at. You must have a fair idea of the intellectual level of the audience and accordingly structure out the presentation. It is indeed a task to consider the audience to determine how best to achieve your objectives in the context of these people. During the presentation, you must be able

to identify their aims and somehow convince them that they are achieving their aims while you are achieving yours at the same time.

iii. When and where it will happen: When you are sure about the place and the timing of the presentation, plan the way you would like to interact with the audience. If you can win them over in the first minute then they are with you till the end. It is a good idea to try and meet them before the presentation actually begins. You can have a chat with them over a cup of tea. This will help to build a rapport with them and thereby establish that special relationship. You may be presenting yourself as a friend, as an expert, or an evaluator, whatever be the role you choose, you must establish it at the very beginning.

iv. The subject of the presentation: Once the subject, on which you are going to speak is decided upon, then structure or format the talk so that it becomes easy for the audience to comprehend what is being said. There should be a careful and deliberate sequential and hierarchical arrangement of thoughts. However, too much attention to structuring may get in the way of the main message.

v. The goal that outlines the purpose of the presentation: If you are not sure at the outset what you are trying to do, it is unlikely that your plan will achieve it. Different objectives cannot be achieved at the same time. It is far more productive to achieve one goal than to clutter with several. The best approach is to isolate the most essential one and remain focused. Focus is the key to a successful presentation. Without focus, you will end up in utter confusion and disorder.

6. a. The ultimate goal of all communication is the expected response from the listener. And individuals respond most readily when they are highly involved in the purpose of communication.

- Listening is more difficult in some situations.
- Physical conditions determine how well we listen.
- Psychological condition determines how well we listen.
- People listen out of politeness.
- Interpersonal communication is impossible without listening.
- To grasp communication one needs to listen.
- Listening is not hearing – it means interpreting as well.

b. Characteristics of well-functioning teams:

- **Purpose:** Members proudly share a sense of why the team exists and are invested in accomplishing its mission and goals.
- **Priorities:** Members know what needs to be done next, by whom, and by when to achieve team goals.
- **Roles:** Members know their roles in getting tasks done and when to allow a more skillful member to do a certain task.

- **Decisions:** Authority and decision-making lines are clearly understood.
- **Conflict:** Conflict is dealt with openly and is considered important to decision-making and personal growth.
- **Personal traits:** Members feel their unique personalities are appreciated and well utilized.
- **Norms:** Group norms for working together are set and seen as standards for every one in the group.
- **Effectiveness:** Members find team meetings efficient and productive and look forward to this time together.
- **Success:** Members know clearly when the team has met with success and share this equally and proudly.
- **Training:** Opportunities for feedback and updating skills are provided and taken advantage of by team members.

7. a. Qualities, which demonstrate interpersonal effectiveness, are:

- Builds and sustains positive relationships.
- Handles conflicts and negotiations effectively.
- Builds and sustains trust and respect.
- Collaborates and works well with others.
- Shows sensitivity and compassion for others.
- Encourages shared decision-making.
- Recognizes and uses ideas of others.
- Communicates clearly, both orally and in writing.
- Listens actively to others.
- Honors commitments and promises.

Interpersonal effectiveness starts with two things. The first involves understanding oneself — understanding what drives one's behaviour, and knowing one's strengths, weaknesses and triggers. Secondly, understanding the impact one has on others. Interpersonal effectiveness is about understanding ourselves in order to understand other people.

b. Shanon and Weavers' mathematical theory of communication (1949) is widely accepted as one of the main source of communication studies. It is a school of thought that sees communication as the transmission of messages.

Shannon and Weaver's model presents communication as a linear process. Its obvious characteristics of simplicity and linearity stand out clearly. Shannon and Weaver identify three problems in the study of communication. These are: level A- technical problems- how accurately can symbols of communication be transmitted? Level B-semantic problems- how precisely do the transmitted symbols convey the desired meaning? Level C- effectiveness problems- how effectively does the received meaning affect conduct in the desired way? A-level problems are the simplest to understand and these are the ones the model was originally developed to explain. Level B problems are easy to identify but hard to solve. Level C problems may at first sight seem to imply that Shannon and Weaver see communication as manipulation.

Section – C

8. Communication is the lifeblood of any institute/organization. It includes the structure through which messages pass and the way information is presented, as well as the actual content of the messages themselves. Whether you are speaking or writing, listening or reading, communication is more than a single act. It is a dynamic, transactional (two-way) process that can be broken into six phases:

The sender has an idea: You conceive an idea and want to share it.

The sender transforms the idea into a message: When you put your idea into a message that your receiver will understand, you are encoding, deciding on the message's from (word, facial expression, gesture), length, organization, tone and style, all of which depend on your idea, your audience, and your personal style or mood.

The sender transmits the message: To physically transmit your message to your receiver, you select a communication channel (verbal or nonverbal, spoken or written) and medium (telephone, computer, letter, memo, report, face-to-face exchange, and so on). The channel and medium you choose depend on your message, the location of your audience, your need for speed, and the formality of the situation.

The receiver gets the message: For communication to occur, your receiver must first get the message. If you send a letter, your receiver has to read it before understanding it. If you are giving a speech, the people in your audience have to be able to hear you, and they have to be paying attention.

The receiver interprets the message: Your receiver must cooperate by decoding your message, absorbing and understanding it. Then the decoded message has to be stored in the receiver's mind. If all goes well, the message is interpreted correctly; that is, the receiver assigns the same basic meaning to the words as you intended and responds in the desired way.

The receiver reacts and sends feedback to the sender: Feedback is your receiver's response, the final link in the communication chain. After getting the message, your receiver responds in some way and signals that response to you. Feedback is the key element in the communication process because it enables you to evaluate the effectiveness of your message. If your audience doesn't understand what you mean, you can tell by the response and refine your message.

The following figure illustrates, the communication process is repeated until both parties have finished expressing themselves. The process is effective only when each step is successful. In other words, ideas cannot be communicated if any step in this process is skipped or is completed incorrectly.

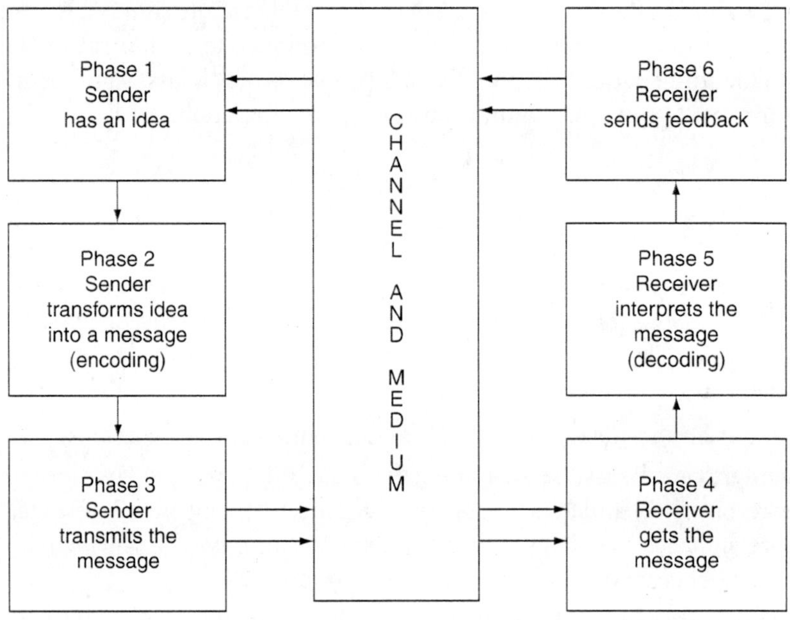

Figure M.2
Repetition of the process of communication

9. Attitudinal change, having clear communication, being empathetic, brain storming, negotiating, and working out the agreeable and best compromise are the basic strategies one can use to resolve the conflict. Precisely these are the principles of conflict management. One may follow the below outlined guidelines to effectively manage the conflict.

   Start with the right frame of mind:

   It is often seen parents in conflict with children tend to view the situation as 'two equals trying together to solve our problems' than to think 'you will do it my way because I say so'. Being in conflict doesn't necessarily mean being mad at each other. It *can* mean an opportunity to show your wisdom, to create a better situation, to help both of you be winners. Having a negative, distrustful attitude is detrimental to this process; believing you must 'win' the argument or otherwise you lose face is a bad attitude; feeling superior or being 'hard-nosed' and feeling inferior or being a 'soft-touch' are both problems. Start by seeing your opponent as a decent, reasonable person who wants to arrive at a fair solution (until proven otherwise). Deal with him/her with respect. Just as you would separate the person from his/her behaviour, separate the person from the conflict the two of you are having.

In this fair and cooperative spirit, invite the other person to sit down and talk it over with you. Even with warring spouses, marriage mediation has proven to be far superior to settling disputes in divorce courts. Lawyers in court do not take a cooperative, integrative problem-solving approach; they take an adversarial, get all you can, let's-prove-who's-wrong approach. If we can control our emotions just a little, however, we can usually work out good solutions. The cooperative, integrative solution approach is not appropriate in all cases.

Have a discussion to understand both sides' problems, conflicts, needs, and preferred outcomes (separating 'positions' from 'interests'). Be empathic:

It is important to make this first meeting as cordial as possible while being honest and open. Persuading the other person to take the 'win-win' approach may take time, especially if the other person is angry. Admit there is a conflict; acknowledge that both of you have legitimate needs and goals. Be respectful and, as much as possible, empathize with each other. Indicate that you are willing to be flexible and open-minded; ask them to be. See if both of you are willing to make a sincere effort to work out an optimal solution, recognizing that neither can have everything he/she wants. If so, arrange to take the time necessary to understand both sides.

Start by clarifying to each other exactly what the conflict or problem involves. Find out what they want. Get all the information the other person has to offer. Ask for all the additional information you need. Don't try to offer solutions now. First, just listen to their side, get all the facts, and give the situation some thought (solutions come next time). Don't try to assess blame but point out anything that seems unfair. Be honest and cordial. Keep on maintaining a good relationship, talk over coffee, or take a walk together. Be as understanding, empathic, and sympathetic as you can be (considering that you may be viewed as the villain).

Gather all the additional information you need and think of several options or plans for resolving the conflict and satisfying shared interests. Try brainstorming:

Drawing upon the things you both agree on and upon your shared goals and interests, draft some plans for changing things and for greater cooperation which will maximize the desired outcome for both of you. Have several plans or ideas (to demonstrate your flexibility).

One person, say a parent or a child, may simply ask the other to join in a rational, adult-like effort to resolve a difficulty between them. They are respectful to each other as equals; both contribute to the solution. There is no force, no threats, no crying or whining or other pressure to get one's way, just logic, respect, and consideration of each other. Both accept in advance that the final 'solution' must be acceptable to both. No one is put down; everyone wins as much as possible.

Both of you present your plans for resolving the conflict; try to integrate the best of both plans. Or, make a fair offer or express a request Negotiate the differences:

Don't present your ideas as the 'ideal solution', be tentative and honestly welcome different or better ideas. Nevertheless, clearly state the logical reasons for the plans or offer you are proposing. Make it obvious that you have considered the other person's needs and preferences. When indicating the outcomes you want, don't just say you want something because it is to your advantage, e.g., 'I need a raise because I bought a new car'. Word your proposals so they seem well justified and are easy to agree with.

Watch out for these common pitfalls in negotiations:

One of the most common mistakes is assuming that one proposal (usually yours) will solve all the problems. So, forget about finding *the best single answer*. In most situations, a good compromise is made up of several changes that benefit you the most (and the other person a little) and an equal number of changes that benefit the other person. So, *don't argue over every proposal made;* the task is to find the best combination of changes. That is why *brainstorming* is so helpful.

What to do if and when the going gets tough:

Keep in mind a saying, 'The relationship is much more important than the conflict'. Stress to the other person the importance of a positive future. Look for the opponent's real reasons. Ask him/her why he/she is resisting giving in on some issue. Maybe the other person will start talking about his/her needs ('interests') and reveal his/her underlying motives. If it is a marital conflict, perhaps the histories of both partners need to be considered.

If the opponent attacks your position or you personally, listen politely and then try to divert his/her thinking into the constructive development of a workable option by saying, 'That's interesting, what other ideas do you have that would improve this plan?' Stick with the win-win philosophy.

Agree upon the best compromise solution available. Try it out:

Consider the pros and cons of each possible solution, based on the criteria you have agreed to use. Do this cooperatively without either person dominating the decision-making process. No solution is possible that will completely satisfy both parties but both parties can be equally satisfied. It takes time to achieve this balance and still have a solution that both parties see as a definite 'win,' not over the opponent but over the problems.

Work out the details of how to carry out the solution. Who does what when? Be specific. What responsibilities does each person have? Decide how to determine if the agreement is working well. Try out the solution for a week or so, then re-evaluate it. Set a date to discuss your progress. Praise each other for making contributions to the solution. Make more changes as needed.

Any method, which reduces the animosity and stress in a conflict situation, is worthwhile. One danger is not taking the time to negotiate well. Another danger is the outbreak of animosity, regardless of how well win-win negotiation is attempted.

10. Let us begin with the basics. Good, effective communication through writing presupposes clear thinking. Only if you have thought through an issue to its last details, you can write effectively. Otherwise, your writing tends to lack coherence, and appears jumpy and illogical.

Next, good written communication requires thorough research. While speaking, we can get away with a casual approach to the issue but when we put it in black and white, the lack of sincere research shows, and very glaringly.

Often, hence, it is argued that for good writing, a six-point programme is necessary:

i. Brain storming to arrive at a precise definition and a statement of the theme to be dealt with. It helps to map out points on loose sheets of paper.

ii. Collecting data through research.

iii. Planning the actual document, its lay out, and final shape.

iv. Putting pen to paper.

v. Editing your draft for grammar, punctuation, spelling and consistency.

vi. Revising, it necessary.

Good communicators use every draft as a stage in the process of writing, and not as a final, finished product. It indeed helps to determine in advance the length of your written communication because you can arrange and organize and explain your points accordingly.

Basically, good written communication requires a unity of effect. We can achieve it if our writing has a clear progression of the beginning–middle–end variety.

It has been observed that an effective beginning, made attractive through a quote/an anecdote/a proverb provides the 'get set, go' effect. A crisp start, in brief, is the need of good communication.

The middle part of the communication should contain all the solid data that is coherently stated through cohesive devices such as 'therefore' 'so,' 'here', 'as a result' (to indicate cause-effect relationship), 'moreover', 'in addition' (to show adding of supplementary details), 'or', 'on the contrary', 'on the other hand', 'nevertheless', (to show contrast) and 'on the whole', 'in brief (to sum up) etc.

Your conclusion should summarize the writing and indicate future possibilities, if any. Please remember that you can start your argument *in medias res*, that is, in the middle. In other words, you need not always begin at the beginning.

You may want to state a case history, for example, analyze it in detail and then come to your theme statement that you would have otherwise stated in the beginning.

In other words, good writing shuttles back and forth through analysis on the basis of its certain premises. You can write deductively or inductively, in other words. Deductive writing would indicate analysis of facts, data, and case histories to arrive at a conclusion while inductive writing means you state an axiom and exemplify it in the rest of your argument. Use either of these styles. You can even blend them for effect.

Please remember that your argument should be structured in paragraphs, a reader can manage comfortably. Solid chunks of information, bound together into a monolith, terrorize more than an atom bomb. Every paragraph should have a theme statement and its relationship with the theme statements of other paragraphs should feed into the overall argument of the entire piece of writing.

Precise vocabulary and a gentle tone with a firm purpose (with a dash of humour, if possible) make your communication a delight for your decoder.

Please remember that in good formal writing, a sentence should never begin with 'and', 'but', 'for example', 'or', 'moreover', et al. These days, with times that are a-changing, such rules of usage are getting lax, but a good writer prefers not to abandon them.

As practice alone makes man perfect, when it comes to written communication, here let us look at

Tips for effective writing

- Be direct and explicit. Remember, nobody has the time to unravel the relevance and significance of your jigsaw puzzles.
- Do not waste too many lines 'introducing' your theme.
- Before writing, you should have outlined the entire, structure of your writing. Stick to it.
- Deal with one relevant issue per paragraph. Don't cram in too many ideas in a paragraph.
- Don't provide too many appendices and/or footnotes. Build all this information into your writing.
- Your presentation should be effective. The page should present a neat, clean, legible look.
- Write several versions, if necessary, of your material. *Revision* helps.
- Copy-edit your writing to avoid spelling, punctuation and grammar mistakes.

11. **The sounds of the english language**: The English language has 26 letters but 44 sounds. Therefore obviously some letters must account for more than one sound.

    All the 44 sounds are produced by the aggressive pulmonic air stream mechanism. The air that is moving out of the lungs is modified at several regions in the vocal tract to produce the different sounds.

    There are 20 vowel sounds in English. 12 of them are called monophthongs or pure vowels where the tongue takes a single position to produce them and the other 8 are called diphthongs or vowel glides, these are produced when the tongue shifts positions. There are 24 consonant sounds in the English language.

    It is convenient to use the phonetic symbols suggested by the International Phonetic Association to represent the sounds of speech. Let us first list out the consonant sounds.

English phonetic symbols for consonant sounds

/ π / as in pen
/ β / as in back
/ τ / as in tea

/ δ / as in day
/ κ / as in key
/ γ / as in get
/ T / as in church
/ δΓ / as in judge
/ ϕ / as in fat
/ ϖ / as in view
/ ⇓ / as in thank
/ □ / as in this
/ σ / as in soon
/ ζ / zero
/ Σ / as in ship
/ Γ / as in pleasure
/ η / as in hot
/ λ / as in light
/ ρ / as in right
/ μ / as in more
/ ν / as in nice
/ N / as in ring
/ φ / as in yet
/ ω / as in wet

English phonetic symbols for vowel sounds

Monophthongs

/ ι: / as in bean
/ ε / as in pet
/ υ / as in boon
/ O: / as in born
/ A: / as in barn
/ ©: / as in burn
/ I / as in pit
/ ℘ / as in pat
/ Y / as in put
/ ℜ / as in pot
/ ∫ / as in but
/ E / as in another

Diphthongs

/ ε#I / as in bay

/ α#I / as in buy

/ O#I / as in boy

/ IE / as in peer

/ YE / as in poor

/ εE / as in pair

/ EY / as in no

/ α#Y / as in now

Model Question Paper IV

Time: 3 hours **Total Points: 100**

SECTION – A (40 POINTS)

Answer any two out of four.

1. a. The classroom communication creates gigantic magnetic field of common and conflicting items of knowledge, beliefs, and values. Explain.

   b. 'You do not have to be best friends to make a team'. Examine.

   c. Explain the importance of nonverbal communication.

   (10 + 6 + 4 = 20 points)

2. a. 'A keen understanding of student psychology lies at the heart of effective communication'. Examine this statement.

   b. Do visual aids improve the quality of presentations?

   c. Briefly explain the communication according to Wilbur Schramm.

   (10 + 6 + 4 = 20 points)

3. a. 'The art of inspiring students is to make tactical use of emotional display'. Explain.

   b. What are the main characteristics of assertive, aggressive, and non-assertive behaviours?

   c. What are the personal competencies require for emotional displays?

   (10 + 6 + 4 = 20 points)

4. a. What is pedagogical communication?

   b. Discuss the process of structuring a lesson plan.

   c. What is psychological contact?

   (10 + 6 + 4 = 20 points)

SECTION – B (20 POINTS)

Answer any two out of three.

5. a. What is the role of the teacher in the pedagogical communication process?

   b. Explain the dimensions of communication.

   (5 + 5 = 10 points)

6. a. What is interpersonal conflict?
   b. Define conflict and highlight the importance of conflict management in day-to-day life.

(5 + 5 = 10 points)

7. a. Explain supportive intention.
   b. Discuss the process of writing in-house official letters, that is, official letters within the organization.

(5 + 5 = 10 points)

SECTION – C (40 POINTS)

Answer any two out of four.

8. Teachers are human and can experience a range of emotions. Can a teacher let his or her emotions reflect in his or her communication?

(20 points)

9. Discuss in detail the process of structuring reports for different academic domains. Explain these principles through the writing of an annual report, a project review and/or a policy statement.

(20 points)

10. What do you understand by 'face work strategies'?

(20 points)

11. Outline effective time management principles.

(20 points)

SUGGESTED ANSWERS

Section - A

1. a. The psychological knowledge of values and beliefs is essential for the teacher for effective communication, and this knowledge is available through psychographics, that is, constructing a psychological profile of the learner. Among the learning community there will be sub-group of values ranging from poor struggling survivors to highly motivated, integrated sustainer, belongers, emulators, and achievers.

   In every full-fledged classroom, every one of these will appear as the values, making the teaching task a challenge.

A teacher by his of her imaginative, effective and empathetic mode of communication shall be able to bridge their cultural and individual difference in values. A teacher must also try to make an attempt to have access to the value system in a relatively ambiguous guise. Ambiguity allows the wstudents to identity with the values.

A teacher has to understand the process of communication method to have access into the value system.

b. The personal relationships we develop on our team make a big difference in how we feel about our work and our workplace, as well as our team. But, contrary to popular belief, you don't have to be best friends to be an effective team. Best friends do not make a best team; best *teammates* make a best team. Being a best teammate is all about thoughtful behaviour. In a sense, it is about treating a teammate as if he or she were your best friend. It doesn't include socializing outside of work, or sharing personal feelings; what it does include is every kind of behaviour you can think of that conveys respect.

One can think about the ways that one demonstrate respect for one's best friend. Do we offer help to our best friend? Do we listen to our best friends without prejudging their ideas or opinions? Are we sensitive towards our best friends when they is experiencing personal problems? Do we accept our best friend's idiosyncrasies? Do we share in our best friend's excitement and offer praise when they have achieved something? The answer can be 'Yes' to all of the above questions. We can think of many more ways of showing respect for your best friends. That's what it takes to be a best teammate.

Instead of taking things personally, looking at things collectively and envisioning a goal is important to make a team. Personal likings and disliking should not play a significant role, which will be detrimental to the success of the team. Hence, looking at things as a matter of fact is important and 'you do not have to be best friends to make a team'.

c. It is important to pay attention to nonverbal aspects of communication as people's actions often do speak louder than their words. In fact, most people can deceive others much more easily with words than they can with their bodies. Words are relatively easy to control; body language, facial expressions, and vocal characteristics are not. By paying attention to these nonverbal cues, you can detect deception or affirm a speaker's honesty.

Because nonverbal communication is so reliable, people generally have more faith in nonverbal cues than they do in verbal messages. If a person says one thing but transmits a conflicting message nonverbally, listeners almost invariably believe the nonverbal signal. Remember, the meaning of nonverbal communication lies with the observer, who both reads specific signals and interprets them in context of a particular situation and a particular culture. Chances are, if you can read other people's nonverbal messages correctly, you can interpret their underlying attitudes and intentions and respond appropriately.

Nonverbal communication is important for another reason: It can be efficient from both the sender's and the receiver's standpoint. You can transmit a nonverbal message without even thinking about it, and your audience can register the meaning unconsciously. At the same time, when you have a conscious purpose, you can often achieve it more economically with a gesture than you can with words.

2. a. The task of education is to determine the structure of a learner's personality with significance to society, because personality is the fundamental propulsive force for the person's to evaluate his of her own behaviour and that of others objectively in any act of communication interaction.

   It is needless to point out the role which the teacher's personality can and must play.

   At the psychological level, the mastery of effective communication entails the constitution of individual operation; then their combination into an integral communicative act; and finally refining the communicative act according to the situation and the purpose of the communication.

   b. Visual aids significantly improve the quality of a presentation. However they must be relevant, and only support what is being orally said. They must add impact and clarity to the point you are making and enhance the verbal message. You should be sure that the audience benefits from these visual aids. Visual aids should be very prudently used. Unnecessary and improper use of these aids may end up in confusing the audience and worse still if you are yourself confused. Before beginning make sure you know when to and more importantly how to operate the equipment.

   Too much information on slides and OHPs should be avoided as it tends to distract the audience's attention from what is being said.

   Some of the visual aids that can be used are:

   - A black board.
   - Charts and real objects that can be passed around.
   - Video, film and 35mm slides.
   - Computer projections (Power-point, applications such as Excel, etc.).
   - Overhead projection transparencies (OHPs).

   Details of OHP and Slide Projector do not form the part of the question. Hence may be considered for omission.

   Visual aids when used properly can enhance the audience's interest and contribute significantly to the success of a presentation.

   c. There is a paradox about the term communication. In order to understand the communication process, we must use various devices to structure our thinking. We call these devices as communication models. Such models are replicas or maps of the events which made up the communication process and are largely the result of the influence of cybernetics on communication theory.

   According to Wilbur Schramm to know how communication works, it would be necessary to study the communication process in general. When two people communicate with each other, at least three elements are involved, the source of the communication, the message or the content and the destination of the receiver. The communicator may be an organization like the news paper or TV station or an individual. The message can be in any form, language, visuals or any other signals that can be interpreted meaningfully. The receiver again, can be an individual or a group.

So communication here means sharing information with a group or an individual.

3. a. The teacher can inspire students by using his or her emotions in a planned and tactical manner. The emotion a teacher displays for effect can be negative or positive. Appropriate emotional displays give a boost to effective teaching characteristics.

   The following techniques will help a teacher to make good use of display of emotions and feelings.

   - To save emotional display for rare occasions.
   - To be explicit about one's feelings.
   - To concentrate on one's nervous system, which matches one's emotions.
   - To practise showing positive and negative emotions.

   b. **Characteristics of a non-assertive person:**

   - Reluctant to express own opinions, and particularly feelings.
   - Often feels used by others.
   - Keeps quiet when others take advantage.
   - Refrains from complaining when services or products are not up to standard.
   - Finds it difficult to refuse the requests of others for time or resources.
   - Acquiesces in the views and desires of the majority even though this conflict with personal wishes.
   - Frequently makes compromises in the interests of harmony.
   - Is unwilling to inconvenience people for the things he or she wants.
   - Is submissive in the presence of aggressive behaviour.
   - Prefers to keep own views private.

Characteristics of an aggressive person:

- Frequently argues with others.
- Frequently gets angry and thinks others need to be put in their place.
- Has no difficulty in complaining when receiving poor quality product and services.
- Usually gets own way in situations.
- Expects others to accommodate own time schedules.
- Has strong views on many subjects and has no difficulty in expressing them.
- Easily and frequently finds fault with others.

- Continually works to personal agendas at the expense of others.
- Rarely feels aware of the needs or feelings of others.
- Competes with others and is angry if not successful.

Characteristics of an assertive person:

The assertive person:

- Is able to express desires and feelings to others.
- Is able to converse and work well with people at all levels.
- Is able to appreciate the views of others and accept any that appear more reasonable than their own.
- Is able to disagree with someone yet retains their friendship and respect.
- Is aware of the needs and desires of others.
- Is able to make concessions to others without feelings of inadequacy.
- Is able to express a concern or a need with minimum embarrassment to both parties.
- Is able to control feelings and emotions even in difficult or emotionally charged situations.
- Is able to refuse a request without feeling guilty or obliged.
- Is able to ask for what he or she wants and can insist on legal entitlements without becoming emotional.

c. • Being attentive to emotional cues and listen well.
- Show sensitivity and understanding for other's perspective.
- Help out, based on understanding other people's needs and feelings.
- Self-awareness – knowing one's internal states, preferences, resources and instincts.
- Emotional awareness – recognizing one's emotion and their effects.
- Accurate self assessment – knowing one's strengths and limits.
- Self-confidence – a strong source of one's self worth and capitates.

4. a. Pedagogical communication is a system of interaction between the pedagogue and the students based on appropriate methods and habits and connecting of exchange of information, exercise of appropriate influence on the pupils for didactic and educational purposes, and the promotion of their mutual understanding. The pedagogue initiates and controls this process:

- Pedagogical communication provides the emotional background for the process of communication.
- Pedagogical Communication is a joint activity.

- Pedagogical communication assumes the form of interpersonal interaction, that is, the sum total of ties and mutual influences arriving in the process of individuals' joint activities.
- Pedagogical communication is based on social works and social control.
- Pedagogical communication is a system of methods.

b. Whether you are sketching an outline or jotting down points for a content subject (history, geography, mathematics, for example) or a skill subject (language studies, for example), effective teaching needs a lesson plan.
It helps to think of the lesson plan as a planned audio-visual presentation. It is useful hence to divide the information into three stages:

i. **Pre-teaching** activities make the learner curious and oriented towards the main topic of the actual lesson dealt with. Often, these activities consist of a quick fire round of question-answer series. You should write out at the planning stage all possible questions and all probable answers.
At times, pre-teaching consists of activities that are framed as leads. In such a case, you have to plan the lesson in such a way that either yours, as the teacher's or the learners' reactions lead to the main argument. You could tell half the story, for example and ask your learners to complete it and then start your teaching, working through these reactions.

ii. During the **actual teaching,** it is necessary to plan in such a way that the multiplicity of media, that writing as a communication skill specially enjoys, is used to advantage, Please see to it that the entire data is dealt with through stages that you cohesively link through markers such as, 'now my next point is', 'my third observation deals with', et al. The learners, thus, understand the progression of the argument. It is the teacher's duty to plan these activities in such an ordered way during the structuring of the lesson plan.

iii. During the **post-teaching interaction,** sum up, and further open up to questioning, the data presented in the lesson.
In brief, the structuring of a lesson plan should look as follows:

	Stage	Time required	Activities involved	Audio-visual aids
i.	Pre-teaching	20 minutes	1. question-answer 2. reading by learners	flash cards, black board
ii.	Teaching	25 minutes	1. reading by teacher	textbook, slides
iii.	Post-teaching	5 minutes	1. summing up through question-answers	cue cards

It is a good practice, moreover, to **maintain a diary** in which you evaluate yourself against every detail. Such a process helps you find out your lacunae, work on them and improve your performance as a teacher.

Such diary entries are often written out as bullet points:

Date	Pre-teaching time was not sufficient.
Time	Student did not get the hang of the idea.
Topic	Questions appeared superfluous to them.
	They took too much time re-arranging themselves into groups.

Planning, in brief, *maketh* a perfect lesson.

c. A teacher must be keenly aware of the fact that due regard, should be given to every individuals though the group may be treated as a single whole. Even a temporary loss of psychological contact with students may have consequences. Regular impairments of mutual understanding between the teacher and the pupils become a rule rather than an exception, are bound to create a gulf between them. This pedagogic tact helps the teacher to establish necessary contacts with his or her pupil's, gives teacher broad possibilities for molding and developing the pupil's personality.

Section – B

5. a. A teacher as an individual cannot afford to have role conflicts, because the post of a teacher is regulated by role expectations and is subject to social control and assessment. Any substantial deviation from the standard is condemned. Teaching behaviour requires tact in communication, that is, we are capable of accurately predicting the expected behaviour, violations of the rules of 'tactful' behaviour leads to serious consequences in pedagogic communication.

6. b. There are four dimensions of communication namely intrapersonal, interpersonal, group, and mass communication. Each of these dimensions contributes to the process of developing good communication skills.

Intrapersonal communication

It is very interesting to know about what goes on inside people as they think, feel, value, react, imagine etc. This dimension is known as 'intrapersonal' and has been the subject of psychological and cognitive studies, which attempt to learn how people respond to information and how they make decisions or store and retrieve data in their brains. It has also been examined about how bias, love, hatred, or even apathy can affect human interaction. How people handle information about their world is the central tenet of this dimension.

Interpersonal communication

Interpersonal communication is a transaction between people and their environment, which includes other people such as friends, family, children, coworkers, and even strangers. Communication is now seen as a transaction in which both parties are active.

The parties are not necessarily equally active—that is more likely in the case of interpersonal communication, less so in the case of mass media and their audiences—but to both parties, the transaction is in some way functional. It meets a need or provides a gratification. To a greater or lesser degree information flows both ways. Like other transactions, this one is likely to be guided by rules or agreement as we see when a teacher communicates with a student, a parent with a child.

It is observed that most people who write about interpersonal communication appear to insist that the more communication you have, the better off your relations will be. However, more may not always be better. It is also seen by researchers that how people see each other ('interpersonal perceptions') may have a significant effect on how those persons will interact.

What happens in interpersonal communication involves so much more than words that we must pay careful attention to people's habits of relating to each other, if we are to be effective in either studying about or participating in these transaction.

Group communication

Not all communication theorists agree on a definition of small group communication—how many people make up a group, what differences there are between dyads and other numbers of people in communication, etc. The field of group dynamics, however, represents a very interesting and special case of communication. It involves theories of leadership and management, small group discussion, and decision-making. A number of the exercises and activities involve group dynamics, group discussion, leadership and management principles are part and parcel of any academic setting. There is no way you can interact in your class without applying or taking into account the principles of group interaction. A teacher and an academic consultant play a vital role in enhancing group interaction and group communication

Mass communication

One of the most popular areas of study in the recent times is that of the mass media – or 'communication', as the term is used in some places—to indicate a broadened view of what once was called simply 'journalism'. At one time it was believed that audiences were a sort of homogenous group, which could be reached through a media source. This very simplified view of audiences was useful to some mass media practitioners but did not explain how complicated are both the process of communicating and the character of audiences. While mass media study is beyond the scope of our chapter, there are many ties between interpersonal and mass communication. One-way transmission over mass media is no longer the only way to view information. As the significance of two-way (or interactive) communication grows, people studying and working in mass media will have to take into account many of the theories and principles of interpersonal communication; and merging of such fields of study is not too far.

Each of the above detailed dimensions individually or collectively contributes to the academic field in terms of understanding communication and sharpening communication.

6. a. During the process of communication certain conflicts may arise due to difference of values, goals etc. The social and educational significance of such conflicts may be different, and depends on the rules providing the base for inter personal relations between the pedagogic and the pupil it leads to tension, emotional distancing, communication gaps eventually block the way to common goal.

   Consisting situation may arise due to Semantic barrier. A semantic barrier in communication commits of a different inter predation by the communicating individuals leading to lack of understanding and, thus, hampering interaction. Semantic barriers are the major cause of conflict.

   b. Conflict is an inevitable part of any relation ship. Conflict takes place between parent and child, wife and husband, teacher and student. Conflict is a very normal phenomenon. However, conflicts do not have to end with someone losing and with both parties hating each other. Unfortunately, many do end this way. That is why we have so many wars, political fights, divorces, lawsuits, business breakups, strikes, effort, time and money-wasting arguments at work, etc. Wise persons are able to resolve disagreements with both parties satisfied and respecting each other. Hence, learning to resolve conflict, which yields a positive outcome, is a real skill.

   Each of us has our own way of dealing with *conflicts* in our lives. Knowing our own style and motives as well as the style and motives of the person we are in conflict with, will help us handle the situation. Also it is obvious that self-serving and hostile underlying emotions are often the cause of disputes. The conflict may be a power struggle, a need to prove you are right, a superior attitude, a desire to hurt or some other motive.

   Conflict is defined as a form of relating or interacting where we find ourselves (either as individuals or groups) under some sort of perceived threat to our personal or collective goals. These goals are usually to do with our interpersonal wants. These perceived threats might be either real or imagined.

   This definition has three elements, which were helpful in explaining the nature of conflict. Firstly, conflict is seen as involving a perceived threat. Perceived is an important word here, as the basis of the conflict may be 'false' or indirect in the sense that there is no real clash of interests or goals between the parties, but the parties nevertheless perceive, and therefore experience conflict. Secondly, conflict is experienced at the interpersonal level that is in our interactions with other people. Thirdly, the dimensions of conflict relating to our interpersonal wants are helpful in linking conflict to the idea of personal and social aspirations. All of these elements are useful to understand the nature of conflict.

7. a. Supportive intentions are the pedagogues underlying divides to provide aid or assistance to students. Here the main important aspect is the intention of the teacher to be supportive. It is this intention that makes message supportive. The supportive intention of the intentions is referred from the behaviour of the pedagogue.

   However, pedagogues need to make their supportive intentions explicit through overt statements of availability. Their overt statements enhance the pupils perception of the clarity, internity, purity and sincerity of the pedagogue intention and, thus, opens the channels of communication between the pedagogue and the pupil.

b. Let us begin our answer with the general observation that official letters within the organization mostly would consist of notices, memos and minutes. These are essentially formal and precise and to the point.

A **notice** is often an invitation to a meeting. So it is necessary to clearly state the notice period, the day, date, time, venue of the meeting, the purpose of the meeting and the actual business to be carried out. Here is an example.

Hyderabad Private School

Banjara Hills, Hyderabad – 16.

February 29, 2011

Notice

A meeting of the Executive Committee will be held in the committee room at 11.30 a.m. on March 10, 2011.

The agenda is:

1.

2.

3.

Signature
Designaton

A **memo** is written almost the same way. Instead of 'Notice', you write 'Memorandum'. Next follows 'To'. On the next line, you have the name(s) and designation(s) of your addressee(s). This is followed by the actual matter of the memo.

Minutes are the official record of the business carried out during a meeting. Essentially a mnemonic, they guide further action. So minutes should have, in addition to the name of the department/unit, a mention of the date/time/venue. Next, minutes should list the names of chairperson(s), members, special invitees, et al. The minutes should include an item-wise record of the discussion and finally, the signature of the authority.

An **agenda** is essentially an official list of activities to be looked at, discussed and dealt with in a particular meeting.

Initially, it should indicate the importance, the urgency, and hence the ordering of items. It should be time sensitive.

It should place routine items at the beginning. Next should follow matters arising from the previous meeting(s).

The new items for consideration are placed next. An agenda, thus, maintains a proper order for a meeting, minimizes discussion, and preserves continuity in the proceeding of the meeting. In brief, it professionally prepares the staff for the issue under discussion. A good agenda makes taking down minutes very easy, for example.

Section – C

8. The answer is yes, in case of positive emotion, where the demonstration of core, kindness, empathy, concern are all so very important for effective communication in teaching and learning. Teachers who make a difference in student's life are those who were transparent and those who were not real individual but 'roles' could not reach out to the students. A teacher without clearly expressed emotions is more like a teaching machine than a teacher.

9. Reports, projects, agendas, policy statements are essentially descriptive in nature.

   A report or a policy statement is unique in nature. It has a clear, defined reader profile but this reader is multiple as the same report, policy statement, et al, may get used in very many committees.

   Hence reports for different academic domains (sciences, humanities, applied sciences) essentially need to **focus.** They have to be very orderly. To make them credible, they have to be objective, evaluative but non-judgmental. They are a written communication that is made of factual information and/or data. Your opinion, if any, has to be supported by this irrefutable data.

   So it helps to clearly determine its purpose. Next, it is necessary to state a clear theme statement. Once your preliminary research work is through, you should think of its presentation that provides to your reader your hypothesis through identifiable topics and sub-topics.

   Your outline should clearly have an introductory unit, a concluding unit and a summary. If a summary collects all your points, the concluding unit can chart out the new directions you may possibly foresee.

   The length of your report should be neither too brief (appears very casual) nor too long. Your report should directly come to the point as your possible future reader—an official, for example, or a bureaucrat—may not have the time or the patience to go through it. So be precise, please.

   Append visual aids, wherever necessary. The layout arrangement, the headers/ footers, numbering, constructing of title (underlining/emboldening it), placement of titles, use of illustrations (pie charts, line charts, computer graphics) make your visual aids which should never attract attention to themselves.

   In brief, the report should succinctly and clearly give a neat picture of the activities it encompasses.

   Any report should be arranged in three parts according to our reference books. They are: front matter, main body, and back matter.

Front matter	Main body	Back matter
Cover (title, number, date, whether confidential) Title page (author's name, designation) Copyright notice Forwarding letter, if necessary Preface Acknowledgements Table of contents List of illustrations Abstract	Introduction Discussion/analysis Conclusions Recommendations	Appendices References Bibliography Glossary Index

Structuring annual reports

School/college annual reports need not be very content-rich. They are more a quantitative statement with a warm note to give their clientele, that is, the students and their parents, a feel-good effect.

Essentially, the tone is friendlier and warmer. The facts are kept to a minimum and are presented in a tabular manner and in a very colourful way designed for easy access.

As a read-it-and-throw-it-away presentation, such reports have a glossy newspaper like feel. Often these reports provide many snaps.

While structuring them, you have to pay more attention to the visual presentation. Give the minimum matter through bullet points. All the financial details should be presented in a tabular format. Use simple, easily accessible English.

Reviewing a project

This kind of written communication differs from a report in two ways:

i. It includes a report, but it goes beyond it through comments.

ii. It is very formal in nature. So the vocabulary and tone, unlike an annual report, reflect this aspect.

You can visualize it in the following way:

Sender's address
Date

For the attention of
Sub: Review of.........

Contents:
i. the report
ii. critical comments
iii. recommendations

Signature and designation of the sender

Please remember that your reader is not going tc have too much time on hand. So 'bold' the important points.

It could look as follows:

Water Conservation Strategies

Progress Review

Aims

- Increasing ground water level
- Storing monsoon water

Plans as stated in report

- Awareness raising
- Central government funding

Limitations

- Appears expensive
- Lacks popular support

Recommendations and suggestions

- NGO participation necessary

Just like a report, a review, too, should identify the problem, its causes, the relative importance of each and the possible solutions along with your opinions and recommendations.

Preparing policy statements

A policy statement is also a kind of a report. So it too should begin with an overview of the past achievements, facts, data.

Next should follow the need for the new policy. A thorough, well-documented and research-backed data, supported by needs analysis, should supplement and strengthen the theme statement.

Mention the policy change and its aim succinctly. Discuss its advantages and indicate possible difficulties and ways to overcome them.

10. A teacher has to be careful in showing his or her supportive intention, because such intentions can implicitly convey negative evaluation of the pupil's impose on his or her autonomy. At times supportive communication can be threatening. Asking questions can challenge privacy, offering advice may undermine autonomy's marking suggestions can imply criticism.

To offset this possibility, the pedagogue has to use certain devices. Face work or politeness strategies are communicative devices for reimbursing the face threats inherent in supportive management. Positive face work aims to protect derive to be evaluated positively; it includes verbal and behavioural devices that express positive regard for the pupil, admiration for the courage or effort shown by the pupil, respect for the pupils' understanding of difficulty and confidence in the capacities and qualities to overcome problems.

Positive face work when used by the pedagogue, results in the following favourable outcome:

- Increase in the pupil's willingness to consider the helper's message.
- Internet in interacting with the helper.
- Liking for the pedagogue.
- Develop acceptance and trust.
- Leads to effective communication.

11. Effective time-management principles:
    1. Setting priorities, listing major goals, rating each goal, and asking oneself what is most important for them to do: It is often seen that people do not set their priorities. Setting priorities will help individuals to plan effectively. It is also essential to identify and list major goals. Rating each goal in terms of which extent one has accomplished is important. Individuals also lack self-introspection and it is required for them to ask themselves as to what they are doing is important for them or not.
    2. List what needs to be done this week in order to reach your top priority goals. Rate each activity: It is very beneficial to review your situation each week, giving a few minutes of serious thought to what actually needs to be done to achieve your goals. It is needed to set one's mind in such a way so as to translate one's major purposes in life—one's aspirations-into concrete actions. Based on one's rather wide-ranging thoughts and feelings, making a realistic list of the learning and work that seems to be required to reach one's 'top' priority goals. Being creative and realistic is also essential. Goals should not be confused with activities.
    3. Observe how you spend your time: It could be an eye-opening experience to simply record how one spends one's 168 hours per week. Noting how one wastes time, spends time on low priority tasks, has trouble getting started, or tends to be inefficient. This kind of information may be useful in setting up a daily schedule so that one will stay on task.
    4. Make a master schedule of fixed activities for the week: A master schedule for the week tells one what time is 'committed', i.e., time periods that one has already scheduled. It includes sleeping, dressing, eating, travel time, meetings or classes, housekeeping chores, time with loved ones, friends or children, and some leisure- relaxation-exercise time. This is one's fixed schedule. It includes the things that one must do. One's master schedule will be pretty stable week after week. The master schedule identifies the hours that are 'free', that one has control over.
    5. Keep a running list of assignments—things one needs to get done this week: Keep track of what needs to be done soon, e.g., get a report written. Note any due dates, the time required (remember many things take twice as much time as we expected), and the importance of the task.

6. Make a 'To-Be-Done List' for every day: One's list of important goal-directed activities, one's inefficient use of time, one's already scheduled time, and one's assignments due this week, one needs to decide on one's priorities for each day of the week. Then start scheduling activities in one's 'free' time, giving priority to the most important. Some activities must be done at a specific time, e.g. an appointment to talk to an advisor. Other activities need to be done but can be done at any available time; they are simply listed to be done (which means one has to leave some 'free' time).
7. Following one's daily To-Be-Done List. Learning to make daily schedule realistic, which means one schedules what can and needs to be done *and* one actually does those things. One has to be flexible; new things will come up each day that requires attention. But the basic point is simple: work on highest priority activities during most of the 'free time' each day.
8. Lastly, one cannot manage time. One can only utilize time. Research has shown that one of the most effective time utilization strategies is to follow Stephen. R Curvey's 'time management Matrix' and learn to put first things first.

Model Question Paper V

Time: 3 hours **Total Points: 100**

SECTION – A (40 POINTS)

Answer any two out of four.

1. a. What do you understand by the term 'supportive communication'? Explain its different features.

   b. Discuss the concept 'team effectiveness'

   c. What are the objectives of socio-psychological training?

(10 + 6 + 4 = 20 points)

2. a. Explain the functional importance of nonverbal communication.

   b. What are the different techniques of interviewing?

   c. Define the term 'empathy'.

(10 + 6 + 4 = 20 points)

3. a. 'Emotions play a significant role in communication'. Critically examine the statement.

   b. Explain how you would go about preparing a 'teacher's handbook(s)' and a 'students' workbook(s)'.

   c. Explain the term 'supportive intention'.

(10 + 6 + 4 = 20 points)

4. a. How can a teacher avoid interpersonal conflict through effective communication?

   b. Explain the verbal aspects of assertive, aggressive, and non-assertive behaviour.

   c. 'How you say it is what counts'. Explain from communication skills' point of view.

(10 + 6 + 4 = 20 points)

SECTION – B (20 POINTS)

Answer any two out of three.

5. a. Discuss the common problems due to ineffective time management.

   b. 'Negotiation is one of the most essential principles of conflict management'. Justify.

(5 + 5 = 10 points)

6. a. Enumerate do's and do not's of good listening.
   b. How many types of interviews are there?

(5 + 5 = 10 points)

7. a. Explain the strategies to improve our listening skills.
   b. 'It is not the strongest of the species that survive, nor the most intelligent, but the one most responsive to change'.

(5 + 5 = 10 points)

SECTION – C (40 POINTS)

Answer any two out of four.

8. Explain the theory of interpersonal needs.

(20 points)

9. What are the barriers to effective communication?

(20 points)

10. Outline the strategies of 'face work'.

(20 points)

11. Define writing as a communication skill. Explain in detail the elements and types of writing.

(20 points)

SUGGESTED ANSWERS

Section – A

1. a. If we define a teacher as a facilitator, then communication is not only a medium of sharing information or passing and knowledge, then supportive communication and interaction are ubiquitous in any institution of learning, because teachers are also providers of support to the students and it has a positive effect on supportive interaction, social relationship and emotional anchoring. Effective support fosters psychological adjustment and perception of self-efficacy, improves coping with upsetting events and enhances task performance under stressful conditions. A teacher needs to understand supportive process if he or she is to facilitate these beneficial outcomes. Moreover, supportive interactions are a primary means through which the social and emotional connections are created and sustained, it leads to the development of personal relationships, supporting communication has a therapeutic value and develops moral character because it displays the highest expression

of the human spirit, so by studying the behaviour, pedagogues acquaint themselves better with the nature and practice of psychotherapy in every day life, it explores the character of moral action and fosters a sense of community in the classroom.

The recent focus on supportive communication owes much to the tradition of interdisciplinary scholarly inquiry centred on the concept of social support, and at the same time the sociological and psychological perspective on social support were being articulated and refined, roughly between 1975–90, scholars in several different academic disciplines were developing research programmes examining what eventually would be called supportive communication, especially the work of Albrecht and her colleagues within the academic discipline of communication, provided much of the initial impetus for an articulation of a communication perspective on social support. This emerging perspective was also informed by a variety of other empirical traditions. These diverse literatures remain largely segregated through the common focus in the varied research traditions on communicative efforts directed at helping others in need. As a result, a distinctive communication or interactional perspective on social support has emerged over the past 10 years in this section, we shall try to understand the concept of supportive communication and then we shall see the facts of communication.

Let us now see the underlying mechanisms through which supportive, messages have their effects. Any explanatory model for supportive messages must account for relationships among three elements: message feature, theoretical mechanisms and outcomes. Message behaviours are verbal and nonverbal components of a helper's behaviour, directed at assisting a target; there are isolated units of behaviour that have characteristics structure. Theoretical mechanisms discuss the actions performed by message features; such a mechanism identifies what the enacted or presence of message components does. Finally, outcomes are the events or states that follow (more or less reliably) from the action of some mechanism; when messages are successful, outcomes reflect the goals which helpers seek to achieve.

At least four features/influence the effectiveness of supportive messages: (a) the presence of a discernible supportive intention, (b) the use of politeness or face work, (c) the informative or prepositional content of the message, and (d) the person-centred quality of the message. Here, we discuss each feature in conjunction with the particular outcomes.

b. Team effectiveness is an important concept, without which the success of the team is impossible. Team effectiveness does not emerge out of vacuum and it is a byproduct of several aspects. When evaluating how well team members are working together, the following statements can be used as a guide:

   - Team goals are developed through a group process of team interaction and agreement in which each team member is willing to work towards
   - Participation should be actively shown by all team members and roles are shared to facilitate the accomplishment of tasks and feelings of group togetherness.

- Feedback is asked for by members and freely given as a way of evaluating the team's performance and clarifying both feelings and interests of the team members. When feedback is given, it is done with a desire to help the other person.
- Team decision-making involves a process that encourages active participation by all members.
- Leadership is distributed and shared among team members and individuals who willingly contribute their resources as needed.
- Problem solving, discussing team issues, and critiquing team effectiveness are encouraged by all team members.
- Conflict is not suppressed. Team members are allowed to express negative feelings and confrontation within the team, which is managed and dealt with by team members. Dealing with and managing conflict is seen as a way to improve team performance.
- Team member resources, talents, skills, knowledge, and experiences are fully identified, recognized, and used whenever appropriate.
- Risk taking and creativity are encouraged. When mistakes are made, they are treated as a source of learning rather than reasons for punishment.

After evaluating team performance against the above guidelines, determine those areas in which the team members need to improve and develop a strategy for doing so.

The team leader can encourage team member's growth, and should be willing to take some risk by having members, whose resources are relevant to the immediate task, provide the leadership.

The team leader should be fair, supportive, and recognized by team members as one who can make final judgments, work with upper management, and give direction to the team as needed.

To assist the team leader in evaluating the level of team development, let each team member answer the twelve questions outlined. This should be followed by a discussion of the questions to determine where and how changes should be made to help facilitate the development of a strong team.

As team members build commitment, trust, and support for one another, it will allow them to develop and accomplish desired results. This commitment, trust, and self-determination by each team member are critical in achieving a sustained high level of performance. Team members will learn to appreciate and enjoy one another for who they are, and will help keep one another on track.

c. Socio-psychological training has two kinds of objectives; first, knowing the laws of communication in general, and second, knowing the special laws of pedagogic communication, which means learning the habits and skills of professional pedagogic communication. Hence, psychologists distinguish between the theoretical and practical aspects of the problem of socio-psychological training. The practical aspects include exercises aimed at helping teachers develop habits and skills of communication with pupils, to act consistently, the ability to achieve muscular relaxation during lessons, the ability to distribute voluntary attention, and the ability of observation special attention is to be given to elocution exercises for improving oral speech standards based on the use of feedback, audio and videotape recording, mimicry and pantomime.

Psychological—pedagogical training may be conducted in the form of professional games, which stimulate the object—oriented social context of the future specialists for professional activity, thereby providing more realistic modeling than in traditional training setups. Communication training as a method of psychological influence enhances the individual's ability for communication and teaching activity, thereby improving his personal characteristics.

2. a. The nonverbal communication is important for a variety of reasons:

    - Nonverbal or verbal factors are the major determinants of meaning in the interpersonal context,
    - Feelings and emotions are more accurately exchanged by nonverbal, rather than verbal means,
    - The nonverbal aspect of communication conveys meanings and intentions that are relatively free of deception, distortion, and confusion,
    - Nonverbal cues serve meta-communicative functions that are indispensable in attaining high quality communication,
    - Nonverbal cues represent a much more efficient means of communication than verbal cues and
    - Nonverbal cues represent the most suitable vehicles for suggestion. We can communicate our true feelings and emotions by nonverbal means accurately and frequently. Messages conveyed nonverbally are often involuntary, or the result of reflex action.

    There are many kinds of non-verbal communication. Of these the most important are kinesics—the movement of our bodies, e.g., smiling; proxemics, the use of space; and our use of time. The proxemic mode concerns spatial relations, and the body orientation. The orientation of two people in a discotheque will be different from that between a professor and a student in a classroom, even though unknown to the two in the discotheque, one may well be a professor and the other a student.

   b. There are different kinds of techniques that are adopted by the interviewers. Some of them are listed below:

      i. Behavioural Interview
      ii. Traditional Interview
      iii. Serial Interview

iv. Panel Interview

v. Stress Interview.

Behavioural interview

This technique is largely adopted for 'on campus' recruiting. It is based on the assumption that the most satisfactory way to predict future behaviour is to ascertain and evaluate behaviour of the past.

The desired behaviour like taking the initiative, planning, motivation, flexibility etc are assessed based on questions regarding a past situation. The questions that might be asked are; 'What did you do?', 'What did you say?', 'What was the action taken?', or 'What was the result?'

The traditional interview

This is the most prevalent technique of interviewing where the interviewee, besides responding to questions is also expected to ask articulate, well-formed questions. An excellent way to prepare for this type of an.

Serial interview

This technique involves a series of sequential interviews with a number of different interviewers. Each of them plays a key role in the decision-making process.

Panel interview

This technique involves a panel of three to ten interviewers, interviewing at the same time. Each of them is assigned to evaluate a particular area. The interviewee should be tactful enough to show equal eye contact and attention to every individual.

Stress Interview

This technique is rarely and deliberately used to test the candidate's ability to be poised and expressive under pressing, compelling or constraining situations.

c. Empathy is the skill of active listening—of approaching an interaction with an open mind. It is the understanding that, regardless of a person's appearance, personality, or history, a common thread exists. We have all experienced pain, love, sadness, joy, greed, lust, pleasure, and contentment. There is an all-permeating similarity we share as we each play our part in the great human comedy. To practise empathy is to not feel for another person, but to actually be another person. In other words, it means to be in other person's shoes. It is to feel a kinship, a bond, a connection and relationship from your own personal background. To communicate with empathy, is to be completely receptive to what another person is expressing, to find out where one is coming from without categorizing, passing quick judgment, or blocking their message by putting up separations, distinctions or walls.

Empathy is important for information exchange in any and all relationships, whether between a stranger, a family member, or between two nations.

3. a. No feature of communication has more meaning and significance than the one identified by the word emotion or affect—love, hate, anger, sadness, courage, anxiety, frustration are emotional states—feelings. Positive or negative emotion constitutes a very general predisposition. Individuals with positive affect are marked by enthusiasm, favourable expectations and general optimism, than individuals with negative affect. The communication-related communicators, because positive emotions are highly correlated with self concept, sensitivity, empathy, and interpersonal skills. The impact of negative emotion in communication can lead to communication apprehension, miscommunication, aggression, etc.

   The impact of negative emotion in teaching is far more critical, for it involves a teacher's overall attitudes about students and teaching. Emotion is the source for the words and expressions we use, and since we know the relation of emotion with communication, negative emotions also disrupt relationships between the teachers and the students indeed, the emotional tie or relationship between the teacher and the taught serves as the channel for all the messages that each arouses in the other.

   Teachers are human and can experience a range of emotions but the question is, should a teacher let his or her emotions, reflect in her communication with the students? The answer is yes, in case of positive emotion (as we shall see in the next chapter on pedagogy and communication) where, the show of love, kindness, empathy, concern—are all so very important for effective communication in teaching and learning. Teachers who have made a difference in our lives were for us real people. Those who were not flesh and blood did not help us internalize whatever they taught. A teacher without clearly expressed emotions is more like a teaching machine than a teacher.

   b. The contemporary models of teaching believe that a textbook, often prepared by a board that may not have the requisite academic leaning/qualifications/interests, may not be sufficient as a teaching/learning aid. Often, hence, are prepared teacher's handbooks and students' workbooks as additional teaching/learning aids. The proliferation of 'special purpose' courses further necessitates such a move.

   A **Teacher's Handbook** gives tips to the teacher for effective teaching. When you are scripting such a teacher's handbook, see to it that it is **self-sufficient.** A teacher, without any further training (which is welcome, if possible), should manage to use this extra resource.

   It is necessary, hence, to provide **clear indications** in a teacher's handbook about how to use it, about how it should supplement and extend the textbook, for example.

   It is essential to provide very many **graded activities,** listed out in detail. These should make both enjoyable teaching and reading, for the experimenting teacher.

Your handbook should have clear indications regarding how to go about the graded activities and how actually to use them.

Your units should not be too lengthy and should address a given point through every possible related activity, e.g., if your handbook deals with 'hotel management English', there could be a unit on 'taking calls'. List all possible responses. Create situations to give your learners to actually try them out.

Your handbook, which covers all related skills, should structure each unit into 'teaching points', 'expressions to learn', 'structures to practice', 'activities', for example.

It helps your reader if you **provide an answer key** as well. Your handbook, thus, becomes a self-instructional material.

Make your handbook very communicative and try to grade activities, specifying the level and the stage when it should be introduced, and how.

In other words, your fellow teacher staying miles away from you should find in your handbook a friend, a guide, and a philosopher who encourages him to think and experiment more, and on his own.

Students' workbooks are visually more effective. Often they are clearly situation-oriented, even for content subjects. They provide a series of activities, mostly with a key. As an author, you are supposed to explain difficult vocabulary, concepts, and structures as the pre-lesson preparation. Most importantly of all, your student's workbook must be photocopying friendly. Students require this kind of freedom. A big, fat bound book may terrorize them and will dissuade them into thinking that it is yet another textbook. Content-rich but entertaining is the nutshell definition of a students' workbook that often has many grids, tables as fill-in-the blank activities.

Essentially a supplement to the course book, it reduces knowledge bits into simple, suitable bytes. So make your instructions very clear and precise. Give extra information, but as entertaining tricks of the trade.

Visually to be very appealing, your workbook should have 'cloze' or 'multiple choice' type of exercises that are non-threatening in nature.

c. Supportive intentions are the pedagogues underlying desires to provide aid or assistance to students. Here, the most important aspect is the intention of the pedagogue to be supportive. It is this intention that makes message supportive. The supportive intention of the pedagogue has to be clear as the variation in the quality of the pedagogues' intentions that affect the pupil. Most of the time, the intentions are 'read off" or inferred from the behaviour of the pedagogue. However, pedagogues need to make their supportive intentions explicit through overt statements of availability, for example when the pedagogue says, 'I am here for you', or 'I really want to help however I can', 'Don't worry I am with you', and so on; these overt statements, enhance the pupil's perceptions of the clarity, intensity, purity, and sincerity of the pedagogue's intention, and is, thus, comforted, and opens up for further communication. It creates affiliation because of the pedagogue's empathy, as well as develops the motivation, interest, and involvement in solving the problem. The pupil may also feel that the pedagogue likes him or her and, thus, value the relationship.

In supportive communication, the pedagogue has to be careful that the supportive intention does not make the pupil feel that he or she cannot manage the problem on his or her own. This implication can negatively affect the target's self-esteem and sense of self-efficacy. Once the pedagogue keeps this in mind, supportive communication is very effective in building interpersonal relationship and a sense of belonging among the pupils.

4. a. The process of communication does not always proceed smoothly and should not be conceived as something devoid of inner contradictions. At times, the communicating individuals enter into an interpersonal conflict.

Communicating parties may hold antagonistic stands, which reflects mutually exclusive values, tasks and goals, evoking mutual hostility and leading to an interpersonal conflict. The social and educational significance of such conflicts may be different, and depend on the values providing the base for interpersonal relations, between the pupil and the pedagogue, it leads to tension, emotional distancing, communication gap, and blocks the way to the common goal.

Conflicting situation may also arise from semantic barriers in communication preventing the establishment of interaction between the pupil and the pedagogue. A semantic barrier in communication consists of a different interpretation by the partners regarding a demand, request or order leading to a lack of mutual understanding and, thus, hampering their interaction. For instance, a semantic barrier in the relations between a pupil and the pedagogue may arise due to the fact that, the child cannot comprehend the teacher's demand as they run counter to his experience, views, attitudes. Semantic barriers arise because of age differences, life experiences, interest and 'adult errors' and its removal is very important in pedagogic communication.

Semantic barrier can only be overcome if the pedagogue knows and takes into account the pupil's age and past experiences and understands their psychology as well as their personal limitations. To reduce semantic barriers, children should be taught to use adult language and adults should be taught to understand children's language. Merely by saying that children should learn adult language, we do not mean the development of the child's speech habits, nor the enriching of his or her vocabulary, or improvement of his pronunciation and spelling, but the meanings and the feelings of the language. The child masters a language as the bearer of meanings in the preschool age, improves and enriches his knowledge throughout the school period. Language like other phenomena of human consciousness has a certain, personal sense, a certain personal significance, which varies from individual to individual. Personal sense is determined by what links the aims of an individual's activity with his motives, that is, by what represents the individual's needs. Communication between two people may have contrary meanings and intentions. For a teacher, a fight between two boys in school is a breach of discipline, whereas, for the student it may be yet another attempt to prevent the bully from teasing him.

A pedagogue has every reason to expect the child to master language not only in its proper context, but also from a personal sense, which would provide a common platform for mutual understanding and respect. But a teacher while expecting a student to learn an adult language with its system of personal senses should also try to understand the personal sense of the learning will be facilitated if he can identify himself with the child. Interpersonal conflicts in pedagogic communication arise mostly due to the pedagogue's lack of ability, or his lack of desire to understand and acknowledge the student's system of interpersonal senses.

b. The verbal aspects of assertive, aggressive, and non-assertive behaviour are outlined as follows:

Non-assertive	Assertive	Aggressive
• Long, rambling statements	• Statements that are brief, clear and to the point	• Excess of 'I' statements
• Fill in words (e.g. may be)	• 'I' statements: 'I' would like	• Boastfulness: 'my'
• Frequent justifications	• Distinctions between fact and opinion	• Threatening questions
• Apologies and permission seekers	• Suggestions not weighed with advice	• Requests as instructions or threats
• Few 'I' statements	• No 'shoulds' 'o ughts'	• Heavily weighed advice in the form of should and ought
• Self put-downs (I am hopeless)	• Questions to find out the thoughts, opinions and wants of others	• Assumptions
• Phrases that dismiss own needs (for example, not important really)	• Constructive criticism without blame or assumptions	• Blame put on others

c. Our words are only a fraction of, the message that we send. In fact, how we say those words often matters more than the words themselves. It is required for each one of us to have an assessment of how we sound like. The following questions proposed by Kris Cole, may help one to understand what one sounds like, she suggests that people should ask the following questions to themselves:

- Is your voice tone harsh, soft, sharp or neutral?
- Is your pitch high or low?
- Is your volume loud, quiet or in between?
- Is your inflexion rising, falling or sing-song?

- Is your voice speed, fast or slow?
- What emphasis do you place on Words?
- Do you articulate clearly or do you mumble?
- How much energy do you speak with?
- What rhythm do you speak with- Modulated or Staccato?

Section – B

5. a. One may encounter many common problems due to ineffective management of time.

Since a lot of people waste time, there must be a lot of problems managing time. First of all, many people have little experience organizing their lives, because parents, teachers, bosses, and friends have done it for them. They don't see the need for a schedule. Also, many people resent any barrier that interferes with their doing whatever they feel like doing at the moment. Thus, a schedule is seen as stifling by some and resisted. Planning their time is too time-consuming for others.

Secondly, some of us are pushed by pressing needs—a need for love and attention, a need to avoid responsibility and work, a need to believe the future will take care of itself (So, I can do whatever I want to right now), a need to escape real life by listening to music, watching TV, or reading a novel, and so on. In some cases, a new determination to schedule your time will get you going. In other cases, greater self-awareness (honestly looking at how you really waste your time) is needed. In still other cases, it seems to be almost impossible to become more controlled until some of the above mentioned basic psychological needs have been satisfied or, more likely, until we realize we are headed for failure, i.e. that our life isn't working out as we had hoped.

Thirdly, as Covey, Merrill and Merrill (1994) point out, many of us spend our days handling what appears to be 'urgent' problems, such as answering the phone or mail, beating deadlines for never read reports, attending meetings, impressing the boss, etc., which are not in a broader sense very important or useful. If your schedule is filled with unimportant urgencies, you won't have time to learn new things, to do long-range planning, to be creative and original, to do research, to exchange ideas with others, to re-think your major objectives, to invent new opportunities, to try to prevent future problems, to help others, and so on. These latter activities result in greater productivity and more benefits to everyone; they are the essence of a thoughtful life. It is said, 'the person who concentrates entirely on sawing wood, is likely to forget to sharpen the saw'. Our goals should be selected with care as aptly stated by Covey, and Merrill and Merrill help us do that.

Fourthly, some people make their daily schedules too rigid and overly demanding. Your schedule should make you feel as if you've 'got it together', not like a failure or an incompetent. It would be foolish to plan every minute of every day. An opportunity—a chance to talk with the boss, a chance to become involved in a project, a chance to meet someone—may appear at any moment. You must be ready to explore any good opportunity;

otherwise, life can become a drag. Priorities and assignments and deadlines change every day; thus, the use of your 'free' time every day must change a little, too.
It is essential to make better use of your time, both in terms of devoting time to high priority activities and avoiding wasting time or spending your time on less important things. It is also required to be time effective, not necessarily time efficient, by selecting the *best* thing to do at this moment from among the infinite possibilities.

b. Negotiation is one of the most common forms of conflict management. Everyday we negotiate something. We negotiate with our work colleagues over where to go for lunch, with our co teacher as to whether she/he can take our class when applied for leave. We also negotiate with ourselves about how to keep certain commitments like a diet or stopping a specific bad habit. It has been widely acknowledged that 'win-win' negotiation is the best kind of negotiation. There are four steps to win-win negotiation that almost anyone can perform with ease. These steps include plans, relationships, agreements, and maintenance.

Establishing win-win plans is simple. One needs to:

- Agree on your own goals.
- Anticipate the goals of the other party.
- Determine areas of probable agreement.
- Develop win-win solutions to reconcile areas of probable disagreement.

Developing a win-win relationship is easy. One needs to:

- Plan activities, which allow a positive personal relationship to develop.
- Cultivate a sense of mutual trust.
- Allow the relationship to fully develop before discussing business in earnest.

Forming win-win agreements is easy. One needs to:

- Confirm the other party's goals.
- Verify areas of agreement.
- Propose and consider win-win solutions to reconcile areas of disagreement.
- Jointly resolve any remaining differences.

Performing win-win maintenance is simple. One needs to:

- Maintain commitment by:

i. Providing meaningful feedback based on performance.
ii. Holding up your end of the agreement.

- Maintain the relationship by:

i. Keeping in contact.
ii. Reaffirming trust.

6. a. **The do's of good listening**

    i. Listen caringly.
    ii. Listen with your body.
    iii. Listen with your eyes.
    iv. Listen with your ears.
    v. Listen with your heart.
    vi. Listen with your mouth closed.
    vii. Validate and confirm the message.

    The donot's of good listening

    i. Do not interrupt.
    ii. Do not contradict.
    iii. Do not criticize or lecture about past behaviour.
    iv. Do not nod your head constantly to hurry them along.
    v. Do not assume that what they are talking about is the total content of their message.
    vi. Do not interrogate.
    vii. Do not use the occasion for self-aggrandisement.

b. Interviews are held for reasons other than just selection for employment. Based on the purpose for which they are held, interviews can be classified as:

    i. Promotion interview
    ii. Assessment interview
    iii. Exit interview
    iv. Problem interview
    v. Employment interview

i. Promotion interview

This type of interview is held when people are due for their promotion. It is an informal one and introduces the candidate to the new responsibilities and persons he/she would have to interact with. Clarifications about the job title, nature of duties, responsibilities, and expectations are made clear during a promotion interview. This type of an interview is held whether there is competition or not.

ii. Assessment interview

It is a method of assessing the employee at regular intervals of time. This interview is more a discussion than a question-answer session. Here, attention is paid to the career development of the employee. Strengths and weaknesses, shortcomings and improvement strategies are generally discussed here.

iii. Exit interview

Such an interview is conducted at the time of resignation. Here the employer gets a chance to find out the reason for the employee's decision to leave, to get a feed-back from the employee about the organization, check all information regarding personal file, cheques, payments, and other benefits.

iv. Problem interview

This type of interview is conducted to alleviate the problems that are either being created by or being faced by an employee. This interview suggests solutions after discussion with the employee about the problems.

v. Employment interview

This is the most conventional type of an interview where people are assessed on their employability skills. Both the interviewer and the interviewee have to make important decisions (whether to employ and whether to take up the employment).

7. a. Some positive behaviours can be cultivated to improve listening. First of all, you must pay full attention to the speaker. This concentration is helped by alertness of the mind and the body. If you are determined to pay attention, you can train and discipline your mind and body to get into the listening mode.

Training for good listening is largely a personal responsibility and can be done by personal effort. Listening skills can be improved by following some of the strategies given below.

i. Maintain eye contact

Eye contact keeps the listener focused and helps you to feel involved.

ii. Interpret the speaker's nonverbal signs

The ears are not enough to listen to the message completely. We need the eyes as well. The speaker's body language can tell a lot about the state of his/her mind. Emphasize upon facial expressions, gestures and posture, and tone and pitch of the voice, to let the listener have an idea about the enthusiasm, excitement, anger or fear, nervousness, or impatience of the speaker.

iii. Stop interrupting

It is not possible to listen effectively while talking.

iv. Ask questions

If you are not sure of what the speaker is saying, ask. But do not ask questions randomly. Ask at suitable moments to get a clear perception. It is quite acceptable to say 'do you mean....?'

v. Do not be judgmental

Keep an open mind; do not jump to conclusions. Avoid making any judgment until the speaker has completed speaking.

b. Darwin observed that, 'It is not the strongest of the species that survive, nor the most intelligent, but the one most responsive to change'. His words are still as relevant today as when they were first thought during the early phase of the 19th century. Indeed, his words are more relevant right now than never before. The explosion of modern information technology is posing a great challenge to the youth.

   Firstly, if one does not change and adapt to the changing needs of the society, one will remain a failure.

   Secondly, in order to prosper and succeed in this period of technological advance, individuals and organizations have to be ready to develop and adopt new skills and approaches. Failing which the individuals and organizations will perish and their very survival may be at stake.

   Soft skills are the emotional sine qua non of the psychological survival. Soft skills are essential for anyone to develop the ability to adapt to change.

   Soft skills are the skills relating to people issues. Unless one gets along well with others, unless one handles the negative emotions of others, it is not possible for one to succeed in life. Interpersonal competencies, communication skills, time management skills are essential to succeed in this era. One may have excellent hard skills, a meritorious track record, and may stand out as an intellectual compared to others. Despite having all the relevant and required hard skills, if one is not responsive to change, and if one remains rigid and inflexible, one may not succeed and also may remain detrimental to the group.

Section - C

8. William Schultz has identified three basic interpersonal needs which underline most of your behaviour around other people. These needs can be best represented as dimensions or continuums along which most people fall. Schultz calls these interpersonal needs the 'need for inclusion', the 'need for control', and the 'need for affection'.

   Inclusion: According to Schultz, the need for inclusion is the need to be recognized as an individual distinct from others. A person with a very high need for inclusion needs recognition and attention from others. Such a person likes to be in the spotlight, to be signed out, to be noticed. At one of the extremes of the continuum, we find the *prima donna*, or the obnoxious little kid who does anything simply to attract some attention, even if it results in punishment. To be punished is better than to be ignored. On the other hand, a person with a low inclusion need prefers not to stand out, would rather not receive too much attention, does not like to be prominent in the public eye.

Schultz holds that people at both extremes are motivated essentially by the same fear of not being recognized as individuals. The people high on the inclusion need will combat the fear by forcing others to pay attention to them. Those low on the inclusion need have convinced themselves that they will not get any attention, but that it is just the way they want it. Most people are probably somewhere in the middle of that continuum. Your needs for inclusion may change as the people you associate with differ, and as the situations you find yourself in change. We may want very little recognition from a professor when we have not done an assignment and do not wish to be called upon, while at the same time we may have a strong need for attention from the person sitting next to us, whom we are interested in getting to know better.

The need for inclusion has some influence on the process of interpersonal communication. Imagine a situation in which two or more people equally something. Much of the energy they are going to spend in that interpersonal context will be spent establishing in the group a position from which they will get the recognition they need. However, if all members are recognition seekers, chances are they will have a difficult time securing attention from one another. Much of the group's time, it can be predicted, will be spent vying for recognition from anyone in authority or from each other. Little else is likely to get accomplished.

A group composed of a reasonable balance of people high and low on inclusion will probably function in a smoother fashion.

Control: The need for control involves a striving for power, for being in charge, for running things, and for influencing one's environment. The need for control is not necessarily related to the need for inclusion. Some people enjoy being in charge of things even if no one is aware that they are running the show. These people are high on control while low on inclusion-power, behind-the-throne types. Some people, on the other hand, may seek leadership or prestige positions not for the power they bring but for the attention they produce. This is why it is not always easy to determine whether a person's behaviour is influenced by one need or the other.

Naturally, some people are quite low on the need for control and are not interested at all in taking initiative, in assuming responsibilities, in making decisions, or in leading a group. As is true for the inclusion need, a mixed group composed of highs and lows on the control dimension, has a better chance of getting things done.

Too many 'leaders' and not enough 'followers' may result in a constant struggle for leadership, and the ensuing climate of competition may not be conductive to accomplishing much. On the other hand, too many 'followers' and no 'leader' may result in apathy, and not much may.

Affection: The need for affection has to do with how close people want to be to one another. Some people like to be very intimate and enjoy warm relationships, even with relatively casual acquaintances. They enjoy telling about themselves on a personal level and expect similar behaviour on the part of others. They want and need to be liked.

Sometimes people high on the need for affection are perceived by others as too friendly or coming on too strong, Affection is closely related to disclosing behaviour, which can have a great effect on our interpersonal relations.

Some people, on the other hand, prefer to keep others at a distance. They do not like to become too friendly too rapidly. They do not wish to be too personal with others and share too much of themselves with people they do not know well. They may have a strong distaste for closeness and intimacy except with carefully selected people. These people are usually perceived as aloof, cold, or 'superior'.

In the case of affection, a mixed group is not the best combination for productive interpersonal relationships. Cold people and warm people do not mix well. Each type makes the other uncomfortable, and they find it hard to figure out each other. Neither is able to satisfy the other's needs.

Interpersonal communication is satisfying to you when you manage to satisfy your needs. In the case of interpersonal needs, you depend solely on others for their satisfaction. If others give you the recognition you seek, or give you a chance to exert influence when you wish to, or provide you with the close intimate atmosphere you like, you feel satisfied and you seek these people again in other interpersonal situations. You tend to avoid, when you can, that type of interpersonal communication situation where your needs are generally thwarted.

An understanding of interpersonal needs is essential, not only in facilitating your insights into group processes, but in helping you predict the situations that will be more or less satisfying and productive for you.

9. The inability to communicate effectively can create conflict and also impede its effective management. Our ability to communicate often degenerates because of barriers. Let us examine what are these barriers to effective communication and why they lead to ineffective communication.

The Barriers and Why They Lead to Ineffective Communication

The Barriers	Reasons for their ineffectiveness in communication.
Criticizing	Criticism is often inappropriate and excessive, leading to defensive and/(or) aggressive responses. It is often justified as a way of getting another to improve or perform better. There are often better alternatives.
Name calling and labelling	Labels tend to put barriers between us and others by creating a 'box' into which we place others. The result is often to distance others from us.
Diagnosing	A more sophisticated form of labelling practised often by professionals of various kinds. It can damage communication for the same reasons as labelling.
Praising evaluatively	Unrestrained praise is often insincere and hollow. It can also be manipulative if the person using it has an ulterior motive. The result is often resentment.
Ordering	If ordering is used with coercion, it will create resistance and anger. Responses can range from sabotage to submission.
Threatening	Threatening has the same effects as ordering, but often more pronounced.

Moralizing	Bolton describes this behaviour as people putting '... a halo around their solutions for others'. (1987). Moralizing creates many problems including resentment, increased anxiety and it often creates pretence in the communication.
Excessive or inappropriate questioning	Questions are unavoidable and valuable tools of communication but when used to excess, create boredom and unnecessary distance between people. There are often better, more direct, ways of communicating.
Advising	Advise is sometimes valuable but when used inappropriately (which is often) it may damage the other's confidence or fail to enhance his or her own problem-solving abilities. It often prevents a full exploration of the issues.
Diverting	Diverting is used often to avoid the unpleasant, unpalatable or the uncomfortable. It creates much tension.
Logical Argument	Logic is necessary but using logical argument when emotions are running high may be inappropriate because it creates distance.
Reassuring	Sometimes reassurance is a way of avoiding the issues whilst having the appearance of providing comfort. It can, in some cases, be very frustrating for the person.

10. A pedagogue has to be careful in showing his or her supportive intention, because such intentions can implicitly convey negative evaluation of the pupil and impose on his or her autonomy. Supportive intentions may imply that the pupil needs help, and is unable or is incompetent to solve his or her problem, or acted unwisely in creating (or failing to avoid) a problematic situation. At times, supportive communication can be threatening. Asking questions can challenge privacy, offering advice may undermine autonomy, and making suggestions can imply criticism.

    To offset this possibility, the pedagogue has to use certain devices. Face work or politeness strategies are communicative devices for redressing the face threats inherent in supportive messages. Positive face work aims to protect the pupil's desire to be evaluated positively; it includes verbal devices that express positive regard for the pupil, admiration for the courage or effort shown by the pupil, respect for the pupil's understanding of difficulty and confidence in the pupil's capacities and qualities to overcome problems. Positive face work when used by the pedagogue, results in the following favourable outcomes: (a) increase in the pupil's willingness to consider the substance of the helpers message, (b) interest in interacting with the helper, revealing potentially sensitive thoughts and feelings, and (c) liking for the pedagogue. Face work achieves these and related outcomes through the mechanism of conveying the pedagogues positive regard and respect for the pupil. Expressions of positive regard and respect by the pedagogue can heighten the pupil's feelings of acceptance and trust, which in turn, enhance the pupil's willingness to discuss sensitive concerns.

    Supportive intentions, along with sensitive face work help cultivate 'supportive conversational environment'—an arena in which upsetting and potentially face-threatening matters can be explored openly. Moreover, these message features should contribute to the pupil's sense of being supported or sense of support availability that leads to coping. Maximally effective supportive messages do more than cultivate trust, acceptance and openness; they also address specific tasks in the effort to facilitate learning, discipline, appropriate behaviour and personality development of the pupils.

An important feature of support message for the pedagogue is its effectiveness in passing informative context. Supportive message can be declaratives like factual statements, observations interactions; or they may be directives like suggestions, proposals, advice, etc.—all intended to enhance the pupil's appreciation or motivation to improve or solve the problem.

Declaratives present information in an adequate and appropriate manner and quantity, expressed in an empathetic manner. Helpful directives present sound proposals and solve the problem effectively and efficiently. Sometimes, there is cognitive or emotional deficit in the learner. In this situation, the pedagogue has to provide 'instrumental support' that would facilitate learning and task accomplishment. At times, the pedagogue may find the pupils lacking information about themselves, lacking confidence, doubt their competence and self efficacy or their likeability and social acceptance. Under these conditions, the pedagogue needs to provide appraisal support to the pupil to be able and competent, and emotional support to makes them feel accepted and loved and to manage their grievances.

However, one thing a pedagogue needs to remember is that, supportive communication is not a commodity or a resource that can be delivered; rather it arises through the interactions occurring in the relationships, besides, the pedagogue may face problems in conceptualizing supportive communication that would serve the purpose.

11. 'Reading maketh a full man, conference a ready man, and writing an exact man', opined Francis Bacon in his famous essay entitled *Of Studies*. This axiom is indeed the motto currently. In the internet era today when words rule the virtual space as well, the Hamlet like exasperation—'words! words! words!'—is no longer valid. In fact, your writing skills speak a lot about you these days.

Defining writing

In other words, despite all the contemporary visual and oral-aural distractions, knowing how to write, and how to write well, is the need of the hour, however boring and dull the staid skill may appear.

Apparently writing appears boring and difficult because, unlike speaking or listening, it is *not an innate or natural skill.* Speaking or listening is inborn to the human species, excluding those who are hearing disabled. In the case of the rest of us, as we grow older, we merely need to refine these skills. Writing, on the contrary, is a skill that is not inborn. We need to consciously learn it, beginning with the alphabet and proceed through orthography, vocabulary, semantics and with a paragraph, and end with a coherent and cohesive discourse. In this sense, writing is a *secondary* skill.

If you want a proof of how writing is not a primary mode of communication the way speaking and listening are, just look around you. Your college peon may be illiterate.

He communicates very efficiently though. He speaks and understands the local language. He may even boast of a smattering of English. He does not know an alphabet of either language, however and the receipt of his pay cheque needs his thumb impression.

As a mode of communication, writing has yet another interesting facet. We start *communicating through writing at a much later stage of our intellectual development.* The best empirical proof of this facet of writing would be observing a growing baby. The phenomenon would prove to you undeniably that writing occurs at a much later stage of human development. A cursory glance/at the history of pedagogy from Rousseau to Piaget, too, proves to us that writing was neither the method nor the mode of transmitting knowledge. Despite the rare handcrafted manuscripts, the primary mode of production and re-production of knowledge has always, everywhere been the oral-aural method, at least until Caxton popularized printing.

It is noteworthy that writing becomes a mode of communication only when a child enters the social sphere beyond the immediate family, that is, the school. Interesting it is hence to note that both these *processes of socialization,* schooling, and consequently writing, enter a child's life at the same time.

So let us re-capture the definition of writing. Writing, we must remember, is a unique tool of communication that is neither innate nor natural, and this secondary type of skill is acquired at a much later stage of development. Unlike speaking or listening, it is, moreover, a more *complex tool of communication.* The co-ordination of mental processes and physical organs involved in the actual execution of this skill is more elaborate than listening, for example. It has, moreover, to be more precise than speaking. The formality/informality binary that writing employs, for example, is far more precise than speaking.

Such a difference is more marked because, unlike speaking as a tool of communication, *writing is not temporary.* Communication through speaking happens, and then literally vanishes in to thin air. The written mode of communication, on the contrary, is ever lasting, permanently available across the barriers of time and space. So we have to be more specific about its *sub-skills* that are listed below:

i. presenting ideas logically and coherently through organization and structuring of ideas
ii. connecting sentences in a cohesive manner
iii. being able to communicate effectively to perform different functions of writing that range from entertainment to information.

A better understanding of these sub-skills of writing emerges once we look at the elements of writing. Writing operates at three levels; namely, word level, sentence level and the discourse level.

These three levels are inter-related interestingly. When we communicate through writing, our word choice is determined by the sentence construction and by the larger discourse. In fact, discourse, the largest unit of meaning, communicates the author's intention to the reader and determines the tone and the tenor of the communication. The way you would write your science textbook, for example, is totally different from the way you would pen a letter to the educational authorities for further grants. The discourses are different.

In the science textbook, for example, you would use more of the passive while you may use more of conditionals in your 'grant' letter. Your words in the science textbook may be technical while your 'grant' letter would use more business-oriented vocabulary. It is, thus, that the discourse defines communicative strategies at all the levels of writing. The skill of writing is represented diagrammatically below:

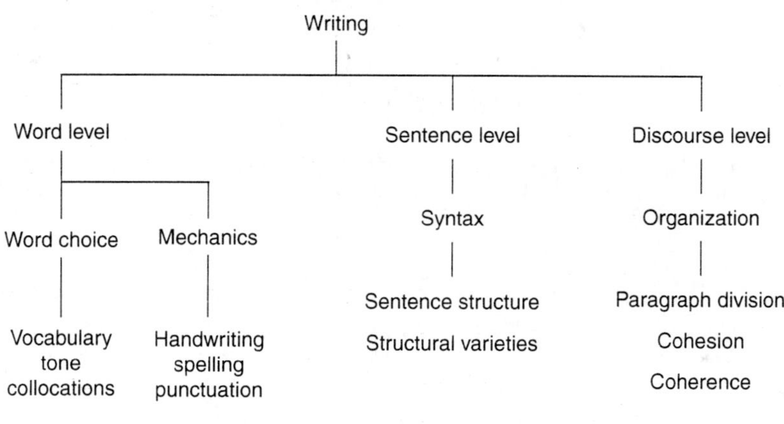

Figure M.3

In other words, right from the most fundamental level, that is, the word, communicating through writing involves making choices that jell, at the sentential and at the discourse level, so as to enable us to convey ideas clearly and logically to our decoders.

Now that we know the basic elements of writing as a communication skill, let us look at the types of writing that we use to communicate through writing. Through its tone, writing can be sub-divided as *formal and informal.*

Formal writing refers to communication used in official contexts, especially when you are addressing colleagues, rank wise higher than you in the hierarchy. Similarly, in the personal context, your writing will be formal when you are writing to decoders distantly related to you or decoders older than you.

Informal writing, on the contrary, is in the personal domain and is used while communicating with decoders you are close to or with decoders who are your age. Rarely used in the official context, it could be used, if at all, while communicating with colleagues you are close to.

Writing can also be sub-divided as *fictional and non-fictional.* Fictional writing refers to writing of novels, short stories and poems. Non-fictional writing is what most communicators need. It consists of cvs, letters of application, reports, brochures, schedules, articles or advertisements, for example.

Non-fictional writing can be further sub-divided in to five types:

i. descriptive: *describes* things/ places/ persons/ processes
ii. expository: *explains* processes/scientific subjects/professions/functioning of institutions, industries

iii. narrative: *narrates* (that is, describes in a sequential and causal order) events/a series of events/natural phenomenon and disasters/ accidents/Journeys/legends/ biographies

iv. reflective: *discusses* issues/abstract ideas/ provides pros and cons of a debate.

v. imaginative: the encoder tries to *identify* with situations/things/people/events that he might not have experienced.

As an M.Ed. trained teacher, you are going to use the descriptive type while writing reports, the expository type while preparing workbooks, introducing stem cell research to your students, the narrative while explaining schedules to your colleagues and learners, the reflective while submitting an article to a research journal, and the imaginative while making your learners explore and express possibilities.

Glossary

Analogue: An analogue is a relatively well-developed theory, frequently a theory from a seemingly unrelated discipline or about unrelated substance, which is used to assist in the development of a theory presently less-developed than the analogue.

Action language: Movements of the body, for example, the way one walks, runs, sits.

Attitude: The predisposition to respond for or against an object.

Axiom: An axiom in a formal theory is identical to a postulate or proposition.

Bandwidths: A network delivers only what will fit down its pipeline. The carrying-capacity, or bandwidth, of different pipelines varies greatly. Telephone lines in most homes are twisted copper wires with a narrow band width. Cable TV uses coaxial cable, a tube of conductors that can carry a hundred times the load of a copper phone line. Long distance phone calls pulse along fiber optic cables capable of carrying tens of thousands of times that of copper. Satellite signals carry more than coaxial cable but less than fiber optics.

Bits: The definition of a bit is that amount of information necessary to reduce the number of possible signal alternatives by one-half.

Body language: A form of non-verbal communication in which messages are communicated by gesture, posture, spatial relations, and so forth; a popular term covering all aspects of non-verbal communication.

Brainstorming: A technique for generating ideas among people.

Channel: The vehicle or medium through which signals are sent.

Code: A set of symbols used to translate a message from one form to another.

Cohesiveness: The property of togetherness. Applied to group communication situations, it refers to the mutual attractiveness among a member's measure of the extent to which individual member of a group work together as group.

Communication gap: The inability to communicate on a meaningful level because of some difference between the parties. For example, age, sex, political orientation, religion.

Communicology: The study of communication and particularly the subject concerned with human communication.

Context of communication: The physical, psychological, social, and temporal environment in which communication takes place.

Credibility: The degree to which a receiver perceives the speaker to be believable.

Decoder: That which takes message in one form (for e.g., sound waves) and translates it into another code (for example, nerve impulses) from which meaning can be formulated. In human communication the decoder is the auditory mechanism. In electronic communication the decoder, e.g., is the telephone, or ear piece.

Decoding: The process of extracting a message from a code, e.g., translating speech sounds into nerve impulses.

Delayed reactions: Reactions that are consciously delayed while the situation is analyzed.

Dialect: A speech variant that is used by persons from a specific area or social class; dialects may be different from the standard language in phonology, semantics, and syntax, but they are intelligible to other speakers of the language.

Dissonance: A psychological state of discomfort created by having two elements (for example, cognition or beliefs), one of which would not follow given the other.

Dyadic communication: Two person communication.

Dysfunctional effects of mass communication: Effects of the mass media that are not in theinterests of the society.

Empathy: A feeling of another person's feeling, or the mass media that are not in the interests of the society.

Encoder: That which takes a message in one form and puts it into another form. In human communication the encoder is the speaking mechanism. In electronic communication the encoder is the telephone mouthpiece.

Encoding: The process of putting a message into a code.

Entropy: A measure of the extent of disorganization or randomness in a system. Entropy is a measure of the degree of uncertainty that a destination has about the messages to be communicated by a source. Entropy is high if the number of possible messages is high and low if the number of possible messages is low.

Ethicizing function of communication: The media's function of providing viewers with a collective ethic or ethical system.

Extemporaneous speech: A speech that is thoroughly prepared, organized in details, and in which certain aspects of style are predetermined.

Feedback: Information that is fed back to the source. Feedback may come from the source's own message or from the receivers in the form of applause, questions, or letters to the editors to the newspaper.

Field of experience: The sum total of an individual's experiences which influences his or her ability to communicate in some views of communication. Two people can only communicate to the extent that their fields of experience overlap.

Group: A collection of individuals related to each other with some common purpose, and with structure among them.

Impromptu speech: A speech which is delivered without any direct prior preparation.

Intrapersonal communication: Communication with oneself.

Kinesics: The study of the communicative dimension of facial and bodily movements.

Laissez faire leader: A group leader who allows the group to develop, progress, or make mistakes on its own.

Language: The rules of syntax, semantics, and phonology; a potentially self- reflexive structured system of symbols that catalogs the objects, events, and relations in the world.

Linguistics: The study of language; the study of the system of rules by which meanings are paired with sounds.

Mass communication: Communication addressed to an extremely large audience which is mediated by audio and/or visual transmitters, and which is processed by gatekeepers before transmission.

Message: Any signal or combination of signals that serve as stimuli for a receiver.

Meta-communication: Communication about language.

Model: A physical representation of an object or process.

Narcotizing function of communication: The media's function of providing receivers with information, the knowledge of which, is in turn confused by receivers with doing something about something.

Negative feedback: Feedback that serves a corrective function by informing the sources that his or her message is not being received in the way intended.

Noise: Anything that distorts the message intended by the source.

Object language: Language that is used to communicate about objects, events, and relations in the world; the structure of the object language is described in a meta-language; the display of physical objects, for example, flower arranging, the colours and colthes we wear.

Olfactory communication: Communication by smell.

Paralanguage: The vocal (but non-verbal) aspect of speech paralanguage consists of voice qualities (for example, pitch-range, resonance, tempo), vocal characterizers (for example, laughing/crying/yelling/whispering), vocal qualifiers ('no', or 'sh' meaning silence).

Paradigm: A philosophical and theoretical framework of a scientific school or discipline within which theories, laws, and generalizations and the experiments performed in support of them are formulated.

Perception: The process of becoming aware of objects and events from the senses.

Persuasion: The process of influencing attitudes and behavior.

Phatic communication: A type of speech in which ties of union are created by a mere exchange of words.

Pictic: The study of the pictorial code of communication.

Pitch: The highness and lowness of the vocal tone.

Positive feedback: Feedback that supports or reinforces behaviour along the lines it is already proceeding in, for example, applause during a speech.

Postulate: A postulate, like a proposition, is assumed and functions as a primary statement in a theory.

Proxemics: Study of patterns of interpersonal distance in face to face encounters.

Proposition: A primary statement of a theory.

Public communication: Communication in which the source is one person and the receiver is an audience comprising of many persons.

Public speaking: Communication which occurs when a speaker delivers a relatively prepared, continuous address in specific setting to a large audience that provides little immediate feedback.

Rate: The speed with which we speak generally measured in words per minute.

Redundancy: One question the information theorist has about the signals in a coding pool is how predictable the next signal will be given that we know all of the signals that preceded it. This is simply trying to determine how predictable (redundant) rather than how unpredictable (entropic) the signals in a message are; that quality of a message which makes it totally predictable and therefore lacking in information. A message with zero redundancy would be completely unpredictable: a message of 100 per cent redundancy would be completely predictable. All human languages contain some degree of redundancy built into them. It is generally estimated to be about 50 percent. All human messages therefore have some redundancy.

Response: Any bit of overt or covert behaviour.

Society: Merely the name for a number of individuals, connected by interaction.

Semantics: The area of language study concerned with meaning.

Sign language: Gesture language that is highly codified, for example a Hitchhiker's gesture.

Tactile communication: Communication through the sense of touch.

Bibliography

Agee, W.K., R.H. Ault and E. Emery, eds, 1979, *Introduction to Mass Communication,* New York: Harper and Row, Publishers.

Ahuja, B.N. and S.S. Chopra, 1989, *Communication,* New Delhi: Surjeet Publications.

Albrecht, T.L. and M.B. Adelman, eds, 1987a, *Communicating social support*, Newbury Park, CA: Sage.

———, 1987, 'Dilemmas of Supportive Communication' in T.L. Albrecht, and M.B. Adelman, eds, *Communicating Social Support*, Newbury Park, CA: Sage, pp. 240–254.

Allport, G.W., 1937, *Personality: A Psychological Interpretation*, New York: Holt.

Applegate, J.L., 1980, 'Adaptive Communication: A Study of Teachers' Communicative Strategies', *Communication Education*, 29, 158–170.

Argle, Michael, 1965, 'Eye Contact, Distance and Affiliation', *Sociometry*, 28.

Aristotle, *Rhetoric and Poetics*, 1954, translated by W. Rhys Roberts, New York: Random House.

Barbee, A.P. and M.R. Cunnigham, 1995, 'An experimental approach to soda support communication: interactive coping in close relationships', in B.R. Burleson, eds, *Communication Yearbook*, Thousand Oaks, CA: Sage, pp. 381–413.

Barlund, Dean C., 1970, *A Transactional Model and Communication, Language Behaviour, A Book of Reading in Communication*, Monton: B. Hague.

Baron and Byrne, 2000, *Social Psychologies* (9th ed.) Allyn and Bacon.

Barron, R.A., 1989, 'Personality and organizational conflict: Effects of the type and behaviour pattern and self-monitoring', *Organizational behaviour and human performance*, 44.

Berlo, David K., 1960, *The Process of Communication, an Introduction of Theory and Practice,* New York: Holt, Rinehart and Winston.

Bloom Field, Leonard, 1933, *An Introduction to the Study of Language*, New York: Henry Holt.

Bormann, Ernest G., 1969, *Discussion and Group Methods, Theory and Practice*, New York: Harper and Row.

Brown, P., and S.C. Levinson, 1987, *Politeness: Some Universal in Language Usage*, Cambridge: Cambridge University Press.

Bryson, Lymon, 1948, *Communication of Ideas*, New York.

Burleosn, B.R., 1994, 'Comforting Messages: Features, Functions and Outcomes', in J.A. Daly and J.M. Wiemann, eds, *Strategic Interpersonal communication*, Hillsdale, NJ: Lawrence Erlbaum, pp. 135–165.

———, 1994, 'Comforting Messages: Significance, Approaches and Effects' in B.R. Burleson, T.L. Albretch and I.G. Sarason, eds, *Communication of Social Support: Messages, Interactions and Relationships*, Thousand Oaks: Sage.

Cooley, Charles H., 1956, *Social Organization,* New York: Scribner's.

Colin, Cherry, 1957, *On Human Communication*, New York: Wiley.

Choi, S.H., 1991, 'Communicative Socialization Processes', in B.B. Schieffelin and Ochs, eds, *Language Socialization Access Cultures*, Cambridge: Cambridge University Press.

Webb, Chriss, 1978, *People and Communication*, London: Macmillan Press.

Kurt, Danzeger, 1976, *Inter Personal Communication*, New York: Pergamon Press Inc.

Devito, Joseph A., 1978, *Communicology, An Introduction to the Study of Communication*, New York: Harper and Row.

Ducks, S., ed., 1990, *Personal Relationships and Social Support*, London: Sage.

Fast, Julius, 1970, *Body Language*, New York: M. Evan.

Fawles, D.P. and D.C. Alexander, eds, 1978, *Communication and Social Behaviour, A Symbolic Interacting Perspective*, Utah, U.S.A.: Addision Westley Publishing Company.

Ferguson, S.D., 1999, *Communication Planning—An Integrated Approach*, London: Thousand Oaks.

Fisher, Aubrey, 1978, *Perspective On Human Communication*, New York: MacMillan and Co.

Fiske, John, 1982, *Introduction to Communication Studies*, London, Routledge.

Hunt, Garry T., 1985, *Effective Communication*, Englewood Cliffs, New Jersey: Prentice Hall Inc.

Giffin, Kim and Bobby R. Patton, 1971, *Basic Readings in Interpersonal Communication Theory and Practice*, The University of Kansas, New York, San Francisco, London: Harper and Row Publications.

Greenberg, L.S., L.N. Rice and R. Elliot, 1993, *Facilitating Emotional Change:The Moment by Moment Process*, New York: Guilford.

Gullery, H.E. and Leathwers and Dale, 1977, *Communication and Group Process (Techniques for Improving the Quality of Small)*, N.Y.: Holt Rhinehart.

Hall, J.A., 1984, *Non-verbal Sex Differences: Communication Accuracy and Expressive Style*, Baltimore: John Hopkins University.

Haslett, B., 1990, 'Social Class, Social Status & Communicative Behaviour', in H. Giles and W.P. Robinson, eds, *Handbok of Language and Social Psychology*, New York: John Wiley.

Hewes, D.E., eds, 1995, *The Cognitive Bases of Interpersonal Communication*, Marwah, NJ: Lawrence Erlbaum.

Jugen, Ruech and Gregory Bateson, 1951, *Communication—The Social Matrix of Psychiatry*, New York: W.W. Norton.

King, S.W., 1975, *Communication and Social Influences*, Addisson: Westley.

Knapp, M.L. and J.A., Daly, 2002, *Hand book of Inter Personal Communication* (3rd edition), California: Sage Publications.

Lindolf, Thomas R., 1995, *Qualitative Communication Research Methods*, Sage Publications, (International and Professional Publishers), Thousands Oaks: London, New Delhi.

Manvell, R., 1966, *The Age of Communication*, Glasgow and London: Blackie.

Mark, L.K. and A.D. Daly, eds, 2002, *Handbook of Interpersonal Communication*, Sage.

McAdams, D.P., 1992, 'The Intimacy Motive', in C.P. Smith, eds, *Motivation and Personality: Handbook of Thematic Content Analysis*, New York: Cambridge University Press.

McLuhan, Marshall, 1962, *The Gutenberg Galaxy*, Toronto: University of Toronto Press.

———, 1964, *Understanding Media*, New York: Mcgraw-Hill.

Mead, G.H., 1967, *Self and society*, Chicago: Chicago University Press.

Mortensen, C.D., 1997, *Miscommunication*, California: Sage Publication, Inc, Thousand Oaks.

Murphy, R. D., 1977, *Mass Communication and Human Interaction*, Boston: Houghton Miffin and Co.

Ng, S.H. and J.J., Bracjac, 1993, *Power in Language: Verbal Communication and Social Influnce*, Newbury Park, C.A: Sage.

Rey, M. R., ed., 1980, *The Relationship of Verbal and Non-verbal Communication*, The Hague: Mouton Publisher.

Robert, Donald F., 1954, *The Process and Effects of Communications*, Urbana: University of Illinois Press.

Ruben, Brent D., 1984, *Communication and Human Behaviour*, New York: MacMillan Publishing Co.

Shannon, Claude and Warren Weaver, 1949, *Mathematical Theory of Communication*, Urbana: University of Illinois Press.

Smith, A. G., 1966, *Communication and Culture*, Holt, Rinehart & Winston.

Stevens, J.D. and Hazel F. Dicken-Garcia, 1980, *Communication History*, London: Sage.

Sullivan, H.S, 1968, *The Interpersonal Theory of Psychiatry*, New York: W.W. Norton & co.